MONTREAL AFTER DARK

Études d'histoire du Québec / Studies on the History of Quebec

Magda Fahrni et/and Nicolas Kenny
Directeurs de la collection / Series Editors

31 A Place in the Sun
Haiti, Haitians, and the Remaking of Quebec
Sean Mills

32 The Pauper's Freedom
Crime and Poverty in Nineteenth-Century Quebec
Jean-Marie Fecteau

33 Au risque de la conversion
L'expérience québécoise de la mission au XXe siècle (1945–1980)
Catherine Foisy

34 From Old Quebec to La Belle Province
Tourism Promotion, Travel Writing, and National Identities, 1920–1967
Nicole Neatby

35 Genre, patrimoine et droit civil
Les femmes mariées de la bourgeoisie québécoise en procès, 1900-1930
Thierry Nootens

36 L'Église et la politique québécoise, de Taschereau à Duplessis
Alexandre Dumas

37 Grossières indécences
Pratiques et identités homosexuelles à Montréal, 1880-1929
Dominic Dagenais

38 Taking to the Streets
Crowds, Politics, and the Urban Experience in Mid-Nineteenth-Century Montreal
Dan Horner

39 Colonialism's Currency
Money, State, and First Nations in Canada, 1820–1950
Brian Gettler

40 Deindustrializing Montreal
Entangled Histories of Race, Residence, and Class
Steven High

41 La guerre d'indépendance des Canadas
Démocratie, républicanismes et libéralismes en Amérique du Nord
Julien Mauduit

42 Countercurrents
Women's Movements in Postwar Montreal
Amanda Ricci

43 Cette science nécessaire
Dissections humaines et profession médicale au Québec
Martin Robert

44 Their Benevolent Design
Conservative Women and Protestant Child Charities in Montreal
Janice Harvey

45 Réinventer Montréal
Ambitions et revers de trois urbanistes des Trente Glorieuses
Frédéric Mercure Jolette

46 Montreal After Dark
Nighttime Regulation and the Pursuit of a Global City
Matthieu Caron

MONTREAL AFTER DARK

Nighttime Regulation and the Pursuit of a Global City

MATTHIEU CARON

McGill-Queen's University Press
Montreal & Kingston • London • Chicago

ISBN 978-0-2280-2477-4 (paper)
ISBN 978-0-2280-2514-6 (ePDF)
ISBN 978-0-2280-2515-3 (ePUB)

Legal deposit second quarter 2025
Bibliothèque et Archives nationale du Québec

Printed in Canada on acid-free paper that is 100% ancient-forest-free, containing 100% sustainable, recycled fibre, and processed chlorine-free.

This book has been published with the help of a grant from the Federation for the Humanities and Social Sciences, through the Awards to Scholarly Publications Program, using funds provided by the Social Sciences and Humanities Research Council of Canada.

Funded by the Government of Canada | Financé par le gouvernement du Canada | Canada | Canada Council for the Arts | Conseil des arts du Canada

We acknowledge the support of the Canada Council for the Arts.
Nous remercions le Conseil des arts du Canada de son soutien.

McGill-Queen's University Press in Montreal is on land which long served as a site of meeting and exchange amongst Indigenous Peoples, including the Haudenosaunee and Anishinabeg nations. In Kingston it is situated on the territory of the Haudenosaunee and Anishinaabek. We acknowledge and thank the diverse Indigenous Peoples whose footsteps have marked these territories on which peoples of the world now gather.

Library and Archives Canada Cataloguing in Publication

Title: Montreal after dark : nighttime regulation and the pursuit of a global city / Matthieu Caron.
Names: Caron, Matthieu, author
Series: Studies on the history of Quebec ; 46.
Description: Series statement: Studies on the history of Quebec = Etudes d'histoire du Québec ; 46 | Includes bibliographical references and index.
Identifiers: Canadiana (print) 20240528484 | Canadiana (ebook) 20240528573 | ISBN 9780228024774 (paper) | ISBN 9780228025153 (ePUB) | ISBN 9780228025146 (ePDF)
Subjects: LCSH: Subculture—Québec (Province)—Montréal—History—20th century. | LCSH: Nightlife—Québec (Province)—Montréal—History—20th century. | LCSH: Urban policy—Québec (Province)—Montréal—History—20th century. | LCSH: Montréal (Québec)—Social life and customs—20th century.
Classification: LCC HN110.M6 C37 2025 | DDC 306/.17142809045—dc23

This book was designed and typeset by studio oneonone in Minion 11/14.
Copyediting by Eleanor Gasparik.

McGill-Queen's University Press
Suite 1720, 1010 Sherbrooke St West, Montreal, QC, H3A 2R7

Authorized safety representative in the EU: Mare Nostrum Group BV, Mauritskade 21D, 1091 GC Amsterdam, the Netherlands, gpsr@mare-nostrum.co.uk

For Daphné

CONTENTS

TABLES AND FIGURES

Tables

Figures

ACKNOWLEDGMENTS

This book owes to the brilliance of Marie-Claire Blais, Leonard Cohen, Dany Laferrière, Hugh MacLennan, Gabrielle Roy, and Michel Tremblay, each of whom informed this twenty-first-century reader about life in twentieth-century Montreal. Inspired – and fuelled by countless espressos – I embarked on a journey that questioned how regulations, at once shaped by environmental and political conditions, transformed Montreal during the second half of that century.

This intellectual journey concludes here, with a book that has travelled between several institutions over the past few years, gathering many debts of gratitude as I engaged with inspiring scholars, archivists, and editors along the way. Since it began as a doctoral dissertation at the University of Toronto, my first and deepest thanks go to my adviser, Sean Mills, whose unwavering support has been invaluable throughout the years. His generosity, encouragement, and sharp intellect were crucial to the completion of this work. I am privileged to have trained as a historian under Sean's guidance, as he has been both a mentor and role model. Throughout my graduate studies, I also benefitted from discussions with outstanding scholars, including LK Bertram, Harold Bérubé, Michèle Dagenais, Brian Gettler, Richard Harris, Marcel Martel, David Meren, Tamara Myers, Steve Penfold, and Will Straw. More recently, my post-doctoral adviser at Simon Fraser University, Nicolas Kenny, has been instrumental in refining some of the book's ideas, seeing Montreal's place within a broader urban history repertoire. And my collaboration with the team at McGill-Queen's University Press, including Jonathan Crago, Magda Fahrni, Kathleen Fraser, and Eleanor Gasparik, was an indispensable part of the journey, guiding this project to completion.

When this project was an idea in its embryonic stage, I received funding for a summer residency at the Canadian Centre for Architecture. Here, I received advice from archivists, who were helpful, considerate, and patient with my requests. The residency also allowed me to meet inspiring scholars from different spheres, including art history and architecture; thanks to Kim Förster, Valeria Téllez Niemeyer, and Lukas Pauer for stimulating conversations. That summer I had the good fortune of meeting equally great archivists at UQÀM and at the Archives gaies du Québec (AGQ). Thanks to Jacques Prince and Ross Higgins who guided me at the AGQ, readily considering some of the themes that piqued my curiosity and interest. (Under very serendipitous circumstances I happened to be on-site when Ross Higgins received the Senate 150th Anniversary Medal in recognition of his years of service to the community – I was witnessing history while crafting it.) The following summer I was a Corsini fellow at McMaster University. There, a few months before the pandemic, I was able to have lengthy conversations about Canadian history with Maxime Dagenais, Ian McKay, and Jodey Nurse. Indeed, like all historians, my research was enriched through stimulating conversations with scholars and the skilful know-how of archivists and librarians. But this was particularly true during the lockdowns caused by the COVID-19 pandemic. Special thanks to Joséphine Waline Ndour and Agnieszka Prycik at the Archives de la Ville de Montréal for digitizing and providing materials that would otherwise have been inaccessible. I am particular grateful for their swift and helpful responses.

In addition to the doctoral residency and the fellowship, the generous funding from several organizations allowed me to visit archives, present early drafts, and dedicate my time to working on this book. The Social Sciences and Humanities Research Council of Canada jump-started my research efforts, and the University of Toronto also provided funds for research travel. The Ontario Graduate Scholarship and the Fonds de recherche du Québec–Société et culture also contributed along the way as this work transitioned into a completed dissertation and, later, into the publication phase. Okanagan College's Grants-in-Aid fund provided funds for travel and to hire research assistants.

Toronto, home to a vibrant intellectual community, was where I met kind and encouraging colleagues who became friends along the way. Among them are Mathieu Arsenault, Chris Baldwin, Ben Bradley, Eriks Bredovskis, Sanchia DeSouza, Joel Dickau, Eric Fillion, Alison MacAulay, Chandra Murdoch, Dan Poitras, Nisrine Rahal, Daniel Ross, Nastasha Sartore, Joseph Stollenwerk, Simon Vickers, and Michael Weaver. In September 2018, Ed Dunsworth and I launched a monthly workshop designed for graduate students to share their works-in-progress, fostering dialogue and debate about Canadian history. Our loose organization, known informally as the Canadianist workshop, brought both camaraderie and structure to the writing process, and I am thankful to all who contributed to its success.

Finally, this book would not have been possible without the constant support of my friends and family in Montreal. Above all, I am especially grateful to Jayla Kennedy, who has been a steadfast companion throughout this interprovincial process. Between finishing the dissertation and publishing this book, we welcomed our daughter. Now, as I close this chapter in my life, Daphné is starting hers. Maybe she'll find a use for this book beyond a bedtime story to get her to sleep – but I won't hold my breath.

ABBREVIATIONS AND SELECT CITY OF MONTREAL BYLAWS

Abbreviations

ADGQ	Association pour les droits des gai(e)s du Québec
AGQ	Archives Gaies du Québec
AVM	Archives de la Ville de Montréal
BAnQ	Bibliothèque et Archives nationales du Québec
CAL	Civic Action League
CBC	Canadian Broadcasting Corporation
CCA	Canadian Centre for Architecture
CHAR	Comité homosexuel anti-répression
COJO	Comité organisateur des Jeux Olympiques de 1976
FCQ	Front commun des Québécoises
FLF	Front de libération des femmes
FRAP	Front d'action politique
GHAP	Groupe homosexuel d'action politique
GMCA	Greater Montreal Council of Arts (Conseil des arts de la région métropolitaine de Montréal)
LDL	Ligue des droits et libertés
MCM	Montreal Citizens' Movement
MFA	Montreal Firemen's Association
MLT	Mouvement de libération du taxi
MNA	Member of the National Assembly of Quebec

MPB	Montreal Policemen's Brotherhood
MTC	Montreal Transportation Commission
PMC	Public Morality Committee
QB	Court of Queen's Bench
QCA	Quebec Court of Appeal
QLB	Quebec Liquor Board
QPP	Quebec Provincial Police
QSC	Superior Court of Quebec
RCMP	Royal Canadian Mounted Police
SCR	Canada Supreme Court Reports
SQ	Sûreté du Québec
UQÀM	Université du Québec à Montréal

Select City of Montreal Bylaws (in chronological order)

1905	Bylaw 333, Anti-loitering
1927	Bylaw 926, Concerning food establishments and restaurants
1937	Bylaw 1448, Concerning noise
1942	Bylaw 1715, Concerning the curfew
1953	Bylaw 2129, Prohibiting the display, distribution, and printing of nude or semi-nude images
1955	Bylaw 2223, Anti-pinball machine
1961	Bylaw 2655, Concerning the Police Department
1967	Bylaw 3416, Anti-mingling
1969	Bylaw 3926, Anti-demonstration
1980	Bylaw 5464, Anti-prostitution
1980	Bylaw 5465, Anti-drinking
1983	Bylaw 6249, Anti-soliciting

MONTREAL AFTER DARK

INTRODUCTION: DUSK

In February 1972, two Montreal journalists embarked on a transcontinental journey to Jocotepec, a small mountain-side town on the outskirts of Guadalajara. Upon arrival they met Licenciado, an old energetic man, who they had come to interview. Licenciado lived in seclusion, on a vast property enclosed by barbed wire, which, as he later told the journalists, gave him privacy and allowed him to spend carefree days enjoying the territory's subtropical climate while reading or farming. Licenciado's routine was simple, and he liked sharing it with Toutsi, a faithful Dobermann that added a sense of comfort and peace to his life. As part of their duty, the journalists observed Licenciado drive around town in a luxurious American car and engage in friendly and lively conversations with acquaintances, shopkeepers, and the mayor. Naturally, "Licenciado," a term long used to address legal professionals in Latin America, was not the old man's birth name. Rather, it was a pseudonym and a reminder of what had been his career.

Rural Mexico offered Licenciado a modest living, and although mundane, it was the desired denouement to a tumultuous life. After all, he once told a Canadian reporter, "I loathe and detest city life. I would love it if I could stay in the country the rest of my life."[1] And escaping the city is precisely what he did in 1958 when he left Montreal and exiled himself to a location that only a handful of people knew about. But the secrecy of his whereabouts, from the moment he left Montreal until he died at the age of sixty-nine in 1976, hinted at a deeper need to evade not just the throng of urban life but also Montreal's criminal underworld. In fact, the two journalists had made the long journey to meet with Licenciado, the one they and all of Quebec knew as Pacifique (Pax) Plante, for an exclusive interview that promised to shed light on his illustrious professional career during which he had waged war on vice, corruption, and organized crime.[2]

After welcoming the journalists into his home, Pax Plante began retrieving memories of mid-twentieth-century Montreal. During lengthy conversations he talked about the city during the 1940s and '50s and described it as wide-open, gripped by an underworld whose racketeering power extracted profits from nighttime establishments. These spaces – late-night gambling dens, brothels, speakeasies, and nightclubs – were connected through an underworld that sustained business by keeping police officers on the payroll and funnelling dirty money to politicians.[3] Plante reminisced about the war he had waged against this underworld, first as the head of the Police Department's Morality Squad and later as assistant chief of police, and the pleasure he took in cleaning up Montreal through waves of successful raids.

At a revealing moment, after Plante had re-emphasized the tenacity of Montreal's underground economy, he disclosed the crux of his crusade: "From the very beginning my slogan was: *Throw the spotlight on 'em!* And if I may share a small memory from college, it might be of these people that Ecclesiastes refers to when it mentions the *lucifugous*."[4] Montreal's lucifugal underworld, Plante contended, sustained a diversified informal economy that comprised sex workers, cab drivers, gangsters, hospitality industry labourers, corrupt police and politicians, nightclub and cabaret artists, and, perhaps most importantly, residents and tourists who consumed night's pleasures. Darkness had been their private playground, and Plante made it his mission to shed light on their social spheres. Propelled by a persevering belief in justice and morality, Plante told the two journalists that the night had been playing host to disreputable activities and desires. Certainly, his crusade was not the first of its sort. Rather, it marked a fresh engagement with old social struggles about what should and should not happen in certain places during the darkness of night. In fact, his slogan, "Throw the spotlight on ... those who flee light," would capture a specific mid-twentieth-century view that was shared by fellow Montreal reformers and technocratic modernists in cities across the globe. Urban life could be vastly improved, each argued, if specific rules and regulations were implemented to manage nighttime's disorder and moral dangers.[5]

This book discusses the period from the 1950s through the 1980s, when the regulation of night loomed large on the agenda of Montreal's civic leaders. It focuses on public and private spaces where nighttime regulation was enforced and contested. It demonstrates that, above all, the regulation of night was a project that would alter urban culture and social norms regarding sex, alcohol, labour, art, and dissent. Chiefly concerned with respectability and moral order, mid-twentieth-century civic leaders believed that by regulating the night they could transform Montreal from a crime-beleaguered city into an internationally ranked, global destination. This process mirrored trends seen in other North American cities, where urban authorities, reporters, activists, artists, residents, and sex workers renegotiated rules and regulations, debating who had a right to nighttime public space, what constituted acceptable behaviour and art, and whose sexual activity sustained the social order versus whose threatened to destroy it.[6] Effectively, this book begins with the coming to power of a municipal reform movement, one that was deeply tied to policing and that was built on a long tradition of moral regulation and suspicion of nonconformity, and it examines how this movement and its leaders would recast Montreal by waging war on the night's disreputable haunts and informal economies. Police amassed information on illicit behaviours, and it used this information to inform politicians and encourage them to further their reformist projects, thus becoming part of a feedback loop that would see the police and municipal politicians mutually reinforcing each other's drive to regulate city space. In fact, the crucial role played by the police was brought home when unionized members of the city's police and fire departments staged wildcat strikes. With their absence, the night descended into chaos and panic. Residents, emboldened by darkness and the lack of protective services, saw a chance to defy the political and economic order, looting stores and setting homes and businesses aflame. The night's dual nature was laid bare: while the authorities viewed it as a time to assert control, organized labour saw it as a time to contest that very control. In this way, the night became a powerful bargaining tool, a time when power both expanded and contracted.

Accounts from those affected by the reformers' regulatory measures reveal an important conjuncture in the histories of urban governance, labour, and sex during a period of social change.[7] Among such stories is one told by a woman who arrived in Montreal precisely when Pax Plante began his ruthless crackdown during the late 1940s. Like hundreds of thousands of mid-twentieth-century rural Quebecers, Rita Picard moved to the province's economic centre hoping to get a slice of the city's postwar economic prosperity. Rather than adhering to the formal economy, however, she, like many postwar migrants who moved to the "big city," chose to earn money in the informal economy. In a tell-all autobiography about her life in the sex industry, Picard writes that when she arrived in Montreal the industry functioned in an organized and somewhat secure environment, within brothels and under the watchful eyes of housekeepers and madams – a position she assumed later in her career.[8] While this lucrative industry had been safeguarded during the early twentieth century, it was completely upended when Plante ordered successive raids and proceeded to dismantle the mechanisms that allowed businesses to benefit from police and political protection. The mass shuttering of brothels displaced sex workers and allowed male pimps to gradually encroach the sex industry. Moreover, the territorial shift of the industry led many sex workers into drinking establishments, where criminal organizations offered limited protection.[9] In response, the city heightened its control over alcohol regulation, thereby prompting sex workers to adjust their practices once again. By the 1970s and '80s, some sex workers found work through massage parlours and call-girl networks, but many were driven to street corners, parks, and public squares, which created another public uproar.[10]

As several Montreal historians have already demonstrated, the sensational Caron Inquiry (1950–54), which brought commercialized vice and corruption into full public view, paved the way for these political and popular reforms.[11] Within the span of a few weeks in October 1954, the inquiry published its report, and a new municipal party, the Civic Action League (CAL), was elected to office. Under the campaign slogan "serving the public, not ourselves," the CAL promised to restore "honesty" in Montreal politics by ending corruption.[12] The party was headed by Jean Drapeau, a thirty-eight-year-old French-Canadian lawyer with strong Catholic and conservative convictions. Like Pax Plante, Jean Drapeau deeply valued justice and morality. Yet, his ambition for Montreal was much greater than his crime-busting partner. He aspired for more than the cleansing of local affairs: Drapeau aimed to elevate Montreal's global profile, hoping that the city might influence global urban culture.

During Mayor Drapeau's first term the tenets of civic reforms produced impressive change as he built on the momentum that Pax Plante had created. After the late-1940s crackdown, Plante, now assistant chief of police under Mayor Drapeau, supervised a series of additional raids on the few – discreet – brothels that remained. Along the way regulation acquired further spatial dimension while remaining fixated on the nocturne, as authorities regulated the night by enforcing the closing time of drinking establishments and by dismantling practices in the taxi industry that allowed revellers to cavort from one clandestine business to another. To be sure, the immediate target of these actions was the informal economy. However, because this economy was so closely tied to nighttime activities, the city realized that further regulation of nightlife could address broader public issues. Consequently, while brothels, gambling dens, and speakeasies were the primary focus of law enforcement, legal establishments such as nightclubs, cabarets, and bars also faced increased enforcement of long-neglected rules and regulations. Therefore, during Mayor Drapeau's first term, the regulation of night became more encompassing, no longer relating only to the informal economy but also to elements that were believed to mar the city's reputation abroad. This book is about this persistent and powerful ideological reform movement and the effect it had on sex, alcohol, labour, art, and dissent as elected officials wrestled to transform Montreal into a global city.

Although Drapeau and his party were unseated in 1957, he returned to power in 1960 under the freshly established Civic Party. Just one month before the election, and recognizing the need for a new start from the somewhat outdated ideas of the CAL, he introduced the Civic Party to electors. At the beginning of this second term, Drapeau, like the mayors of other major North American cities during the 1960s, turned his attention to the idea of police reform. He stated that if the city was able to clean up its Police Department, the rest would follow, and that is precisely what the Civic Party set out to do.[13] Montreal hired police reformers who proposed solutions to combat the department's problems with corruption and incompetence – issues that were brought to light by the Caron Inquiry. Their initiatives paved the way for the department's restructuring, resulting in better-trained officers capable of effectively managing the most disorderly aspects of city life. The alliance between police and elected officials would grow over time, strengthening the link between authority and governance. Essentially, the city expanded its influence over the night as officers conducted raids on illegal spots and monitored drinking establishments thought to be catering to sex workers, queer community members, and gamblers.[14] But early on, in a matter of months during the early 1960s, the Civic Party had become the emblem of modernism in Montreal, not only by tackling issues like police reform but also through its commitment to urban redevelopment. In fact, for many in the province the Drapeau era has been read as axiomatic of the Quiet Revolution, mirroring the powerful zeitgeist of 1960s Quebec.[15]

Under the Civic Party, Drapeau governed the city he loved for over a quarter century, holding an outsized expectation for it. His party ushered in an unprecedented construction boom that completely recast the city's landscape and its skyline. He played a key role in transforming the city, which ultimately benefited from his determination to promote megaprojects. Its swift transformation required supporting new transit infrastructure, including the building of a vast subway system and an adjoining climate-controlled underground city that included miles of shops, restaurants, bars, and theatres.[16] Where the automobile was more suitable, the city made major public investments in street widenings, acting to make Montreal a "metropolis of progress."[17] Around the same time, it launched *Montréal* (1964–68), a periodical designed to promote the city abroad. In its inaugural issue, Drapeau allowed himself to wax poetic about Montreal's recent metamorphosis in no less than five European languages: "Today, Montreal is in the midst of its most stimulating period in history. Already one of North America's greatest cities, it is moving ahead boldly with enthusiasm and dynamism to become a leading world metropolis." The following year, sensing that he was on the cusp of greatness, he rearticulated that statement: "Indeed, what we have been witnessing in recent years is not a point of arrival but a point of departure."[18] These efforts seemed to culminate with the 1967 world's fair, which drew millions of visitors to Montreal. The event was an emphatic realization of Montreal as a desirable global destination, the sum of which gave the impression that anything was possible for the city as it buzzed with cultures from around the world.

Amidst the colonial celebrations of Canada's Centennial, crowds flocked to Expo 67's site to see a host of visual and aural spectacles under its strikingly modernist theme, Man and His World.[19] That same year the city proudly unveiled a comprehensive and large-scale master plan for metropolitan Montreal, *Horizon 2000*. The audio-visual report offered an optimistic outlook on the year 2000: in space-age sounds and images it presented an expansive city of seven million inhabitants.[20] During the 1960s Montreal seemed oblivious to the possibility of its decline.

In Montreal, night, a natural period of darkness, evolved into a battleground where ambitions could be observed. Notwithstanding its contradictions and its historical links to the informal economy, city reformers recognized the potential that nighttime held in propelling Montreal toward achieving global metropolis status. While it remained a moment for rest, it also was in the process of being incorporated into the expansionary tendencies of consumer capitalism. Socialization in legitimate spaces, like restaurants, cabarets, cafés, and theatres, enhanced Montreal's image as a sophisticated and cultured city. Indeed, night symbolized not just vice, crime, and darkness but also an extension of the public realm, an environment and time for consumption and of socialization.[21] And like in cities across the globe, residents spent their hard-earned cash in the formal nighttime economy.[22] In fact, the reformist movement did not condemn nightlife outright. It embraced the illuminated city – bright boulevards, neon signs, and high culture – as an integral part of global modernity. And this could be seen, for example, in the development of strategies designed to enhance the nighttime economy and in the city's attempts to reimagine, reinvent itself as a place of consumption of high cultural forms based in the nighttime economy. As this economy flourished, it was inevitably shaped by the city's negotiation with the environmental realities created by night.

For instance, members of the Public Morality Committee (PMC), the reformist group that was responsible for the Caron Inquiry, drove around, night after night, noting which establishments were open and registering the sorts of activity transpiring within or outside of them. As previous research has shown, the committee's concerns reflected a middle-class perspective on urban regulations, as their reports fixated on late-night entertainment and sexual activities.[23] Its members would have seen sleepless gadabouts gallivanting around the city, searching for the next clandestine

Figure 0.1
Scene of Sainte-Catherine at night, 5 May 1964.

business. When one of their own, Jean Drapeau, became mayor, that approach was expanded. He, too, drove around the city in his black sedan, actively seeking out nuisances – ranging from commercial streets cluttered with newspaper boxes and pornographic images to noisy discotheques and nightclubs – the sum of which motivated him to work tirelessly, often for eighteen hours a day. In fact, while on official business abroad, he gained new knowledge about urban environments after dark. Reportedly, he would embark on "a relentless 10-mile hike through the night to study his hosts' street lights, parks, traffic systems and garbage operations," which took place after his late-night dinners and lasted until 3 a.m.[24] Like most busy politicians, Drapeau's sleeping habits were erratic. Nonetheless, after several decades in power, he could confidently proclaim that Montreal looked nothing like it did in the days of his youth. Because his vision for Montreal was crisp, he had been able to direct the enactment of, or amendment to, bylaws that prohibited a wide range of visual and aural nuisances against public morality, respectability, and order.[25] Regulating urban forms and civic spaces was essential in legitimizing authority; in return, the transformation of urban space stimulated new types and levels of consumption that set the stage for a sense of civic pride that corresponded with the administration's worldly ambitions.

Crucially, the formal integration of the nighttime economy into consumer capitalism was part of a strategy to offset industrial decline as the city's old economy transitioned into a new service-based economy during this period.[26] For instance, "Focus on Montreal," in the aforementioned periodical *Montréal*, promoted the city's link with the world by reviewing internationally renowned figures who toured the city, thus contributing toward making its high culture a defining and pleasant feature.[27] Therefore, the political interest in the nighttime economy, where macroeconomic and cultural shifts came to terms with a specific political-legal entity and local cultural practice, partially explains the ferocious attitude that the city held toward nighttime's informal economies. Throughout this period, city policies recreated night spaces so that people's actions and desires would be directed, if not outright controlled. And it was the ongoing pursuit of this clandestine realm, which operated under the cover of night, that had a swift impact on what Montreal was, and what it would become.

As a voracious reader of Western history, Mayor Drapeau understood the era's historical moment, which allowed him to envision a future in which Montreal would be the North American hub for Western high culture. He perceived how Montreal fit into the contemporary period and how future historians might see it as a city that had made substantial contributions to the international community during the second half of the twentieth century. Indeed, in the mid-1960s Drapeau claimed that Montreal did more for the arts than any city on the continent, which was paramount to the city's global prominence: "Being a metropolis imposes obligations as well as privileges ... the movement to make Montreal a great world city has definitely been launched. In the future, no list of great cities will be complete without a mention of Montreal."[28] Clearly, that belief was rooted in his love for Western art and culture. He admired men of letters and collected their poems, compatriots like Octave Crémazie, Paul Morin, Louis Fréchette, and

Albert Ferland.[29] In fact, his short-lived fine dining establishment, Le Vaisseau d'Or (1969–71), honoured famous Montreal poet Émile Nelligan. And he once declared, during a passionate political speech, that "artistic life within the metropolis should be a veritable industry."[30] This love for the arts paved the way for the creation of the Greater Montreal Council of Arts (GMCA), which was directly attached to his office. The GMCA openly exhibited his penchant for high culture, allocating funds for many plays, operas, ballets, and orchestral works and compositions. Indeed, the Civic Party, a populist party, perceived the arts in a binary of either low or high culture, which impacted the vision it held for Montreal's future and the way it managed the night.

Drapeau, however, tirelessly pursued another iteration of high culture – the 1976 Summer Olympic Games. He claimed that the event would be nothing short of Montreal's pinnacle of achievement since it had been founded as a French missionary colony in 1642. That summer, for the length of a few weeks, the Games created a unique spirit of international celebration, one that was broadcasted worldwide on television and in print media.[31] The event – ultimately marred by a scandalous financial fiasco, artistic censorship, and a ruthless crackdown on queer nightlife – also led to the planning of permanent structures that not only outlasted the Games but also solidified Mayor Drapeau's legacy. In a very real sense, the Olympic Games not only raised Montreal's global profile but also connected it to ancient history. And, in another way, this connection was strengthened a few years later, albeit with limited global outreach, when Drapeau personally travelled to Cairo to negotiate the 1985 exhibition *The Great Pharaoh Ramses II and His Time*, North America's first important display of Egyptian antiquities in over two decades.[32] Certainly, Drapeau boosted the city's global image by organizing events of various sizes, which, he claimed, improved the lives of Montrealers. These projects gave him confidence and pride in speaking about his city's high culture, especially when he welcomed tourists, international celebrities and entertainers, dignitaries, politicians, royalty, and, toward the end of his political career, the Pope.[33] His vision for the city was as grand as his love for it and this involved opening it up for the world to see.

In 1986, during the final year of his eighth mandate – a reign that overlapped with seven Canadian prime ministers and nine Quebec premiers – the seventy-year-old mayor announced that he would not seek re-election.

By then he had solidified his place as one of the most remarkable politicians in Canadian history. Indeed, no twentieth-century Canadian politician at any level of government produced such lasting monuments and memories for his or her constituents.

The paragraphs above offer insight into how this history represents a tale of Montreal's exceptionalism. But as I alluded to earlier, this story is also about one iteration of the larger phenomenon of imagining the urban future during the mid-twentieth century. This was a period when issues like the nature and workings of economic globalization, the role of cross-border finance in urban development, and social or class polarization was being renegotiated, which shifted the focus toward rich and prosperous cities. As Dutch sociologist Saskia Sassen stresses, under the supremacy of globalization, cities organize life as much or more than nations.[34] Indeed, Montreal offers a specific and powerful example through which to think about the major transformations that Western cities experienced during this period.

***

In Montreal, politicians knew that their city's transformation into a modern and vice-free metropolis hinged on its ability to control the night. Put another way, reformers wanted nighttime activities to be brought into the formal economy, one that was free from sin and transgression, and that evoked a certain soundscape and visual aesthetic. As mayor of Montreal, Drapeau paid careful attention to noise and visual aesthetics and used this intimate knowledge to develop new regulations for the city, which altered the night and its economies. This approach effectively demonstrates French philosopher Henri Lefebvre's notion that "political power knows how to utilise and manipulate time, dates, time-tables" and American sociologist Murray Melbin's claim that "a change in the temporal order jolts the social system."[35] Control over the night thus emerged as a struggle between competing ideas about the urban political economy. Regulatory measures created temporal order, and temporal order allowed authorities to assert control over the unruliest aspects of city life. The dual effective of nighttime regulation allowed authorities to partially crush informal economies and end norms deemed inferior, which in turn allowed greater space for the formal economy to claim the night, thereby attracting a different, reputable clientele. In other words, it was the municipal administration's view that a city that could not govern and regulate the nighttime environment was a city in disarray, and a city in disarray would deter deep-pocketed investors, entrepreneurs, and tourists from selecting it as a place to spend money.[36]

Examining mid-twentieth-century Montreal's relationship with the night encourages us to think about the urban in a way that evokes broad categories. Indeed, a major part of this book considers the civic governance of sex, which offers a unique perspective on the intertwining histories of urban regulation, politics, law, and culture. During the second half of the twentieth century, particularly under the Civic Action League and the Civic Party, Montreal revised the boundaries of moral acceptability by engaging in what American historian Anne Gray Fischer calls "sexual policing" – the targeting and legal control of people's bodies and their presumed sexual activities.[37] Sexual policing refers to more than simply enforcing prostitution laws per se, or the narrowly defined exchange of sex for money. It amounted to enforcing vaguely termed bylaws that reinforced public order and social hierarchies. Reflecting both the biases of many officers and the structures of non-heteronormative life, nighttime policing often posed a special risk to socially and economically underprivileged individuals, especially those marginalized by race, gender, and sexuality. Authorities used anti-loitering, anti-prostitution, and anti-soliciting bylaws to forge nighttime "cleanup campaigns." Effectively, local bylaws were created to address broad concerns about sex as a prime cause of public disorder. Each one aimed to regulate public behaviour and to maintain control of city space, but the agenda was much more expansive. In times of extreme anxiety, authorities raided nighttime venues like bathhouses, cabarets, nightclubs, and bars because they saw each one as representing a threat to the social order. These raids mostly targeted women, transgender people, or gay men and were based on reports that severely overestimated each community's position in the sex industry. While Montreal's social reformers believed in the tenets of respectable heteronormativity, their vision was wide. During the second half of the twentieth century, it expanded to other alleged forms of moral decay, like erotic films and literature, protest art, and the yellow press, and would even lead to the city's outlawing of tarot reading and pinball machines.[38] Civic authorities regarded each of the above as a bold and dangerous element that resisted the reform movement's rational structures.

And it was under this scenario that municipal regulation became increasingly pervasive and comprehensive.

Because political and police control over night was deeply entangled in urban policies and legislative processes, this book also shows how the history of nighttime regulation and control was dependent on the shifting boundaries of jurisdictional authority. As already mentioned, to integrate night into the formal economy the municipal administration created and amended numerous bylaws. These provided a ready tool for police officers to justify crackdowns and raids on disreputable or nonconforming behaviours, the sum of which allowed the city to articulate a rhetoric of "progress" and "development" that it would circulate across the globe. During the second half of the twentieth century, Montreal enacted bylaws regulating behaviour, sex, alcohol, and freedom of speech in public space, each of which was a direct challenge to federal and provincial spheres of influence. To borrow the words of art historian Lynda Nead, these campaigns related to a "visual economy of public display and viewing" and were about who occupied the streets, how they behaved, and what they looked like.[39] This process not only exploited the vague nature of the Canadian legal system but also defied legal conventions, complicating relationships between the city and federal and provincial authorities. For instance, during the politically charged year of 1969, the city enacted an anti-demonstration bylaw under the premise that it was regulating the use of public space, even though it had long been clear that the right to assemble and express political opinions – what the bylaw was actually targeting – falls under exclusive federal authority. In the 1980s, the city used a similar approach to curb street-based sex work even though prostitution laws also fall under federal authority. City lawyers held fast to the claim that Montreal's 1980 anti-prostitution bylaw and its 1983 anti-soliciting bylaw regulated public space and not prostitution per se. But the city did not have much success in its arguments; the courts, both the Superior Court of Quebec and the Supreme Court of Canada, tended to side with the provincial or federal government in constitutional disputes, striking down municipal bylaws as ultra vires.

The second half of the twentieth century was a period of urban growth for Montreal. In 1951, driven by the postwar baby boom and both intraprovincial and international migration, the city's population reached one million.[40] The city's expansion was a historical moment that made regulation more complex as well as more important. This book demonstrates how the battle for increased nighttime law enforcement was grounded in an urban political economy that was based in morals policing, itself a response to the city's growth. Although the administration's anxiety over vice and immorality evolved over time, depending on the historical moment, one thing remained clear: Montreal's transformation was rooted in a heteronormative vision of urban space, one that believed that illicit, immoral, and unruly behaviours had to be expelled from public view to make way for a respectable urban culture and modern projects. Therefore, throughout the second half of the twentieth century, as the city's landscape was being redeveloped and its image recast, the night became a key battleground between diverse groups wrestling to shape the city's future.

The night was thus a time and space in which different rules applied as the municipal administration repeatedly tried to impose its authority over it. The expansion of municipal control over nighttime was bound up in norms and codes that have deep historical roots in heteronormativity and moral regulation. Historians have examined how certain categories such as "nuisance," "vagrant," and "prostitute" are political categories born of racialized municipal codes, policing, and official and unofficial practices of segregation that take us to the heart of the operations of an urbanizing settler colonialism.[41] Clearly, the policing of sexual activities did not begin in the mid-twentieth century. On the grandest scale, the mid- to late-twentieth-century policing of it was just the latest chapter in a long history of repression. What this book reveals, however, is the way in which nighttime surveillance of nonconforming behaviour could not be disentangled from the vision the administration held for Montreal and its place on the global stage. For that reason, and as I have already elaborated, the civic effort to recast the city's image had deep connections to notions of heteronormativity and morality. However, the night was also a moment when heteronormative values and morals could be challenged, whether on the stages of cabarets, in dark and dingy tourist rooms, or on the streets through public protests. Although it is impossible to qualify the success of these challenges, many who defied urban authorities, conventions, and norms spoke proudly about exercising their freedom.[42] Illustrating these connections underlines the value of doing a kind of urban history that overlaps with and learns from wider scholarship, connecting social, legal, and political history.

***

This book shows how Montreal's mid- to late-twentieth-century transformation was enabled by three interrelated processes. First, a greater control of the night was implemented. From the 1950s to the 1980s, basic arrangements regarding alcohol, sex, labour, noise, and protest experienced serious upheavals as the city expanded its authority. Second, municipal authorities operated with heteronormative frameworks that understood nonnormative displays as a threat to the social order. Over the course of several decades municipal leaders and police took steps to regulate and control the night by enacting bylaws and enforcing them in nightspots and in public space where women and queer community members of different races mingled. And third, because the night was a time when different rules applied, and when power expanded and contracted, it could also transform into a moment to contest the political order. Because the administration's project prioritized urban visual aesthetics over helping the most marginalized, nighttime became a terrain where the boundaries of authority were vociferously contested. Night thus became a time when the struggles over the future of society played out.

Chapter 1 begins by looking at how an informal nighttime economy took root in early twentieth-century Montreal. It shows how social reformers repeatedly tried to curb illicit nightlife – to no avail. Eventually Pax Plante and Jean Drapeau started a process that would uproot the city's most famous brothels and gambling dens, and dismantle a network of police and political corruption. The process, however, went much further as reformers strictly enforced rules and regulations that pertained to the press, liquor, taxi and the hospitality industries. In the span of a few months Montreal's nighttime economy underwent serious reorganization.

Although Montrealers voted Drapeau out of power in 1957, they reelected him under the newly formed Civic Party in 1960. During his second and third terms, the gamut of the postwar economic boom produced an era of prosperity that permitted the city's rapid transformation into a global city. Its recasting involved the bulldozing of sections of low-income neighbourhoods to make way for new urban infrastructures, which marked a moment of reassessment of rules and regulations, including the police's role in enforcing them. Chapter 2 explores this transformation through two key developments: the restructuring of the Police Department and a noise-abatement campaign. The restructuring of the Police Department, effected by police reformers from London and Paris, aimed to eliminate corruption and to professionalize the Montreal workforce, which placed a greater set of demands on officers and brought civil servants into the department. During those years, the city also was being reshaped by urban development. As was the case in cities around the world, this development was linked to modern sounds brought on by industry as well as commercial, residential, and leisure activities. The city at night echoed with such relentless and pervasive sounds that a significant noise abatement campaign emerged. This effort led to a revision of the city's anti-noise bylaw, which granted police greater authority to detain and prosecute those responsible for the disturbances. While the night remained a concern for city officials during the early 1960s, it took on a different significance than in previous decades, as law and order, along with social norms, continued to shape the city's politics during this period.

Chapter 3 looks at the Civic Party's further reorganization of the nighttime economy in preparation for Expo 67. Weeks before the world's fair, and following police and news reports about dishonest practices in drinking establishments, the city passed a highly controversial "anti-mingling" bylaw, which prohibited drinking establishment employees from drinking, dancing, and sitting with customers. Effectively, elected officials thought that the bylaw could curb problems relating to prostitution and swindling. The bylaw was successful insofar as it allowed the city to monitor employees – particularly women in nightclubs, bars, and cabarets – who transgressed the legal barrier outlined by the bylaw. Further, the bylaw's loose framework also allowed local police to uphold moral norms and heteronormativity within the city's nightspots. Ultimately, police enforced the bylaw not necessarily where officers found dishonest employees but, rather, in nightspots where Montrealers of different economic background, race, and sexual orientation mingled. By further regulating establishments serving alcohol, officials claimed to have made the nighttime economy more honest, which enhanced Montreal's reputation as a suitable and safe tourist destination. However, the anti-mingling bylaw would have a profound ripple effect as it was cited as one of the reasons that pushed the province to form an inquiry into the alcohol beverage trade (Thinel Commission, 1968–71), which led to the modernization of provincial liquor legislation.

Chapter 4 shows how the Civic Party's project of rule relied on the city's protective services by focusing on the police and fire departments' strikes of 1969 and 1974. The chapter highlights two key facts. First, it shows the fundamental role of the police and fire departments in upholding the civic administration's vision and ambition for Montreal. Without these two departments, the administration's hegemonic structure collapsed. This was on clear display at night when Montrealers reaped the benefits of an unprotected city by engaging in acts of political protest, theft, vandalism, and arson. Second, because of their role as custodians of order, unionized members of the police and fire departments held a bargaining power unequaled by other sectors – an especially important fact in an era of political unrest and labour activism. Leading up to the strikes, unionized members of the Montreal police and fire departments were vocal in advocating for their cause. Paradoxically, once the strike began, their inaction triggered chaos and panic, allowing anarchy to take over the city at night and giving Montrealers a glimpse of life without protective services. In this sense nighttime played an irrefutable role in the bargaining process and shaping discourses around police funding.

Chapter 5 looks at the conflict over appropriate forms of nightlife and art in Montreal in the lead-up to the 1976 Summer Olympic Games. During the mid-1970s the civic administration continued to demonstrate an intolerance of different ideas and lifestyles, exemplified by its crackdown on protest art, queer nightspots, and visible forms of sex work. Nighttime reproduced some forms of power, while also providing opportunities for resistance. Once again, the city was concerned with optics in an increasingly connected world. The pre-Olympic cleanup campaign was a general attempt by the Civic Party to reaffirm hegemonic orthodoxy through surveillance, order, and so-called security in public space. Experiencing the administration's rueful approach to urban order and its repressive tactics, however, activists organized and challenged the hegemonic structure by organizing public demonstrations and protests. By stifling subversion in leftist art and sexual discourse, municipal authorities gave momentum to activists who brought their challenges to the Quebec Superior Court.

Chapter 6 examines why, at the tail end of Jean Drapeau's political career, the Civic Party launched an intense crackdown on street-based sex work. The chapter examines the administration's response to the proliferation of sex work in the late 1970s and early 1980s. During this period, the sex industry's visibility on city streets increased following a 1978 Supreme Court of Canada ruling that soliciting had to be "pressing and persistent" in order for sex workers to be charged. Because local police officers could not provide evidence that sex workers had been "pressing and persistent" during transactions, Montreal – like other Canadian cities – enacted its own anti-prostitution and anti-soliciting bylaws to circumvent the Criminal Code. This pan-Canadian contest over the right to prosecute sex workers led to passionate debates about the boundaries of the criminal justice system and the place of sex work and pornography in society. Under these circumstances the governance of nighttime public space became a terrain where profound questions about gender and the right to the city emerged, not only in Montreal but across the nation as well.

1

RED LIGHTS AND REFORMERS

Since the early nineteenth century, Montreal, like many other North American cities, had been a town where clandestine sex and alcohol could be purchased. Authorities were of two minds regarding the criminal underworld as they tried to strike a balance between regulating and punishing individuals for their behaviours. For instance, in the case of sex workers, they punished some women for prostitution, yet offered protection to others because they understood the sex industry as a "necessary 'evil' that could protect respectable women from the worst excesses of men's sexuality."[1] It was under these circumstances that a Red Light district, a densely populated space charged with sexual desire and transgression, flourished in Montreal. The Red Light district, dominated by the criminal underworld, was a popular destination for thrill-seekers from other neighbourhoods and from out-of-town; and like other segregated vice districts of the nineteenth century, police tolerated and protected this underground economy organized around race-based hierarchies and heteronormativity.[2]

At the turn of the twentieth century, as the hours of commerce expanded into the night and the pleasure-seeking public swelled, the Red Light district's popularity grew. As we will see below, throughout the first half of the twentieth century, both urban politics and global conflicts swayed how Montreal authorities governed the district. And although moralizers and reformers tried to stamp out vice there for more than half a century, their efforts fell short due to corrupt politicians and police officers who allocated limited resources to combat organized crime. Consequently, and under the leadership of Camillien Houde, who intermittently held the position of mayor between 1928 and 1954, Montreal's nightlife flourished as one of the continent's most active and uninhibited from the 1920s to the 1950s.[3]

Montreal by night, however, underwent a significant transformation beginning in the mid-twentieth century when prosecutors and reformers started to pay close attention to the relationship between municipal authorities and the criminal underworld. Chief among those involved was city attorney Pacifique (Pax) Plante, who was promoted to head the Police Department's Morality Squad in the mid-1940s. As the head of this unit, he ordered officers to enforce the laws that his predecessors simply refused to uphold – like the closing time of drinking establishments and the regulations that controlled the taxi industry – and he directed surprise raids of gambling dens, speakeasies, and brothels to dismantle Montreal's tenacious underground economy. This ruthless approach agitated his enemies, and in 1948 he was suspended then dismissed from the Police Department. In a way, Plante's efforts culminated after these events with the establishment of a judicial inquiry into the Montreal Police Department, commonly known as the Caron Inquiry (1950–54). The inquiry shifted events from the darkness of night into the daylight of the courtroom, proving beyond question that corruption among city politicians and police had fuelled illegal markets and immoral activities.While much more than the corruption probe was at stake during the municipal election campaign of 1954, Justice Caron's final report, delivered weeks ahead of the election, gave ammunition to a new reform party. Headed by mayoral candidate Jean Drapeau, the Civic Action League (CAL) was elected to office on a platform that promised to eradicate corruption from Montreal. This was the beginning of a pivotal moment in Montreal's history like no other.

The (re)invention of Montreal during the 1950s, under the CAL, happened in many official ways, but one of the most important was the reorganization of the nighttime economy. This chapter shows how the dramatic period of transition between Montreal's two longest-serving mayors, Camillien Houde and Jean Drapeau, was a struggle over nighttime governance. In Mayor Houde's city the underworld functioned largely unrestrained in nightclubs, brothels, and gambling dens – all of which were protected by city councillors and senior police officers who had been bought with bribes.

However, when Mayor Drapeau was elected, honesty, morality, and respectability became the guiding principles of urban governance. These principles held the promise of transforming Montreal into a global city, and to this end, his party generated a gendered and sexualized discourse about the city's appearance and about how it should look, especially at night. Ultimately, the city at night became a battleground over changing ideas of moral order.[4] Throughout its mandate, from 1954 to 1957, the CAL coordinated with the Police Department to clear non-normative behaviours from the city, which included seizing pinball machines and pornographic literature as well as shutting down dingy alleyway speakeasies and lavish brothels. Although seemingly disjointed, this multi-faceted approach should be understood within a single ideological framework.[5] Altogether, this chapter argues that regaining control of Montreal's nighttime economy – and purging it of illicit and disreputable activities – allowed Mayor Drapeau to mould Montreal into his vision of a modern city. By destroying the informal economy and rigorously enforcing laws and regulations to control nighttime, the municipal administration put an end to an older version of Montreal nightlife, which incensed its habitués and those whose livelihoods depended on it.

Nighttime in Ville-Marie and the Red Light District

Throughout most of the modern era, the flickering flame of lamp and candle cast a feeble candescence into the unknown darkness of the night. But during the nineteenth century, technological change in the quality of light began transforming how night was experienced, especially in urban centres of economic and political importance. Historians have illustrated the interplay between cities, modernity, and industrialization to show how night was filled with contradictions during this period. These contradictions are characterized by liberty and restriction or fantasy and fear, and were marked by many factors like one's class, race, sex, or religion and the way authorities upheld regulations.[6] Equally important was the increasing organization of daytime work and nighttime leisure under industrial capitalism. Along with new sounds, smells, and textures, this new system of production profoundly moulded the daily rhythm of people as they became bound to factory time.[7]

Mid-nineteenth-century nocturnal Montreal was not unlike most industrialized cities. During this period, residents grew accustomed to and dependent on luminescence created by gaslight. Later – as the economic, demographic, and industrial capital of Canada – Montreal witnessed electric light for the first time. And by the end of the century, it witnessed the industrialization of light, which spread across urban space to delineate central landmarks like main streets, train stations, churches, squares, and public buildings.[8] Industrial light gave the city a certain legibility and navigability after sundown, but on the whole, night still retained darkness so that it remained filled with unknowns. Around each street corner one could find criminal activity or romance, religious processions or friendly bootleggers.

In the first half of the twentieth century, industrial light began expanding from public landmarks to places of commerce, like cafés, taverns, cinemas, theatres, and bars, which gave rise to new patterns of work and leisure.[9] Nighttime leisure would cement a network connecting a world of taxis, hotels, restaurants, and nightclubs, with alcohol consumption, sex, and dancing as their nuclei. Within the Canadian context this rise in commercial amusement can be understood in the number of motion picture theatres, which doubled from 1930 to 1950.[10] Other commercial establishments, like taverns, restaurants, and nightclubs, were also on the rise, especially in prohibition-free Montreal.[11] In these alcohol-fuelled establishments Montrealers and tourists interacted and were wowed by talented performers – male, female, queer, drag, and racialized – who took the stage to play music, dance, sing, and act. Even children as young as three would entertain half-drunk audiences at an hour that matched their age.[12]

In some tearooms, jazz bars, speakeasies, or queer nightclubs, heterosexual whites sought sensual novelties by "slumming."[13] Slumming often occurred in Black clubs, like the Terminal Club, Rockhead's Paradise, and Café Saint-Michel. Audiences would see and hear sizzling entertainment as jazz and drag coexisted, sharing nights.[14] Famous nightlife columnist and cultured man-about-town Al Palmer claimed that there was "no color line [back] then," as interracial crowds and acts mingled in Little Burgundy nightclubs.[15] But while many Black club owners relied on a white clientele for the bulk of their business, white club owners made Black patrons feel distinctly unwelcome downtown, sometimes outright refusing them entry. Although no formal segregation laws existed in Canada, Blacks were often barred from these venues as well as other public places like restaurants, theatres, and dance halls.[16]

For a century, however, Montreal's uncontested epicentre of nighttime entertainment was its Red Light district. Palmer noted how this district was also a magnet for slumming: "It is not unusual for Montreal's Upper Strata to organize an evening in the district for the simple purpose of mingling with the shady characters."[17] The Red Light district's perimeter varied over time, stretching at its more expansive from Sherbrooke to Craig (present-day Saint-Antoine) streets, and from De Bleury to Saint-Denis streets. It was a place where people from various social classes and ethnicities mixed: a bustling hub, teeming with numerous clubs and bars and illegal gambling dens and brothels.[18] It was a space of leisure in which growing commercial venture attracted and required creativity, investment, and labour, which offered the promise of substantial financial returns. During its heyday, in the early twentieth century, many young women and men came to the district to find adventure, anonymity, and, of course, money.

While many women migrated to the city to work as domestics or in laundries and sweatshops, sex work earnings would have been an attractive proposal for some, especially those under social, labour, and economic constraints.[19] Brothels, lodged in tenement rows or in walk-up apartments, could serve as a workplace and a residence for women who chose to work in the sex industry. Guiding clients to the covert establishment would be a red light hanging in the portico. As times, the district's visual display of the sex industry was clearer, such as when men queued along sidewalks while sex workers – standing in the doorway or at a windowsill – waved them in one at a time. Not all women, however, boasted the freedom to pick the industry in which they worked; for some, entering the sex industry was not a choice but a product of their limited options.

Gradually, as nighttime practices became entrenched into cultural systems, administrators and social reformers began arguing that leisure and entertainment was a rejection of work ethic, discipline, and authority.[20] Throughout its history, the Red Light district had enemies: moralists and magistrates, residents and government officials, who, at various moments, formed uneasy allegiances to curb perceived immoralities. Such was the case in the 1920s, when social reformers embarked on a campaign to curtail the sex industry. In 1924 a civic organization named the Committee of Sixteen

(1918–26) hired detectives from Chicago – itself a city notorious for its underworld – to investigate sin in Montreal.[21] Upon inspection the two detectives, George O. Hadick and Alexander Schwaren, concluded that Montreal was "the most wide, the most open town [we] have ever seen … the rottenest town [we] have ever been in."[22] The detectives had in large part confirmed the allegations made by the Committee of Sixteen: there was collusion between the Police Department and the criminal underworld. Soon thereafter, the Quebec Superior Court commissioned an inquiry to discern how Montreal's Police Department and its elected officials protected criminals from prosecution. Held over several months in 1924–25, the Coderre Inquiry revealed rampant corruption and a deplorable situation within the Police Department and at City Hall. However, the municipal administration dismissed all recommendations and instead opted to uphold the system that combined surveillance and toleration of vice in the Red Light district.[23] The Coderre Inquiry failed to make an appreciable dent in municipal problems. Therefore, unlike most North American cities that had been swept by reformist policies during the early decades of the twentieth century, Montreal and its Red Light district weathered the storm.[24]

Despite what American crime-busters had to say about vice in Montreal, the Red Light district was home to a heterogeneous community. Many working-class families lived there, and unsupervised children played in its streets.[25] Unchaperoned teenaged girls wandered alone or in groups looking for fun. And, as historian Tamara Myers writes, though they did meet misfortunes and danger, they also found jobs, temporary lodgings, and pleasure in the district.[26] "Cobblers, grocers and restaurant keepers go about the task of educating their children in these surroundings, and if they are not unaware of the goings-on they are at least indifferent to them," wrote one *Maclean's* reporter.[27] Numerous residents remembered how madams and gambling kingpins made the district a welcoming and safe neighbourhood.[28] To be sure, this does not mean that it was devoid of violent crime. In the criminal underworld, disputes were settled violently whenever and wherever possible. The same organization could be friend or foe depending on the time, the place, and the circumstances. For example, Charlie Feigenbaum, who had helped the police in a drug trafficking investigation, was shot six times in broad daylight in 1933 after crossing notorious gambling kingpin Harry Davis.[29]

Adding to the Red Light's liveliness was its location between Chinatown and the Quartier Latin. The latter served as the city's francophone student district and home to Université Laval's Montreal campus from 1876 to 1919.[30] By being close to a university campus, and by virtue of its proximity to the port, the Red Light district thrived as an important site of both homosexual and heterosexual sociability. Alcohol and drugs fuelled mixed-race transients, and students roamed the neighbourhood at night looking for cheap brothels, vaudeville theatres, jazz clubs, and restaurants. Taxi drivers who were well acquainted with the city's underbelly and its discreet pleasures knew that this was the place to drive rambunctious youths who wished to purchase sex. This arrangement was advantageous for multiple parties since the drivers would often get a cut from the business they brought to an establishment.[31]

The heads of the underground economy made heaps of money through alcohol, sex, and gambling by paying off the right police officers. Meanwhile, officers were familiar with the women and men of the Red Light district and took advantage of certain privileges before making an arrest, relying on insider knowledge to build a case, especially against bootlegging venues like speakeasies and blind pigs. Indeed, co-operation ensured smooth business for the underground economy, benefitting many affiliates. Sex workers, in particular, found protection from the justice system and hostile clients, thanks to powerful and influential madams. It is paramount, however, to stress that the sex industry entailed many dangers, being a perilous universe with clear hierarchies, which involved the risk of sexually transmitted infection, unwanted pregnancy resulting in abortion, substance abuse, and violence.[32] Profits, not benevolence, guided business. Effectively, well-to-do madams were business owners and their industry was managed by housekeepers. Apart from the sex workers themselves, clients would have interacted mostly with these housekeepers as they were the ones who kept order. Some large brothels employed two or three housekeepers who would split twenty-four-hour shifts among themselves.

Elsewhere in the district, bookmakers connected with gamblers via telephone. Often, employees of restaurants, nightclubs, and taverns acted as intermediaries by placing bets for clients over the phone.[33] Gambling kingpins like Harry Davis, Harry Ship, Julius Silverberg, Vic Cotroni, or Armand Courville controlled a small army that contributed to the underground economy by funnelling money through 250 gambling dens. Meanwhile, the clientele inside these establishments reflected Montreal's mid-twentieth-century diversity as French, British, Chinese, Polish, Russian, Czech, and Jewish gamblers intermingled around tables, especially around the most popular game, a Middle Eastern dice game called barbotte.[34]

At the political centre of this "wide-open" city was a colossal and flamboyant character, Montreal mayor Camillien Houde. In 1928, Houde, a Conservative member of the provincial legislature since 1923, challenged and defeated Médéric Martin – Montreal's third-longest-serving mayor and well-known Liberal. From that moment forward, Houde would serve on and off as mayor until 1954.[35] The man universally known as Monsieur Montréal was described by eminent Montreal writer Hugh MacLennan as capable of expressing the city's "spirit of wit, tolerance, perversity, cynicism, gaiety, bawdiness, gallantry, delight in living and – make no error here – dignity."[36] Although he is mostly known for right-wing populism, Houde's politics were never anchored in any concrete philosophy. In fact, his scandalous political contradictions reached an apex during World War II when he – a royalist who held his interactions with the Queen in high regard – openly encouraged young men not to register under the National Resources Mobilization Act. Because he had defied the federal government's campaign, Houde was arrested and remained interned for four years (from August 1940 to August 1944) at Petawawa and Fredericton, the sum of which made him a wartime hero in the eyes of many French Canadians.[37]

During World War II sailors stationed in Montreal's port made their way up Saint-Laurent Boulevard toward the Red Light district.[38] The demand on nighttime shows was great, especially from audiences eager to forget the nightmare of war. Montrealers, tourists, military men, dock workers, and many others flocked to the district to experience the wide-open town. Montreal was officially focused on war production, and because of this economic influx, other sectors – like the nighttime economy – were rolling too. Indeed, during wartime, Montreal held the extraordinary benefit of full employment and prosperity, which in turn led to the increase in population. Fondly remembering those years, American burlesque performer and stripper Lili St-Cyr (who arrived in Montreal during the winter of 1944) said that men and women from all over the world would mingle, dance, and relax in Montreal nightclubs. Those who came to see her shows were awestruck by the romanticism, passion, and sexual seduction she conveyed onstage. In an amusing anecdote, illustrating the impact of her shows on patrons, a team of scientists undertaking nuclear research in collaboration with the Manhattan Project – presumably those from the Montreal Laboratory – named a radiation detection instrument the "Lili" and an improved version of it the "Superlili."[39]

During the war, the provincial government tried but failed to curtail vice, and nightlife more generally. It limited the number of liquor permits for Montreal, but this solution was futile because hundreds of establishments already had permits. Moreover, Montrealers and tourists could easily find alcohol in clandestine and after-hour speakeasies and blind pigs. Gambling thrived as well. Since unofficial economies by definition escape official documentation, we can only guess at the size of Montreal's, but by way of example, journalist William Weintraub later estimated that gambling grossed $100 million a year, making it the city's second-largest industry, right behind the manufacturing of women's clothing.[40]

Many "clean" police officers who monitored the city's underground economy at an arm's length found that this wartime commotion had become hard to manage. Authorities believed that sexual activity corrupted youths, and for that reason the Police Department's Juvenile Morality Squad was expanded. The squad intervened where misbehaving youths could be found – in theatres, parks, and restaurants, and at dance halls and known gay hangouts. This juvenile delinquency panic led to the successful passage of a curfew bylaw in September 1942.[41] This municipal bylaw enabled squad members to interrogate any child in public space after 9 p.m. While officers largely arrested boys for nighttime loitering, girls were arrested at a higher rate for other offences such as disturbing the peace, violations of public morality, and indecent or immoral behaviour. As Tamara Myers notes, the delinquency panics of the 1940s and early 1950s provided the impetus to expand, coordinate, and fully fund police efforts.[42] Alongside dealing with general criminal activity and moral panics, police officers also faced other challenges during wartime, like safeguarding strategic locations (such as factories) from foreign enemies and special nighttime surveillance (during partial blackouts imposed as a shield against enemy attack).[43] The transformation of police officers' roles evolved quickly during the war. In fact, it was so swift that in 1943 members of the city's Police Department demanded the right to unionize, leading to a short-lived police strike.

Policing of sex intensified during the war as moral panics over sexually transmitted infections were translated into national security concerns. In mid-January 1944, the Canadian Army pressured Montreal authorities to clamp down on the Red Light district because cases of syphilis and gonorrhea had surged to an epidemic level (nearly three times the national average). Army officials threatened to remove cash-suffused troops from the city and make Montreal completely out-of-bounds for its personnel if things remained wide-open.[44] According to Major-General Ernest James Renaud, the principal source of infections could be traced back to nighttime establishments where civilians and military personnel mingled: brothels, rooming houses, hotels, restaurants, taverns, dance halls, and nightclubs. Renaud also blamed nighttime labourers such as taxi drivers, bartenders, concierges, maîtres d'hôtel, and pimps for facilitating connections and transactions. Montreal chief of police Fernand Dufresne responded to the army's demand by increasing surveillance by the Night Patrol and the Morality Squad in "problematic" areas.[45] While there was a general emphasis on brothels in the Red Light district, the issue – as the major-general and the chief of police both recognized – was much larger and concerned the whole of Montreal's nighttime economy. However, Mayor Adhémar Raynault (a political protege of Quebec premier Maurice Duplessis, who served during Camillien Houde's internment) held off on a city-wide cleanup because he was of the mind that brothels acted as a necessary evil, holding back the proliferation of crimes. Shuttering brothels, he claimed, could lead to a rise in a multitude of other problems.[46] One municipal judge echoed the mayor's logic when he told a *Maclean's* reporter: "For me, [brothels are] the lesser evil. Close these places and you send the girls on the street. That is worse."[47]

In a surprising twist, and because they had no other choice, brothels alongside gambling houses agreed to cease activities on 2 February 1944. "Fortunately," wrote Chief Dufresne to the chair of the Montreal executive committee, "we did not have to take the radical and illegal means that we previously discussed." He continued, explaining how and why these estab-

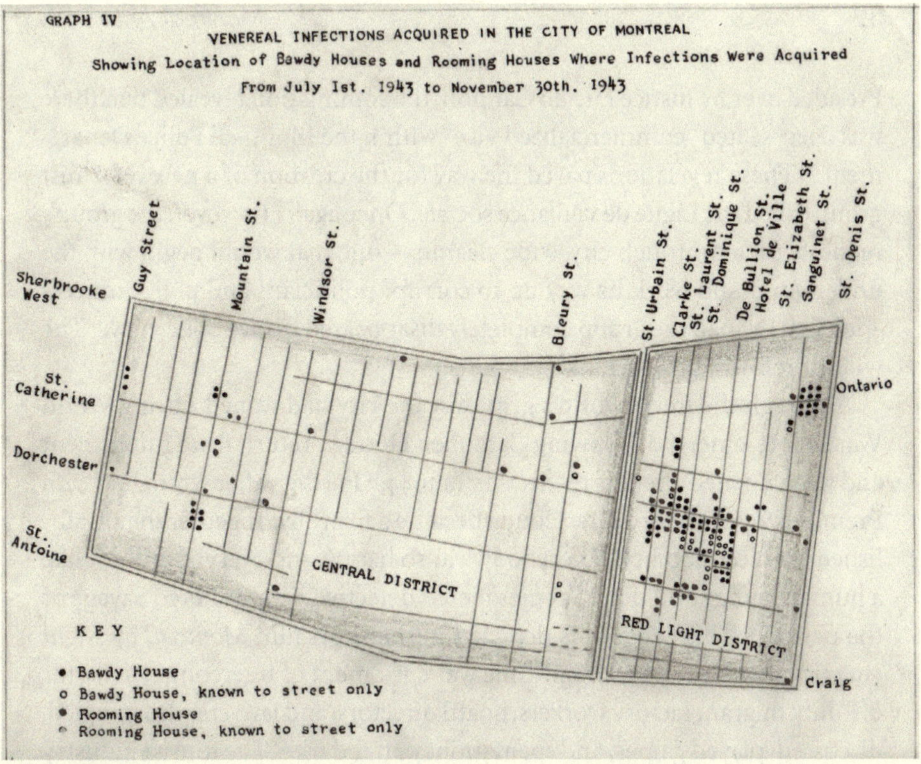

Figure 1.1
A 1943 map showing bawdy houses and rooming houses in the Central and Red Light districts, believed to be sources of venereal infections.

lishments had closed their doors: "Municipal court judges decided to impose very heavy prison sentences and fines on those whom the police would arrest and as a result, almost all brothels and gambling houses have closed."[48] The Police Department's official narrative likely concealed certain truths about the events because the underworld always had been able to dodge prison sentences and fines. In fact, some tabloid journalists contradicted that narrative by reporting that sex workers still conducted business, albeit in a more discreet fashion. Meeting the journalists in nightclubs and bars, the sex workers scoffed at the dominant claim that all brothels had closed.[49] Obviously more was happening behind the scenes than the official version acknowledged.

Later that year, a commission was launched to investigate the Montreal divisions of the Quebec Provincial Police and the Quebec Liquor Police.

Presided over by Justice Lucien Cannon, the commission revealed that there was deep-seated "commercialized vice" within the Montreal Police Department.[50] These revelations paved the way for the creation of a new reformist group called the Ligue de vigilance sociale. Once again, however, the group's requests for a thorough city-wide cleanup – one that would begin with the underworld and work its way up to corrupt politicians and police officers – fell flat; by 1946 the group completely disappeared from public view.[51] The will for reform, however, did not perish.

Although the underworld's grip over the city had waned during World War II, it re-emerged following Camillien Houde's return from internment and strengthened after his re-election in 1944.[52] Further, after wrangling with Premier Duplessis for years, Houde became a firm ally. Together they established political stability. "Everybody was so happy, and everybody lived like a human being should live," remembered detective-sergeant Fred Savage of the period.[53] This zeitgeist is depicted in the short film *Montreal by Night* (1947), which shows how nighttime was a moment of interconnectivity for off-duty migrant factory workers, board directors, and lawyers who mingled, discussed, played games, and spent money after dark.[54] The tourist industry reflected this liberty too. Brochures and articles lauded the city's good restaurants and shopping opportunities and referred to its cosmopolitanism as adventurous, exotic, and exciting: "The city's reputation for wickedness may have been exaggerated but its lights could hardly be brighter, its shows more sumptuous, its dusk to dawn gayety more spontaneous – or its night club business bigger business."[55] But as historian Nicole Neatby notes, the travel writers would begin to recognize the limits of the city's "racy" pleasures. In newspapers and magazines they wrote about Montreal's bad reputation as "Canada's largest and gaudiest playboy [where] night life … is gay and practically uninhibited."[56] Stuart Keate of *Maclean's* echoed this view writing that Montreal was known as one of the "most gaudy, bawdy cities in North America."[57] Houde's personality had dominated city politics from 1944 to 1954 and during this period his administration, along with the Police Department, became entangled in these aspects of Montreal nightlife, profiting from clandestine sex, alcohol, and gambling.

Crime-Busting Reformers

Throw the spotlight on … those who flee light.[58]
– Pacifique (Pax) Plante

Montreal at night remained wide-open until city attorney Pax Plante burst onto the scene. During his youth, Plante had been an earnest and dedicated student. While his classmates cheerfully traipsed from lecture halls to the Red Light district, he remained studious and befriended Lucien L'Allier, Claude Robillard, and André Laurendeau – men who, in their own right, would also go on to play significant public roles in Quebec's future. Eventually, he earned a law degree, which enabled him to indulge in life's finer things. In fact, he gained recognition for his sartorial elegance and dapper lifestyle, which included a love for luxurious goods like silk clothing and rare wines; not shying away from that reputation, he repeatedly told reporters that yachting was his favourite sport.

As a zealous law clerk at the municipal court, Plante had seen how corrupt politicians and police officers enabled commercialized vice in the city.[59] To shake things up he decided to set himself up for promotion after a position opened following a series of sensational events: Harry Davis, the underworld's uncontested kingpin, was murdered by gunshot on 25 July 1946, and following a great amount of scandalous publicity, Chief Dufresne fired Arthur Taché of the Morality Squad on 30 July. Plante seized this opportunity by securing a nomination from Pierre Des Marais, a city councillor who would later become the chair of the executive committee. He told the politician that he could uproot the "whole comedy" that he had seen on display at the municipal court during his eight years as attorney. With political backing, Plante replaced Taché on 9 August and headed the Morality Squad.[60] Over the years journalists would report that Plante's stylish demeanor and lavish allure was "pure radio-serial gangbuster stuff."[61] They noted that his by-the-book attitude denounced *any* connection to the underworld – from medical professionals administering sexually transmitted infection tests for madams, to fund-seeking reverends who organized clandestine bingo "lotteries." Hard-core criminal organizations soon sent death threats and plotted his assassination. Fearful for his life, but not deterred, Plante surrounded himself with bodyguards.[62]

As the head of the Morality Squad, Plante immediately pursued regulations that effectively ended business for after-hours establishments, something that his predecessors had refused to enforce. Although most nightclubs, restaurants, hotels, bars, and cabarets owned legal alcohol permits, many brushed off the section of the permit regulating the time when drinks could be served. Business owners viewed the Quebec Liquor Board's 1941 law – which banned the sale of alcohol in Montreal between 2 a.m. and 8 a.m. – as a nuisance that limited profits for no apparent reason other than effecting moral control over the population. And they were right. When it was introduced, wartime Quebec premier Adélard Godbout stated that the law was enacted to promote the temperance cause.[63] According to Al Palmer, however, throughout World War II and up until Pax Plante's rigorous enforcement, the regulation had been a mere suggestion: "The legal curfew hour in Montreal is two ayem [*sic*] – but don't pay too much attention to it. Most spots stay open till the last customer has left."[64] Jazz musician Fred McHugh recollected that he and his bandmates performed at all hours: "Every night you would go somewhere. The clubs were open twenty-four hours. We used to play in the Black Magic Room of the Chez Paree on Stanley Street. We used to get out of there at nine o'clock in the morning. The regular band would finish at four. It was open to musicians to jam, and all the night people would come by – taxi drivers, waiters, hookers, and dancers."[65] The city's core never slept, it seemed. Yet, Plante valued temporal regulation as highly as any other rule because rowdy, intoxicated revellers frequently disrupted the peace at a time when law-abiding individuals would have been asleep. In fact, during his tenure, Plante heard from hotel owners about embarrassing incidents involving loud brothel and gambling den hustlers who kept hotel guests – representatives of countries the world over, including royalty, diplomats, and ambassadors – awake at night.[66]

Although Plante energetically pursued his duties against the informal economy and its underworld, his focus was emphatically on dishonest public officials. Police corruption was a paramount issue. For example, corrupt officers leaked police plans about oncoming raids, and armed with that knowledge, offenders used stand-ins to take the fall on their behalf and buried all damning evidence before the police arrived. (Stand-ins were paid to undergo the ordeal of an arrest, with possibly a few days in jail after a quick guilty plea. Meanwhile, officers made no attempt to unearth evidence or discern the mastermind behind the clandestine business.)[67] The 1925 Coderre Inquiry revealed that one or two brothel employees were routinely charged and fined. Madams settled those fines on-the-spot and negotiated their employee's release. Meanwhile, sex workers continued to work in rooms that police deliberately avoided.[68] It was easy to see how these "raids" were elaborate charades designed to persuade the public that something was being done to combat commercialized vice. In reality, however, corrupt officers did not disrupt the regular course of business.

Soon after heading the Morality Squad, Plante began upending these practices. He targeted the city's most infamous gambling dens to prove that he – unlike his predecessors – could monitor Montreal's nighttime economy without being bought by the underworld. As other historians have argued, the media was central to this project as it invigorated public support. At first, Plante notified the press after a raid. But later, he would do so in advance, enabling reporters to arrive on time and witness the Morality Squad in full action; this flair for showmanship made for sensational stories and photographs.[69] Under these circumstances, Plante won a national reputation as a hard-hitting and incorruptible opponent of the city's underworld, something the Police Department had failed to achieve in half a century. Moreover, a large segment of the electorate welcomed the media's attention on those whom Plante labelled the "lucifugal." As media exposure of widespread immoral activities increased, the public's call for the moralization of urban spaces became more fervent.[70]

Plante's approach had been successful because of his belief in justice and morality, but also because of his sophisticated understanding of the nighttime economy. Officers who spent their nights patrolling the city amassed new and often-unusual knowledge about the underworld, and they used that knowledge to enhance their efficiency in the field. For example, Plante started targeting taxi drivers because they acted as key intermediators, enabling an interconnectivity between illicit businesses. During the postwar period Montreal saw a boom in the taxi industry, and many drivers became intimately connected to door attendants, waiters, sex workers, bootleggers, bookies, and police officers.[71] The city responded to this development by modernizing the structures governing the industry. In 1946 it enacted a lengthy bylaw that mostly defined how taxi drivers could not behave: no unnecessary honking, no soliciting, no parking outside designated zones, no driving in search of passengers (cruising), no smoking, and much more.[72] Taxis often caused traffic jams while idling outside busy nightclubs, restaurants, and cafés, where they awaited sex workers and clients destined for hotels. Therefore, when Plante took control of the Morality Squad, he increased police surveillance by closely monitoring taxi drivers and ensuring strict enforcement of that bylaw, even the sections that some officers found superfluous.[73] Plante also required drivers to have their permit and licence visible to passengers.[74] This initiative received a mixed reaction from drivers. Some claimed that identification cards gave the public reason to be suspicious of them; others, claimed Plante, had congratulated him because it restored public confidence and encouraged business. "My program was introduced to convince the public of [taxi drivers'] honesty," he told the *Montreal Star*, "because many women have told me personally that they're afraid to ride a taxi at night."[75] Plante knew that nighttime public space constituted a moment of uncertainty for women, and his approach had the benefit of making the industry both honest and safe. Later, he would claim that the taxi industry had been the most robust "fortress" of the informal economy because it threaded different illicit spheres together.[76]

As the paragraph above indicates, Plante aimed to increase regulatory measures to better inform authorities about nighttime activities, but this process also brought in focus patriarchal control of city space. Although gendered and moral concerns over public space were not new, Plante's effort to stamp out the sex industry marked a significant turning point in the city's sex history. Under his supervision, officers were instructed to charge women under the Criminal Code's vagrancy provision and the sections relating to nightwalking and prostitution.[77] Sociologist E. Nick Larsen has observed how the implementation of these anti-vagrancy laws reflected significant class and chauvinist biases, which excluded male customers from regulation while offering more protection to upper- and middle-class women compared to their lower-class counterparts.[78] The very wording of the Criminal Code placed the burden of proof on the accused when it came to charges of vagrancy and prostitution, for it was up to her to provide a "good account" of herself. If not, she bore the assumption of guilt. Although intended to be used against sex workers, vagrancy laws were applied loosely, which made it nearly impossible for unchaperoned women to be in public space at night. Police reports of monthly charges laid by the Morality Squad during the late 1940s confirm this bias since women account for nearly all cases involving nighttime loitering and vagrancy.[79] Moreover, police departments across Canada applied these laws irregularly by targeting women who were not of the dominant race, religion, or ethnic group. In some jurisdictions officers used the law to their financial advantage because they would be paid overtime for court appearances.[80] As legal historian Constance Backhouse shows, the history of policing sex workers and vagrants essentially amounted to policing "'undesirables and misfits' who were thought to threaten the social order."[81] Reform and repression thus went hand in hand, as police officers often used the vagrancy article to control "dangerous" classes and clear streets of women they considered "undesirable."[82]

In a revealing example, Rita Picard recalled having been victim of such a police stunt in 1948. After finishing her shift at a restaurant, and to blow off steam, she went to a cabaret on Stanley Street with a friend. The duo ordered drinks and sat at the bar waiting for the performance to begin. Suddenly, ten police officers raided the establishment, and in the whirlwind of things, both women were stuffed into a police van. Despite having committed no crime, they were charged under the vagrancy article and spent the night in jail; and upon bad advice from an officer, she pleaded guilty.[83] Because some officers protected the underground economy – sex work, gambling, or the traffic of clandestine alcohol – they devoted their time to shaking down establishments where customers indulged in anodyne leisure. This ruse, which made women like Rita Picard the target of choice, allowed officers to extort money from those who had been caught in a raid and, at the same time, inflate police statistics and provide evidence to the public that surveillance was efficient and effective.[84] Not only was sexism entrenched in the law but the law also allowed officers to reinforce the long-standing idea that women who go out at night were, simply put, indecent women.

But in mid-March 1948, only a year and a half after Chief Dufresne had placed him as head of the Morality Squad, Pax Plante was charged with gross insubordination by Montreal's new chief of police, American-born Albert Langlois.[85] At the root of this fiasco – characterized by irregular documentation and dubious claims – was the question of authority among police rank. Chief Langlois had pressured Plante to charge an officer of the

Morality Squad with soliciting during a brothel raid. Plante believed that this charge was unfounded and only served to discredit the integrity of "his" Morality Squad and benefit Chief Langlois who could then claim to be the Police Department's sole and incorruptible authority. Plante responded by submitting a sizable 550-page report filled with statistics, photostats, charts, newspaper articles, names, and dates that showed how Montreal "was literally sold out to commercialized vice" from 1932 to 1945. The report clearly illustrated that an extensive cleanup campaign had begun once Plante took control of the Morality Squad. The evidence, however, was not enough to protect him from Chief Langlois's commanding authority; because he refused to follow orders, Plante was suspended.[86]

In a statement following his suspension, Plante declared, "I have always said that if my work were interfered with I would tell the whole story to the people of Montreal and leave the verdict up to them. I accept this suspension in the hope that it will bring to an end the considerable and intolerable pressure which has made it impossible for me to continue."[87] In May 1948, he was dismissed from the department and was forced to surrender his police badge, his revolver, and the keys to his beloved black Buick.

Plante's dismissal lit a fuse that led to explosive revelations of corruption among municipal politicians and police officers. With the help of *Le Devoir* news director Gérard Filion, Plante wrote a series of newspaper articles that were published from 28 November 1949 to 18 February 1950 and detailed how municipal authorities tolerated, fostered, and protected Montreal's underworld. Gérard Pelletier was the series' editor, famed cartoonist Robert LaPalme was its illustrator, and Jean Drapeau was hired as legal counsel to the paper to protect against defamatory libel. In these articles Plante elucidated two truths about commercialized vice: the underworld could not exist without police protection, and conversely, police protection of the underworld could not exist without corrupt and negligent politicians.[88] As far as Plante was concerned, he had been dismissed from the Police Department because he had derailed this system. Plante certainly loathed the underworld, but he placed the blame on authorities who were at best passive and at worst complicit in the proliferation of Montreal's underground economy. In the final article of the series, Plante listed the culprits and accused those governing the city since 1940 – members of both the municipal administration and the Police Department – of corruption.[89] Following the transformation of these articles into a book, which became an overnight success, the public came to recognize the ways that corruption influenced municipal affairs.[90] Later, Jean Drapeau would recall the prolonged effect that corruption and immorality had on the city's development: "[To] put an end to the scandalous collusion between certain elements of the administration or of the police with the underworld, we chased out of Montreal the greater number of the promoters of this systematic debasement; especially, I am convinced, we gave back to the people of the Metropolis both their self respect and that of others."[91]

In 1950, during a meeting at the Windsor Hotel, the Public Morality Committee (PMC) was founded with the purpose of investigating the corrupt state of politics in Montreal. In contrast to the Ligue de vigilance sociale, the PMC was mostly made up of French-Canadian men, notably nationalists from the Société Saint-Jean-Baptiste and Ordre de Jacques-Cartier, businessmen, and well-known public figures like wealthy printer and councilman Pierre Des Marais and intellectual François-Albert Angers.[92] Committee members and partisans held a common goal: to eradicate commercialized vice from the city and restore its honour and reputation. To this end, they advocated for an inquiry into the role of the underworld by submitting a hefty 1,000-page petition containing close to 5,000 indictments in order to investigate the city administration and, in particular, the Police Department. Almost instantly, the Superior Court of Quebec accepted its request for an inquiry and placed Justice François Caron at its head.

On 11 September 1950, a probe began into commercialized vice and police corruption in Montreal. Attendees joined en masse to hear testimonies from the seamy side of town and reporters echoed the inquiry's scandalous *coups de théâtre* in newspapers. A few months into the inquiry, however, cash-strapped appellants could no longer pay court clerks and stenographers. Justice Caron requested that the city pay for those fees, but city attorneys argued against it because it would set a precedent. A couple of weeks later prosecutors reconvened after Plante and Drapeau announced that they had managed to collect enough money through fundraisers in the city's working-class parishes.[93] In April and May 1951, critics of the inquiry submitted a counter-petition for a probe into Plante's Morality Squad, and later, a group of police officers obtained a temporary injunction.[94] Both of those were dismissed, however.

In the end, the three-year-long inquiry cost $500,00 and involved some 373 witnesses, 4,000 court dossiers, and 1,000 special exhibits. Altogether, it set a record in Canadian jurisprudence for length. And although it ended on 2 April 1953, Justice Caron withheld the result of the inquiry for some months. The report was finally published on 8 October 1954 and landed like a bombshell on Montreal's political scene that autumn. It created what former mayor Raynault described as a collective hysteria.[95] In total, fifty-eight police officers and five former members of the city's executive committee were charged and fined, including executive committee chair Joseph-Omer Asselin, ex–chief of police Fernand Dufresne, and then–chief of police Albert Langlois.[96] Although the report exonerated Mayor Houde, the scope of the inquiry was enough to set ablaze a political movement that would reshape the city.

***

Whether calculated or not, the publication of the Caron report weeks before the municipal election paved the way for the reformers' electoral success. Members of the PMC carried the momentum from the courtroom to the ballot box by recognizing the power that they could yield under a political party. And although the inquiry had cleaned house in the Police Department, nobody could argue that it had completely rid Montreal of corruption. As Plante would later explain to a journalist, the path to reformism could only materialize if the PMC presented a candidate for mayor. PMC members fulfilled this mission by reorganizing and launching the Civic Action League (CAL), a political party that introduced both a compelling platform and a youthful candidate for mayor, thirty-eight-year-old prosecutor Jean Drapeau.[97] The CAL's platform promised an honest administration, promotion of taxpayers' interests, and transparency in municipal politics. This much was made clear by the party motto, "serving the public, not ourselves," which promised electors that members of this party would eradicate greed and corruption from municipal politics.[98] But the CAL's reworking of politics would not go unanswered. On election day, henchmen from Montreal's underworld challenged it with tactics that varied from payoffs to ballot-rigging, and from intimidation to outright violence. The sum total of the day's events, argued a *Montreal Herald* journalist, had made the 1954

Figure 1.2
Taking his position at the mayor's seat, Jean Drapeau (centre), with executive committee chair Pierre Des Marais (left) and crime-buster Pax Plante (right), 25 October 1954.

election the roughest in the city's recent history.[99] In any case, the CAL emerged victorious. Drapeau won the election, and Pierre Des Marais, a prominent member of the PMC, returned to council as the executive committee chair. Along with Plante, the non-hierarchical trio immediately set to work on various reforms (see fig. 1.2).[100]

Montreal's new mayor, Jean Drapeau, was born at the height of World War I on 18 February 1916 to working-class parents, Alberta (Berthe) Martineau and Joseph-Napoléon Drapeau. Although he followed in his father's footsteps in local politics – Joseph-Napoléon served as city councillor from 1944 to 1970 – Jean held a stronger, loving bond with his mother. He emphasized the adulation he held for her by proclaiming that her death was the single most important event of his life.[101] In his youth, Jean developed a profound love for the arts through Berthe, who enthralled the household with her performances of grand opera arias while playing the piano. Her talent was such that she was occasionally invited to sing at the midnight Mass at Notre-Dame Basilica. When she grew too tired to entertain, Jean delved into books, gaining a mastery of French and immersing himself in tales of Roman Catholic missionaries. At a time when his peers frolicked in the playground, he aspired to become a priest, dreaming of joining the White Fathers to evangelize Africa. His local church, which enlisted him as an altar boy from an early age, influenced such ambitions. By his teenage years, when his mastery of French developed into a passion for public speaking, he became known as the Mark Antony of his Rosemont parish. Young Jean would gather a group of friends and pretend to be a politician, captivating them with his political speeches: "If I were elected …," he mused. Passersby and neighbours stopped to listen, spellbound by the teenager's words.[102]

A lifelong resident of the modest Rosemont neighbourhood, Jean Drapeau was profoundly influenced by the nationalist writings of turn-of-the-century intellectuals Henri Bourassa and Canon Lionel Groulx. More than anything, it was Groulx's understanding of Quebec history within a subaltern framework that shaped his convictions. Groulx articulated a nationalism that was grounded in the permanent fusion of language and religion and the duty to defend the established network of Catholic institutions. This position presumed that religious, ethnic, and racial minorities posed a threat to the nation. In the 1930s global atmosphere of antisemitism, for example, Groulx played an important part in a rather virulent public campaign against Jewish shopkeepers and students in Montreal, and in opposition to Canada's aid to persecuted Jews in Europe.[103] Antisemitic campaigns were bolstered by individuals like notorious fascist Adrien Arcand and civic groups like Jeune-Canada, a right-wing nationalist movement that Jean Drapeau associated with. Drapeau would read the antisemite press of the 1930s and he kept a list of Jewish-owned shops to avoid in Rosemont.[104] "Our nation's worst enemy is the Jew," he wrote in 1934 to intellectual–activist lawyer Anatole Vanier, "once defeated, his entourage of cartels, trusts, and usurers will disappear."[105] Over the following decades, Drapeau often made references to the nation – though he remained cryptic about whether he meant the Québécois or Canadian nation – when he allowed himself to wax poetic about Montreal's development and its historical trajectory.

Seeing himself as the heir to nationalist figures of the past, Drapeau pursued a law degree at the Université de Montréal where he rubbed shoulders with the next generation of Quebec's intelligentsia. During his degree he sharpened his academic virtuosity by partaking in immensely popular campus debates. He won the Villeneuve trophy – an award handed to the best debating team from a francophone university – three years in a row from 1938 to 1940, with partners like future Quebec premier Jean-Jacques Bertrand.[106] His classmates described him, teasingly, as authoritarian, a Canadian Gauleiter who cursed democracy and loathed censorship and war profiteers.[107] After earning his degree in 1941, Drapeau began a serious, although unsuccessful, political career. As a co-founder of the anti-conscription party Bloc populaire (1942–48), he ran for Parliament in 1942 and for the Legislative Assembly in 1944 but was defeated on both occasions.[108] He continued to practice law as a defence lawyer, making a name for himself at murder trials and during the violent Asbestos strike of 1949.

Thus, by the mid-1950s, Drapeau emerged from relative obscurity as a prominent populist municipal politician. His ascension to power did not mark the end of the PMC campaign. Instead, as historian Mathieu Lapointe explains, it became a pivotal moment when the campaign was transformed through the wielding of authority.[109] As hinted at in the above paragraphs, Montreal's young intellectuals had been striving to gain power since the 1930s, forming "neo-nationalist" intellectual alliances, which could be traced to turn-of-the-century intellectuals and early twentieth-century political movements. On the one hand, Drapeau's ascension in local politics was similar to that of his predecessors, Médéric Martin and Camillien Houde. Like them, he based his appeal on the simple but effective notion that he personified the city itself and that a vote against him was somehow a vote against Montreal, or at least against the French-speaking part of the city.[110] On the other hand, the CAL had connections to a new and broader French-Canadian intellectual movement that extended beyond mere populist sentiments. If there was a second act in Drapeau's life it began here, in the mid-1950s.

As for Pax Plante, following the election, he assumed a new role within the Police Department. This development came after Justice Caron's ruling, which declared Plante's dismissal from the department unjustified. With the suspension of Chief Langlois, his assistant Tom Leggett took on the role of acting chief of police until the outcome of Langlois's appeal. As a result, Plante filled the position of assistant chief of police on 16 December 1954, which granted him supervision over the Morality Squad.[111] As the first order of business, Plante summoned the Police Department's captains and ordered them to visit the city's night haunts – bars and nightclubs – to warn owners that they would lose their liquor permits if sex workers were found soliciting on the premises. Historian John Gilmore notes that the warning was obeyed: hardly a few weeks after the election, by the end of November 1954, sex workers had almost entirely vanished from Montreal bars and nightclubs.[112] Over the following months the CAL and the Police Department refined their crackdown on the nighttime economy. They ensured that taxi drivers, performing artists, nightclub owners, and others involved in it followed the law. This, the reformers believed, would dissipate the notion that Montreal was wide-open. A new trajectory toward international recognition took shape.

"What Virtue Has Done to Montreal": The Civic Action League, 1954–57

The inquiry had exposed the geography of vice and corruption, and to recast Montreal as an "honest" city, Drapeau believed that his administration had to clamp down on both the space and time that illicit activities took place. Over the following months the Police Department effectively built on the work that Plante had started in the late 1940s and began enforcing laws regulating the hours of operation for establishments with liquor permits and the taxi industry. In fact, after a year in power, Drapeau discussed these issues at length when he told journalists that "the cleanup campaign, initially launched externally, was pursued internally."[113]

As previously mentioned, many establishments chose to openly violate the law that banned alcohol sales between 2 a.m. and 8 a.m. They had been able to conduct business in such a way because the enforcement of liquor laws was the sole responsibility of a special unit within the Quebec Provincial Police (QPP), which left city police without any authority over the sales of alcoholic beverages (granted that an establishment held a liquor permit in the first place). Consequently, Mayor Drapeau resorted to an indirect strategy to regulate licensed drinking establishments: he enforced bylaw 926, which mandated businesses to obtain a city permit for selling goods. Created in 1927, the bylaw regulated the health and safety of restaurants and of establishments like taverns, cafés, boarding houses, and hotels – where food-stuff or beverages were held, prepared, cooked, stored, sold, transported, delivered, or given away.[114] He realized that the bylaw could serve as a versatile tool, giving authorities the ability to regulate establishments that held a provincial liquor permit. Therefore, if an establishment violated liquor laws by selling alcohol beyond the permitted hours, city police would use bylaw 926 to padlock its door, claiming that it was a nuisance, unsafe, or unhygienic. As a result, establishments that otherwise would have remained open, closed at 2 a.m.

After strengthening these temporal parameters, Plante then focused on suppressing sex work. As geographer Julie Podmore argues, up to the mid-twentieth century the spatial concentration of the sex industry within the Red Light district allowed the heads of the industry and authorities to manage it, which prevented its proliferation into public spaces. During World War II, however, when the army pressured the city to close brothels, sex workers moved elsewhere, into hotels – particularly those that offered "tourist rooms."[115] Now, the city's latest drive would reshape the landscape of sex work again by forcing women out of circumscribed workspaces and onto streets or into drinking establishments. This created new clandestine commercial networks, built on basic trade patterns and arrangements that had begun to emerge in the late 1940s. While brothels were structured around a certain hierarchy that could exploit vulnerable sex workers, the latest reorganization of the city's sex industry removed the relative protections and basic commercial and administrative infrastructure previously afforded by brothels and their well-connected madams. This resulted in deteriorating labour conditions for sex workers who became dependent on male intermediaries, such as pimps, bellboys, taxi drivers, and waiters – men who facilitated communication between buyers and purveyors of sexual services.[116] One individual recalled how this reorganization led sex workers into gay nightclubs too, which heightened police surveillance over those covert community spaces.[117] And later, a probe into organized crime revealed how gangs – supported by henchmen, door attendants, pimps, and managers – used the formal nighttime economy to profit from sex work.[118] Thus, in the span of a few weeks, the reformers had radically transformed Montreal from a wide-open to a "closed" city by removing the mechanisms that made the sex industry safe. In the wake of the 1954 municipal election, both Rita Picard and famed madam Martha Adams temporarily relocated to Ontario.[119] In fact, the cleanup campaign drove sex workers out of the city en masse, as many sought safer working environments in mining or industrial cities across Quebec and Ontario.[120]

The transformation had profound consequences for everyone in the city, not just those who made a profit from the informal economy. Most notably, it had a devastating impact on the livelihood of nightclub and cabaret employees, which included bartenders, waiters, kitchen staff, cigarette girls, performing artists, doormen, and many others (it was estimated that in the early 1950s, 7,500 people found employment in Montreal's 170 nightclubs and music lounges).[121] In an interview with historian John Gilmore, two jazz musicians stated that the latest initiative drastically cut their gigs, leading to a two-thirds decline in their incomes.[122] Elsewhere, Mademoiselle X, a mysterious contributor for *Le Magazine Maclean*, wrote with poetic nostalgia about working as a performing artist in cabarets and nightclubs during the early 1950s: "The gradual decline of Montreal cabarets over recent years has caused a chorus of lamentations because of its regrettable impact on commerce and the economy. The metropolis, once Canada's most colourful, bustling city, is now a boring site. Montrealers and tourists alike evoke with nostalgia the gaiety of yore: cafés overflowing with cheerful crowds, exciting variety shows, the bustle of the streets at night."[123] Mademoiselle X not only described how the temporal restriction on alcohol sales restricted profits, particularly for those who could no longer rely on profitable and extended late-night shifts, but also noticed that it had led to a rise in fraud. Cash-strapped industry workers, she noted, had turned to defrauding and swindling customers to recoup losses. The reorganization of the nighttime economy shifted things in such a way – as reported by an array of performing artists – that a third of Local 382 of the Hotel and Restaurant Employees and Bartenders International Union had been thrown out of work.[124] Another musician went so far as to tell Gilmore: "You can say what you like, but there was a lot of work for everybody when [the underworld was] running things."[125] Within the span of a few years, Montreal's nighttime economy had suffered substantial loss.

Expectedly, the loudest rebuke and challenge concerning these reforms came from the business sector. Montreal-based members of the Province of

Figure 1.3
Cabaret performer, 1955.

Quebec Licensed Café and Restaurant Owners Association united to protest the enforcement of closing times on Saturday and Sunday nights. This state of affair, claimed their spokesperson, was deadly for business because it kept tourists and touring performers away from the city and local customers at home. Although it was a "new" way of doing business, many law-abiding establishments followed regulations and adapted to reforms. However, in some establishments liquor laws were actively contested as patrons believed that they were entitled to consume drinks until dawn. In a stunning act of defiance, belligerent clients at the high-end Mansfield Café refused to obey the law. The ensuing battle between waiters and clients forced the manager to phone Montreal Hydro to cut off the establishment's electricity for several hours; it was the only way that he could get revellers to understand that drinks would no longer be served past 2 a.m. Writing about Drapeau's first term, William Weintraub argued that the regulation of after-hours establishments had been the administration's "most sweeping reform."[126]

Come mid-May 1955, Drapeau's Rosemont home was assailed with a brick, an incident he immediately pinned on the business leaders of the nighttime economy. This act, according to him, was "definitively because of the closing time of the city's nightclubs."[127] The Montreal section of the Province of Quebec Licensed Café and Restaurant Owners Association swiftly condemned and distanced itself from the violent incident. The next week, the association met with the mayor and asked that police stop meddling with business and that the city to allow owners to close establishments at their preferred time. Members of the association confronted the mayor and argued that the 1941 provincial liquor law regulating the hours of sale was obsolete and impractical for business, that it would lead to a drop in tourist revenue and an increase in criminal activity. "You're choking us out of business!" griped one member. Cognizant of, but indifferent to the effect this had on business, the mayor responded: "we don't want to persecute you: all we want is for you to observe the law."[128] These, and similar incidents, made the front-page headlines of Montreal dailies. On 5 June 1956, for example, *Le Devoir* announced that Pax Plante had revoked fifty-seven municipal permits from cabarets, nightclubs, and restaurants "for tolerating immorality or having remained open after lawful hours, or for both."[129] The regulation of the nighttime economy was of prime importance for reformers, and it captivated the public's attention.

During its mandate from 1954 to 1957, the CAL collaborated with the Police Department to eradicate illicit activities within the city. But reforms did not start and end with the regulation of illicit businesses. In key instances authorities also waged battles against "obscene" literature and "immoral" games. A year before Drapeau took office, city council had made amendments to a public artworks bylaw. The amendment prohibited any depictions of nudity or semi-nudity "in any street or public place, in front of theatres or moving picture halls, or in lobbies of theatres or moving picture halls in windows of stores, occupied or not of booksellers' shops, of newsstands, of taverns or hotels, in tramcars or at any other place where they might be seen by the public, … which have not been previously submitted and approved by the Director of the Police Department."[130] Of course, these regulations were not intended to curb high culture or the private consumption of art. Rather, they were intended to regulate and manage a distinctive and degraded form of mass commercial culture. Throughout the following years, vendors who sold obscene literature were subjected to fines and charges. Police raided pharmacies, cabarets, newsstands, and restaurants, and seized everything that they considered pornographic or obscene.[131] For the most part these publications provided lurid coverage of the latest gossip about vice, corruption, and criminality as well as sexually focused content. For example, *Allô Police* (est. 1953) had been launched to capitalize on public interest in crime and corruption, and *Midnight* (est. 1954) had been started by a teenager as a guide to goings-on within Montreal nightclubs and, more generally, about the semi-illicit pleasures of nightlife.[132] Nevertheless, authorities viewed these publications and their imagery as a form of cultural poison that created dangerously motivated and suggestible audiences, a threat to the very foundations of public order.

In March 1955, the CAL enacted another bylaw, one prohibiting pinball machines and bagatelle games. Pinball machines were perceived as a form of gambling due to their unpredictable nature and the potential for players to win prizes or rewards based on their performance, which resembled elements of chance commonly associated with gambling activities.[133] This viewpoint was fiercely debated, however. At a trial three witnesses – an American representative for the machine manufacturers, a skilled player, and a mathematician knowledgeable in calculus – argued that pinball was a game of skill. But Municipal Court Judge Ernest Simard was unimpressed: "It is not the player that has control of the machine, but the machine with its complicated mechanism, which controls the player." Throughout the following years, and until the Canadian Criminal Code was amended, Morality Squad officers seized machines during raids and charged owners and players who tried to evade the gambling bylaw.[134]

Montreal's 1955–56 budget, adopted at the same meeting when council passed the bylaw prohibiting pinball machines and bagatelle games, highlighted the importance of nighttime regulation. It doubled the business tax for establishments where alcohol was served and allocated 10.6 per cent of its budget, the largest to any single service, to the Police Department.[135] To be sure, the sum of this process had little effect on the hard-core crime ring, which was still very much in business (although less visible than before). In any case, by the end of the year, the Morality Squad had made close to two thousand arrests for a wide range of offences, including loitering, vagrancy, prostitution, lotteries, and gaming.[136]

At this point it is important to emphasize that while the crackdown on vice and immorality created an important cultural upheaval, it was only one facet of the reformist agenda during Mayor Drapeau's first term. The modernization of the city's crumbling infrastructure was another defining aspect of that term, and it was facilitated by postwar prosperity, scrutiny over tax rolls, and generous loans. Working in piecemeal fashion, the city bulldozed, demolished, and restored elements that had been marring Montreal's image. Administrators eyed aging infrastructure and rundown tenements with keen interest and began working on thoroughfare and street resurfacing, traffic congestion, and public parks – things that had been neglected for years. Particularly important for public works – which received $10.5 million from the 1955–56 budget, the second-largest amount after the Police Department – was the widening of Dorchester Boulevard (present-day René-Lévesque Boulevard). The project transformed Dorchester from a "decrepit, rundown, narrow" street into an alleyway for skyscrapers, which reoriented the city's central business district away from the port.[137] And as the next chapter demonstrates, the need to demolish vestiges of an inadequate past, rebuild and reconstruct infrastructure and homes, not only made the city appear modern but also made its soundscape loud, another signifier of modernity.

Urban renewal projects sparked varying opinions on the city's future. In 1954, weeks before Jean Drapeau was elected, city councillor Paul Dozois submitted a report that identified thirteen "slum" sectors in Montreal. The report suggested initiating a major slum clearance project, beginning with the Red Light district due to its deteriorating housing, juvenile delinquency, and high crime rates.[138] It proposed to address these issues by using the National Housing Act of 1954 and bulldozing the sector to replace it with state-of-the-art affordable housing. Typical of slum clearance projects, it promised to increase public revenues through property and business tax. The Dozois Plan, presented on the eve of the 1954 election, did not come up for vote until 21 June 1955. Once in power, however, the CAL spoke out against the proposed project.[139] Mayor Drapeau regarded the Red Light district as a blank canvas, an opportunity to engineer a project that would elevate the city's global reputation. He proposed that the district be transformed into Radio and TV City (Cité des ondes) – a neighbourhood dedicated to both telecommunications and high culture, akin to New York's Radio City Music Hall (est. 1932). The project included a museum of natural sciences, a planetarium, and ample parking spaces. But its key component was its potential for new offices for Radio-Canada and the Canadian Broadcasting Corporation (CBC). Families that would be displaced for the project were to be relocated in another part of town as part of a garden city project called Family-City. These elements formed the core of the proposed project, which also aimed to fulfill the immediate radio and television needs outline by the 1957 Royal Commission on Broadcasting (Fowler Report). But for reasons explained below, Radio and TV City was a pipe dream that never materialized.[140]

Drapeau's dream of turning Montreal into a hub for high culture began to take shape in April 1956, five years after the Royal Commission on National Development in the Arts, Letters and Sciences issued its 1951 Massey Report advocating federal funding for arts and culture. Montreal's city council voted in favour of bylaw 2325, which created the Greater Montreal Council of Arts (GMCA). Through the GMCA the mayor was able to mastermind the city's, and by extension a large portion of the province's, cultural effervescence.[141] The GMCA was attached to the mayor's office and its duties included maintaining and promoting artistic and cultural life as well as administering grants and subsidies.[142] During its first three years, it allocated money to twelve plays, two operas, two ballets, four works for orchestra, and for the Canadian League of Composers to present two concerts of original Canadian compositions. The GMCA exhibited a penchant for high culture, and according to its first president, Léon Lortie, it made Montreal an attractive and modern city to tourists.[143] Thus, while authorities clamped down on perceived forms of "low" culture, they defined acceptable cultural productions. In Drapeau's mind, the GMCA was precisely what Montreal required in order to attain the status of a sophisticated, reputable city.

As the mayor elevated the city's status by promoting megaprojects and high culture, he ignored mounting protests, which eventually contributed to his 1957 electoral defeat. Not only had he been selling his dream for Radio and TV City to other politicians but also, from the very beginning, he had delayed, prevented, and meddled with the Dozois Plan. He overlooked its overwhelming approval by both city council and the public. In fall 1956, Premier Maurice Duplessis made a fateful visit to City Hall to discuss provincial-municipal business.[144] By then, Paul Dozois had left municipal politics for a seat in Quebec's Legislative Assembly and was the minister of municipal affairs for Duplessis's Union nationale provincial government. Still, after meeting with Premier Duplessis, Drapeau refused to sign the housing plan into action and explicitly stated that "the Dozois project will not be built so long as I am mayor."[145] The battle lines had been drawn.

With the 1957 municipal election looming over the city, widespread discontent with Mayor Drapeau was evident. The mayor was roundly jeered at the Forum during the Stanley Cup final that spring. That same season, Pax Plante, one of Drapeau's closest allies, had to step down from his position as interim chief of police. This occurred when the Quebec Court of Appeal overturned Justice Caron's ruling and reinstated Albert Langlois as chief of police. Despite his permanent return, Langlois remained embittered and openly defied Jean Drapeau's orders for the police.[146] The two factions clashed as Drapeau and Des Marais steadily "peppered" Langlois with requests for reports on the Police Department's monitoring of the taxi, sex, and gambling industries.[147] Moreover, organized labour threw its support behind another candidate following both the CAL's privatization of waste management (a process that slashed 230 permanent jobs) and after hearing that Des Marais had advised the City of Saint-Michel's police to use tear gas against strikers.[148] The CAL, however, retained strong support from Catholic Church leaders and from the middle-class, property-owning conservatives who believed in its reformist goals. Finally, the press began to turn on Drapeau, criticizing him for mishandling a public health issue: after campaigning to have children immunized with the new polio vaccine, he told journalists that his own three sons would not be inoculated.[149]

For these various reasons, mayoral candidate Senator Sarto Fournier pulled ahead and won the 1957 municipal election. Fournier, a seasoned politician who had served as a Liberal member of Parliament from 1935 to 1953, ran a savvy municipal campaign that was supported by Premier Duplessis.[150] Fournier's Greater Montreal Rally (GMR) articulated the city's need for a master plan and its electoral pamphlet placed a great emphasis on fi-

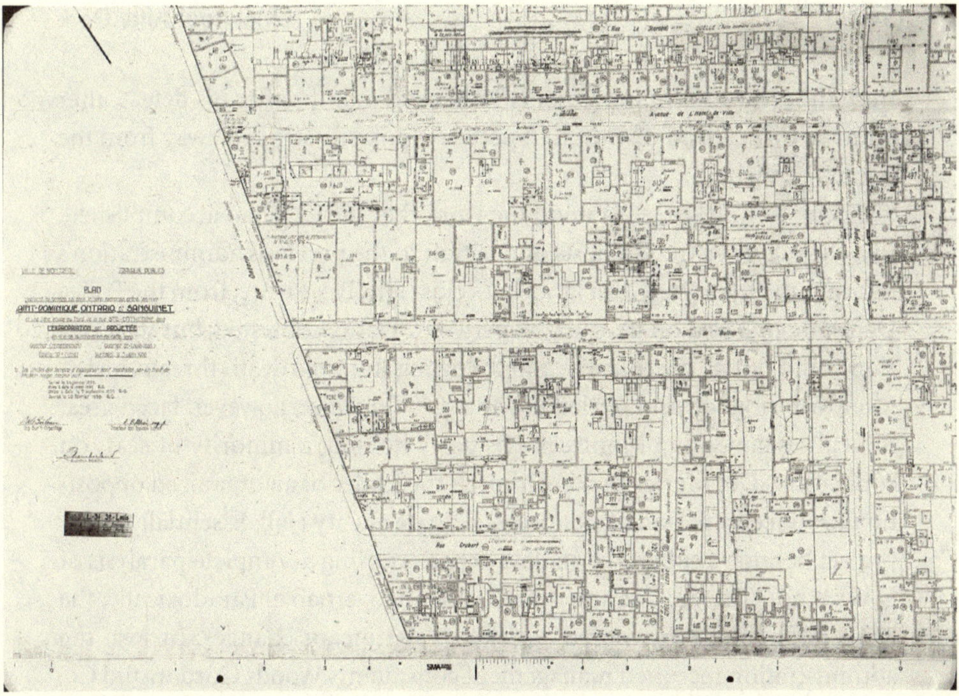

Figure 1.4
Red Light district expropriation plan stretching from de Sanguinet to Saint-Dominique streets and from Ontario to Sainte-Catherine streets, 20 February 1958.

nance, taxation, traffic, housing, social and cultural works, economic activity, and safety.[151] Electors expressed their dissatisfaction with Drapeau's political style and his vision for Montreal – at least for the time being – by voting him out of office. This allowed the GMR to lay the groundwork for the Dozois Plan in the Red Light district, leading to what would eventually become the Habitations Jeanne-Mance (see fig. 1.4).[152] In the aftermath, Drapeau never conceded the election and did not make the traditional concession speech at City Hall. Instead, he claimed that the election was stolen. A few months later, he gave a vindictive speech before CAL supporters at the Théâtre Saint-Denis claiming that electoral fraud had been enabled by a corrupt, hateful, and wealthy opposition made up of anglophone journalists and the yellow press.[153] During another speech, when he tried to clarify his thoughts, he warned that "racial politics" were likely to emerge in Quebec if the anglophone press and English-speaking citizens were to "remain aloof from the great reform movements."[154] Several months after his defeat, after bouts of dismay and distress, Drapeau temporarily stepped away from the public spotlight.

The GMR quickly set to undo the work that the CAL had accomplished. In a clear demonstration of its opposition to the previous administration's reforms, the GMR fired Jean Drapeau's close ally, Pax Plante, from the Police Department based on irregular paperwork. Plante contested, but the decision could not be overturned, and following multiple death threats, he left Montreal for good and settled in Mexico.[155] Fournier, however, faced great difficulties governing Montreal. His party holding a minority of seats on council and Des Marais making himself the leader of an organized opposition produced a period of political stalemate at City Hall. Essentially, every project became a subject of endless debate, causing a complete paralysis of governance. The city became practically ungovernable. Paradoxically, the city's difficulties engendered a series of significant changes. In 1959 the administration recruited management consultants Woods Gordon and Co. to conduct a study on the administrative problems beleaguering the city, including its Police Department. The firm's 750-page report, submitted months before Fournier's term ended, found that Montreal's administration had organizational weaknesses primarily because it could not keep up with the city's rapid growth and expansion.[156] Much of what it touched on would be addressed over the following years, under Jean Drapeau.

In the meantime, however, the transfer of power from Drapeau to Fournier scarcely changed things for labourers relying on the nighttime economy. Throughout 1958, and under pressure from residents and newspapers, the executive committee called on chief of police Albert Langlois to crack down on nightclubs that sold clandestine alcohol and advertised indecent shows. Eventually, Chief Langlois convened one hundred club owners in a municipal courtroom and publicly stated that raids would last so long as drinking establishments harboured illicit activities, particularly "shows involving erotic dancers." Following this meeting a new unit called the "Shadow Squad," comprised of undercover officers, patrolled the nightclub and cabaret scene to observe ongoings and to censor performers when necessary.[157] By 1960 the Police Department was still monitoring what was referred to as the lawless "jungle" of the night in vast operations that took officers from male-only taverns to high-end nightclubs to erotic cabarets.[158] Owners of drinking establishments claimed that this constant surveillance was bad for business and repeatedly tried to have authorities deregulate the liquor law. Harry Blank, member of provincial Parliament for the riding in which the Red Light district was located, had to contend with them. Blank kept a watchful eye on these developments, but he also proposed to business owners that they improve their establishments and "appeal to a higher-class clientele."[159] Indeed, this was an age when elected politicians at all levels understood the importance of appearance and the role of the nighttime economy in attracting the wealthy.

Conclusion

The scope of the Caron Inquiry had far-reaching effects, beginning with the momentum it offered to urban reformers. In the wake of the inquiry, reformers laid the groundwork and articulated a discourse that would profoundly transform the city at night. Effectively, the Caron Inquiry gave concrete evidence to back up what everyone already knew: police and political authorities protected the criminal underworld, and the underworld could not be disentangled from the nighttime economy. The inquiry's report, coupled with the absence of long-time mayor Camillien Houde from the election ballot, gave PMC members and CAL candidates the space they needed to promote their reformist agenda. When Montrealers elected Jean Drapeau to his first term, they triggered what one reporter claimed was the "most ruthless house cleaning any Canadian city ever saw."[160]

While many of the immediate reforms were the culmination of a number of "moral" concerns, the goal was not simply to make Montreal a puritanical city. It was part of a greater urban strategy: a step toward making Montreal a global city. Upon assuming power the CAL brought about a significant transformation through extensive public investment projects. Simultaneously, at night, under Pax Plante's leadership, zealous police officers enforced long-standing laws and new regulations to curtail what previously had been customary behaviours. The nighttime economy was under a new system of governance. This resulted in sex workers, taxi drivers, performing artists, business leaders, and the heads of the criminal underworld being compelled to adapt their practices accordingly. These significant cultural changes had broad repercussions, including on the economy, labour, and tourism. Despite the strength of the reform movement – or, more accurately, because of it – the CAL experienced a resounding defeat during the 1957 election. Maurice Duplessis's powerful Union nationale backed Sarto Fournier, a candidate who, much like the majority of the electorate, opposed the impact of the changes he observed around the city.

2

FROM POLICE REFORMS TO NOISE ABATEMENT

Ever since the Caron Inquiry, the debate over appropriate nightlife had been raging. Upon being elected in 1954, Drapeau was not of the mind that the city should be closed after dark: "we [the reformers] have been wrongly labelled. We don't want Montreal to be a closed town. We want it to be a lively town within the law." Indeed, the reformers celebrated the economic value of Montreal's playful nightlife culture, albeit within so-called moral boundaries. His successor, Sarto Fournier, mayor under the Greater Montreal Rally from 1957 to 1960, partially echoed this sentiment when he promised a less puritanical, more liberal Montreal that would remain "wide open but honest."[1] Both mayors envisioned the nighttime economy, in the mid-twentieth century, to be completely integrated into the formal economy. Understandably, following Fournier's victory over Drapeau in 1957, police continued to enforce city bylaws in areas that resisted different aspects of this vision. This enforcement was especially noticeable in the police's raids of places where youths and performing artists played jazz, danced, and engaged in drug use, and in spots frequented by the queer community, where men were deliberately entrapped to meet arrest quotas.[2]

Beyond nightlife, this moralizing strategy could be observed in the ongoing and idiosyncratic battle over "obscene" literature – a battle that led police to enforce the public artworks bylaw against thirty vendors who possessed and sold *Time*'s 11 January 1960 issue on population explosion. The news magazine's cover was demonstrably obscene, the city claimed, because

Figure 2.1
The nighttime view of Montreal includes several skyscrapers under construction, including (from left to right) the CIBC Tower, Place-Ville-Marie, and the CIL House, June–August 1961.

it featured a Black woman breastfeeding her naked infant. In the uproar that ensued over the issue's censorship, Chief of Police Albert Langlois penned an open letter defending his department's activities. Meanwhile, newsvendors challenged the city's public artworks bylaw, arguing that it contradicted the Criminal Code sections on obscenity.[3] Whether this rigorous enforcement was ultra vires or not mattered little as this moralistic vision was ultimately supported for a number of years by a permanent committee comprised of civic authorities, religious leaders, and members of the public.[4]

In 1960, amid reforms to Montreal's political and electoral system, the essence of which is explained below, Jean Drapeau returned to office after campaigning on projects that promised to modernize Montreal's transit network. Chief among those was the transformation of Décarie Boulevard into a sunken highway and the development of a subway system. Indeed, during the early 1960s the city's transformation was multi-faceted, and one of the determining factors, as with most North American cities, was the growing dominance of automobiles and the pressure exerted by drivers in local politics. As a majority, drivers steamrolled city politics, forcing politicians to improve roadways, create new boulevards, and expand existing ones.[5] During the 1962 election, Drapeau's party campaigned on ongoing transit projects and planned to modernize the Police Department, another critical aspect of city governance.[6] The result was a landslide victory, with Drapeau receiving 87.8 per cent of the votes. Backed by a clear mandate, the administration initiated a construction boom. In its hypergrowth, Montreal of that era typified the energy and cacophony that many major Western cities underwent in the second half of the twentieth century. In fact, Montreal executive committee chair and Civic Party member Lucien Saulnier went so far as to state that "in this present decade we're in the process of building, in a way, a new city whose appearance will easily throw into the shadows everything that has happened since the last world war."[7] During the early 1960s, the city was teeming with heavy machinery as it was being reimagined by politicians, technocrats, planners, and architects. These men carried a vision of the modern city, and through relentless effort, they laboured to shape Montreal into the image of their dreams.

As was the case in the mid-1950s, the city's structural and political evolution had a significant impact on the formal nighttime economy. To be sure, revellers could still enjoy alcohol-fuelled nights and watch routines by performing artists along the city's main drag, Saint-Laurent Boulevard.[8] Amid the hypergrowth of the early 1960s, however, downtown nightspots were demolished and replaced with modern structures, a change that drew lament from a diverse group of observers – from internationally acclaimed artists and left-leaning poetic journals to the right-leaning Chambre de commerce du district de Montréal.[9] Conveying a nostalgic sentiment, famous American burlesque performer and stripper Lili St-Cyr contemplated this change when she described Montreal's ebullient atmosphere in the 1940s and '50s. "I felt a great joy of belonging to and participating in that unique universe," she reflected, and declared that because of this sense of belonging she considered Montreal her "real homeland."[10] However, when she returned to the city in the mid-1960s she discovered that that Montreal no longer existed. To her dismay, most of the places that made her feel at home – cosmopolitan hubs of cultural exchange where sexual energy and desire fluttered in the night – had been bulldozed, replaced by vacant lots or modern buildings. "My Montreal was not this new city," she longingly wrote.[11]

Like the city itself, the night was undergoing a transformation. Montreal, during this era, was a polyphonic and bustling city, alive with the energy of its people. This development was observed by a police officer who plainly told a journalist, "when I was a rookie [in the 1940s], nobody was out on the streets at all hours. If anyone was, we'd book him."[12] While this officer conceded that arresting folks simply for being in the streets at night was no longer conceivable, tensions persisted around which behaviours were considered acceptable and which were not. On the one hand, city residents, musicians, tourists, and artists enjoyed the flourishing cultural scene enabled by the GMCA.[13] On the other hand, although changing mores determined new ways of policing and regulating late-night public space, it did not stop officers from profiling women and men based on racist and sexist presumptions. During this era, for instance, police continued to arrest women under the Criminal Code's vagrancy provision and the sections relating to nightwalking and prostitution.[14] Certainly, officers would have observed a growing number of city residents engaging in aimless nighttime activities like cruising, wandering, and loitering. Concurrently, there would have been a noticeable rise in nighttime labourers – individuals who played a key role in creating what both Saulnier and St-Cyr called the "new city." At night, Montreal was filled with modern machines and sounds, which demanded modern regulations and, crucially, a modern police organization to enforce them.

The contrast between efforts to control undesirable nightlife noise and allowance of nighttime construction noise underscores the tension between Montreal's past and future, between the disorderly and illicit city and the fast-paced construction of the new city. Mid-twentieth-century urban development placed new demands on Montreal, encompassing not only spatial but also temporal growth as construction became part of the twenty-four-hour cycle, no longer confined to typical workday hours. Inevitably, Montrealers found themselves at the centre of debates surrounding noise, gauging whether soundscapes were productive, unnecessary, or unbearable. Often, the source of the sound determined how residents and police reacted.

In this chapter, the importance of nighttime regulation is explained through the lens of the city's early-1960s transformation. It focuses on two pivotal developments, both of which highlight the modernist challenges that the city confronted in tailoring its status as a global city. The first development involves the reorganization of the Police Department, which aimed to silence police critics by tackling the issues raised by the Caron Inquiry. The Caron Inquiry was unique to Montreal, but police reforms were not. Like other North American cities, Montreal politicians recruited police reformers who believed in modern and professional law enforcement in order to manage the challenges of a growing urban environment.[15] In fact, and as the *Montreal Gazette* reasoned, the success of ongoing urban developments was intricately linked to the professionalization and capabilities of the city's Police Department: "It is beyond question that Montreal's Police Force has to be reorganized, and modernized. It is a force that has, in various ways, lost touch with the higher standards of training and performance that combatting modern crime demand."[16] Rather than seeking the help of Pax Plante, as he had done in the past, Drapeau entrusted this reorganization to two high-ranking police reformers from Europe: Andrew Way, commander of the London Metropolitan Police, and André Gaubiac, retired chief of the Paris Municipal Police. Way and Gaubiac familiarized themselves with Montreal by spending considerable time with the Night Patrol and surveilling how local officers conducted business. Eventually, Hull's chief of police, Joseph-Adrien Robert, joined the duo and was appointed Montreal chief of police. Once Way and Gaubiac left, Robert supervised the overhaul of the Police Department as he introduced a technocratic approach to policing and advocated for reforms that the Europeans had conceived. Supervising an established "professional" Police Department, Robert kept a watchful eye on Mayor Drapeau's city. His approach involved intense raids on nighttime venues, especially those that catered to clandestine or non-normative behaviours. Indeed, Mayor Drapeau and Chief Robert enjoyed a close relationship, perhaps mirroring the one the former had held with Plante. And this close relationship, Drapeau believed, facilitated city governance and improved Montreal's image, which helped recast it as a modern metropolis.

The second development discussed in this chapter is the 1965 amendment to the city's long-standing anti-noise bylaw. Like officials in cities the world over, Montreal authorities had to deal with the problem of late-night noise complaints.[17] Solving this problem demanded a delicate equilibrium that ensured the tranquility of residents as well as the progress of urban developments. The interplay between what constituted legitimate sounds and transgressive noise was left to the interpretation of the average Montrealer, which resulted in different norms and notions about what was thought appropriate. Importantly, the issue was not only what is proper and what should be avoided, and even prohibited, but also where and when sounds became noise. Noise, once thought a necessary by-product of progress and economic success, was perceived as an unfortunate consequence of urban modernity and in need of regulation.[18] During the second half of the twentieth century, not only did Montrealers experience far-reaching changes in the acoustic environment of their city but also the city itself expanded and evolved. The pace of life in Montreal was set by the pace of its development. Therefore, whereas the early-twentieth-century noise-abatement campaign produced the city's 1937 anti-noise bylaw, the public uproar during the early 1960s highlighted the bylaw's deficiency as residents fought against noise, particularly nighttime noises, derived from construction sites. The tsunami of noise complaints concerning heavy machinery that found its way to City Hall showed that the problem of nighttime noise was neither localized nor elitist. Ultimately the anti-noise bylaw was revised to give greater power to police. "On complaint from any citizen or upon simply witnessing such violation," it read, police could arrest, on sight, labourers engaged in construction or excavation works between 10 p.m. and 7 a.m.[19]

Both these developments portray how the early 1960s was a period when authorities reassessed rules and regulations and, crucially, strengthened the police's role in the enforcement of them. As recent studies suggest, the reaction against urban noise in the nineteenth and early twentieth centuries focused on "obtaining quietness as a private commodity" and was influenced not only by the time and location of the noise but also by who was responsible for making it.[20] Just as with after-hour clandestine activities observed in chapter 1, noise was perceived as a threat to the social order. Whereas the former concerned proscribed behaviours, the nuisances examined in this chapter mostly emerged out of a hegemonic problem: since authorities were in the process of creating a new city, they allowed construction sites to operate late into the night. Of course, during this era other notable noises annoyed Montrealers – stereos, airplanes, sirens, and much more – but on the whole, the city bylaw already addressed, or simply could not address, these sounds. Therefore, stunned residents found it difficult to accept official reassurances and claimed that the city could, at the very least, act on the issue of nighttime construction.

A New Political Era

After his 1957 defeat, Jean Drapeau did not curb his political ambitions. In 1959 he published *Jean Drapeau vous parle*, a book that conveyed his French-Canadian nationalist views on two pressing issues: constitutional reform and economic life. Touching only minimally on municipal affairs, Drapeau reviewed contemporary failures by provincial and federal leaders, giving the reader the impression that it foreshadowed a renewed foray into provincial or federal politics.[21]

Indeed, Drapeau stalked bigger game than Montreal. From 1957 to 1959, he embarked on a province-wide promotional tour with members of the Public Morality Committee. Their intent was to extend municipal anti-corruption politics, and its momentum, across the province and effectively pose a challenge to Maurice Duplessis and the Union nationale.[22] Gradually, Drapeau also became engrossed in the tenets of corporatism and met with Raymond Barbeau, founder of the right-wing nationalist party Alliance laurentienne.[23] Drapeau's decision to lay the foundation for the CAL's transformation toward provincial politics was both insightful and opportunistic. In September 1959, despite being weakened by a flu, he campaigned for weeks during a provincial by-election in Lac Saint-Jean for an independent candidate on behalf of the CAL. His message, however, flatlined with voters.[24] Following this defeat, Drapeau left the Quebec political sphere and shifted his focus back to Montreal as an election loomed over the city.

Weeks before the municipal election of October 1960, and in a surprise turn of events, Jean Drapeau and Lucien Saulnier mutinied against the CAL. Both politicians recognized the need for a well-organized party that could break away from the now-outdated principles and philosophy of the CAL – especially Des Marais's strong grip over it. Drapeau and Saulnier created a new party, the Civic Party, and introduced it to the electorate alongside a group of acolytes and star candidates, including Joseph-Napoléon Drapeau and Gérard Niding. Eager to capture the CAL's political base, the party presented a sixteen-page electoral platform that revisited earlier CAL promises to combat vice and corruption. This, of course, completely enraged loyal CAL members. In fact, Drapeau not only abandoned the party that had propelled his political career but also left it in financial disarray by racking up bills right before his exit, which led one embittered member to describe the move as highly strategic, Machiavellian.[25] In the Civic Party, Drapeau and Saulnier found freedom, which allowed them to develop dynamic and appealing initiatives, particularly in the realm of urban development. Additionally, the Civic Party was committed to fight unemployment through extensive public works projects, including a subway, which was the largest of these initiatives.

Part of the Civic Party's sudden popularity resided in the fact that many Quebec Liberal Party members publicly endorsed it. Elected to the Legislative Assembly in June 1960, the Liberals had defeated the Union nationale in what was one of the most significant elections in Quebec history, the springboard to the so-called Quiet Revolution.[26] The Liberals led the province into a new era that would be characterized by the modernization of the education system, increased government intervention in the economy, the nationalization of hydroelectric resources, and a renewed focus on social welfare programs. And it was with this support that a few months later, during an abnormally peaceful municipal election, Jean Drapeau was re-elected to City Hall with 53 per cent of the vote after campaigning on policies that echoed his mid-1950s reforms. The Civic Party won forty-six of the sixty-six council seats.[27]

But this new political era was not determined solely by Drapeau's re-election. A referendum on the city's political system was held alongside the election, and the outcome marked another significant development. Dating back to 1940, the political system known as the "regime of the ninety-nine" had been imposed by then–Quebec premier Adélard Godbout after the province placed Montreal under trusteeship following its financial default.[28] The system was an innovative coalition of interests, insofar as it was built on the idea that spending at City Hall would be under control if council membership was increased from thirty-five aldermen to ninety-nine councillors.[29] Within this system, one-third of council was elected by property owners in eleven new wards (Class A councillors), one-third was elected by all householders who paid water or business tax in the same eleven wards (Class B councillors), and one-third were non-elected representatives who were appointed by thirteen designated public bodies – including universities, the Chambre de commerce du district de Montréal, and unions (Class C councillors).[30] The city's executive committee, made up of the mayor plus two representatives from each Class, elected a chair and vice-chair. Because the three categories of councillors came from remarkably different interest groups, however, the council chamber at City Hall quickly became notoriously heterogeneous in ideas and concerns. If anything, the system, dominated by male representatives of the wealthiest groups in the city, institutionalized the historical link between elites and urban governance.[31] And although the trusteeship ended in 1944, the system remained.[32]

All of this explains why the electorate overwhelmingly voted to abolish Class C representation in 1960.[33] During the following election, in 1962, Class A representation was abolished and four-year mandates for municipal administrations was established going forward. Under the new system, the mayor was given the power to choose the executive committee in the same way that a prime minister selects a Cabinet. With a majority in council, and without the checks-and-balances of an opposition, the municipal administration could work in secrecy and shield itself from public debate. The sum of these adjustments marked the beginning of a new political era.[34]

Police Reforms: European Imports

During the mid-century, a time preceding the Caron Inquiry, the Police Department earned a reputation for tolerating the informal economy, leading to the perception that it was "no place for an honest man."[35] As seen in chapter 1, this problem was recognized by successive police chiefs who considered ways to improve the department's public image, especially once the Caron Inquiry exposed officers' tolerance for illicit activities such as gambling and sex work. In fact, police reformer Andrew Way later pointed out how this reputation framed the prevalent apathy and the mutual distrust between the police, the civic administration, and the public throughout this period. "The department had been neglected for years by the city," he opined to a reporter, "and when you neglect an organization all sorts of undesirable things creep in."[36] Moreover, and despite employing close to 3,000 police officers by 1960,[37] Montreal's police services did not reflect the diversity of its population, which added to public distrust. As Tamara Myers notes, it predominantly mirrored the city's working-class French-Canadian, Roman Catholic majority, which compounded the normative framework with which officers patrolled the city.[38]

Although the Police Department underwent piecemeal reorganization during the first half of the twentieth century, leaders of the civic reform movement believed that a more thorough overhaul of the department was critical for the city's ambitions, especially in the fallout from the Caron Inquiry. Many observers noticed that police corruption had not ended following the inquiry but instead continued into the 1960s as officers enforced bylaws unevenly.[39] And with Chief Albert Langlois resigning as soon as his old enemies – Drapeau and former PMC members – regained power in 1960, the search for a new chief of police started then, if not earlier.[40]

Weeks after the Civic Party's 1960 victory, Jean Drapeau embarked on a furtive air trip to Europe with one idea in mind: to end corruption within the Montreal Police Department. He scouted the help of two seasoned police officers, one English and the other French, for an assignment that promised to restore public trust in police. In early December, on the other side of the Atlantic Ocean, he awarded a year-long contract beginning on 1 January 1961 to two men who had never set foot in Montreal.[41] Making the transatlantic journey to Montreal were Andrew Way, a commander in the London Metropolitan Police, and André Gaubiac, retired chief of the Paris Municipal Police. Despite knowing little about the city itself – or precisely because they knew little about it – Way and Gaubiac were brought to Montreal to examine its Police Department with an experienced and impartial eye, and to make recommendations for its improvement.[42] This undertaking would appear as a minor achievement on their resumés. Andrew Way had joined the Metropolitan Police during the interwar period; throughout World War II and after, he served with the special police corps of the Allied Military Government of Occupied Territories, notably in the Free Territory of Trieste.[43] As for André Gaubiac, he had made a name for himself supervising a "drastic overhaul" of the Paris Municipal Police in response to acts of political terrorism arising from the Algerian War in the late 1950s.[44]

The city housed the urbane and pipe-smoking duo downtown, in suites on the eighth floor of the Windsor Hotel.[45] Montrealers were at once intrigued and fascinated by the European officers. For example, Way and Gaubiac were invited as guests of honour by the Canadian Club of Montreal and the Kinsmen of Montreal to inform members of the public on the kind of police reforms they envisaged for Montreal. Initially, Way and Gaubiac were bemused by the local population's wonder, but as residents began to ask questions, they noticed recurring themes, some of which made the officers uncomfortable and embarrassed. Much of the questioning shed light on Montrealers' self-perception and a certain colonial mindset, suggesting their curiosity about how French-Canadian cuisine, women, and language compared to Europe's. Presumably, this curiosity aimed to gauge how Montreal ranked among the world's biggest cities. In any case, residents – who were eager to see a shakedown of their Police Department and keen to see their city measure up to the likes of London and Paris – wished the two men success when crossing paths on the streets.[46]

Initially, minimal information about the kind of reforms Way and Gaubiac imagined came to light. Nevertheless, journalists readily wrote about their involvement with the Montreal Police Department whenever possible. For example, on an eventful January night, they reported that the duo had become acquainted with Montreal's nightlife by observing a large-scale raid of a dance hall on Laurier Avenue as part of a campaign to stamp out teenage drug use. The raid involved several dozen officers of the police flying squad, the RCMP, and the social welfare squad. Remarkably, and ironically, on the same night as police were raiding the dance hall, hospitality industry workers held a press conference railing against what seemed to them an injustice, pure and simple.[47] The Committee of Night Workers, which claimed to represent some 40,000 people, lamented the state of the city's nightlife and argued that unemployment within the industry was estimated at 2,500 or more due to the "rigid enforcement of the [liquor] laws." Amid rising unemployment and falling profits, many in the liquor trade still clung to the hope that police raids would end and that liquor laws would be eased or amended. "It is a most urgent question," read the statement by the committee, which included waiters, taxi drivers, entertainers, musicians, and restaurant employees. "The authorities must work out a new law, appropriate to modern life in our province and designed to meet the future population growth and expansion of the tourist industry."[48] For industry employees, the modern city was not just a city with modern infrastructure but a city that offered the freedom to consume goods and services without rigid moral regulations. Nevertheless, there was no reprieve in sight for their industry. The line between the informal and formal economy was rigid, and authorities – civic, provincial, and federal – were of no mind to loosen regulations. That cold January night saw rules and regulations both enforced and contested.

Only a few weeks later, after a late-night meeting with Way and Gaubiac in attendance, the executive committee announced increased funding for police. Following recommendations from Way and Gaubiac and approval of the Montreal Policemen's Brotherhood (MPB) – the trade union representing police officers – the city announced that it would hire an additional three hundred officers over the next year. Indicating the first aspect of police reform, the city revealed that new personnel would be subject to strict hiring requirements: improved levels of physical fitness, education, and training. Beyond a greater emphasis on professionalism, the city also announced that civil servants would replace traffic bylaw officers, which would grant police greater freedom to address "real crime." In its early stages, police reorganization looked a lot like the reorganizations taking place in other cities as Montreal placed a great emphasis on the "professional crime-fighting model."[49]

Days later, after an outing with the Night Patrol, and reviewing the means at the patrol's disposal, Way and Gaubiac expressed their bewilderment to a reporter. They failed to understand how a city like Montreal had so few officers on the night beat – only two hundred – and they were equally taken aback by the equipment that was available to those officers. In short, they claimed that Montreal was poorly protected at night.[50] Way and Gaubiac essentially echoed what Woods Gordon and Co. reported in 1960: the city administration and services had to keep up with Montreal's rapid expansion and growth. The report also highlighted, quite crucially in the context of this chapter, that police services were excessively centralized. One journalist went so far as to describe the reorganization of the Police Department as a struggle "against poor standards, distracted interests, divided loyalties, and discouraging moods."[51] As criminologist Jean Turmel notes, the decentralization of the Montreal Police Department was all the more important considering the revelations from the Caron Inquiry.[52] After all, Mayor Drapeau had brought in Way and Gaubiac to rebuild public trust in police services.

During the summer of 1961, about halfway through the police reformers' undertaking, tangible changes in the reorganization of the Montreal Police Department took shape. First, the duo requested that a third member be added to their team to steer the ship after their departure.[53] In May, following a recommendation from the QPP, Joseph-Adrien Robert, the police chief of Hull, joined Way and Gaubiac. Pundits perceived this decision as astute because Robert, who had been Hull's police chief from 1937 to 1960, held a reputation as an incorruptible public figure during a 1943 corruption probe.[54] In a matter of weeks, the administration would announce that Robert was to become Montreal's chief of police by year's end. "There is much more to this appointment than the naming of a new head of the Montreal police," reasoned the *Montreal Gazette*, "the appointment is part of a process to remold the force."[55] As well, the city acted on some of the police reformers' recommendations when it enacted a new policing bylaw in 1961. The bylaw "concerning the Police Department" defined in precise detail the duties and general responsibilities of the chief of police and police officers.[56] It also partially tackled the problems exposed by the Caron Inquiry by allowing different sections to police each other's territories and paved the way for civil servants to gradually replace police staff.[57]

Another issue soon became apparent to police reformers, and it concerned the political strength of the MPB. A few days after Robert became chief-in-waiting, Way and Gaubiac sent a strictly confidential memo elaborating the reasons why a trade union is "totally incompatible with the conception of an efficient police and utterly unsuitably in a disciplined service, the very nature of whose work requires complete flexibility of direction and control."[58] Foreshadowing the intense labour conflict between the city and its protective services in 1969, Way and Gaubiac expressed concern regarding the bargaining powers of the MPB:

> It is sine qua non that police must exercise complete impartiality at all times, and as the servants and guardians of the general public, must treat all law-abiding citizens, irrespective of their race, colour, creed or social position, equally and with unfailing patience and courtesy. We consider that the militant attitude of the Brotherhood under its present

> leaders is responsible in a large measure for the present bad feeling that exists between the Department and the general public, a situation which we maintain is disastrous for both. Under the existing regime this trade union outlook is unlikely to alter unless sweeping changes are introduced. [It is] within the Department and its administration that the worst effects of the power of the Brotherhood are to be found, and it is here that positive action must start before any hope of improved public relations and effective policing can be expected.[59]

Recognizing the impossibility of disentangling labour and politics, Way and Gaubiac argued that the Police Department could restore its public image by dissolving the MPB. This demand, however, was not acted upon.

A year after Way and Gaubiac had arrived, the Montreal Police Department had seen much change. To begin, services were decentralized. For instance, the Morality Squad, a source of much controversy, was divided into four sections with overlapping jurisdictions, allowing each squad to monitor the others. Police stations gained more authority, and recruitment and training methods were improved. Civic leaders firmly stated that they would not tolerate police protection for nightspots like brothels, speakeasies, and gambling dens. But as their previous means of extra income suddenly vanished, police officers embarked on a prolonged campaign to improve their salaries.[60]

At year's end, when Gaubiac had left for personal reasons and Way was eyeing his own departure from Montreal, Chief Robert settled into his position and closely monitored drinking establishments, making sure that officers upheld laws and regulations.[61] This approach partially relied on the creation of the Social Security Squad, which was charged with eliminating the protection racket.[62] It also relied on co-operation with officers of the Quebec Liquor Board (QLB), which announced a desire to crack down on illegal practices in nightspots across the city. The QLB chair told members of the press that the board had been receiving complaints from the public concerning watered-down drinks.[63] These developments – what amounted to the authorities' further control over the nighttime economy (and would intensify in the lead-up to Expo 67 with a heightened regulation of women's behaviours in drinking establishments) – gave authorities the impetuous to

Figure 2.2
Police officer in uniform, c. 1962.

claim that the war on vice, immorality, and corruption was ongoing, and it would be won with a forceful assertion over the nighttime economy.

The criminal underworld, however, continued to assert domination over drinking establishments. In fact, in 1962 the police raided nightclubs in an effort to curb the "recently-revived protection racket."[64] Performing artists and gay nightclub-goers recalled that throughout the 1960s many Montreal nightspots were still entangled in protection rackets, offered by both the police and the mafia. Reportedly, police would receive envelops stuffed with money and agree to both turn a blind eye to the establishment's goings-on and warn managers when raids were about to go down.[65] But amidst rising criminal activity, Chief Robert grew resolute in his mission to eliminate illegal practices within the nighttime economy. His approach, however, remained dubious. During a multi-day cleanup drive, for instance, an officer fired his revolver, "hitting [a] man in a hand. A woman standing nearby was struck in a knee by a ricocheting bullet."[66] Although crime-reporter Paul Dubois claimed that Chief Robert had "dealt a death blow to organized crime and sown great fear in the ranks of the city's underworld," Montreal residents themselves would have been equally terrorized by the trigger-happy Montreal Police Department. Throughout the following years, raids on the city's nightclubs and cabarets continued and intensified.[67]

In 1962, between Christmas and the New Year, the city quietly reinstated the Police Department's Night Patrol. Dressed in plain clothes, the dozen men who were part of the patrol oversaw the preliminary investigation for all major crimes between midnight and 8 a.m.[68] In 1963, the Night Patrol arrested 562 individuals. In fact, the unit was so successful that a newspaper ominously predicted that "if the riffraff were to learn, overnight, that our police have decided to go on strike, we would witness a swarm of cutthroats roaming the streets, who undoubtedly would subject law-abiding citizens to a very unpleasant time."[69] While crime scenes belonged to the Night Patrol, another nocturnal unit, handpicked by Chief Robert, patrolled the city streets. The intent behind this second unit, whose constables were described as youthful and "tough," was to regain the respect of hoodlums and to make Montreal streets "safer."[70] As described in the city's newspapers, the range of police work in the 1960s expanded. Articles at times described in gruesome detail murders, brawls, and gangland settlements; but would still describe how night retained a certain mundaneness. "Flashing lights, lonely people trudging home, hippies, a few dead beats, a boy and girl aware of no one but themselves, a noisy group of kids growing suddenly quiet as the dead-giveaway green Ford passed by."[71] By the mid-1960s some core methods of nighttime policing would significantly change. These additional demands, alongside the period's political atmosphere, would give the Police Department's union great advantage when it came time to bargain for new contracts.

With the assistance of Chief Robert, the European police officers' recommendations amounted to sweeping changes in four areas for the Police Department: organization and role; administration; personnel; and, finally, communications, mobility, and buildings. These recommendations included enhancing the level of education, constant training, and a development program as well as implementing stricter promotion criteria.[72] The aspects were interrelated. In fact, Way and Gaubiac contended that training should be required for promotion and that selected officers be sent for special courses with the RCMP, the FBI, the Traffic Institute at Evanston, and elsewhere.[73] Way and Gaubiac attended some of the meetings and took part in the discussions to help foster a new police code that was implemented in 1962, which outlined the Police Department's hierarchy, ethics, and disciplinary action.[74] By November 1963, their recommendations had been wholly approved.

Over the following years, the model was tested and gradually modified to align more closely with the North American model of police administration. For example, in 1960 the basic course for police cadets was extended from twelve weeks to sixteen weeks. In 1968, it was prolonged to forty-three weeks.[75] Some officers had to complete additional training, while others needed to adapt to new roles. Administrators also faced an immense task of decentralizing all sections, adopting new methods of management, and implementing these administrative reforms with the support of the Montreal Policemen's Brotherhood, whose members often felt overwhelmed by the scale and pace of change. The transition period was challenging but not marred by the scandals of past eras. Nevertheless, as chapter 4 clearly shows, such reforms placed significant demands on police officers, which disgruntled many of them. In the meantime, as the city prepared for Expo 67, raids and gender- and race-based profiling created a feedback loop that would see the police and municipal politicians mutually reinforcing each other's drive to regulate nighttime city space.

A Decent Night's Sleep: Anti-Noise Bylaw 1448

Drapeau would be one of the first mayors of a Canadian city to understand that municipal affairs concern not only the local but also national and international contexts. Amidst rapid urbanization, population increase, and high levels of industrial activity, the city expanded. During the early 1960s, the civic administration promoted Montreal's urban development as a sight to behold: a global destination for both tourists and investors. For example, it bought a sixteen-page coloured advertisement in the *New York Times*: "In every direction, the attention is captured either by an emerging structure or the demolition of an obsolete property to make room for the next establishment. Linked with this creative activity promoted by private financial sources an extensive public works program is carried out by a progressive Civic Administration fully aware of the potentialities of its community. Road improvements, street widening, expropriations for urban renewal projects and the long awaited subway are an integrated part of this colossal reshaping of a fascinating Metropolis."[76]

The construction transformed the city, drastically. Colonial buildings and tenement rows were demolished to create skyscrapers and highway superstructures. One architect told a trio of journalists that during the early 1960s, "we looked for the land that was the cheapest. We simply never thought about the people."[77] In fact, foreign architects started viewing Montreal differently, perceiving it as a city that was being reimagined.[78] Although the "colossal reshaping" was a contentious ordeal, an affair that caused a lot of noise and disruption for residents, the city's advertisements portrayed both the destruction and construction as equally impressive sights.

Of course, the noise created by all this work was not a new issue for Montrealers. On the grandest scale, mid-twentieth century noise was just the latest chapter in a decades-long history. Trains, tramways, loud merchants, and the bustling industrial innovations of the late nineteenth and early twentieth centuries were part of the urban soundtrack. Historian Bettina Bradbury puts this into perspective in her description of the industrial landscape: chunky factory chimneys towering over the pre-industrial spires of the city's churches and the new sounds enveloping the landscape, from whistles to horsecars and construction work to screeching railway brakes.[79] At times, some of these sounds, like bells and steam whistles, were designed to help residents navigate the city and its potential hazards. Over time, however, many sounds began to acquire more bothersome connotations, redefining urban life, which led to noise-abatement campaigns and to enactment of Montreal's anti-noise bylaw in 1937.[80]

By the early 1960s the vehicle horn, designed to signal imminent danger, was seen as a pervasive nuisance: "an infernal noise, day and night," wrote one columnist in *La patrie*.[81] Like many urban centres, Montreal's sonic ecol-

Figure 2.3
Poster presented at a tourism competition centred around the theme "City of Montreal." Members of the selection committee consider the image's visual stimuli – skyscrapers, lights, and movement on a city street.

ogy was rapidly transformed by increasing traffic, individual mobility, and consumption.[82] In pursuit of a solution, an investigative journalist turned his attention to Paris, where noise-reduction efforts had proven successful in the 1950s. He interviewed André Gaubiac who was, at the time, chief of the Paris Municipal Police. The Frenchman disclosed that his capital had effectively tackled the problem by taking a two-pronged approach: consistent public education and ruthless enforcement of the city's anti-noise bylaw. Debates and conflicts over the regulation and control of urban soundscapes was an aspect of urban growth that was not unique to Montreal.[83]

Figure 2.4
Snow-covered Notre-Dame Street and its sidewalk in front of what was then the Palais de Justice (courthouse), now known as the Édifice Ernest-Cormier and home to the Quebec Court of Appeal, 1964.

Chief Robert adopted a similar strategy when he urged residents to cease honking at night. Meanwhile, city council proposed establishing new regulations to curb honking from 10 p.m. to 6 a.m.[84] Remarkably, this emphasis on nighttime tranquility, which trumped safety issues, raised important questions. In fact, just a few months before this attempt to silence vehicle horns, city council had introduced a system for nighttime waste collection, which would have been just as disruptive, or perhaps more so, for sleeping residents. In discussing this choice, Lucien Saulnier, chair of the executive committee, stated that collectors were instructed to minimize noise, and he argued that nighttime collection was for the benefit of the daytime city, which would "improve the appearance of the city for tourists, and generally make for greater cleanliness."[85] Alongside nighttime honking and waste collection, residents also expressed grievances regarding noises caused by air conditioners and snowplows, which significantly impeded their ability to get a decent night's sleep.[86] Clearly, during the early 1960s, the city's orderliness, appearance, and cleanliness were tied to the night in intricate and multiple ways.

That said, in the early 1960s, one of the greatest uproars regarding nighttime noise concerned abuses on the part of contractors. City councillors reported that contractors completely ignored the bylaw banning night work, which led to myriad complaints about late-night construction in residential neighbourhoods.[87] One daily newspaper went so far as to assert, "the night has almost ceased to exist for the past few months wherever there is construction. And there is currently a lot of construction happening in Montreal. So, a lot of noise."[88] Modern urbanization could not take place without the development of a transport system – like the transformation of Décarie Boulevard into a sunken highway and the metro network (fig. 2.5) – and those living near these large constructions sites were at the mercy of that promised progress to improve their city.[89] Construction created a major nuisance for Montrealers, albeit tolerated during the daytime hours; what sparked complaints was construction noise late into the night. The city's historical past was being erased and the future envisioned, and such work involved modern heavy machinery like piledrivers, excavators, loaders, cranes, and trucks. Altogether this transformation created a sensory overload for Montrealers at a time when their senses should have been resting.

Eminent writers noticed and described this transformation too. "I observe that Montreal is transforming at a fantastic rhythm," wrote Hubert Aquin in 1963. "Leave for a year (or even less), and upon your return, three neighbourhoods have emerged, and new streets have sprung."[90] Hugh MacLennan described Montreal in a comparable manner in *Return of the Sphinx*, as one of the novel's main characters, Gabriel, contemplated the parallels between mid-1960s Montreal and London after a blitz.[91] Making way for modern and avant-garde buildings, Gabriel's architectural firm made a profit from the hurried destruction of Montreal's historical past. Architectural evidence of the new Montreal was noticeable almost everywhere in the city.[92]

Figure 2.5
Excavation and construction of Berri-de-Montigny metro station, 19 January 1965.

Montreal newspapers gave noise complaints ample space in their editorial sections, especially as the amount of heavy machinery increased in the city. One individual described the sheer madness of the timing: "It's not so much the volume of the racket but the timing – at 2 a.m. for instance – and the senselessness … many people are driven up steep walls by construction noise – and not just blasting. Compressors can cause conniptions when they are used to power cement tamping on the 13th floor of the latest tall apartment structure at 3 a.m."[93] All kinds of construction disrupted sleep. Construction projects on Saint-Hubert Street and Châteaubriand Avenue kept residents awake all night too.[94] In response, Mayor Drapeau ordered police to monitor noise levels.

By 1963 city councillor John Lynch-Staunton reported a noticeable improvement in the enforcement of work hours and the elimination of noise. However, and taking into consideration residents' need for rest, Lynch-Staunton pressed his colleagues for a bylaw that would limit nighttime noise between 10 p.m. and 7 a.m. (with restricted hours on weekends). He wrote to Mayor Drapeau, proposing either an amendment to the 1937 anti-noise bylaw or the creation of a completely new bylaw. Whichever option was chosen, the councillor recognized that a comprehensive solution needed to be found to deal with construction noise.[95] Thus, councillors introduced a motion to establish a bylaw requiring contractors to obtain a special permit for night work.[96] In response, and knowing that such a bylaw might itself be a nuisance for contractors, the mayor requested police to monitor noise levels, again. Clearly, noise was an issue that meshed the economy and politics. "If the contractor is worried about a completion deadline, a mere fine on conviction after the job is finished is peanuts," wrote the *Montreal Star*. "City hall takes a lenient view of noise if it gets a big building finished earlier for quick tax revenue."[97] Nevertheless, it was against this backdrop that throughout the summer of 1964 politicians and police initiated a noise-abatement campaign, targeting contractors who deliberately violated the anti-noise bylaw.

Before the city made any changes to its 1937 anti-noise bylaw, Councillor Paul-Émile Sauvageau raised a series of questions that brought into sharp relief the sum of Montreal's transformation. He pondered why the city would regulate nighttime noise at major construction sites but overlook other disruptive nighttime noises such as music from nightclubs, the clatter of sewer hole covers, or the sirens of emergency vehicles. "If we want to ban noisy night-workers," stated Sauvageau, "why do we tolerate loud jazzbands in night clubs with their windows open until the wee hours of the morning, particularly during the summer?"[98] The nighttime bustle, from construction work to music venues, highlighted the fundamentals of urban life and the weighty subject of the nighttime political economy. As Councillor Sauvageau aired his grievances, he told council members that the polyphonic sounds, which emanated from the nightclub down his street, led him to phone the police on repeated occasions. However, and to his dismay, by the time the police arrived at the establishment, the sounds had somehow ceased.[99] Suspicious of the historical link between club owners and members of the Police Department, and energized by the problem's simple solution, Sauvageau produced a radical, impossible plan – one that was perhaps conceived during a sleepless night – which aimed to make Montreal the "Noiseless Capital of the World."[100] While defining noise in a universally objective and purely scientific way is impossible, Councillor Sauvageau's concerns reflected long-standing middle-class views on acceptable behaviours in public space at night.[101]

Finally, in 1965 city council unanimously ratified the executive committee's amendment to the anti-noise bylaw. The amendment added the following paragraph to the bylaw: "Any constable of the City shall, on complaint from any citizen or upon simply witnessing such violation, arrest on sight any person infringing the provisions of this article and who is unable to show a special permit authorizing the carrying out of such works, between ten (10) P.M. and seven (7) A.M."[102] The amendment encouraged officers to immediately arrest personnel working on construction sites at night. Council also decided to increase the maximum fine from $40 to $200. To be sure, it was a drastic measure to prevent noise, yet it was a desirable one. Because noise had a profound effect on residents close to construction sites, it received positive reviews. "Montrealers will finally sleep at night," *Le Journal de Montréal* proclaimed on its front page the day following the amendment's enactment.[103] Other journalists and writers also allowed themselves to wax poetic about the restoration of nighttime's tranquility.[104]

However, contractors seemed to be impervious to the new regulations. Residents who had to contend with noisy construction sites claimed that police were either lenient, complacent, or unaware about which sites held a special permit for nighttime construction.[105] One resident told a reporter that when police paid a visit to the construction site across the street, labourers ceased their work. During this pause, the resident deduced, they must have been replenishing their two-stroke engines because once the officer left, the labourers resumed their work. Fuelling the resident's frustration was the byzantine and convoluted process to find out if a contractor had a special permit: "When one seeks information, a call is made to the City, which strongly advises you to contact the local police station. And the local

Figure 2.6
View from Notre-Dame Street of Saint-Laurent Boulevard (left to right) in 1965. The Hydro-Québec Building shines brightest on the right. In the foreground, a dark, vacant lot marks the future site of the Palais de justice (courthouse).

police station strongly advises you to contact the City. You are then transferred between various lines, and you realize with astonishment that the question you are asking falls outside the jurisdiction of any office."[106] Within the span of several months and with construction in full bloom for Expo 67, the amendment served little purpose. However, historical documentation may be tainted by bias: it mostly reveals when noise complaints reached the public sphere; residents who were satisfied with police enforcement of the bylaw seldom took the time to write and congratulate police for its action. At the same time, authorities seized editorial space to congratulate residents who had refrained from complaining about noise: "I have words of high praise for the hundreds of thousands of uncomplaining Montrealers who endured the inconveniences of subway construction over the last four years," wrote Montreal Transportation Commission (MTC) chairman Lucien L'Allier. "Most people who had to endure the noise and disturbances have sympathized when we explained our problems to them. They realized just how much the job we had to do means to Montreal."[107]

Conclusion

Incredulous and incensed with the result of the 1957 municipal election, Jean Drapeau orchestrated a successful return to Montreal politics in 1960. That year Montrealers could not have known that Drapeau's rule was to last for more than a quarter-century, and that over those decades he would cement his legacy as a powerful mid-twentieth century reformer. The elections of 1962 and 1966 gave the dynamic mayor unprecedented majorities, which practically eliminated any opposition in civic politics. Within the span of a few years, from the mid-1950s to the mid-1960s, the city had clamped down on perceived decadent social and moral behaviours. Then, it began to promote itself as a safer destination for moneyed tourists and business entrepreneurs by investing in high culture and modern infrastructure.

To illustrate the forces reshaping early-1960s Montreal into a new city, this chapter tells that story from two important vantage points. To begin with, and mirroring developments in Western cities, Montreal brought seasoned policemen to restructure police services and thus recover from the consequences of the Caron Inquiry. In fact, Drapeau was so pleased with this restructuring that he recommended Andrew Way be included in Her Majesty's New Year's Honours.[108] "Seldom has so much been done in such a short time by so few," claimed Drapeau at a reception held to honour Way. "We have now a solid working plan of reorganization for a modern, scientific and effective Police force," he continued.[109] By 1966, a new police chief had arrived on the scene: Jean-Paul Gilbert. Unveiling an extensive reorganization of the Montreal police, he too acted on the recommendations made by Way and Gaubiac: the Police Department was decentralized to make way for "the large-scale use of modern, proven methods of crime-busting."[110] But as chapter 4 shows, after only a few years, this reorganization collapsed when the Montreal Policemen's Brotherhood revolted against those in power during a bitter labour conflict. Consequently, the reforms conceived by Way and

Gaudiac would be reversed, and the Police Department was once again centralized to make enforcement more efficient.[111]

As in other cities, police engaged in struggles to establish control over every inch of space, which seemingly escaped officers during the 1960s. Hospitality industry employees organized and continued to lobby against the closing time of drinking establishments. Meanwhile, contractors refashioned the city on schedules that roused residents from their night's sleep. Noise, as a source of public debate, was an important facet of Montreal's own evolution. It was tantamount to the city's future. Examining how police reorganization and noise regulation became political issues gives greater insight into the changes that characterized 1960s Montreal. Of course, noise in a vast city like Montreal will never cease to be a topical issue, so long as people sleep, work, and socialize in close proximity to one another. But in the early 1960s, nighttime noise was a by-product of the city's transformation into a large, modern metropolis. As it was being reshaped, so too were the regulations governing its territory.

Montreal had lost its ebullient and boisterous wide-open characteristics during this period. When American burlesque performer and stripper Lili St-Cyr returned to Montreal in 1965, after leaving for Nevada and California in 1951, she observed the city's transformation, and noted that it was "becoming very conscious of its image."[112] Many nocturnal activities became antithetical to this image. Over several years, police raided nightspots and apprehended people for running or frequenting brothels and gambling houses and partaking in non-normative activities like loitering and homosexuality.[113] In the wake of these changes criminal organizations occupied other spaces, rendering bars, nightclubs, and hotels into semi-legal zones. Clearly, the Civic Party believed that by refining Montreal's image it could make the city an attractive destination for upmarket, cosmopolitan, global tourists. Effectively, it was setting the scene for what would be one of its highest achievements, the 1967 world's fair, commonly known as Expo 67.[114]

3

HUSTLING DURING EXPO 67

A bizarre and unexpected event prompted the Bureau International des Expositions to award Montreal the 1967 Universal and International Exhibition. In 1962, the chosen host, Moscow, stated that it did not wish to have the spotlight on itself. Therefore, in lieu of attending an event meant to mark the Russian Revolution's fiftieth anniversary, Expo 67 visitors would travel to Montreal to celebrate the Canadian Confederation's centennial anniversary. It was an unforeseen twist for the Bureau International des Expositions, but the outcome allowed Montreal to formulate a plan to host the world. With the support of provincial and federal governments, much of the site of Expo 67 took shape on an archipelago of artificial islands on the Saint Lawrence River.[1]

Preparations for the mega-event, however, moved beyond the islands as the city fast-tracked urban renewal projects in neighbourhoods where tourists and reporters might set foot during the fair. For example, in December 1962 the municipal administration voted to expropriate properties in Victoriatown – a neighbourhood situated southwest of the city's downtown core – to make way for Expo 67's Autostade.[2] Victoriatown had been home to roughly 1,500 residents of Italian and Irish descent and was surrounded by rail lines, abattoirs, port-related industries, and a dump.[3] This was the city's largest urban renewal project since the completion of the Habitations Jeanne-Mance housing development in the Red Light district. Coincidentally, the city planned to relocate a number of Victoriatown families to the

Habitations Jeanne-Mance, as the former's space was redrawn for Expo transit and industry.[4] In Little Burgundy, home to a vibrant Black community, the city began purchasing properties to clear that neighbourhood of low-income tenements and further extend the city's road network.[5] Throughout this process, the city masked Little Burgundy's poverty from onlookers by erecting seven-foot-high, blue-and-white fences around its perimeter.[6] At stake in both these cases was Montreal's new international reputation as a modern metropolis, a global city. Effectively, because Expo's site was so close to the city's downtown, officials embarked on a crusade to make the city's image as immaculate as the event site itself, hoping that this would enhance the overall experience for visitors and tourists. Like fairs held before and after, Expo 67 was designed by planners as an ideal representation of modern life, and the city seized this opportunity to reimagine its territory accordingly.

While visitors experienced Expo 67's bright displays during the day, they travelled to the city centre in the evening to enjoy all that Montreal's nightlife had to offer. Throughout the summer of 1967, the city at night was meant to be a hive of activity, echoing Expo's general hubbub. But according to reports, many drinking establishments – where tourists, performing artists, bartenders, and locals mingled – were undermined by fraudsters who used "every known method – plus a few they invented themselves – to part customers from their money."[7]

At the heart of this struggle, which had emerged in the aftermath of the 1950's crackdown, lay two deceptive practices. The first was the manipulation of light and darkness by owners and managers. Often, they would shroud their establishments in near-darkness, allowing their employees to set prices at exorbitant rates, shortchange customers, or even pickpocket them. The second, far more widespread scheme, involved "B-drink hustlers" – typically women hired as servers, hostesses, or performing artists – enticing men into buying them expensive drinks.[8] Once the drinks were flowing, the hustler focused her attention on her patron and devoted herself to sustaining the relationship for as long as possible. While the client's drink always contained alcohol, hers was a "phony" – a watered-down drink charged at full price. The gist of this scheme lay in the conspiring relationship between the B-drink hustler and the bartender. Because these hustlers often worked at the establishment, some employers required it as part of their jobs, while others paid them a per-drink commission on top of their regular wages. In the end B-drink hustlers, bartenders, managers, and owners all made considerable profits from this racket.[9]

As I discuss throughout this chapter, indignant male patrons exposed these frauds by telling their stories to the media. They seethed at the ongoing theft and price gouging, and warned other men about paying for phony drinks. What upset customers most was that they were vulnerable victims, unwilling or unable to dispute capricious and costly outcomes, especially once they realized that their drinking companion was not a genuine sexual connection but had been planted to extract as much money as possible. B-drink hustlers cultivated sexualized interactions with male patrons, but they were inevitably caught between the expectations of their employers and those of their customers. Men, expecting adulation from women in bars, instead became victims of deception, which left them feeling both confused and frustrated. Therefore, in the lead-up to Expo, police stepped up raids on establishments serving alcohol and started waging war on the circuit of shady nightclubs, bars, and hotels that fed the local and tourist economies in the 1960s.[10] Ultimately, and as a representative for the Montreal police told reporters, in the months leading up to Expo, "cheap night clubs catering to cheap people doing cheap things" would be seeing a whole lot of his colleagues.[11]

This chapter shows how the city reorganized the nighttime economy when it decided to confront and dismantle these fraudulent schemes in preparation for Expo 67. To achieve this, the municipal administration enacted a highly controversial "anti-mingling" bylaw, which banned employees of establishments serving alcohol from drinking, dancing, or sitting with customers. However, the bylaw was more than a tool to protect customers. Because authorities knew that sex workers constantly drifted in and out of the hospitality industry, depending on economic circumstances, and would generate additional income by finding part-time jobs like serving, dancing, or hosting, they outright stated that the bylaw would be used to uproot the sex industry from such establishments. "The real purpose behind [this bylaw]," revealed executive committee chair Lucien Saulnier, "is to fight prostitution."[12] Effectively, the bylaw was enacted to eradicate sex from the hospitality industry. But as American historian Amanda Littauer notes, B-drink hustlers created a professional subculture in which they purposefully

Figure 3.1
People walking among the modernist structures and pavilions of Man and His World, the fairgrounds of Expo 67, with the Saint Lawrence River and the Montreal skyline in the background.

blurred the line between commercial and casual sex.[13] Consequently, when officers patrolled nightspots and eyed women who "mingled" with male clients, they had trouble deciphering which women were employees, customers, and sex workers. In fact, as several court cases involving the anti-mingling bylaw reveal, this patriarchal control of nightspots led to the arrest of women not because of any concrete evidence related to sex work but because of mundane acts like taking a seat, dancing, or chatting with customers. And because the bylaw was enforced so assertively, it became the source of intense contestation as legal scholars, lawyers, business owners and employees, and judges debated whether Montreal exercised power beyond its legal authority.[14]

The push to regulate (sexual) behaviour in nightspots was a conspicuous evolution of mid-1950s reformism and, accordingly, further disrupted the nighttime economy. This was especially the case for women who were continually (mis)identified as duplicitous B-drink hustlers – a term that became indistinguishable from sex work in the press and in the minds of authorities

Figure 3.2
Sainte-Catherine Street's Casa Loma nightclub with illuminated marquee announcing performers, 19 April 1966.

and residents.[15] Nevertheless, the anti-mingling bylaw allowed city authorities to claim that they had responded to the threat of fraudulent behaviours, which were especially prevalent in dark and dingy nightspots. By further regulating drinking establishments, officials claimed to have made the nighttime economy more honest, which enhanced Montreal's reputation as a suitable and safe tourist destination during and after Expo 67.

Beyond affecting thousands of workers employed in establishments serving alcohol, the bylaw was partially responsible – and this was not intended – for the modernization of the provincial liquor legislation, which had been in effect since the establishment of the Quebec Liquor Board (QLB) in 1921. In 1968, the Quebec government launched an inquiry into the sale of liquor and liquor laws in an attempt to find a balance between "order and revenue." There were several reasons behind the inquiry, but chief among them, in the context of this chapter, was the fact that Montreal's municipal administration had enacted a bylaw that concerned alcohol control, which fell under provincial jurisdiction. Therefore, while commissioners investigated how to reform the liquor market, they also considered the complicated legal structure that had led Montreal authorities to enact the anti-mingling bylaw.[16] When Justice Lucien Thinel submitted the inquiry's report in 1971, he alluded to the bylaw by recommending that liquor legislation should be "strong enough so that no municipal laws take precedence over that of the provincial board."[17] By scrutinizing the murky road to the anti-mingling bylaw's creation – and its subsequent termination – this chapter underlines how the regulation of sex, promiscuity, and darkness shaped municipal and provincial policies in the lead-up to, during, and after Expo 67.

The Trouble with Darkness and Intimacy

In December 1966, *Maclean's* published a colourful sixteen-page report on Montreal proclaiming that the city had, fairly suddenly, "become one of the world's great cities." It attributed this overnight success to a host of factors like migration patterns, politics, and urban development. Ultimately, however, the study concluded that Montreal was a great city because of its culture, which it evaluated by describing the stylish middle-class office workers who sustained the city's five thousand bars and restaurants. Women and men who worked downtown enjoyed the cafés and international cuisines available to them during office hours. After work, they enjoyed rambunctious cinq à septs. However, because many of these workers were commuters, this atmosphere was far from a twenty-four-hour affair. In fact, and still according to *Maclean's*, the city underwent drastic change once these commuters returned home. At night, after workday hours, it claimed that Montreal transformed into a sombre place. As part of the report one contributor wrote with fear and fascination about his experience at night, leading him to claim that the nighttime city was equally busy but with different characters and attitudes that revealed how "under all that gaiety Montreal is a violent town."[18] Although the intrepid contributor wrote with superficial knowledge about Montreal's distinct nighttime communities, his observation evoked a persistent problem with the city's image: the city was urbane during the day and perilous at night. Montreal had been transforming at an extraordinary rate since the mid-1950s, yet if one scratched the surface that glamour faded quickly.

Any suggestion that Expo 67 was a glamorous and modern urban achievement was complicated by the undercurrent of anxiety that ran through the festivities. In March 1966, a few months before *Maclean's* published its report, the Montreal police, QPP, and RCMP established a special brigade to counter the threat of sex work, gambling, and drug and alcohol trafficking in nightspots. They acted on internal reports that suggested that international criminal organizations would descend on Montreal to lay the foundations of their businesses during Expo.[19] According to one source these criminal organizations had been renting apartment units by the hundreds for incoming sex workers said to be numbering three thousand.[20] Tabloid newspaper coverage of Expo exposed issues concerning social order, as articles exploited stories to create panic regarding security and moral standards. Articles sensationalized stories involving not only sex workers but also incoming pickpockets, counterfeiters, motorcycle gangs, gangsters, and pests, amplifying concerns and anxieties.[21] Moreover, reports discussed how the event would attract "undesirable" youths, including loitering hippies, rock concert–goers, and drug users. Historian Greg Marquis's study of the federal Commission of Inquiry into the Non-Medical Use of Drugs (Le Dain Commission) shows that the event helped create Montreal's new drug scene, much to the ire of Jean Drapeau and the Civic Party.[22] Teenaged users hung around squares and parks, and at the Expo site itself, while those of drinking age went to coffee houses, discotheques, and bars. The authorities' crackdown on nightspots thus began with articles and corresponding police reports that informed the public about perceived undesirables and lawbreakers who tried to reap the multi-faceted and urban benefits of a world's fair.[23]

City officials, knowing that tourists would spend time and money in the nighttime economy, started focusing on the threat posed by B-drink hustlers, commonly referred to as "B-girls."[24] Found in establishments serving alcohol, these hustlers were commonplace in mid-twentieth-century North

American cities.[25] In their usual practice, the hustlers would mingle with male customers and appear to be sexually available. Once engaged in conversation, the hustler might ask him for a drink or wait for him to offer. An unspoken agreement between the bartender and the woman meant that unless (or until) the customer objected, the tender would continue supplying phony drinks to the woman, charging the man more for each subsequent drink. After the first drink, a typical customer quickly lost control of the situation – and to keep the drinks and cash flowing, hustlers encouraged and managed their admirers' attraction to their bodies. The customer would pay for a B-girl's high-priced scotch, crème de menthe, or champagne, and she received diluted tea, coloured sugar water, or ginger ale. This racket allowed her to consume drinks by the dozen, amounting to several hundred over a week, a pace that would be impossible to sustain with real cocktails.[26]

B-drink hustlers mastered the art of attracting, engaging, and exhausting their customers and used spatial positioning to avoid or cut off unprofitable encounters, since they could afford to accept men's attention only so long as the drinks kept coming. They cared a great deal about earning money, which they did by receiving a percentage of the income they helped the establishment generate. "In some clubs," recollected a transgender B-drink hustler, "drinks were sold for $1.80, which was expensive … We received about 60 cents [per phony]! I once made $360 in a day! Do you understand? Can you imagine?"[27] Underpaid performing artists often participated in this scheme after their performances, sitting down with clients to converse over drinks or demand tips. In 1965 and 1966, B-drink hustlers, including women and drag performers, were arrested and charged with fraud. However, all were acquitted due to a lack of incriminating evidence.[28] Despite that, it is important to emphasize that hustling drinks was not the primary goal of most performing artists; when talking to reporters, Montreal's cabaret and nightclub artists, professionally trained and representing racial and ethnic diversity, primarily discussed their artistic endeavours, exhibiting a sense of pride in their craft.[29]

Many establishments used discreet methods to entrap men. On occasion, they would charge customers after they took a seat with one of their female employees. Sensational stories about ordinary clients, like one man who received a $190 bill for champagne he shared with an employee in a Drummond Street cabaret, revealed the costly outcome. Another article reported that an Eastern Townships college professor was handed a $160 tab for buying a few drinks and spending an hour and half with a performer; another told the story of a New Yorker who was handed a $110 bill for talking to and spending less than an hour with a female employee.[30] Thus the B-drink hustle was amplified by tourists who warned others of the systematic money heist and of the "rudeness and belligerent insistence on tips by club personnel."[31] As the director of the Montreal Municipal Tourist Bureau noted in the months leading up to Expo, these practices tarnished the city's image and held the potential of becoming "deadly for business."[32]

Although the issue was one of petty theft or dishonesty, tabloid articles like those published in *Allô Police* allowed the Civic Party to articulate a discourse about the need to control women working in nightspots. Put another way: the same tabloids that Mayor Drapeau had so openly loathed in the 1950s now allowed him to legitimately develop a regulation that would remove "undesirable" women from the nighttime economy. As in other cities, the concern was not for women who had to resort to this work to supplement meagre incomes, or the fact that it must have exposed them to some dangerous situations. Rather, the concern was for male victims.[33] To this end, authorities identified several factors that sustained the fraudulent scheme – coming to the conclusion that, most often, it was the establishment's darkness and intimacy that was to blame, particularly in small and dingy venues that offered erotic shows.[34] The venues' darkness created a state of confusion for clients who, during transactions, could not decipher bills or the ridiculous price rates, and the intimacy allowed employees to pickpocket and rob them. Undercover agents from the QPP noted that certain nightclubs were too dim and, at times, simply did not have any light. For instance, during one police check, an owner told officers to stop searching for a light switch. "There are no lights here," he revealed.[35] Montreal's chief of police Jean-Paul Gilbert told reporters in jest that he did not expect "these places to be lighted up like soda fountains [b]ut something must be done."[36]

Before elected officials passed a bylaw, however, police raided the city's "B-girl row" on Sainte-Catherine Street and Saint-Laurent Boulevard. QPP Chief Joseph-Adrien Robert led the crackdown, which produced hundreds of charges and arrests. "Clubs that serve juveniles, hoodlums, and prostitutes, clubs that tolerate disorder and water their drinks or in any way violate the law," he announced in the aftermath, "can expect daily visits from our men

– and full scale raids." Unlike the Montreal Police Department, which Robert had led from 1961 to 1965, the QPP could keep law and order in establishments serving alcohol by revoking liquor permits or charging those who broke liquor laws. Meanwhile, the new chief of police for the Montreal Police Department, Jean-Paul Gilbert, corroborated that "everyone in the city is influenced by Expo these days – including the police."[37] Detectives and officers working for both Robert and Gilbert collaborated and acted on every complaint they received, which led the *Montreal Star* to conclude that "seldom has the heat on the city's dives been so intense."[38] Despite clear jurisdictional boundaries, including the fact that municipal authorities had no legal control over liquor permits and laws, Chief Gilbert sent a request to the Montreal executive committee asking it to come up with a plan that could give his officers the power to end fraudulent schemes.

On 8 February 1967, the executive committee drafted an anti-mingling bylaw. Because this draft only regulated female employees' behaviours, it showed that authorities were more serious about uprooting those who bridged the gap between sex work and casual pickups than they were about protecting clients.[39] One month later, however, the executive committee amended the bylaw's wording so that it applied to all employees, and council passed it. Bylaw 3416 made it "unlawful for any employee of any establishment dispensing alcoholic beverages or for any entertainer thereof to mingle with the customers of the establishment, to drink, dance or sit at the same table or counter with a customer."[40] Later, Chief Gilbert reported that it had been inspired by bylaws enacted in New York City, Chicago, New Orleans, Miami, Los Angeles, and San Francisco.[41] And like authorities in those cities, Montreal was hopeful that the bylaw would end soliciting and dishonesty in nightspots. Members of the executive committee told journalists that it was a step against sex workers, against women and transgender performers, and against nightclubs that served phonies.[42] Though he did not support the bylaw outright, Quebec Liquor Board chair Judge Marc Lacoste supported the essence of the pre-Expo crackdown, guaranteeing that the board was ready to shoulder its responsibility to protect Montrealers and tourists: "Take notice, you who hold permits, that you must supervise the persons responsible for your establishments and that on founded complaints, the Board will use its powers to suspend a permit for the period it determines. If an establishment ... houses a shameless system of exploitation of tourists or a category of the underworld, drug addicts, commercialized vice, or habitual illegalities, the permit holder will be duly summoned and the law will follow its course."[43]

From the start officers applied the bylaw indiscriminately and ruthlessly, meaning that performing artists like dancers, musicians, and singers who stepped off the stage to join friends, family, or admirers in the audience – whether for a drink or a conversation – were equally targeted.[44] Within a matter of days, police arrested and charged employees for mingling and managers for allowing it. "They say that the bylaw was adopted to fight prostitution," wryly noted a writer for *Le Monde du Spectacle*, "but it's a pretty funny way to crack down on prostitution. Everyone knows that 99.9 per cent of Montreal's prostitutes never set foot on a cabaret stage. Someone around here must be kidding."[45] Later, a cabaret owner would claim that the bylaw had reduced business to the brink of bankruptcy and contended that authorities did everything in their power to "have cabarets disappear, that's clear!"[46]

As chapter 1 showed, Mayor Drapeau largely ignored business owners who claimed that rules and regulations were bad for business; instead, he persistently claimed that people had to follow laws that upheld order, honesty, and morality. A decade later, he held the same position. Like the reforms that he had led in the 1950s, this one concerned public perception in two distinct ways: apprehending perceived criminals and upholding Montreal's image as an honest and moral city. Certainly, Drapeau and members of the city's executive committee saw how the bylaw could restore the city's image and its international reputation, which is what counted most to them. For others, like cabaret owners, the anti-mingling bylaw not only transformed business but also threatened the connectivity of urban life.

Though the terms of the bylaw clearly did not target the sex industry per se, authorities constantly claimed that it was an effective tool with which to combat prostitution. And given the police crackdown on the nighttime economy, that held some truth. Sex workers confirmed that in the lead-up to and during Expo 67 they had to steer clear of nightspots, because they feared that officers would charge them – not under the anti-mingling bylaw, but under the article of the Criminal Code that punished prostitution and acts that were believed to be connected to it: vagrancy, solicitation in public places, and loitering.[47] Police presence had become pervasive.

Two prominent madams, Martha Adams and Rita Picard, revealed more about the authorities' practices during this period. Born in 1930 in Disraeli, a small community in the Eastern Townships, Martha Adams had been one of the cabaret performers who saw her livelihood vanish as police increased cabaret raids.[48] Contrary to newspaper accounts, she recalled mingling with friendly customers and hustling genuine drinks: "Between dances, we had to 'mingle' as we called it then, meaning taking a seat with people who were alone ... So, I'd go and sit with them, and the bartender would serve us champagne. I'd never had any before and I'd take two glasses and, by the time I headed back to the dance floor, I was tipsy. But every time I'd sweat out the alcohol."[49] She also revealed that throughout the early 1950s, mingling led to generous tips, especially from wealthy tourists from out-of-province and the United States. When reformers upended cabaret work in Montreal, however, she saw no other choice but to move to Ontario to pursue her line of work.[50] Rita Picard, freshly out of prison, also described Expo 67's atmosphere. Like many other sex workers, she could not work in nightspots due to intense police surveillance and raids. But the alternative, at least for her, was not particularly bad. She rented a penthouse on Sherbrooke Street where, along with five employees, she serviced over two thousand clients throughout the event – including diplomats, businessmen, and tourists from around the globe.[51] For other sex workers, however, the heat on the city's nightspots led them to other urban hubs like New York City and Vancouver.[52] While sex work might have been entangled in the nighttime economy, as these women noted, it did not mean that all women who worked in the hospitality industry were sex workers. Still, the emphasis placed by elected officials and the media on the bylaw's potential to remove sex workers from the nighttime economy created the perception that most women employed in the hospitality industry were somehow involved in sex work (fig. 3.3).

Although drink hustlers found sex work tempting, they hesitated to cross what they viewed as an ethical line between selling drinks and selling sex. But sometimes the line between the two was lost. Ultimately, the anti-mingling bylaw could not, as elected officials claimed, be an effective tool to combat prostitution since it did not help officers decipher who was or was not selling sex. For instance, at Bar des Arts, a cabaret located at 286 Sainte-Catherine Street West, police officers enforced the bylaw to arrest five female employees and the manager. The night's events, described during the trial,

Figure 3.3
A 1969 cartoon satirizes the idea that women working in alcohol-serving establishments are also engaged in sex work. The caption reads "Tourist season is afoot: police enforce the 'famous 3416,'" while an officer warns, "Hey! No mingling!"

gives insight into the kind of scenario that fuelled frustration among employees and owners:

> Constable Gaudreault testified that … he entered the premises in question, followed shortly after by Constable Dufour and both sat at a table and both remained in the club for the purpose of making observations and subsequent arrests for a period of at least an hour and a half.
>
> **Colette Hargray** … was sitting at a nearby table with two men and was drinking from a glass, though the officer could not testify if it was an alcoholic beverage. Later, she got up on the table where she had been sitting with two clients of the establishment and danced on the table. She told the officer that she worked in the kitchen of the establishment and later was arrested there.
>
> **Monique Kemp** … stated she was acting as waitress and serving clients but, at certain times, she would come and sit at a table with four or five young people.

> **Jeannine Fournier** ... was described by the witness as a waitress and dancer with the cabaret and, while acting in this capacity, from time to time, would come back and hold a conversation with three men at a table and, finally, when there was a free chair, she sat down with them.
>
> **Dawne Kye** ... though she was not present [during trial], evidence was taken concerning her activities at the time and place in question. Testimony was given to the effect that the defendant was a waitress-dancer employed by this establishment and, from time to time, after serving other clients, she would come back to this particular table and sit on the knee of a client.
>
> **Lucie Russel** ... the testimony is to the effect that she was a waitress but between serving clients at different tables, she would come back and sit at a table with two clients of the establishment.
>
> **Leo-Paul Champagne** ... he was arrested by the senior officers at time of the raid as being in charge of the establishment. Constable Marcel Dufour corroborated the testimony of Constable Gaudreault concerning the other defendants and with respect to Leo-Paul Champagne, he testified that he was at the bar of the cabaret and seemed to be in charge of the establishment. Sergeant Poitras who was in charge of the Police operation, testified that on his arrival there with other officers, around 21.00 hrs, that Constables Gaudreault and Dufour pointed out to him the foregoing defendants and he arrested them. He also stated that the female defendants were permitted to use the coat room to secure additional clothing.[53]

Effectively, this trial reveals how the court relied upon plainclothes police officers to provide evidence of transgression, which required extensive and sexist monitoring of nightspots.

The bylaw was enacted to address the problems that reformers deemed persistent within the nighttime economy: dishonesty, swindling, and sex work. But as the trial above reveals, officers were limited in their ability to identify lawbreakers. Those who monitored nightspots may have been confused or uncertain about the exact roles played by women in drinking establishments. Essentially, authorities tightened their grip over the nighttime economy by studying how women behaved in nightspots, leading them to enforce the bylaw against a prosaic and harmless nighttime culture.

The bylaw, claimed authorities, specifically targeted dishonest drink hustlers and prostitutes. But these identities were discursive. Yet, this lack of clarity did not dimmish the intensity with which they enforced the bylaw. For example, before Expo had started, nightclub singer Joan Hill Sabatini was charged under the bylaw for sitting at a table with a client. She petitioned for a writ of evocation at the Quebec Superior Court wherein she claimed that the bylaw was unconstitutional because it contravened the Canadian Bill of Rights.[54]

Years after Expo 67, Quebec historian Robert Rumilly stated that Montreal was the capital of world and that Man and His World was its epicentre during 1967.[55] "It was stupendous … like everybody was on this great collective high," recalled a bartender who worked at Expo's Bavarian beer garden two decades after the event. A secretary in the Expo administration stated that it "surpassed everything that ever happened in Canada," and a *Gazette* journalist observed that "the city became a lot more open to new things," concluding that "it became genuinely cosmopolitan after Expo, and Montrealers became much more sophisticated than they ever were before."[56] Many recollected how the event set Montreal's international reputation as a global city. Overlooking the event's colonial controversy and celebration,[57] many pundits agreed that the event was a smashing success; it had been a celebration of world culture and a demonstration of the time's most memorable artistic creativity. Playing a part in this success were architects like Frei Otto and Buckminster Fuller, musical acts ranging from the Supremes to Luçiano Pavarotti and Marlene Dietrich, and dignitaries, heads of state, and royal family members, whose presence enticed others to see and experience the mega-event. Between 27 April and 29 October 1967, Expo drew fifty million visitors to Man and His World.[58]

By the time Expo's activities were in full swing, the city's nightlife had undergone a profound transformation. This transformation was, in part, shaped by officers' enforcements of regulations in low-income neighbourhoods and the relaxation of those same restrictions in the city's swankier nightclubs. For instance, repeated raids by the police – as many as half a dozen in a single evening for some venues – were enough to scare clients from heading off the beaten track, which led one nightlife journalist to conclude that the "night club business is shot in Montreal."[59] For authorities the goal remained simple: keeping tourists in areas that magnified Montreal's

Figure 3.4
A bright full moon between two Expo 67 structures: Buckminster Fuller's geodesic dome (left), which first served as the United States pavilion and then as the Biosphere, and ARCOP's Man the Explorer pavilion (right).

splendour. Therefore, tourists were gently corralled to Man and His World's restaurants, discotheques, beer gardens, concert hall, theatre, and enormous amusement park, which, taken together, provided ample entertainment. By keeping tourists and visitors at the site, the city brought much-needed revenue to Expo, which eased some of the debt accrued in building it. Thus, while authorities enforced the bylaw in low-income or disreputable neighbourhoods, they ignored it where wealthy tourists blended with Montreal's elite at Man and His World. There, establishments served alcohol past the lawful hour as well. As one journalist remarked, "Montreal police on Expo duty haven't bothered the performers … there seems to be no barrier to 'mingling' between employees and customers on the site."[60]

Racial prejudice also played an active role in how the Police Department regulated the nighttime economy during Expo. In one instance officers raided the historically Black Harlem Paradise and charged six women under the anti-mingling bylaw. On the same night, they raided Sahara, a nearby cabaret, where they charged a twenty-one-year-old Arab dancer whose performance "had particularly captivated [the officers'] attention."[61] The Arab nightclub, owned by Fawzia Amir, was subject to numerous police raids during the 1960s because it promoted belly dancing.[62] Throughout 1967, officers policed racialized women's behaviours differently, and as research shows, Blacks were prosecuted at a statistically higher rate than any other racial or ethnic group in Montreal during that year.[63] A couple of weeks after the raids at Sahara and Harlem Paradise, two police officers returned to the latter to apprehend women. Disguised as sailors, the officers did not charge anyone under the bylaw since they did not witness any mingling. However, upon leaving Harlem Paradise, they were solicited by a pimp who asked the supposed sailors if they "would like some women" and "quoted them a price of $25 for each of them." After having been ushered into a nearby tourist room, the officers charged a sex worker for prostitution and the pimp under the Criminal Code's bawdy-house law.[64] Although the officers' stakeout at Harlem Paradise had failed to achieve the desired effect, a coincidental encounter in public space was enough to convince the Police Department that the venue, and its neighbourhood, should be monitored. Less than two weeks later, officers returned to Harlem Paradise. And this time they enforced the anti-mingling bylaw to charge two employees for "molesting" a patron who wished to leave, a third one for mingling, and the club owner for permitting his employees to sit with the customer.[65]

The extent of the Police Department's racial prejudice was mocked at the end of that year during the "African Ballet Affair."[66] The affair unfolded when Les Ballets Africains (Guinea's national dance company) stopped in Montreal during its North American tour. After performing in Quebec, Joliette, Sherbrooke, Ottawa, and Sorel, the dance company, comprised of thirty male and thirteen female performers, was set for a residency at Place des Arts from 5 to 20 December 1967. On the first night, undercover agents, seated in the front row, observed attentively; they took notes and snapshots of the performance – especially during the three scenes when female dancers performed topless. The following night, during the show's intermission, Lieutenant Detective Paul Boisvert issued a summons to five underage dancers, to the troupe's director Sekou Sakho, and to the show's producer

Elise Pouliot, under provisions of the Criminal Code's "sexual offences, public morals, and disorderly conduct." Although the Police Department did not invoke the anti-mingling bylaw in this case, the manoeuvre was connected to the city's wider cleanup project. Numerous artists, activists, and even a clergyman wrote about the absurdity of the whole affair and commented on the way that Jean Drapeau was killing artistic culture in Montreal.[67] After public uproar, the municipal court dropped all charges, including the one against Pouliot, who had been charged with producing an indecent show. In his statement, Municipal Court Judge Henri Beaulieu argued that police officers had overlooked the cultural and artistic value of the show: "It appears that the young girls were chosen for their dancing ability, not to satisfy or whet the audience's sexual appetite."[68] The Morality Squad's coarse analysis of the performance – its sexualization of African artistic expression – exposed latent racist codes and attitudes that Black Montrealers faced throughout the mid-twentieth century.[69]

In the years following Expo 67, police officers continued to enforce the anti-mingling bylaw, but in a different way, targeting queer drinking establishments and employees, thus reinforcing heteronormative boundaries. Notably, it was used against five employees of the Hawaiian Lounge after they shared drinks with clients; the manager was also arrested for allowing mingling.[70] Moreover, police constantly raided cabarets like Béret Bleu and Chez Paree, which were known gay hangouts. Eventually, a municipal court judge had both historic establishments closed after receiving police reports that disclosed, amongst other things, that Chez Paree employees had been charged some three hundred times under the city's anti-mingling bylaw. Although a legal challenge followed, each establishment's fate was sealed.[71] Elsewhere, in a spectacular and coordinated raid, police arrested over a dozen employees at the Cave des Moines because they had witnessed men, dressed in drag and as monks, dancing with the clientele.[72]

The sum of these raids, which led to thousands of charges and arrests, reveals how police operations could not have been randomized. Rather, officers assessed the need to monitor or raid certain venues based on the clientele's socio-economic status, race, sexual orientation, and gender identity. Sometimes, however, officers were more discreet. Dressed as civilians, they entered establishments and waited until they observed non-normative patterns of behaviour. All of this led to legal challenges. At the Quebec Court of Appeal, three female performers argued that the City of Montreal acted beyond its powers because the power to regulate, punish, or prohibit behaviours was a provincial authority. Further, they contended that the power to regulate did not include the power to prohibit acts that have nothing to do with the consumption of alcohol. However, Chief Justice of Quebec Lucien Tremblay and Justices Paul Casey and Garon Pratte dismissed these constitutional challenges.[73]

To gauge public opinion on the anti-mingling bylaw, *Le Journal de Montreal* decided to hold an informal street vox pop. The tabloid interviewed five men, each of whom stated his staunch opposition to the bylaw: "I fail to understand why I can't sit with my buddies who work at a licensed establishment," said one. "I work at a bar," revealed another, "and to be frank this bylaw is stupid because no one can stop me from sitting with someone. The police have been enforcing this bylaw and it's doing a lot of harm."[74] One of the daily's journalists published articles that lamented the way multiple reforms, like the anti-mingling bylaw, forced Montrealers to self-police.[75] Roused by outrage and claims of an undemocratic handling of nightspots, these individuals demanded that the municipal administration cease its interventionist creed to save the nighttime industry. They cared little about whether or not the bylaw would help Montreal's image on the global stage, and they probably cared just as little about those who had been scammed.

By the end of the 1960s, some establishments were forced to close because of insurmountable legal fees following anti-mingling court cases. A famous business owner who lost large sums of money challenging the bylaw in court recalled with nostalgia the halcyon days of Montreal nights. "The good times are over!" he exclaimed resentfully, "The anti-mingling bylaw is driving the industry to the ground."[76] Like the reforms initiated during the mid-1950s, those administered during the mid-1960s allowed the municipal administration to strengthen its rule over night and thus have Montreal's nighttime industry align with "honest" urban practices. While City Hall could claim that regulations had, in fact, ended forms of criminal activity, they had also brought an end to a nightlife culture that many business owners, employees, and performing artists depended on. As one embittered jazz musician later told historian John Gilmore, "Expo cut the throat and let the blood out of the city."[77]

Montreal Nightlife and Liquor Reforms

After Expo 67 had come and gone, and as the city continued to regulate its nighttime economy, the Quebec government formed an inquiry to look at the multi-faceted issue of alcohol consumption in the province. The inquiry was formed in a tense atmosphere after employees of the QLB had gone on two strikes – a first one lasted eleven weeks from December 1964 to February 1965, and a second from June to November 1968.[78] Toward the end of the second strike a "scandal" erupted in the suburbs of Quebec City when a chief of police seized a shipment of nearly ten thousand bottles of spirits that the QLB was allegedly sending to New Brunswick despite the ongoing strike.[79] Although it was later proven that the shipment was not illicit but in fact destined for the Quebec market, Quebec Premier Jean-Jacques Bertrand announced the formation of a Royal Commission to probe Quebec's liquor market and the government-owned body overseeing it.[80] Nearly a half-century had elapsed since the QLB's creation in 1921, and needless to say, Quebec society had undergone profound transformations during this period. Headed by Justice Lucien Thinel, the inquiry investigated Quebec's alcohol commerce dating back to 1964, aiming to enhance the affordability and effectiveness of its monitoring. To achieve this goal, the inquiry included two other members, Quebec City accountant Marcel Belanger and Montreal economist Otto Thur.

Montreal had a lot to gain (or lose) from this inquiry. Throughout the early twentieth century, Quebec's liquor laws were the envy of Canadians who opposed the temperance movement. Journalist Al Palmer would even claim that "there is more personal freedom in Quebec than in any other province and your right to drink what and when you please has been safeguarded by the sanest set of liquor laws in the Dominion."[81] Although Palmer conflated the leniency of liquor enforcement with the actual freedoms guaranteed by the law, he nevertheless touched on a widespread sentiment among people who lived in or visited Quebec: the province offered more freedom than any other Canadian province when dealing with alcohol consumption.[82] The probe eventually found that liquor laws were violated, not so much because of negligent officers but because the QLB had not evolved alongside Quebec's social mores. For instance, under the Sunday Observance Act, alcohol could not be sold in theatres on Sunday. Later, the commissioners would state that this act was "neither applied nor applicable," leading them to suggest that it needed to be repealed as part of sweeping reforms.[83]

For Montreal's municipal administration, there was no widespread disagreement over specific and mundane details such as the one above. Rather, another issue elicited its attention, one that it believed should be at the heart of liquor legislation reform: the fact that the policing of liquor permits and laws remained under the authority of a handful of Sûreté du Québec (SQ) officers. The Civic Party contended that these officers – though they benefitted from the SQ's intelligence – were ill-equipped and could not prevent local criminal organizations from seizing control of Montreal's nighttime economy. The party based its knowledge on Montreal Police Department reports, which claimed that gangsters and lawbreakers of all kinds persistently trafficked sex, drugs, and stolen goods in establishments serving alcohol.[84] Therefore, city authorities saw an excellent opportunity when the inquiry announced that its main objective was to tie alcohol consumption to "order and revenue." Liquor reform could allow the Montreal Police Department, and by extension members of the municipal administration, greater control over the nighttime economy.

As the inquiry was underway, the Montreal Police Department submitted a report to the city's legal team in which it underlined the importance of order, control, and surveillance in establishments serving alcohol. The report would be used as the city's basis for listing its own recommendations to the inquiry. In the end, the legal team recommended the following reforms to the commissioners: reforming accounting systems for establishments holding liquor permits; designated areas for performances; clearer distinction between establishments serving meals and those selling alcohol; better illumination of drinking establishments; and clearly visible QLB permits posted next to city permits.[85] Unmistakably, the city believed that implementing a law that emulated Montreal's own anti-mingling bylaw was a good thing. But the city went even further when it evoked the need to bolster its knowledge about the hospitality industry and its workforce. To that end it recommended a carding system for employees that would identify them by name, photo, and fingerprint.[86] Furthermore, in its review of lighting standards, it claimed that under current laws clients could engage in lewd behaviour. "Semi-darkness," the report argued, "yields to an atmosphere in which order and moral standards cannot be held."[87] Therefore, the city evoked the need for proper permits and illumination, both characteristics of honest labourers and respectable establishments.

Within the Quebec context, effective liquor control raised issues relating to legislative powers and responsibilities. In short, the division between provincial and municipal authority. Therefore, a small, but not insignificant, change happened in 1967 when Quebec attorney general Justice Minister Jean-Jacques Bertrand granted special authorization for some officers of the Montreal Police Department to patrol establishments serving alcohol. As previously mentioned, for most of the twentieth century local police departments held no authority over the control of alcohol in cities and could only act in cases involving clandestine sales or when liquor had been sold to underage clients. But to help local police units maintain order during Expo 67, Bertrand eased restrictions that had kept alcohol control under provincial authority. Armed with special permits some officers could assess and monitor the threats that had been "posing particular problems to the Police Department."[88] As the Thinel Commission was underway, a similar and more consequential transfer of power took place. In July 1970, the new Quebec attorney general, Justice Minister Jérôme Choquette, gave the Montreal Police Department the right to act on matters concerning alcohol legislation. Choquette granted these rights to the department after receiving a special request from Montreal's chief of police. Later, Choquette proudly recalled his decision: "I gave the authorization to all officers of the Montreal Police Department … to inspect offences that could be committed concerning alcohol and, also, to handle cases without my authorization as attorney general so that they could clean up Montreal."[89] The Montreal Police Department had submitted its recommendations to the Thinel Commission earlier that year, and before the end of the inquiry, the Quebec government had transferred the power wholesale to the department. Chief Gilbert's other recommendations, however, would be addressed at the end of the inquiry. In the meantime, it was becoming clear that liquor legislation reform would address the needs of Quebec's metropolis.

The Thinel Commission's 359-page final report was submitted in February 1971. The commissioners offered recommendations for a new regime based on a balance between "order and revenue." Within this new regime was a section that would address the provincial liquor legislation's historical weaknesses, which had led to fraudulent schemes like B-drink hustling and price gouging. The commissioners stated that this legal loophole had led Montreal to enact, understandably so, an anti-mingling bylaw: "Some cabaret owners employ [B-drink hustlers], waitresses or dancers, in order to encourage customers to drink and to extort large sums by being offered drinks with low alcohol content. In addition, these procedures often lead, according to police, to unacceptable behaviours in public space. To prevent these abuses, and given the silence of the QLB on this point, the City of Montreal had to adopt bylaw 3416, which prohibits female staff from mingling with customers." Therefore, concluded the commissioners, monitoring the behaviour of hospitality industry labourers should be the responsibility of the body overseeing alcohol legislation, not municipalities, which is why they recommended incorporating a text inspired by the anti-mingling bylaw into the provincial legislation with offenders receiving "the most severe criminal and administrative penalties."[90]

After receiving the Thinel Report, the Quebec government decided to split the QLB into two bodies. The commission's goal had been to find a balance between order and revenue, and in July 1971, the QLB was divided along those lines. Since the state believed that profitability rested on modernizing Quebecers' shopping experience, it tasked the Quebec Liquor Corporation (known as the SAQ, Société des alcools du Québec) with managing revenues.[91] The SAQ shrugged off the QLB's monochromatic image by designing sleek and colourfully attractive stores where clients could see and handle products. Although the SAQ became the exclusive importer and wholesaler of spirits, wine, and beer, the wine monopoly was broken up and opened to retailers, like food stores and supermarkets.[92] Meanwhile, employees of the Liquor Permit Control Commission – notably its inspectors and investigators – were tasked with upholding the law by issuing, renewing, suspending, and cancelling permits where applicable.[93]

The commission addressed the legal limitation that had allowed Montreal to enact its anti-mingling bylaw. In this regard, and clearly acting on recommendations made by the Montreal Police Department, an anti-mingling provision was enacted into law: "No employee of an establishment in which a cabaret permit is used and no person who participates in a performance there shall mingle with the customers of the establishment, drink or dance with them or sit at the same table or counter with them."[94] Unlike Montreal's bylaw, however, the law targeted employees – not owners – meaning that performing artists remained subject to policing while owners could uphold a criminal system without punishment.[95] Additionally, the commission enacted another provision mandating a registration card for all employees of a establishment holding a bar or cabaret permit. Minister Choquette was pleased with these reforms as he agreed that local authorities now had the tools to remove "undesirables and criminals" from the nighttime economy.[96] By the late 1970s, after further reforms to liquor legislation, the article remained and was mainly used against female erotic dancers.[97]

The legacy of the anti-mingling bylaw stretches far beyond the late 1960s and '70s. It remained on the books until 1993 when an owner, Pierris Zoumboulakis, was accused of "letting his staff mingle with the clientele."[98] His lawyer, and future leader of the Civic Party, Clément Bluteau, convinced the courts that the bylaw was unconstitutional since it violated the right to freedom of expression guaranteed by the Canadian Charter of Rights and Freedoms.[99]

Conclusion

Reformers made the regulation of women's bodies and sexual behaviour a top priority in recasting the city's appearance. They observed how Montrealers and tourists had mingled in the city's drinking establishments and, driven by the desire for friendly or romantic companionship, had fallen victim to unsavoury schemes. By monitoring employees – particularly women – in nightclubs, bars, or cabarets, the anti-mingling bylaw attempted to further regulate drinking establishments at a moment when it looked like Montreal might finally become a global city. By further monitoring and regulating nightspots to safeguard clients from swindlers and sex workers, authorities reformed the nighttime economy into a lawful, appropriate, and secure marketplace. Yet, the bylaw's limited framework upheld heteronormative and moral norms since it was enforced in nightspots where Montrealers of different economic background, race, and sexual orientation mingled, and not necessarily where officers found swindling B-drink hustlers. As this chapter demonstrates, officers repeatedly visited and charged employees working in Black, working-class, and gay drinking establishments located in different neighbourhoods. Eventually, and after accruing legal fees, many establishments were forced to fold, which threw hundreds out of work.

The chapter also reveals the link between the anti-mingling bylaw and reforms to Quebec's liquor legislation. By tracing the history of liquor law reform back to Montreal's anti-mingling bylaw, we see how the Civic Party forced the Quebec government not only to act on matters that were specific to the metropolis but also to cede powers to the Montreal Police Department. Indeed, the Civic Party showed how it could both influence provincial politics and dictate the contours of new laws governing alcohol. Later, and as with Expo 67, the city would "clean" its image in a series of similar crackdowns in the lead-up to the 1976 Summer Olympic Games, which once again forced Quebec's intervention. But before turning our attention to that mega-event, it is necessary to first look at the very workers who were charged with maintaining order in the city, and the municipal administration's efforts to also keep them under control.

4

STRIKES AND NIGHTTIME DISORDERS

On the night of 4 September 1969, at the same address where the Public Morality Committee was founded in 1950, a shrine to romantic Montreal poet Émile Nelligan opened its doors. The establishment, whose rich decor recreated the opulence of a late-nineteenth-century Golden Square Mile mansion, was adorned with souvenirs, manuscripts, portraits, and a bust of the famous poet.[1] Le Vaisseau d'Or, named after one of Nelligan's poems, displayed the passion of the venue's owner, Jean Drapeau, for high culture. Accordingly, on that opening night a coterie of Montreal's elites headed to the establishment for a seven-course dinner. The city's elite would have heard about the mayor's newest project by word of mouth, and many of them had been invited to its launch. Over the following weeks, the masses would have been made aware of the establishment's existence – having seen hundreds of ads for it in the dailies. In *La Presse* they appeared in a section on Montreal's culinary scene, and in *Le Devoir* they appeared alongside a potpourri of ads for plays, erotic cinema, and university courses.

While the clientele's perfumes and the aromas from the establishment's kitchen made Le Vaisseau d'Or rich with scents, it was not, like most nighttime establishments, rich in revelry. Under strict directives from the owner, an embargo on light and noise limited the moments when the dining space was lit and when clients could feast and talk. "Since … Le Vaisseau d'Or features music as well as high cuisine," the menu outlined, "one is asked to speak in a low voice. In an effort to minimize conversation with waiters, the menu provides you with a full description of its different items, as well as an order form where you may indicate your choice with a mark at the proper place. We appreciate your contribution to the success of the evening. The procedure outlined will foster your own enjoyment."[2] This arrangement gave the establishment's twenty-piece orchestra, conducted by Jean-Eudes Vaillancourt, the freedom to perform pieces by Bach and Vivaldi uninterrupted.[3] To the discontent of many patrons, the owner placed an emphasis on his guests' behaviour – silence, order, and timeliness – rather than on haute cuisine. In fact, unlike other musically inclined establishments, the staff at Le Vaisseau d'Or quickly reprimanded clients who spoke during the musical performances. In a way, Drapeau had crafted his ideal version of nightlife at this establishment, seamlessly blending diverse facets of high culture. But Drapeau, the proprietor, could not have envisaged how the lines of the eponymous poem would so accurately presage his establishment's fate. Just over a month after it opened, the establishment was wrecked and ransacked during a day-long police and firefighter wildcat strike:

> She was a massive ship, hewn in gold,
> With masts that fingered heaven, on seas unknown.
> Under redundant sun, with scattered hair
> Was prowed outspread Venus, bare.
>
> But then one night she hit the huge reef
> in waters where the Siren sings
> and this ghastly shipwreck tilted its keel
> to the depths of the chasm, that immutable tomb.[4]

On the morning of 7 October 1969, 2,400 firefighters and 3,700 police officers walked off the job. That evening during a special newscast, a CBC anchor prompted his audience to consider "what happens when a metropolis has no policemen, no firemen." The anchor told his audience that Montreal coped easily during the day. The trouble started, he remarked, as night fell and things spun out of control into what the national public broadcaster labelled a "Night of Terror."[5] The outcome of the strike would be surveyed over the following days: death, injuries, violence, and arrests, plus nine bank holdups, thirty other armed robberies, and 494 complaints involving

Figure 4.1
The orchestra performs for diners at Le Vaisseau d'Or, c. 1969.

Figure 4.2
Jean Drapeau poses in Le Vaisseau d'Or stairwell's "hall of poets," September 1969.

$853,882 worth of reported damage – including at Le Vaisseau d'Or.[6] Quebec's provincial police, the Sûreté du Québec, offered some protection to Montrealers during the strike as it responded to hundreds of emergencies.[7] Nevertheless, and to the horror of Montreal's elected officials, the Night of Terror was an event – one of a handful in the city's history – that made international front-page news.[8] Night, darkness, and chaos gave editors the world over a facile imagery with which to play, one they juxtaposed with the law and order that reigned in global cities during the brightness of day.

The context of the firefighters and police strike is significant. In 1960s Quebec, strikes took place in the private sector as meat packers, truckers, and factory workers walked off the job and in the public and para-public sectors as government employees, teachers, and health care workers did the same. The power of the labour movement was centralized in Montreal due to the presence of major trade union headquarters, including the Fédération des travailleurs du Québec (FTQ) and the Confédération des syndicats nationaux (CSN). Historian Sean Mills places this period within a transnational context by showing how, whether peaceful or not-so-peaceful, overlapping strikes and protests made the province's metropolis and its streets the setting for a new political culture.[9] Montreal was one of many cities in the world where the intense confrontations of the 1960s redefined the conditions of women and men and led to an explosion of new political subjects that included students, youths, women, and queer, racialized, and post-colonial actors.

A clear example of this redefinition occurred during the occupation of Sir George Williams University's computer centre in protest of systemic racism against Black students. Like many other challenges to authority during this period, the occupation of the university ended in a confrontation, with the anti-riot unit's intervention and a violent mass arrest. And because a fire broke out during the bedlam, firefighters also arrived onsite to allay the heat.[10] The event not only shook the Black community to its core but also showed how the Civic Party relied on the city's police and fire departments to crack down on, or clean up after, opposition during the 1960s. A few months after the Sir George Williams affair, however, the city's already tense atmosphere was thrown into chaos when those same officers and firefighters elected to go on strike after a breakdown in talks while bargaining for new labour contracts. And as we'll see, just as protestors used symbolic space to convey their message – like the occupation of a state-of-the-art computer centre – the city's workforce made strategic use of temporality, using the night to fight back at Drapeau and his political regime.

This chapter reveals how city employees made use of the spectre of nighttime anarchy to achieve better working conditions. The night became a tool to negotiate with, one that was used by both the municipal administration and city employees. Leading up to the strikes, trade union leaders representing the Montreal Policemen's Brotherhood (MPB) and the Montreal Firemen's Association (MFA) strongly defended their members' cause, but paradoxically, once their members went on strike it was the unions' passivity that generated chaos. Indeed, the wildcat strikes cannot be disentangled from the night because it was the fear (and reality) of nighttime chaos that allowed members to improve their bargaining power and thus gain better settlements. By scrutinizing not only the centre of municipal power but also the administrative forces operating in the background – like firefighters, police officers, and trade union leaders – we gain new perspectives on municipal governance.[11] Clearly, the municipal administration's hegemonic structure collapsed without the city's protective services. As police and firefighters positioned themselves as the keepers of order, their unions gained unmatched power during negotiations. And as order faltered, Montrealers were left to fend for themselves, caught between opportunists of chaos and their struggle to preserve their homes, goods, and livelihoods. The lasting result of these disputes was not just labour victories but substantial increases to police funding, which underscored the municipal administration's priorities and its determination to restore order (in fact, between Drapeau's first mandate in 1954 and 1970, funding for the Police Department increased by 418 per cent).[12] The same did not hold true for firefighters, however.

Eventually, the sixteen-hour 1969 strike was resolved when the provincial government intervened, which involved the mobilization of the Sûreté du Québec and the Canadian Army. In the aftermath, and to defuse the city's politically charged atmosphere, the Civic Party enacted an anti-demonstration bylaw, which prohibited assemblies in order "to prevent riots and other violations of order, peace and public safety."[13] But because the Civic Party's answer to protest and dissent was so draconian, activists from different factions began seeing elements of totalitarianism in the way that it was governing Montreal. They reacted defiantly by organizing nighttime protests, the most significant of which were the rallies organized by the feminist Front commun des Québécoises (FCQ) in November 1969 and the rally organized by labour leaders in the context of a strike at *La Presse* in October 1971. The city, however, enforced the bylaw with force by sending the anti-riot unit, resulting in violent confrontations, mass arrests, and death. Many quickly realized one of the most remarkable aspects of these events: in the span of a few weeks, police officers had gone from challenging the powers at City Hall to enforcing a bylaw that prevented residents from doing the same. Over the following months and years, civil rights activists would challenge the legitimacy of the anti-demonstration bylaw both on the streets and in the courts.[14] The echoes of protest politics resonated deeply in Montreal's streets and literary scene. Few captured this era's turbulence as powerfully as Marie-Claire Blais. In a poignant and gripping way, *St Lawrence Blues* (1973) dramatizes the late-1960s and early-1970s political atmosphere of Montreal. It takes the reader on a picaresque journey through Montreal's streets and culminates with a huge demonstration against injustice – what Blais poetically refers to as a "night of justice."[15] This work of fiction, like many others of that period, showed how the night was a moment of political defiance.

Another labour conflict would rock Montreal in 1974. In October of that year, firefighters elected to go on strike, again. Feeling like the city had abandoned them, firefighters went on strike after a complete breakdown in talks during which union leaders tried to get the city to index wages to the rampant rate of inflation.[16] This second strike lasted a whole weekend, which allowed vandals and arsonists to roam the streets and destroy properties, homes, and businesses. The nighttime firestorms would hit Montreal hard and left hundreds of residents destitute, which forced the provincial government to intervene, again. But unlike the mobilization of troops in 1969, this strike was resolved when the provincial government guaranteed that it would contribute funds for the firefighters' new contract.

From the Night of the Strike to the Night of Terror

7 October 1969 was the most beautiful day of my life.[17]
– Jean-Guy Ménard, police lieutenant and executive committee member of the Montreal Policemen's Brotherhood (MPB)

At 5 a.m. on Tuesday, 14 December 1943, Montreal's police and fire departments began an eighteen-hour-long strike. Alongside many blue-collar workers, the striking officers and firefighters were pursuing their right to unionize. During that strike, a crime spree took hold of Montreal in what newspapers branded the "Night of the Strike." Vandals, burglars, and arsonists dotted Montreal's wartime landscape with crime scenes, the most important of which was a fire on Chambord Street where striking firefighters stood watching while five fire marshals attempted to bring the flames under control.[18] The event forced federal authorities to place seven hundred soldiers from Camp Borden, Ontario, on high alert from December 1943 to February 1944. In the end, and upon request from Quebec Premier Adélard Godbout, the municipal administration yielded to both departments' demands.[19]

While this episode might seem like a distant and unconnected story, it nevertheless frames the political struggle for power in 1960s Montreal. In fact, the morning after the 1969 strike ended, Quebec premier Jean-Jacques Bertrand, chair of the Montreal executive committee Lucien Saulnier, and trade union leaders all recalled 1943 and drew parallels between the two strikes.[20]

In the years leading up to the 1969 strike, Montreal chief of police Jean-Paul Gilbert noted a shift in tone within the Police Department's labour culture: "We began to see the change in about 1964 … Up until that point the police were not like other unions. They had a sense of duty and responsibility toward society."[21] But the 1960s was a time of intense confrontation between the old and the new. In Quebec, these contestations mostly took place in Montreal, and because these upheavals created volatility and violence, many officers grew cynical about the changing nature of their work.

Although these upheavals transformed the nature of police work, the average officer's workload had remained more or less the same until January

1967. That month the municipal administration enacted three new policies that destabilized the workforce. The first policy instructed the department to have one constable per police car; the second slashed pay grades, which made salaries inferior to Toronto's Police Department; and the third had the city cease its contribution to the Montreal Policemen's Brotherhood (MPB) pension plan. Since labour contracts would expire in 1968, union leaders pushed the municipal administration to hold talks. The latter, however, claimed it was too busy dealing with Expo 67 to begin negotiating contracts, and instead compelled union leaders to wait until the end of the event. This cavalier response was met with anger and frustration, and it quickly dawned on union leaders that they could gain some leverage if they meddled with the event.

Before ending, Expo 67 was held up by a number of well-coordinated wildcat strikes. Organized labour presented a bold challenge to the municipal administration, and it was orchestrated, not by unionized police officers, but by six thousand employees of the Montreal Transportation Commission (MTC) and taxi drivers. During the strike, a nighttime riot erupted when it was announced that labour contracts would not be signed in 1967. On the streets, conductors, drivers, inspectors, and attendants displayed their frustration.[22] Members of the radical taxi faction Comité d'entr'aide embarked on parallel protest as they drove down to City Hall shouting "We want justice!" and "We want to talk to Drapeau!"[23] When it became clear that nobody would step outside City Hall to meet with them, taxi activists regrouped and held a spontaneous street protest as well.[24] Because it brought Montreal's bus lines and its brand new metro system to a halt, it was the MTC strike, more so than taxi activists, that made life difficult for Montrealers and Expo tourists alike.

The MTC strike paralyzed the rhythm of the city for several days. Some encumbered citizens coped with the lack of public transit by carpooling with neighbours or walking, despite autumn rains. City activities had been disrupted by the labour movement and Jean Drapeau made the extraordinary claim that it was "truly criminal … some people will die and others will have their lives cut short [because of it]."[25] The transit strike ended in mid-October when Quebec Premier Daniel Johnson stepped in and signed a highly contested back-to-work order. In the end, it had been a worrisome episode for

Mayor Drapeau, demonstrating how his power rested upon the strength and obedience of the city's services.

Incidentally, it was the financial strain created by Expo 67 that generated tension between cash-strapped Montreal and city employees. In 1968, a year when labour contracts would be renegotiated, the Civic Party announced its first budget crisis: a deficit of $28 million.[26] Labour unions expected the administration to slash spending. On 23 February 1968, 1,500 police officers expressed their concern by walking on City Hall. Once they reached the building, they pounded on the walls and on the windows, and hurled insults and threats at the men nestled inside, which included Jean Drapeau, chief of police Jean-Paul Gilbert, and executive committee chair Lucien Saulnier. The officers were embittered and felt that the new labour contract should mirror the role that they played in a climate of social unrest, viewing themselves as custodians of law and order. "Suddenly it was the police who were in the streets," remarked Jean Drapeau's biographers, "engulfed in all the classic passions of a mob." Later, Chief Gilbert disclosed that it had been the single most frightening night of his career: "I will never forget that night as long as I live. I was scared, I can tell you. The mayor, Saulnier – we were all scared. I can still hear the echo of the pounding. And their chant: 'Dra-peau au po-teau!' [Drapeau to the stake!] over and over. I had the impression of a bad dream, of a *coup d'état*." Petrified by the possible outcome, he also recalled how the officers had nearly brought down the municipal administration.[27] Although Drapeau, Saulnier, and Gilbert were accustomed to protests, this marked the first time that they, themselves, had been exposed to potential violence. Eventually, the mayor gathered courage and walked up to the mob in an attempt to calm the officers' spirits. He anguished over the scene and asked them to consider the optics of dissenting police, but his plea inspired no shame.[28]

As mentioned at the beginning of the chapter, the streets of Montreal were the crucible of a revolutionary political culture, which sometimes led to violent confrontations. And one of the era's most violent (and important) incidents happened in 1968 when inexperienced police officers cracked down on Saint-Jean-Baptiste Day revellers, leaving over one hundred women and men injured. The night's events, however, started earlier when a stage had been erected in front of the municipal library on Sherbrooke

Street to give VIP guests a prime view of the annual parade. Guests included Jean Drapeau and Liberal Party of Canada leader Pierre Elliott Trudeau.[29]

With increasingly separatist protests taking hold of the city, the presence of Trudeau, an opponent of the Quebec sovereignty movement, was seen from the revellers' perspective as an antagonizing manoeuvre. Therefore, when the parade started – and sensing that a confrontation might arise – officers began arresting activists associated with the sovereignty movement, many of whom had gathered nearby. In retaliation, the crowd pelted officers with rocks, threw projectiles toward the stage, and chanted "Tru-deau au po-teau!" (Trudeau to the stake!). Officers quickly manoeuvred toward the riotous crowd, causing it to move across the street into La Fontaine Park where the festivities were thrown into complete disarray. Bystanders, and people who had been nestled in nearby nightclubs, cafés, and private residences, also suffered under the merciless wrath of nightstick-wielding officers as police raided adjacent properties in search of agitators. Police crushed young and old and took close to three hundred into custody during what became known as the infamous and bloody "Lundi de la matraque" (Nightstick Monday).[30] The short documentary *Taire des hommes* depicts vivid images of the bedlam. In the film's closing moments, Jean Drapeau rides in a black sedan, while Jacques Couture – a respected priest, activist, and future leader of the opposition at City Hall – speaks over the footage, his voice marked by the memory of the police brutality he suffered that night, offering a sobering reflection on Montreal's political landscape: "If our society accepts outcomes like this, we're screwed. Even with great achievements like Expo, the metro, Place des Arts. When people are unjustly attacked, flogged, and disrespected in holding cells ... well I find it very serious. It's a sign that our society is really sick and if we're not addressing this problem, well then, I believe it's hopeless. We may need more comprehensive solutions."[31] The following day, as parade attendees were kept in holding cells or nursed wounds, Canadians went to the polls and elected Trudeau as the head of the first majority government in a decade.

In the aftermath of the fiasco that was Nightstick Monday, the Police Department created an anti-riot unit that would be equipped with protective shields, three-foot-long clubs, special face guards, and, later, tear gas in order to respond adequately to large and volatile crowds.[32] Police depart-

Figure 4.3
Nightstick-wielding police officers clash outdoors with a large crowd during the infamous "Nightstick Monday," 24 June 1968.

ments in cities like Los Angeles, Chicago, and New York, which had recently acquired military training and equipment (like grenade launchers for tear gas) and protective gear (like vests, helmets, and gas masks), influenced Montreal's decisions.[33] The experiences of other urban centres offered both warnings and examples to follow as the department worked out its future. In fact, in the 1968 atmosphere of rebellion, in which strikes and riots broke out in places as diverse as Mexico City, Paris, Rio de Janeiro, and Tokyo, the president of the MPB coolly stated that any future clashes between Montreal's new anti-riot unit and protestors would leave "bodies in the streets."[34] By early 1969, the anti-riot unit had been on-site and praised for its decisive action during events like the Sir George Williams University incident and Opération McGill français.[35] The squad's role had been to prevent and suppress any type of public protest that could paralyze the flow of the city. And it played that role particularly well according to a senior observer from the

Toronto Police who claimed, after studying several American anti-riot units in action, that "none compare with Montreal's for deftness and effectiveness."[36] The Police Department upheld law and order with diligence and proficiency – until the labour contract expired.

30 November 1968, the day that the police and fire departments' labour contracts expired, marked the beginning of an arduous bargaining process.[37] The first order of business for MPB and MFA union leaders was to restore salary parity with the police and fire departments of metropolitan Toronto, which until recently had long been in place. Union leaders argued that Montreal's atmosphere of protest made jobs demonstrably more difficult than in any other Canadian city.[38] Cash-strapped Montreal, however, argued otherwise. Bargaining hit a dead end in January 1969. Therefore, the MPB filed for arbitration; the MFA did the same less than a month later.[39] Both unions, however, waited several months before hearing a verdict from the arbitration tribunal.

As they waited, a massive city-wide strike loomed over Montreal. The Civic Party voted to withhold pension plans from blue-collar and white-collar employees, which pushed labour leaders to call for a general strike. To reduce a deficit swollen by years of big spending, the municipal administration had made the decision to freeze city contributions to pension funds and pay the money at some future date. But with a general strike looming over the city, the Civic Party backtracked and released the funds.[40]

Early autumn 1969, however, produced a series of events that made the city's atmosphere even more tense. On 29 September 1969, shortly after 5 a.m., explosives were detonated at the mayor's home. His wife and son, who were sleeping at the time of the attack, escaped unscathed. Drapeau, who was reportedly at Le Vaisseau d'Or when the bomb exploded, had a theory. Someone had tipped off a terrorist cell about police no longer guarding his house. In the aftermath, the Drapeaus temporarily relocated to the most logical place imaginable – above Le Vaisseau d'Or at the Windsor Hotel – and coped with the trauma by adopting Duke, a Bullmastiff that acted as a watchdog over the family.[41] A few days later, on 2 October, the unions received the verdict from the tribunal, which vindicated the city's position and maintained that salaries would be kept inferior to demands. The following day, notices were posted in police stations informing MPB members that assemblies would be held at the Paul Sauvé Arena to "take cognizance of the verdict."[42] As for the MFA, the outcome had been predictable because the presiding justice on its tribunal had worked for Drapeau and Saulnier as the city's personnel director, which was a clear conflict of interest according to the union.[43] The following morning union leaders met. They stated that the worst was about to happen after the "rotten" verdict, which is why they appealed the decision.[44] But the issue remained in limbo for several days.

Less than a month after it had opened, the mayor's restaurant had become a gathering site, not only for Montreal's elite but also for activists and protestors. Everyone knew that the mayor spent evenings in a makeshift office upstairs where he could see – from a bird's-eye view – how customers were treated. Inside the chic establishment, for which he had signed a ten-year lease, Drapeau hoped to meet with and make a profit from wealthy Montrealers. In a very real sense, there was no clear division between his office at City Hall and the one at his restaurant. For instance, the Civic Party would make tourism a principal component of its electoral platform in 1970. And the following year, in a televised interview, Drapeau revealed that Le Vaisseau d'Or had been opened "to attract a clientele – made up of fifty per cent tourists."[45] Patrons, many of them tourists from different provinces and countries, were captivated by the establishment's atmosphere. Religious leaders, politicians, magistrates, health care professionals, diplomats, and entrepreneurs wrote commending letters to Mayor Drapeau. "My family and I look forward to visiting you again very soon and, of course, to partake of many gourmet meals at Le Vaisseau d'Or. Incidentally, your autographed menu is now safely secured as one of our treasured mementoes of world personalities and places," wrote one American college professor. In what was surely a time-consuming venture, the mayor responded to each letter he received with a thoughtful and personalized comment.[46]

Montrealers recognized this conflict of interest. Those whom Quebec writer Malcolm Reid calls the "shouting signpainters" began staging protests in front of the restaurant. They were likely audible over the orchestra's music, or, if they were not, they certainly gave the restaurant's patrons an unwelcoming salute by lingering outside, shouting slogans, and holding placards and posters.[47] Some of these protestors, however, like firefighters and police officers, had a few more tools at their disposal. For instance, following a rowdy assembly on Saturday, 4 October 1969, 1,200 firefighters marched from their meeting hall on the corner of Saint-Laurent Boulevard and des Pins

Figure 4.4
Halting traffic in front of the Windsor Hotel, home to Le Vaisseau d'Or, firefighters refuse to keep marching on, 4 October 1969.

Avenue to Dominion Square (fig. 4.4). On their way, they stopped at the restaurant and spontaneously chanted "We want Drapeau!"[48] Such incidents rattled Drapeau: "If people keep targeting Le Vaisseau d'Or I'll go bankrupt. I don't want to go bankrupt!"[49] Indeed, the firefighters recognized the fact that city politics could not be disentangled from Le Vaisseau d'Or. Driving through the city in fire trucks, they pulled up in front of the restaurant. Inside, the orchestra paused while the firefighters, feigning an emergency, arrived in protective gear to inspect the exits, the kitchen, and smoke detectors. Meanwhile, outside, the trucks' red lights bounced off the neighbouring windows while sirens wailed into the night.[50] A few days later, at the apex of the disruption, shots were fired inside the establishment.

Bargaining had stagnated for nearly a year, and on the eve of receiving the result of the MPB and MFA appeals, Chief Gilbert met with leading police officers and chief inspectors.[51] He reported to City Hall that he did not "feel" like a strike was in play. That quickly change, however, when the appeal tribunal's decision was released on 6 October. Police officers with five years' experience were offered an annual salary increase that was still several hundred dollars below the pay grade for comparable service at the Metropolitan Toronto Police Force. Upon hearing the news, they started clearing out of police stations. They made their way to the Paul Sauvé Arena for a general assembly where union leaders would discuss the "distasteful" and "rotten" decision rendered by the appeal tribunal.[52]

That Day

That Tuesday was an unusually beautiful, clear, and crisp autumn morning. The weather on 7 October 1969 at 7 a.m., when Jean-Paul Gilbert and Lucien Saulnier were sitting at their offices, was, by all accounts, perfect. The men might have sensed that a metaphorical storm was brewing, however, when they received copies of the dailies, which reported on profound dissatisfaction among MPB members. And if they were not worried then, soon they would be upon hearing that sixty officers of the anti-riot unit were convoying from station to station announcing a wildcat strike and establishing picket lines.[53] "That's the way, not by going to Le Vaisseau d'Or or City Hall, [the strike] is the way to go about it boys," a firefighter told the convoy encouragingly.[54] At 8 a.m., radio contact within the Police Department was interrupted.[55] By the time most Montrealers arrived at work, Canada's largest police force – about four thousand strong – had walked off the job.

Soon enough, the firefighters joined the police officers in a wildcat strike. At 10:30 a.m., the MFA received the verdict on its appeal. Frustrated by its result, the union opted for a wildcat strike as well, and members joined those of the MPB at the Paul Sauvé Arena. Altogether, there were nearly six thousand police officers and firefighters on strike. In fact, one police officer later expressed how the magnitude of the situation dawned on him when he saw the firefighters arrive at the arena: "I was struck by the sight of firefighters because I live in their district, and they were the same firefighters who are supposed to protect my family. Meanwhile, there were no police officers present to safeguard the citizens of Montreal."[56]

By lunchtime, as the crowd swelled, MFA president André Plante alerted Lucien Saulnier via a wired message that the atmosphere at the arena was

Figure 4.5
Young and energized, the striking police officers and firefighters cheer during an assembly at the Paul Sauvé Arena, 7 October 1969.

getting rowdy and out of hand (fig. 4.5).[57] Upon receiving this information, and sensing a potential for unrest, Saulnier publicly begged Montrealers to find a safe hideout and, most importantly, to co-operate: "The citizens must not panic; they must think of their security and of their belongings in the greatest possible measure and I advise all go back home after their work and be calm and vigilant."[58]

Saulnier, a Montreal businessman, city councillor from 1954 to 1972, and chair of the Montreal executive committee from 1960 to 1970, was at the centre of the day's events. As calamity fell upon Montreal, Mayor Drapeau was nowhere in sight. He was neither at City Hall nor at Le Vaisseau d'Or. In fact, he was not in the country but on an economic promotional trip to St Louis, Missouri, taking part in a Canadian trade show. Although the mayor initially cancelled the trip after his house was bombed, federal officials convinced him to deliver his address to businesspeople as planned, with the promise of returning to Montreal on Tuesday night. Upon landing at the Dorval airport, he joined Saulnier at City Hall. Along with the rest of the executive committee, the men remained there until the following morning.[59] But before any of this took place, Saulnier did what he could in Drapeau's absence, assuming leadership with confidence. That afternoon, he made his way to the arena where, upon arriving, he was instantly jeered by a sizable share of the city's protective services workforce. Unchaperoned, he spoke for several minutes about safety, order, and law, but brought limited insight to the men who simply wanted to hear about competitive salaries and better working conditions. By the time he returned to City Hall, he had a good gauge of the volatile mood in the city.[60] While he would later state that he did not sense any immediate danger, he did sense that honest dialogue might break down, which is why he phoned provincial authorities to request army troops in Montreal. However, the provincial government declined this initial request. Instead, it sent five hundred SQ officers to Montreal and indicated that another three hundred would be en route. Alas, the officers coming from far away were underinformed about the city and its geography, and the protection they could offer was limited at best. In the meantime, the strikers idled at the arena and spent most of the day into late evening playing cards, chatting, drinking, and eating.

That Night

Then came the night. Subsequent news articles reported that on that morning people had ignored traffic laws. In the afternoon there had been some dozen heists.[61] And – as had been the case during the 1943 strike – complete chaos reigned at night. Several times throughout the night the SQ received phone calls alerting them of violent riots. Immediately, they dispatched an anti-riot squad (fig. 4.6). Upon arrival, however, they discovered empty streets. Meanwhile, the pranksters reaped the benefits of unpatrolled streets elsewhere. Further complicating things, the SQ's radio contact was interrupted.[62] At one point, in the centre of the action – at the intersection of Metcalfe and Sainte-Catherine streets – a marauding gang ambushed an SQ cruiser. They were able to extract the officers out of the car and beat them violently, enucleating one officer's eye and breaking an arm of the other.[63] But the SQ had to deal with more than the population's volatility; it also had

Figure 4.6
An anti-riot squad of the Sûreté du Québec attempts to disperse a nighttime crowd on Peel Street, 7 October 1969.

to contend with MPB members who were enraged by their confreres' strike-breaking. At dusk, close to two dozen MPB members, many of them from the anti-riot unit, embarked on a successful campaign to locate and commandeer SQ cruisers. They drove vans – at times against traffic – and plotted: "Someone needs to give those scabs a lesson to let them know that we don't need them here. They need to be removed from the streets. And if need be, we'll teach them a lesson."[64] Dressed as civilians or in uniform, armed and allegedly under the influence of alcohol, MPB members forced SQ officers out of their cruisers, stuffed them into the backseat or left them on the curb, and drove the vehicles to the Paul Sauvé Arena.[65]

The day's escalating development was noticed by those in power. MPB president Guy Marcil glorified the "thin blue line" separating society from chaos and anarchy.[66] With the lack of a capable police force, it was a battalion of some 110 to 150 soldiers of the Royal 22nd Regiment of the Canadian Army – called into action by Quebec Justice Minister Rémi Paul after he realized the extent of the chaos – that provided limited protection to the city.[67] Some, however, felt glee and liberation in the absence of police. "The crowd, both the demonstrators and those who were watching," explained famous Quebec writer and sociologist Marcel Rioux, "seemed to feel a certain liberation, a certain country-fair mood. At the same time, there was an extreme tension."[68] Rioux had wandered downtown, around Sainte-Catherine Street, and though he saw lawlessness, he was struck by the prevalence of mass jubilation. What made the day's development so spectacular was not simply the prosaic exploitation of the city's lawlessness by mobs of looters and vandals – although that certainly helped many dailies sell copies over the following days – but rather, the multiplicity of nighttime contestation: how private groups, political grievances, and labour disputes all intertwined on city streets.

Like any other weeknight, Montrealers gallivanted from store to store downtown. But on that Tuesday night, men and women who otherwise were alienated by consumer society saw the windows along Sainte-Catherine Street in a new light and congregated for a once-in-a-lifetime opportunity to obtain luxury goods.[69] Indeed, an astounding contrast lay before onlookers who saw neighbours and colleagues carrying ultramodern electronic equipment and haute couture items in a frenzy of pillaging and arson. The bright neon lights of department stores oriented those who, caught in the hysteria, made their way through Sainte-Catherine Street's shopping area: "Jewelry stores, clothing stores, electrical appliance shops – and anything that stood in the path of the mob were hit after nightfall … Fur coats, electric razors, skis and hundreds of small items from dozens of jewelry stores were stolen by laughing bearded youths."[70] The fact that looters targeted sites for the affluent – as opposed to pharmacies or hardware stores, for example – shows that people were looking for expensive goods and for things they otherwise could not afford. And, as in other instances of mass looting, the culprits seldom distinguished between chain stores or independent businesses, locally or foreign owned. Historian David E. Nye, in his research on the history of blackouts, describes the collective hysteria and social pressure to "dig in" when law and order collapse as a "break in the flow of social time."[71] Although Montrealers did not experience a blackout during the Night of Terror, the event had, much like a blackout, disrupted the city's flow of social time and for that brief moment Montrealers dug in.

Earlier that evening a procession of seventy-six taxis and automobiles, stretching as far as the eye could see, made its way to City Hall.[72] The group of cabbies and political allies known as the Mouvement de libération du taxi (MLT) met, as they did every Tuesday, to strategize and advocate for fair labour rights within the taxi industry. The location of their meetings, the schoolyard of the École des Beaux-Arts, served as a vital hub for political involvement and cultural mobilization. It was a site of collaboration and mingling for diverse individuals, including students, radical activists, and social animators. In the months leading to the Night of Terror, the MLT had been particularly frustrated with the Murray Hill Limousine company's monopoly of taxi services at the Dorval airport, a contract that had been given to wealthy English-speaking business owner Charles Hershorn. This frustration was compounded by the fact that Murray Hill also possessed the exclusive privilege of parking in designated areas at the city's most luxurious hotels, namely the Ritz-Carlton, the Sheraton-Mt Royal, and the Windsor. According to reporter Nick Auf der Maur, the battle between the MLT and Hershorn had become "a rallying point for left-wing activists. It was ideal, a microcosm of everything wrong in Quebec."[73] And as sociologist Jean-Philippe Warren notes, although all three levels of government could be blamed for the structure of Montreal's taxi industry, it was Jean Drapeau and the Civic Party that endured most of the protests. "MURRAY HILL AND JEAN DRAPEAU ARE INFURIATING US – LET'S INFURIATE THEM," roared taxi drivers.[74] For a year, the MLT, like the protective services workforce, attempted to meet with Civic Party members. But on that Tuesday, when Lucien Saulnier rejected yet another request for a meeting, the MLT decided to act.

The MLT procession drove southbound along Saint-Denis Street until it reached Notre-Dame Street, at which point it caused disruption by slowing the flow of traffic, honking, and circling City Hall. Although noisy, the motorcade was orderly and peaceful up to this point. After its second lap, however, it made its way toward the second of its three targets that evening: the Murray Hill garage located at 1380 Barré Street in Griffintown. The well-documented violence started when the convoy reached the garage. The MLT and its allies – about four hundred–strong but swelling to eight hundred at the height of the riot – trashed Murray Hill's property and destroyed four buses by showering them with Molotov cocktails.[75] "Many felt – and did not hide from the fact – that the city and the night belonged to them," wrote a *Le Devoir* columnist about the event.[76] As the violent protest was underway an SQ van carrying eight officers and a Fire Department car carrying a handful of firefighters arrived on-site. "You're strikers too, don't get mixed up in this, forget Murray!" argued one individual to the cadre of firefighters.[77] The firefighters stood back and reached an entente cordiale with the protesters by informing them that their goal was to save lives and nearby properties, but not Murray Hill itself.

According to a journalist, the aural environment was absolutely surreal at this point: "Rock music from portable radios and screaming newscasts from several stations were mixed with the sounds of exploding fire bombs and shotgun and rifle fire." The site was primarily lit by the incendiary flames of Molotov cocktails that had been hurled at the business. It was after 10 p.m. when an employee of Murray Hill, a security guard, shot at the crowd and wounded twelve. The guard's shots killed an undercover SQ officer, thirty-three-year-old Robert Dumas, who had infiltrated the MLT. After being shot at, the crowd dispersed and left for its third target: the capitalist landmarks in the heart of the city. The immediate conclusion of the confrontation at Murray Hill had left injured bodies scattered and the property heavily damaged and covered in ash. News reports remarked that the scene resembled a war zone.[78]

The final denouement on 7 October sent a clear message. Joining looters and vandals, protestors also began stealing from stores and businesses. During the pillaging, parts of the Queen Elizabeth Hotel, Sheraton-Mt Royal Hotel, United States Consulate, IBM office, and McGill University were damaged.[79] But like Polaris, Le Vaisseau d'Or at the Windsor Hotel seemingly guided those who had waited for a night like this one. Upon reaching the establishment, the crowd made its way inside and completely upended its interior, from the vestibule to the kitchen, and from the dining space to the stage. The following morning, amid shattered glass and broken chairs and kitchen equipment, the cleanup crew discovered a cartridge case that had been fired from a .38 Smith & Wesson revolver.[80] Miraculously, they found that the bust of Émile Nelligan had survived unharmed, emerging as one of the few items to endure Le Vaisseau d'Or's wreck.[81] Thirty years later, the

Figure 4.7
Bust of renowned poet Émile Nelligan, at the bottom of Le Vaisseau d'Or's spiral staircase, c. 1969.

restaurant's cashier would proudly tell *La Presse* that, despite complete lawlessness, she had rescued all $10,000 from the till and hand-delivered it to Jean Drapeau at City Hall the following day.[82]

At this point, in the middle of the night, there was a very real possibility that the conflict would expand and destabilize other parts of the province. Because the scale of the disorder was dangerously intensifying, Justice Minister Rémi Paul began elaborating a plan that would end the strikes. At 10 p.m., Jean-Jacques Bertrand's Union nationale government met during an emergency session at the National Assembly in Quebec City.[83] It unanimously passed a special law that resembled the 1967 back-to-work order delivered during the MTC strike. The legislation laid out heavy fines, loss of accreditation as a trade union, and risk of imprisonment if members did not resume their duties by midnight. Premier Bertrand gave insight into the government's decision during the second reading of the Bill: "I hope that firefighters and police officers realize the seriousness of their action, that they realize they've failed to uphold their responsibilities, which is uncharacteristic of them, and I once again urge them to obey [the law] before this one is passed. This law is based on the principle that the State has duties to fulfil for the common good. When laws are broken, when authority is challenged, when a climate of anarchy and chaos is created, the State has no right to fail in its responsibilities, the State must act, the State acts."[84]

With the back-to-work order passed, a battalion of the Royal 22nd Regiment that had arrived remained garrisoned on the city's outskirts in Saint-Hubert.[85] The military personnel would remain in the area and patrol Montreal until 13 October. In the end, this military operation involved 587 personnel, cost taxpayers $11,333.45, and, in the scheme of things, served as a dress rehearsal for the following year's October Crisis.[86]

At 11 p.m. MFA president André Plante ordered his members back to work.[87] Twenty minutes after midnight MPB president Guy Marcil did the same when he read the back-to-work order to the officers at the Paul Sauvé Arena. The province's intervention in the labour conflict had been successful. One traffic officer later stated that it was not the fear of impending fines or imprisonment that brought them back to work. Rather, it was the sheer violence that unfolded before their eyes that night.[88] By 12:30 a.m. employees of the fire and police departments had returned to their stations, and as one reporter put it, "Montrealers were once again protected, after a few hours of complete anarchy."[89] In the darkness of night, the disciplinary power of the state had been temporarily removed, and as the sense of community broke down, the fractures of society became clear. On a night when most Montrealers had barricaded themselves in their home, thousands had contributed to the rebellion, violence, pillage, and protest.

The extent to which the police and fire departments had been able to outmanoeuvre the municipal administration became clear a few weeks later. With very little public opposition, the police and fire department unions signed a new contract on 29 October – a day that, as I explain below, would be remembered not because of this "truce" but for a huge nighttime protest.[90] The contract awarded to the Police Department represented a significant salary increase. The city bumped the department's share of the city budget from about 8.6 per cent in 1968–69 to 11.2 per cent in 1970–71.[91] It boosted first-class constables' annual salaries to $8,750 – $270 above what the arbitration tribunal had offered. Taking into account fringe benefits, it was effective parity with Metropolitan Toronto Police officers.

The strike had shown the fragile nature of the city's authority over its own protective services. And as political scientist Andrew Sancton remarks, Montreal simply could not afford to pay competitive salaries, even to its most essential employees because of over-expenditures related to Expo 67.[92] In fact, the city was much more reticent when it came to providing salary increases for the Fire Department. The ongoing and enduring debate between the Civic Party and the MFA would result in tremendous consequences half a decade later, specifically during the infamous Red Weekend when bargaining turned sour, again. But in the immediate aftermath, Drapeau orchestrated the city's return to normalcy, starting with the cleaning of his own restaurant.

Restriction on the Freedom of Assembly: Nighttime Demonstrations, Protests, and the *La Presse* Lockout

During the late 1960s, demands had been mounting for a provincial language policy, one that would explicitly address whether immigrant parents could have the right to send their children to English-language school. Many francophone Quebecers viewed this as a problem because if immigrants continued sending their children to English schools, they reasoned, then they would be integrating into the language and culture of the dominant power. On 10 September 1969, tensions boiled over when a pro-francophone group staged a protest in the neighbourhood of Saint-Leonard, which had a large concentration of Italian Montrealers. This protest led to violent confrontations and caused considerable property damage.[93] After that riot the Quebec government introduced Bill 63, "An Act to Promote the French Language in Quebec," which fell short of meeting the demands of pro-francophone advocates because it did not compel parents to send their children to French-language schools. Amid the tense atmosphere, a massive protest unfolded, orchestrated by a coalition of workers' and citizens' committees. When night

Figure 4.8
A protestor douses a mound of political effigies with fuel before setting them ablaze, 29 October 1969. The top one is of Lucien Saulnier, who – as the Nazi swastika suggests – was perceived by protestors as an authoritarian figure.

fell on 29 October, twenty-five thousand protestors converged from four different rallying points into a unified and jovial march. The procession's more militant participants, however, stopped at Square Victoria to light a bonfire and to burn effigies of politicians (fig. 4.8). Later, when they reached La Fontaine Park, they burned several other effigies under the watchful eye of police.[94] By 11 p.m. most protestors had returned home.

The protest's considerable size and its violent message moved Lucien Saulnier to phone the city's legal team and ask it to create a bylaw that would put an end to disorderly behaviour. Put another way: he wanted the legal team to conceive a solution that would cease political unrest in Montreal, especially since there were growing reports that "subversive activities" menaced civil liberties.[95] In the end the city's legal team drafted the bylaw "relating to exceptional measures to safeguard the free exercise of civil liberties, to regulate the use of the public domain and to prevent riots and other violations of order, peace and public safety." Whereas the Civic Party believed that the bylaw would restore order, critics saw it for what it was: an instrument that further increased City Hall's power and muddled the meanings of civil liberties, order, and peace. For this reason, on 8 November, when members of the executive committee presented the bylaw to city council, elected officials inside City Hall could hear the ringing of sirens, helicopters, and protestors. And although members of council could not see them, perhaps they had heard that protestors were once again setting fire to their effigies, and symbolically burning the bylaw.[96]

A few nights later, when the time came to vote on the bylaw, the *Montreal Gazette* reported that Mayor Drapeau gave the most impassioned speech of his career. He pounded his desk and warned councillors that "demonstrators are preparing revolution in our home!" During the voting process, Councillor Abraham Cohen, a World War II veteran and progressive lawyer, stood as the Civic Party's only dissenting member: "[I spent 60 days on the front] and I could now spend the same 60 days in jail for standing by my right to demonstrate. I always knew in the war exactly what I was fighting for. I was there so that people could demonstrate and speak freely at home … always."[97] His testimony failed to move the members, and the bylaw passed with near unanimity. Because the bylaw ostensibly contradicted the Canadian Bill of Rights sections on freedom of speech and freedom of assembly and association, federal politicians of different stripes, including Liberal Prime Minister Trudeau and former Conservative Prime Minister John Diefenbaker, suggested that the bylaw was illegal and encouraged citizen-led court challenges.[98]

Once enacted, the bylaw gave politicians the power to ban any march, parade, or demonstration that had the slightest potential of leading to violence. However, there were certain limitations on its usage. Specifically, it could only be employed for a period of thirty days, beginning whenever city council decided to invoke it.[99] Incidentally, city council wasted no time, invoking it within less than twenty-four hours, effectively making any type of public assembly or demonstration on public property, including parks and streets, illegal for the next thirty days. The Vietnam Moratorium Committee's plans for a candle-lit march downtown was the first to be declared illegal. A spokesperson, speaking passionately on behalf of the committee, described the city's undemocratic turn and informed journalists that the committee, in addition to its opposition to American imperialism, would oppose "the undemocratic regime in the City of Montreal."[100] But the city permitted some assemblies to proceed, notably Eaton's Santa Claus parade and the Grey Cup parade, both planned before the bylaw was passed. While the Grey Cup parade proceeded more or less as planned, Eaton's cancelled its parade at the request of police and "out of respect for the spirit of the bylaw."[101] Significant about this two-tiered system was that authorities had banned the nighttime protest; the daytime parades, promoting a festive and commercial atmosphere, had been exempted.

While most Civic Party members hoped that the bylaw would quell the city's politically charged atmosphere, activists publicly denounced it as an infringement of civil rights and quickly organized to test the limits of what they alleged was an undemocratic and repressive municipal administration.[102] The most audacious act of defiance was organized by the Front commun des Québécoises (FCQ) and took place two weeks after the bylaw was enacted.[103] Sociology student Louise Harel, who later served as interim leader of the Parti Québécois, informed journalists that the FCQ was intended for "free women who want to show their opposition to an unfair and illegal bylaw," and artist Lise Landry echoed her remark when she told journalists that the FCQ had been formed "solely for the purpose of protesting against the anti-demonstration bylaw."[104] Their resolve culminated in the planning of a night march from the Monument-National to City Hall.

On a frigid and windy November night, FCQ members stepped out of the Monument-National and onto Saint-Laurent Boulevard. Journalists and photographers had gathered to see how the city would respond to this defiance. As soon as the women stepped outside, anti-riot officers – who had come prepared with helmets and weapons – moved towards them. The officers had a clear mandate: to enforce the anti-demonstration bylaw and arrest those who dared defy it. Because it was immediately clear that the march to City Hall would not proceed, the women reorganized the demonstration into a peaceful sit-in protest. Thirty demonstrators chained themselves to one another with padlocks to evoke Montrealers' unfreedoms and began chanting "Liberté, liberté!" and "Long live the illegal police strike!"[105] It evoked the irony and the injustice of the city's legal system, which had allowed police the freedom to demonstrate but not members of the public.

Within minutes, 137 demonstrators were arrested and brought to jail. Many of them were renowned public figures, notably Ginette Letondal, Marie Savard, and Denise Boucher.[106]

All demonstrators, ranging from artists to clerks, domestic workers to students, were released overnight on a $25 bail after officers noted and filed their personal information for a later court date. In all, the riot police had allowed the demonstration to last twenty-five minutes. Although short-lived, the resistance to the anti-demonstration bylaw extended far beyond November 1969. First, it set the stage for the Front de libération des femmes (FLF), which would become the most public manifestation of second-wave feminism in Montreal.[107] Second, when the women appeared in municipal court, they triggered a long legal battle against the bylaw by arguing that it was ultra vires – that is, beyond the legislative powers of the city – because it touched on an exclusively federal jurisdiction.[108] In April 1970, a Social Welfare Court judge, reviewing the case of twelve juvenile girls who were arrested during that protest, declared the bylaw ultra vires because it assumed a power that falls exclusively into the constitutional orbit of Parliament.[109] Although the city appealed the decision, it was again declared ultra vires on 18 June 1970.[110] At this point all women who had participated in the FCQ's protest had paid the $25 fine, except Suzanne Corriveau and Lise Landry; both chose to spend eight days in jail rather than, in their words, "[contribute] to the coffers of the authoritarian and fascist Drapeau-Saulnier administration."[111] As social historian Dominique Clément notes, challenges to the anti-demonstration bylaw contributed to the early days of Canada's rights revolution and would soon "lead to a moment in history that revolutionized Canada's rights culture."[112] The City of Montreal, however, was determined to keep its bylaw and eventually it appealed to the Supreme Court of Canada.

In autumn 1970 all eyes were on Montreal as Pierre Elliot Trudeau's federal government deployed the army and then invoked the War Measures Act in response to the kidnappings of Labour Minister Pierre Laporte and British diplomat James Richard Cross by the Front de libération du Québec (FLQ). As historian Sean Mills highlights, 1960s Montreal was a hub of intense activism, with various political factions adopting different styles and approaches to achieve social change. The FLQ emerged as one of the most radical proponents of this political activism, engaging in some of the era's most violent actions. Armed robberies financed their revolutionary agenda, and strategically placed bombs targeted symbols of imperial power and affluence, instilling fear in a significant segment of Montreal's population. The streets of Montreal had been the site of political violence that stemmed from the most radical aspects of social change, but more than anything it was the FLQ's political kidnappings and its public demand to reject the established order that led the federal government into action. For several weeks during what became known as the October Crisis, authorities held incredible power over Montreal; no distinction was made between private and public space, and night became a time of total control under the standing curfew. Police raids and searches resulted in numerous seizures and hundreds arrested, many of whom were released without charges. The October Crisis is significant for a host of reasons that go beyond the scope of this book, but it is significant to note the way it intensified debates around Quebec nationalism and the methods of achieving political change.[113]

The War Measures Act changed the idea of night, but despite its significance, it did not stop Montrealers from heading to the polls on 25 October to participate in a municipal election. During the final three weeks of what was his most active campaign since 1960, Drapeau took the strongest position possible against the FLQ. He framed the election as a choice between order and chaos by confusing voters into thinking that the opposing party, the left-wing Front d'action politique (FRAP), was closely tied to the FLQ.[114] He was able to convince voters that there was a relationship between the two groups because a number of FRAP candidates and organizers were jailed under the War Measures Act. In the end, Drapeau received 92 per cent of votes and all fifty-two seats in council were awarded to the Civic Party. The result of the 1970 election was unequivocal and would remain the clearest mandate that Drapeau received during his extensive political career. It was a powerful showing because residents overwhelmingly voted for the party that represented law and order at a moment when Montreal faced great political uncertainty.[115]

In 1971 the municipal administration showed how far its power stretched during the bitter lockout at *La Presse*. After six months of bargaining with typesetters, management decided to lock out its employees. The tense dispute escalated over the course of a few months, during which the employees received support from many left-leaning groups, including Quebec's three major trade unions, queer activists, and members of the Parti Québécois. This culminated with the three unions calling for a huge demonstration in support of *La Presse* employees in October 1971. Montreal's Police Department immediately identified the demonstration as having the potential for violence. Jean-Jacques Saulnier, the recently appointed chief of police and Lucien Saulnier's brother, referred to it as a "monster protest" at one point, and a "Nouveau 'Murray Hill'" at another. He sent a report to the executive committee and recommended invoking the anti-demonstration bylaw. The executive committee not only invoked the bylaw but also declared a large perimeter around *La Presse*'s office off limits to the public.[116] The demonstration planned for 29 October would be vastly larger than the one organized by the FCQ two years earlier, but the message remained the same. Both protests revolved around a common theme: opposition to the municipal administration and its anti-demonstration bylaw. "The atmosphere among protestors was that the desire to defy Drapeau's anti-demonstration bylaw was as strong as that to denounce [*La Presse*'s owner] Power Corporation," wrote one reporter for *Le Devoir*.[117] And like the FCQ's protest, this one would be nocturnal too, and head southbound toward the city's centre of power.

By nightfall somewhere between eight thousand and fifteen thousand protestors gathered at Carré Saint-Louis, the city's symbolic centre of rebellion. The square, mostly known as a left-friendly space where people exchanged ideas, drugs, sex, and art, saw its usual rebellious crowd blend with trade union leaders and activists. Because the march was held at night, it brought together a coalition of vastly separate groups that would not have been possible during the day: Université de Montréal's union, recently unemployed Canadair workers, firefighters, the truck driving union known as the "Gars de Lapalme," and many other unionists and citizens.[118] At 8 p.m., the large crowd started moving to the square's edge under the command of Parti Québécois MNA Robert Burns and the presidents of the main trade unions. As the march headed down Saint-Denis Street, the men steering it told the crowd that they would turn west on Dorchester Boulevard so that they could make their way to University Street and end at the Tour de la Bourse, the heart of Montreal's financial district.[119] But awaiting the crowd several blocks away were hundreds of police officers who had been ordered to enforce the bylaw. The Police Department's anti-riot unit had installed powerful floodlights, which beamed onto the empty street's pavement. The scene meticulously set by the police was reached by the procession half an hour later.

The violence started because of a tactical decision to place buses along Dorchester Boulevard, which meant that the crowd could not move westward like organizers had planned. And because police officers blocked the southbound route, demonstrators were effectively trapped in a cul-de-sac. As tensions mounted between protesters and police, it became clear that there would be no peaceful outcome. "After an endless face-to-face," wrote union leader Louis Laberge about the quandary, "we heard someone yell 'GO!' and the police came charging at us, with an incredible brutality and great blows ... The motorcycle unit also charged at people who left the scene. At one point, we had to hide behind a car to avoid an officer who drove at us several times."[120] According to activists, what unfolded was nothing short of a planned attack on organized labour.[121] Later, Captain Wilfrid Bouchard, who trained anti-riot officers based on "books put out by the Chicago police, the FBI, and the Canadian Armed Forces," disclosed that the evening turned out to be one of the toughest jobs his unit ever faced.[122] Once the dust had settled, it became possible to survey the extent of the damage: incinerated buses and police cruisers, injuries, and death. Ambulances rushed from the scene to different hospitals, and despite the paramedics' attempt to ease the load on medical professionals, the injured overloaded the city's emergency rooms. Tragically, the fracas led to the death of FLF sympathizer Michèle Gauthier, who succumbed to an asthma attack.[123]

In the aftermath, labour leaders all but declared class war during a mass rally organized by the Common Front (an alliance of the province's three major trade unions). Laberge spoke adamantly to a crowd of fourteen thousand: "We give serious warning to the wealthy and to the established powers that this first victim [Michèle Gauthier] might be followed by others, but in the future the victims won't only be on *our* side."[124] Many wondered why and how police officers had accepted orders to crack down on strikers when, in 1969, they had been on strike. October 1971 was, in the words of Auf der Maur, "one of the most profound and important contemporary turning points in the Quebec historical process," and clear proof of, according to labour leader Yvon Charbonneau, "collusion of the political and economic powers." Just as the city was entering a new moment of labour turmoil (which led to a province-wide general strike in 1972), labour leaders read the MPB out of the labour movement.[125]

The Red Weekend: The Firefighter Strike of 1974

I'm not proud of last week. I am too proud of my city to rejoice in what happened … But I cannot accept that we hold the Civic Party accountable for this tragedy.[126]
– Jean Drapeau (November 1974)

In 1974, the municipal administration and firefighters found themselves embroiled in yet another labour dispute. It began with the inflation crisis of the early 1970s, which eroded the prosperity achieved in the 1960s. As with many other places in the Western world, Montreal experienced the end of post–World War II economic expansion with a dramatic stagflation during the 1973–75 recession. The embargo of Saudi Arabian oil led to a surge in petrol prices, which had a profound impact on businesses. And the growing rate of inflation set the conditions for a creeping conservatism in social and political affairs.[127] While this was the global context in which the firefighters' union and the city started bargaining, other, decidedly more local issues framed the affair. In 1971 and 1972, Montreal firefighters went on strike for a week when salaries fell far below those of the Toronto Fire Department; however, a firefighting team kept guard throughout these strikes, and facing the dual threat of heavy fines and the dissolution of their union, the rest of the workforce headed back to fire stations.[128] In July 1973, an arbitration tribunal recommended increasing salaries by 4.3 per cent. However, this was a trivial, borderline-insulting, offer according to the MFA because the city raised salaries 12.5 per cent for police and 11.6 per cent for blue-collar workers when inflation hit 14 per cent that year.

Other issues – at once local and global – also had a bearing. The 1974 municipal election was Drapeau's chance to hold an unprecedented fifth consecutive term, and he hit the campaign trail with vigour alongside Civic Party candidates under the slogan "Together for tomorrow." Aside from campaigning, Drapeau was equally, if not more, busy preparing the city for the 1976 Summer Olympic Games. For the second time in less than a decade the world's attention would be fixed upon Montreal, and once again the event's masterminding fell to him. Planning for the Olympics consumed Drapeau's time day and night as he made sure everything would be ready on time. It was all but official policy that routine city business be placed on the backburner. But as had been the case during Expo 67, union leaders used the Olympic Games as a vehicle for demanding better wages and labour conditions. For example, the employees of the city's public transit authority went on a wildcat strike, again, and despite a back-to-work order from the courts, the union remained on strike. After forty days of disorder, Liberal Premier Robert Bourassa convened the Quebec labour minister, trade union leaders, and Jean Drapeau. After a long night of bargaining, the strike ended on 19 September 1974 when salaries were indexed to the rate of inflation.[129] As the mayor returned to the campaign trail and to the Olympic dossier, an unexpected strike by Montreal firefighters caught him off guard.

Firefighters started pressuring the Civic Party with work-to-rule action in late August. Because this failed to achieve the desired effect, the firefighters decided to use more drastic tactics, especially after the city abolished eighty firefighting jobs and closed nine fire stations without warning. What began with small acts of vandalism, like puncturing hoses and sabotaging city equipment, would quickly escalate to more serious criminal activity. After two fire stations were set ablaze on the night of 8 October, the city placed on-duty police officers at fire stations.[130] The police left no doubt that it would not side with labour during this conflict, as had been the case with the lockout at *La Presse*.

Finally, a strike began at nightfall on Thursday, 31 October, when firefighters scheduled for the night shift did not clock in. It was the beginning of a weekend-long strike wherein all but 55 of Montreal's 2,400 firefighters went on strike.[131] It would be revealed later that those who chose to stay behind had received anonymous phone calls threatening violent retributions if they did not walk off the job.[132] As had been the case during the 1969 strike, many firefighters headed to the Paul Sauvé Arena, overnighting and receiving the latest news from union leaders.

As the personnel settled into the arena, fires began to sweep pockets of the city. With fires raging, Jean L'Abbé, president of the MFA, sensed that a dire situation was imminent. He took the stage and announced his change of heart. He begged the firefighters to consider the events unfolding across the city. MFA members responded by heckling and jeering. "I appeal to your common sense and implore you to return to your stations," he pled. "The city is burning all over the place. I also ask [Premier] Robert Bourassa to intervene in what has become a wild conflict. I implore him to engage with Jean Drapeau."[133] Although the firefighters refused to co-operate, his last wish was granted: he was awarded the opportunity to speak with Premier Bourassa and Labour Minister Jean Cournoyer live on CKAC during Matthias Rioux's talk show. Throughout the weekend, the talk show, hosted by the former union leader and future provincial labour minister, served as a middle ground between the MFA, municipal, and provincial leaders. Each took turns calling in to express their perspectives to the public. During that initial conversation, however, Labour Minister Cournoyer explained that the City of Montreal was the exclusive body responsible for the fire brigade and that there was nothing the Liberal government could do. In the midst of an extremely tense situation, and sensing that the Quebec government could no longer stay idle, Rioux cheekily retorted to his guests: "It seems as though the municipal administration has, once again, brought the government of Quebec to its knees!"[134]

Since no headway was made during the first hours of the strike, Jean L'Abbé returned to the Paul Sauvé Arena with a stunning announcement. He and the rest of the MFA's executive committee had resigned because, as far as they were concerned, there was nothing more to do if those in power refused to bargain.[135] At 3:30 a.m. on 1 November, L'Abbé left the arena and returned to CKAC's building after agreeing to speak as the MFA's spokesperson, not as its president. With a beer in hand, L'Abbé spoke candidly about the futility of bargaining with Drapeau as thousands of listeners, including Premier Bourassa and Labour Minister Cournoyer, listened attentively.[136] "This municipal administration, which supposedly stands for law and order," wrote *La Presse* columnist Marcel Adam, "pushes upstanding civil servants toward vice, disorder, and criminality."[137] And as fires raged across the city, the municipal administration did not attempt to speak with MFA leaders but instead requested help from neighbouring fire brigades.

Unlike the 1969 Night of Terror, the nighttime vandalism seemed more random.[138] Each newspaper reported that out-of-control fires, riots, and vandals had raged across town from Plateau-Mont-Royal to Verdun to

Figure 4.9
One of the nighttime fires during the Red Weekend, 1974.

Rosemont.[139] The dry and windy environmental conditions were particularly favourable for the spread of fires, which swept across homes, businesses, and public space. The wind would have carried the pungent odours of things burning across the city as well. Squinting to cut down glare, thousands who were not busy extinguishing the bright flames stood still and marvelled at the extraordinary heat coming from them. Montrealers, like twenty-one-year-old student Nick Paré and his friends, banded together, co-operating to save lives and homes. He described the heat and the public rage to a journalist:

> About 20 of us ran down to the fire station (a block south on Montcalm) and broke in. There was a cop there and he pulled his gun on us. Some guys put him up against the wall and some more police came in after us and cooled him down. My cousin started the fire truck and drove it up the street. None of us knew what to do … All the time the (striking) firemen were going at the hoses with axes and scissors and

punching holes in the compressor. They were harassing us – trying to get in our way.

It was the middle of the night but it was light out because of the fire. Flames were jumping right up over these new buildings. And it was so hot a T-shirt was all you had to wear. If you got water on you it would dry right off.

I'll never forget it – firemen trying to stop us from saving the buildings and even the people who lived in them. I blame Drapeau too. Is it true what he said: "They can have another night of this before I'll give in."

Could he really have said that?[140]

Friday afternoon, Matthias Rioux was back on-air with sleep-deprived Jean L'Abbé. The men listened to callers who overwhelmingly supported the firefighters – out of thirty-five callers only three agreed with Mayor Drapeau's aggressive bargaining tactic.[141] During daytime on Friday the fires diminished, but as soon as dusk hit, they amplified at an alarming rate – especially in Saint-Jacques Ward. The extent of those fires was observed by another CKAC reporter who boarded the station's small Cessna 182 Skylane plane to get a bird's-eye view of the destruction on the following morning. Circling over the city the reporter poignantly described the destruction and exhaustion: "It was a terrible night … I know now what despondence and helplessness mean. Everyone was exhausted. I wondered how it would end. The wind, the raging fires, and embers; it created a climate of terror and looked like a warzone. We knew that people were sleeping in houses that were at risk. I don't want to be cynical, but the sound was at once amazing and pathetic too. For example, we recorded and aired a woman's wail that made one of our editors cry."[142] The fires, wholly uncontained during the night, had spread across neighbourhoods.[143]

Finally, the mayor made a noteworthy public appearance when he spoke to Matthias Rioux on CKAC Saturday afternoon. While Drapeau thought CKAC was an excellent venue to deliver his message and campaign, he was completely blindsided by Jean L'Abbé's impromptu phone call and his request that the mayor negotiate the MFA's contract live on-air![144] The mayor was infuriated by the ambush. Nevertheless, he agreed to sit with the MFA along with the provincial government later that night, away from public scrutiny. At the stroke of midnight on Sunday, 3 November, as he entered the Hydro-Québec building and made his way past Jean-Paul Mousseau's gigantic *Lumière en mouvement dans la couleur*, Jean Drapeau knew what had to be done. He made his way to Premier Bourassa's office knowing that he would have to sign a new contract for the firefighters. Bourassa implied that a hefty bill would result from the fires that had been raging along Coloniale Street, Saint-Michel Boulevard, and in Saint-Jacques Ward, and which he had seen glistening from the vista of his seventeenth-floor office. Standing above the city and overlooking the contrast between the flames and the darkness of night, Bourassa concluded that Drapeau's stubborn idiosyncrasy had reached its limit. But when Drapeau exited Bourassa's office, the mayor had effectively won his gamble: Bourassa told him that the province would cover the difference between the arbitration tribunal's report and what the city was willing to pay. This settlement was exactly what Drapeau wanted to hear. Meanwhile, in another room, adjacent to where Drapeau and Bourassa had been negotiating, Cournoyer and L'Abbé waited. As they observed the fires raging across the poorest neighbourhoods, L'Abbé allegedly turned to the anxious labour minister and told him not to worry "because the only things burning are cockroaches and bedbugs; no one's in danger."[145]

Finally, at 2:30 a.m. on Sunday, 3 November, the provincial government, the municipal administration, and the MFA signed what one journalist called a "truce" and what Cournoyer stated was Bourassa's way of ending a "social problem."[146] By 4 a.m. the firefighters were on the streets extinguishing the remaining fires. Astonishingly, there had been no casualties.

After the Fires

The Red Weekend was another event that defined the power struggle between Quebec and Montreal, and it ended when Bourassa caved to Drapeau's demands. Indeed, it was the financial compensation offered by the province that ended the sixty-hour conflict during which eighteen fires destroyed 150 family homes and many businesses. Like the strike of 1969, the mayor and the MFA had not found common ground; instead, they let chaos reign. During the darkest of hours, when Drapeau failed his constituents and firefighters punctured hoses, police cruisers escorted fourteen suburban fire brigades from Verdun, Côte Saint-Luc, Outremont, LaSalle, and Ville Saint-Laurent as well as the Canadian Ski Patrol into the city.[147] And despite their limiting the magnitude of the fires, Drapeau refused to recognize the help that they had provided. In fact, it was a suburban brigade that, early on Saturday morning, extinguished two arsons at Drapeau's brother-in-law's hotel on Drummond Street.[148] In the aftermath, Quebec ordered Montreal to pay for the services it had received.

It was a cruel twist of fate that the hardest-hit neighbourhood was also one of the city's poorest. The overnight fires in Saint-Jacques had reduced homes to rubble and left hundreds destitute. Bearing the pain and suffering of a conflict over which they held no influence, members of the community saw their livelihoods, goods, and properties vanish over the course of a few nights. Alline and George Allain and their three young boys spent Saturday night huddled together in La Fontaine Park after someone had set fire to the grocery store below their apartment: "It's all gone, all gone. Eight rooms full of furniture – everything we had – all gone."[149] Another victim, Monique Beaudoin, told a journalist, "Everything we owned was in there, and we sure don't have any insurance. My husband isn't working now, so I don't know what we'll do." Having gone without food for three days, she was clearly frustrated by the firefighters' response to the labour conflict. One elderly couple suffered a similar fate; although they were able to find a new apartment, their rent had increased by a whopping 61 per cent – an unforeseen expense for the retirees.[150] And one visually impaired man, who lived alone and lost all his belongings, told a journalist, "I starved myself to collect what I had. I ate so many eggs to save money to buy a camera, typewriter, sound system, and television."[151] In the immediate aftermath, many Saint-Jacques residents relied on the Society of Saint-Vincent de Paul of Montreal and Sacré-Coeur Church for shelter, food, clothing, and, above all, comfort.[152] By Sunday, 3 November, over 150 families had applied for aid.

The city's infrastructure and its citizens were seemingly defenceless without protective services, but also defenceless because that workforce had gone on strike. On Saturday there had been only one daytime fire – at Hotel de LaSalle. It was a bold attempt on an establishment owned by Mayor Drapeau's brother-in-law. Otherwise, the daytime was uneventful. It was a lull that permitted fire crews from out-of-town to extinguish flames and

Figure 4.10
The remains of an apartment on Rivard Street after the Red Weekend fires, 1974.

embers – leftover residue from the previous night. On Saturday night, however, the fires had resumed with unforgiving ferocity. Roving terror and disorder characterized nighttime for Montrealers during that weekend. Saint-Jacques residents spoke about the weekend's violence by evoking the contrast of the flames against the night's dark skies. Patricia Harris, who lost all her belongings except two of her six cats, compared the Red Weekend to her own experience during the nighttime bombing raids against London during the Blitz. And Louise Bélland was stunned by the swiftness of the blazes: "The violence and the speed of the fire was unimaginable, incredible. The fire spread at the speed of light; it burned all the old wooden buildings." And according to news outlets, the outcome looked the same as the MLT riot at the Murray Hill garage – like "the end of some terrible battle in a terrible war."[153]

A few days later, Jean Drapeau returned to the campaign trail with his usual showmanship, telling people how, even in the wake of the Red Weekend, nothing would stop Montreal from becoming "one of the first, if not the first ranking city in the world."[154] Trade union leaders and journalists rejected this civic boosterism and stated that he and the Civic Party should hold full responsibility for the tragic event.[155] But despite strong opposition, Montrealers remained convinced that Jean Drapeau was a capable leader and he was re-elected. The mandate, however, was a far cry from the 1970 election when the Civic Party won one of the largest victories in Montreal's political history. In 1974, the Civic Party secured only thirty-six of fifty-five council seats, and Drapeau's share of votes dropped significantly, from his previous high of 92 per cent to 55 per cent. This election also marked the emergence of the Montreal Citizens' Movement (MCM), a new social-democratic party that obtained one-third of the seats at city council. Led by priest Jacques Couture, the MCM garnered 40 per cent of the votes by presenting a less radical discourse than the FRAP. The party's rise was fuelled by concerns about Mayor Drapeau's increasingly autocratic tendencies, which had been noticed since the 1970 election.[156] In the wake of these developments, Montreal's "New Left" had mobilized itself, seeking to address and counterbalance the perceived concentration of power in Drapeau's hands. By June 1974, francophone and anglophone intellectuals, activists, members of the New Democratic Party and the Parti Québécois, and trade unionists had united to found a new political party with the simple idea of improving Montrealers' quality of life.[157]

***

Who were the winners and who were the losers of the Red Weekend? While all parties might claim that they had won – after all, the MFA had been awarded a raise that the city did not have to pay in its entirety, and the provincial government had been able to contain a "social problem" – it was obvious that the real losers of that weekend were those whose fates placed them in the parties' crossfire. Montrealers were left without firefighters, and their care was thwarted by complex jurisdictional politics, leaving them caught in the middle. While only one firefighter was eventually charged with mischief (for a fire that razed a three-storey building), as a whole, firefighters transformed their image from background figures of municipal order into rebellious dissenters.[158]

Amid the aftershock and ashes, many wondered who would pay for the damages. Others wondered where the working-class people of Saint-Jacques would find shelter or aid. Answers came a year later when Fire Commis-

Figure 4.11
Two Saint-Jacques residents survey the fire damage caused on Plessis Street during the Red Weekend, 1974.

sioner George Allison, the special investigator appointed by Justice Minister Jérôme Choquette to determine the root causes of the Red Weekend, submitted his report. He traced the history of labour disputes and argued that the Red Weekend had been the logical evolution of the 1969 and 1971 strikes and the absence of disciplinary actions against firefighters during those strikes. Moreover, Allison also noted the criminal and unsolvable origin of many fires, highlighting the significant evolution from 1969 and 1971 to 1974. Finally, individuals who tried to contain arsons had been obstructed by striking firefighters who violently sabotaged the equipment and assaulted and threatened them.[159] His report recommended, as did the federal government, that civil and criminal proceedings be taken against MFA members and leaders.[160] To offset the costs of the damages, the tribunal ordered the MFA to pay $1 million plus interest to the victims. But as Jean L'Abbé later told Labour Minister Jean Cournoyer, the MFA was able to raise these funds through tax-deductible contributions, which meant that Canadian and Quebec taxpayers footed a significant part of the bill.[161]

Conclusion

In November 1971, the mayor's three-hundred-seat establishment closed for good. After undergoing repairs following the Night of Terror, Le Vaisseau d'Or had faced financial hardships – in part due to sewage backwater flooding; in part due to a costly dispute over rent at the upscale Windsor Hotel.[162] The establishment had been a manifestation of Jean Drapeau's own dreams and wealth. Upon its opening, Montrealers perceived the mayor's latest endeavour as yet another display of his penchant for high culture and authority. As an advertisement for the establishment asserted: "While awaiting the Montreal Opera, Le Vaisseau d'Or takes pride in offering opera lovers the greatest Canadian voices accompanied by the Concert Orchestra of Le Vaisseau d'Or conducted by Jean-Eudes Vaillancourt."[163]

The establishment's "discipline dining" was a business model based on precise organization. But more to the point, it allowed Drapeau to mingle with elites, discuss politics, and elaborate power by awarding jobs to people who had been loyal to him. The establishment was more than a restaurant: it was a space where the well-connected could experience high culture – the most respectable form of culture in the mayor's mind. This interconnectivity was mocked in the poetically titled *La démocratie à Montréal : ou, Le vaisseau dort* (1972) by journalist Marcel Adam. The book reviews the Civic Party's civil rights record and makes the argument that Montreal of the early 1970s was not a democratic city, citing as examples Nightstick Monday, the anti-demonstration bylaw, and the lockout at *La Presse*.[164] Although the book is a fierce polemic against Jean Drapeau and the Civic Party, this view was echoed, as we have seen, by civil rights activists, students, feminists, writers, trade union leaders, and residents who were caught in the crossfire created by the Civic Party's conservative economic agenda. Had Adam published the book two years later, the inclusion of the 1974 Red Weekend would have added depth to his thesis. That labour conflict was another example of failed Civic Party labour policies, resulting in catastrophic loss for hundreds.

The events covered in this chapter illustrate the profound importance of nighttime as a moment that produced new forms of protests. The night was a tool in the bargaining process for the labour movement, and some unions achieved great gains because of it. In the absence of transit employees, police officers, and firefighters, the nighttime city became ungovernable. Vandals, arsonists, rioters, protestors, and ordinary citizens broke social norms in the absence of public safety personnel. At the same time, the night explains why authorities could implement new rules and regulations that bent democratic conventions, extending their power during an era of social unrest. The creation of the anti-riot unit and the enactment of the anti-demonstration bylaw were both direct responses to a series of nighttime events that had presented a significant challenge to the administration. Organizing demonstrations, sit-ins, and marches at night had fostered greater social connectivity and allowed various activist groups to unite and present a strong political opposition. However, the cover of darkness also provided an opportunity for vandals to influence the dynamics of many of these nocturnal protests. Finally, these developments characterize the transition toward a new police culture that would come to shape Montreal in the following decades and century, one that would receive sizeable funding. Indeed, nighttime events transformed the political culture of the city.

When his restaurant closed, Drapeau's vision of "respectable" culture would extend in the way that he managed street art and the culture of nightlife. In the nights leading up to the 1976 Summer Olympic Games, perhaps the apex of his personal achievement, he refined Montreal's image to the world. Again, Montreal's image was grounded in respectable visual aesthetics. Drapeau's instruction that the Police Department and city employees clear the city of "low-art" and sexual "deviants" furthers the thesis that nighttime order was at the centre of his politics during the mid-1970s. Out of this contest over art and culture emerged fiery debates about privilege and the right to the city. The mayor believed that the city should be recognized and celebrated for its high culture. That position led civic authorities to reason that non-normative expressions should be hidden from view.

5

CENSORSHIP, REPRESSION, AND THE 1976 SUMMER OLYMPIC GAMES

During a rainy night from 13 to 14 July 1976, under the pretext that it contravened municipal bylaws, city employees censored the public art exhibition *Corridart dans la rue Sherbrooke*. Under cover of darkness, the employees furtively stripped Sherbrooke Street of the installations, mangling the art pieces before loading them into dump trucks. A few days later newspapers reported that Mayor Drapeau himself had ordered the nighttime destruction after he had seen *Corridart*. He would later claim that its content was worthless, that it was an eyesore and "an incredible pollution of Sherbrooke Street," which is why he had it dismantled.[1]

Consisting of seventeen visual art projects, two performance areas, and two gallery exhibits, *Corridart* had been installed a week earlier on 7 July. The artists taking part in *Corridart* felt that its portmanteau title fittingly described the light-hearted and festive five-and-a-half-mile-long "corridor of art" they had created on Sherbrooke Street, which was intended to add excitement to the 1976 Summer Olympic Games. In fact, the exhibition was part of the event's Arts and Culture Program and had been funded by a small grant from the province as well as by the artists themselves – not by the municipal administration.[2] Laurent Lamy, head of the Visual and Plastic Arts sector, considered *Corridart* to be the Games' most important art display, which is why he was horrified when he saw it being censored. "One of the artists called me at 2 a.m. and asked, 'what's going on?'" he recalled during an interview. Perplexed, Lamy jumped out of bed and went to see for himself.

Arriving minutes later, he, too, wondered what was happening. He saw police officers guarding city employees who had been tasked with dismantling the artworks. The city's show of force led Lamy to describe the destruction as "a wicked re-enactment of the Night of Broken Glass" and declared that it had been "a calculated move that could not have been possible in the light of day: maces, saws, chainsaws!"[3] The destruction appalled artists, organizers, and critics, and it would soon cause an incredible uproar about the freedom of expression and censorship in Montreal. (fig. 5.1)

Artist Françoise Sullivan recalled her bewilderment, too, when she heard that city employees had trashed her freshly installed artwork *Legend of Artists*. Best described as a walking tour along Sherbrooke Street – between Aylmer Street and De Lorimier Avenue – her exhibit charted and celebrated the spaces where she and her contemporaries had spent many nights debating politics, art, and social change. The artwork was a historical survey that threw light on bygone cultural hubs, ones that had represented spontaneous and exuberant forms of urban life and that had spurred the city's artistic efflorescence.[4] Above all, and quite crucially, her artwork exposed the brute character of Montreal's mid-twentieth-century reformism because it revealed how urban policies and speculative investment had decimated the city's artistic network. It was ironic, she later reflected, how those mid-century nightspots and *Corridart* suffered similar fates under the very same mayor. Sullivan, and at least one other critic, would go as far as to connect *Corridart*'s censorship to sexual violence. "They acted in a barbaric way too," she told filmmakers, "like thieves in the night. It was like a rape, really."[5] While this was a brash, and perhaps crude, way to reflect on the manner that authorities had despoiled public artworks, Sullivan nevertheless touched on the municipal administration's merciless enterprise, one that was particularly perceptible at night.

The context of *Corridart*'s destruction is significant. In the summer of 1976, the mayor's decades-long dream had materialized as Montreal captured the world's spotlight, playing host to the Olympic Games. In fact, St Louis, Missouri, and Montreal were the only North American cities to host both a world's fair and the Olympic Games in the twentieth century, underscoring these cities' cultural, economic, and global significance. But in the lead-up to that event, and in anticipation of international delegates and the press landing on the Island of Montreal, authorities refined the city's appearance.

Figure 5.1
Official poster advertising Corridart as part of the Arts and Culture Program of the 1976 Summer Olympic Games on which the word "CENSURÉ" (CENSORED) has been stamped.

They wanted Montreal to appear as an immaculate expression of modern urbanism. Which is why, when artists mounted *Corridart* and used the high-profile 1976 Summer Games to critique the controversial nature of Montreal's swift mid-twentieth-century urban reformism, the city (re)acted. In other words, the city would not allow protest art to ruin the event. It is important to reiterate that despite Mayor Drapeau ordering the censorship of *Corridart*, he was not a philistine. As previous chapters have emphasized, he was an avid patron of high culture and enjoyed its most traditional aspects, like fine dining, operas, ballets, and orchestras. However, his dilettante interest in arts and culture prevented him from appreciating the value of alternative cultural expressions, like discotheque culture or modern art, which is why he vehemently opposed any attempts to redefine the subject. In fact, *Corridart* was not the first time his administration censored artworks. In the past he instructed police to confiscate erotic films like *I, a Woman* (1965) and *Quiet Days in Clichy* (1970). Indeed, the 1960s and '70s was a period when art and culture were redefined, expanded, and diversified, which created problems of classification and judgment. At times, the city's regulation of artworks left some perplexed and others, like the chief of the Morality Squad, advocating for the legalization of prostitution because officers constantly had to "distinguish between nudism, pornography and art."[6] Ultimately, the mayor understood the profound meaning of art and its power for social change, which is why he felt the need to respond to *Corridart*'s commanding message opposing unregulated growth. However, and sensing that he would face significant backlash if the censorship took place in broad daylight, he arranged for the mission to be swift, covert, and performed under cover of darkness.

As the Games drew near and the city prepared to welcome international delegations, camera crews, Olympians, and tourists, it refined the parameters of conformity.[7] At night, in the shadow of the event that authorities would later claim was a glorious success, the city purged "undesirable" elements from public view to safeguard the immaculate image sold in international magazines and newspapers. *Corridart* is an example of an effort to clear nonconformity from the streets, but it was not the only one. Reportedly, employees of the organizing committee for the Summer Games, known by its French acronym COJO (Comité organisateur des Jeux Olympiques de 1976), received specific instructions to confine and hide a different set of "nonconforming elements."[8] This simultaneous crackdown attempted to dismantle the city's gay networks and the night scene that allowed members of the queer community to experiment with their sexuality, talk, dance, and find a home in the city.[9]

As earlier chapters have shown, Jean Drapeau's control over the city took root in his attempt to bring moral order to public space, which required the policing of nightspots, parks, squares, and streets. This continued in the lead-up to the 1976 Olympic Games as the mayor seized the opportunity it provided to refine the city's image. Once more, night was a moment that enabled crackdowns on, and censorship of, nonconforming elements that did not fit into the city's global mould. The contest over who or what had the right to public space took place in or near the downtown district because it was where authorities hoped that out-of-towners would spend money.[10]

I begin this chapter by showing the ways that architects and artists influenced urban life. As Quebec art historiography shows, two strains of art influenced social change during the second half of the twentieth century: techno-pop art and political art.[11] The following pages focus on the second strain by providing two examples of 1970s political art in Montreal: *Montreal, plus or minus?* (1972) and *Corridart dans la rue Sherbrooke* (1976). Both exhibitions are characterized by their playful artworks, illustrating the disequilibrium of modern urban life. And although a lot has been written about each event, their kinship, as art historian Johanne Sloan remarks, remains elusive.[12] This chapter reconciles this schism by considering both exhibitions as part of a unified act of public contestation, one which actively challenged Jean Drapeau and the Civic Party's policies. I achieve this by placing their coordinator, Université de Montréal professor of architecture Melvin Charney, at the heart of the narrative. At first glance, *Montreal, plus or minus?* might appear an odd choice to include in a book about nighttime governance during the Drapeau years. But because the exhibition challenged the mayor's vision of Montreal and commented on the sorry state of city politics, it captured how residents had come to feel about the city's rapid mid-twentieth-century make-over. And although Drapeau never saw the exhibition, he knew that disillusioned artists mocked his political project.[13]

In the summer of 1976, Charney attempted to spur further political debate with *Corridart*. *Corridart*'s exhibits, selected after a call for submission (open exclusively to Quebec artists) and months of planning, also highlighted the social, political, economic, and environmental dangers of unbridled development. This time, however, the authorities censored the exhibition's message, an action that they tried to justify by arguing that *Corridart* was "downright provocative and blasphemous – showcasing a foul and unliveable city."[14] Notwithstanding the exhibition's provincial source of funding, the city's action reaffirmed its control over public space during the Olympic Games. Therefore, historicizing *Corridart*'s censorship requires not only an overview of the 1976 Olympic Games but also of its interconnectivity with the broader trajectory of political art.

Elsewhere, the same governing strategy was deployed in attacks on the gay community. Starting over a year before the Summer Olympics, and spanning the course of several months, the city coordinated crackdowns on dozens of gay night spots like Aquarius, Baby Face, and Lime Light, and used its authority to repress gay activism. In fact, queer bathhouses, editorial rooms, bars, and nightclubs in cities playing host to 1976 Games events – Montreal, Toronto, and Ottawa – were raided by police.[15] Raids were conducted under the vague terms of the "bawdy-house" law, and the full extent of this pan-Canadian effort can be observed in the criminal statistics put out annually by Statistics Canada: between the years 1974 and 1982, the bawdy-house offences fluctuated drastically, hitting a high of 1,143 in 1975 and a low of 269 in 1982.[16] As community historian and activist Ross Higgins notes, those in power asserted dominance over public and social spaces before and after the 1976 Olympics. In the end, after intense repression and violence, Montreal's queer community emerged somewhat triumphant when the Parti Québécois provincial government amended the Quebec Charter of Human Rights and Freedoms in 1977 to include sexual orientation as a prohibited ground for discrimination.[17]

Examining Montreal at night during the mid-1970s connects ongoing discussions in art history, urban governance, and queer history.[18] Throughout this period, artists and gay activists fought the city's repressive actions and the merging of political and police forces, which they referred to as "drapolice," by organizing nighttime street protests and taking the civic government to court.[19] As Montreal embraced its global moment, authorities increased their control over acceptable sex and art at night, reshaping urban spaces and profoundly influencing the city's politics and culture.

The City as Œuvre: *Montreal, plus or minus?* (1972)

Like many things, space is moulded according to political and historical context, and in mid-1970s Montreal, the power of financial elites had come to dominate it. According to one estimate, construction projects downtown exceeded $1.2 billion during this period.[20] Two projects were symbolic of the era. The $200-million Complexe Desjardins, constructed from 1972 to 1976, which held the promise of revitalizing a long-neglected block. Nestled between the historic Red Light district and Place des Arts, the block had been home to rows of low-rise cheap clothing stores, novelty shops, and rundown rooming houses known for their poverty, petty crime, and sex workers.[21] In the end, the project displaced 360 residents, and although Mouvement Desjardins supported a relocation plan for evicted residents (including compensation and rent subsidies), the city's Planning Department rejected the financial institution's involvement. In 1972, another $200 million project materialized under similar circumstances.[22] Conceived over a period of fifteen years, the Complexe Guy-Favreau preyed upon a slate of low-rise buildings in Montreal's Chinatown. Although the project was for a federal building, it seemed, according to one critic, "fairly certain that Jean Drapeau played a key role in the expropriation of the Chinatown block."[23] Despite community protest, the city expropriated residential and commercial property to clear six acres for the federal building. Community hubs were demolished, including two Chinese churches, a school, several grocery stores, and arts and crafts stores. Furthermore, a food processing plant and Chinatown's main employer, Wong Wing Noodle Company, was forced to move in the process.[24] High rents and further encroachment would continue to threaten and alter the district so that by the time construction was completed, surveys revealed that the community was considerably reduced.[25]

As the city spearheaded plans for development – which pushed unwanted communities further from the central business district and increased land value and tax-generating businesses – residents, artists, and intellectuals became more responsive to and critical of local politics. Among the clamour one intellectual stood out: Université de Montréal professor Melvin Charney. After sojourning in New York and Paris – where he improved his French and drew connections from different intellectual circles – Charney returned to Montreal in the mid-1960s to begin a career that examined the relationship between art, urban identity, and history. His activism, notably in the Saint-Antoine district where he fought development and gentrification, was a testament to his profound belief in social justice. Charney's strength lay in his ability to seamlessly interlock artistic, linguistic, and social spheres, which explains how he – an anglophone Jew of Polish and Russian heritage – became the driving force behind politically engaged artists at a moment when Montreal's art scene was heavily shaped by Quebec nationalism.

Charney's ability to link different spheres was clearest when he coordinated art exhibitions. At the Montreal Museum of Fine Arts, renowned for exemplifying high culture, he headed the popular art exhibition *Montreal, plus or minus?* The exhibition brought together a heterogeneous cohort of eighty artists that included architects, social activists, community organizers, intellectuals, photographers, and students. Each presented their perspective on the essential aspects of urban life: human-scale communities and green environments, characterized by laneways and parks. Charney asserted that the exhibition served as a thoughtful reflection on the planning history of Montreal during a time when conversations about planning were scarce.[26] By presenting it as a historical reflection, Charney aimed to shed light on the "large-scale" and "inhumane" economies of land development. These developments, Charney argued, originated with settler colonialism, gained momentum during the Second Industrial Revolution, and reached its zenith during post–World War II economic expansion – the golden age of capitalism. "The real subject of the exhibition," he states in the exhibition catalogue, "is the relationship between the physical presence of the city and people's lives. The early destruction of Indian culture and the destruction of housing for the building of a super highway in 1972, the 'housing crises' and the profusion of high-rise apartments, violence and culture, are all interconnected in Montreal."[27] Across the city, automobiles had replaced pedestrians, pavement replaced greenery, and corporate skyscrapers replaced housing units. He challenged the municipal administration's vision of Montreal by asking how space is produced, by whom, and for whom.

The exhibits extended beyond the Montreal Museum of Fine Arts. Mauve, a feminist group, challenged the objectification of women and drew attention to capitalist consumption by using dance, mime, music, and street theatre performances within shopping centres across metropolitan Montreal.[28] Tom Shively designed "Caribbean of the North," a gargantuan geodesic dome à la Buckminster Fuller, to cover the hills of Montreal's South Shore for a greenhouse effect, which would recreate the tropical climate for winter vacationers and allow "Québec dollar$ [to] be spent in Québec."[29] Like other grassroots protest campaigns of the period, this one brought activists who looked to make the kinds of changes and worlds that were once unimaginable. The artworks were meant to raise critical questions about development and destruction, inclusion and exclusion – fundamental issues that questioned the politics of Drapeau's reformism and modernism. Perhaps the most poignant exhibit was the bus tour "Green Spaces." Its route presented sightseers a not-so-picturesque tour of modernism and revealed the remarkable ways that state projects had destroyed communities. This was exemplified by stops along stretches of the Trans-Canada Highway in Little Burgundy and the Maison de Radio-Canada in the Faubourg à m'lasse.[30]

The exhibition, described by *Artscanada* as a succès de scandale, divided critics.[31] During its eight-week run, it attracted 52,300 visitors, a commendable turnout for a summertime exhibition.[32] Many who saw it, however, could not understand its artistic value or merit. One federal urban planning adviser described it as "defeatist, fatalist – expressing a cul-de-sac in the view of the city's future."[33] Gilles Toupin, art critic for *La Presse*, held a divergent opinion, however, writing that the exhibition's timely political statement would certainly be seen as a turning point in Montreal history. And when he interviewed Charney, he asked whether this was part of the ongoing cultural *rattrapage* (catching up) discourse, which had overtaken the province within the context of the Quiet Revolution. The architect rejected that premise, asserting instead that it was a display of everyday living in Montreal. To this end, Charney conceded that holding the exhibition over a four-mile stretch across neighbourhoods or on a street would have been truer to this goal – which is exactly what he would do a few years later for *Corridart*. He told Toupin that for *Montreal, plus or minus?* there had been "a few attempts at censorship, but I resisted."[34] Little did he realize the prophetic accuracy in his statement. Ultimately, Charney's work was a sincere attempt to renew critical debate on the topics of urban planning and modernism, which he did by examining how speculative development and city planning overlapped in Montreal. The questions he raised were part of a discourse that characterized the era and to which municipal elected officials would have to respond.

***

In 1970, Montreal was selected to host the 1976 Olympic Games. At the time, Drapeau told the International Olympic Committee that, unlike most cities, Montreal did not need to secure financial guarantees because he was "staking the city's reputation on the Olympics."[35] That reputation had been taking shape for a number of years, certainly since the resounding success of Expo 67. And as with Expo 67, Drapeau wanted to create an unforgettable event that would bestow global glory and prestige on the city. According to Drapeau, for this vision to materialize, a lasting landmark was needed, a monument that would inspire pride in residents and awe in visitors. That landmark became the Olympic Village and its Olympic Stadium. The site, which could accommodate four hundred thousand people per day, began taking shape when City Hall seized parklands and displaced low-income tenants in the east end. A pocket of the Hochelaga-Maisonneuve neighbourhood and its residents had a similar experience for the 1976 Summer Olympic Games to that of Victoriatown for Expo 67. With limited time available, City Hall favoured a fast-track construction, which led to dangerous working conditions and a dozen work-site deaths.[36] While it is not this book's goal to review how Montreal erected the site for the Summer Olympics, it is noteworthy that out of this messy and deadly process emerged a coalition of more than a hundred community organizations. This coalition further contributed to the broader array of critiques aimed at the municipal administration.[37]

But perhaps the most stunning facet of the Olympic fiasco concerned its source of funding. Montreal had set off without having secured federal or provincial funding, and since private capital would not fund the event, the city started grabbing money from public coffers with brazen confidence.[38] By May 1974, city council abolished public bidding for tenders when it voted to vest power in its executive committee, and it soon emerged that this had helped to further the private interests of engineers, contractors, and architects. Quite rapidly, and as had been the case during the 1950s, explosive headlines claimed that collusion and corruption swamped City Hall.[39]

In early 1973, the Quebec government intervened and appointed a joint committee for the review and control of revenues and expenses related to the Summer Olympic Games. Meanwhile the federal government gave an important nod of approval on 23 July 1973 when it authorized the printing of Olympic coins and stamps to help finance the event. It also coordinated an "Olympic Lottery" – a haphazard bid to pay for the soaring cost of the Olympics. From the very beginning, however, the federal government made it clear that it would not contribute to a deficit if one were to occur, and although it allocated $260 million to fund the games, the likelihood of a deficit increased over time.[40] Later, a planning consultant would claim that the profits derived from the sale of coins, stamps, commercial licences, and lottery tickets were beneficial but that local labour disputes, inflation, and the oil crisis of 1973 constricted spending power.[41] By November 1975, the skyrocketing cost (see table 5.1), the lack of proper administrative control, and the delay in carrying out the work, forced the Quebec government to intervene. It entrusted itself with the ownership of the Olympic facilities and the responsibility for continuing its construction under the Olympic Installations Board (Régie des installations olympiques).[42]

After the Summer Olympics had come and gone, the Quebec government would order the Commission of Inquiry into the Cost of the 21st Olympiad. The Malouf Report, presented in 1980, offered six main reasons why the Games had drifted so far from the initial projected cost: administrative irresponsibility, poor fiscal planning, lack of a masterplan, acquisition of lavish and superfluous installations, architectural difficulties, and the choice of French architect Roger Taillibert who not only held a patronizing attitude toward Quebec professionals and labourers but also refused to revise his blueprints in order to reduce costs.[43]

But before this inquiry was held, when the Quebec government created the board in November 1975, it seized control of more than the Olympics. It effectively ended Mayor Drapeau's vision for the city's greatest event by making it clear that governing the city was a shared responsibility. In an interview decades later, Melvin Charney argued that when Drapeau lost power over the city, he had been incensed and vindictive, and that was why he became determined to show, once and for all, who ruled Montreal.[44] In the midst of corruption and fraud, the essence of which made its way into newspapers across the globe, everything fell into place for a ruthless cleanup campaign beginning in November 1975.

Table 5.1
Cost of the 1976 Montreal Summer Olympic Games: selected years, 1969–75 (projection) and 1976 (final), with percentage increase over that time

Date	Total projected cost (CAD)	Percentage increase relative to initial projection
4 December 1969	$120,000,000	–
23 November 1972	$310,000,000	258.0
26 April 1974	$309,505,100	257.9
4 February 1975	$610,600,000	509.0
16 July 1975	$730,000,000	608.0
	Total final cost	
1 August 1976	$1,333,028,000	1,111.0

Note: The "final cost" does not take into account completion of the Olympic Stadium, which remained unfinished during the Olympic Games and was estimated to require an additional $137 million; it also does not take into account $176 million of Olympic activities outside of Montreal. That amount was paid by the governments of Ontario, Canada, and Quebec as well as several municipal administrations.
Source: Malouf, *Rapport de la Commission d'enquête sur le coût de la 21e olympiade*, 24–9.

Pre-Olympics Raids

Sometimes it takes vicious repression to make people fight back.[45]
– *The Body Politic* (1976)

As we have seen in earlier chapters, nightclubs, brothels, bars, and cabarets attracted sizable crowds and produced great economic activity during the early to mid-twentieth century. But following the election of Jean Drapeau in 1954, and in the lead-up to Expo 67, the city completely transformed this night scene. Authorities clamped down on illicit activities, which paved the way for a greater integration of the nighttime economy into the formal economy. However, because the struggle over acceptable behaviour was an ongoing battle, municipal authorities continued to police sex during the 1970s. And although authorities had been monitoring gay sex since at least the first Canadian law condemning homosexuality in 1841, the process by which they did so evolved – especially after the decriminalization in 1969 of certain sexual practices between consenting adults (federal Omnibus Bill C-150).[6] Therefore, in the lead-up to the Summer Olympics, authorities considered different ways to crack down on businesses that advertised queer-friendly storefronts and where people continued to resist heterosexual dominance, like bookstores, cinemas, bars, discotheques, restaurants, and taverns. For this reason, police raids were conducted under the broad bawdy-house legislation, which legally defined any place that is kept, occupied, or resorted to by one or more persons for the purpose of prostitution or the practice of acts of indecency. Using the legislation's vague terms "acts of indecency" or "indecent acts," police asserted power over downtown, reinforcing heteronormativity in the process.

In Canadian cities, gay activism had been growing throughout the late 1960s and early 1970s.[47] In Montreal, this activism was informed and propelled by intellectual developments that blurred the boundaries between art, politics, music, and sexuality, particularly evocative in art and counterculture journals like *Sexus* and *Mainmise*. In 1971, after becoming disillusioned by the commodification of gay (night)life, members of *Mainmise*'s editorial team founded the Front de libération homosexuel (FLH). The FLH's activities, however, ended abruptly one night when police raided its office and arrested sixty people, forcing it to dissolve.[48] In the aftermath, other queer liberation groups like Gay McGill and COOP Femmes became popular activist hubs. The former raised funds through monthly dances that drew thousands to the university's campus, even attendees from San Francisco. Members also founded Androgyne, a downtown bookstore stoked with feminist and queer literature, and launched the lesbian periodical *Long Time Coming* (1973–76).[49] Meanwhile, the francophone lesbian group COOP Femmes also held dances to raise awareness about issues like abortion, daycare, employment, and, of course, the struggle for gay rights.[50]

The pre-Olympic cleanup campaign would dismantle these hubs, striking at the heart of the city's queer community and the spaces that had been providing comfort and empowerment, and where members could develop their sexuality based on a shared search for pleasure and excitement. It was an effort that combined modern political and economic interests since it primarily acted downtown, aiming to refine Montreal's "tourist-friendly" image. According to *Gay Times*, a source close to the city's Police Department revealed that "there [was] indeed a master plan to clean up the city prior to the Olympics," and this forceful initiative started eighteen months before the start of the Olympics when police officers busted into Aquarius sauna on 4 February 1975.[51] During that raid, officers charged thirty-five men with being "found-ins in a bawdy-house"; later, these officers testified that the establishment encouraged sexual activities because it sold gay magazines and lubricants. As the principal body governing bawdy-house economies, police used their discretion in whether or not to use bawdy-house laws and, in so doing, drew on a long history of selective enforcement. Aquarius continued operating for two more months before a fire destroyed it and resulted in the deaths of three people. Despite suspicions of arson, the Fire Department ultimately ruled the fire's cause as unknown.[52]

By spring 1975, community members formed a Marxist organization called the Groupe homosexuel d'action politique (GHAP).[53] GHAP communicated important community updates by circulating its bulletin and leaflets in gay nightspots and at dances organized by Gay Montreal. At times, when it did not have enough funds to print a bulletin, members relayed important messages by word of mouth or by etching graffiti inside bars and discotheques.[54] GHAP was committed to social justice and articulated its worldview in opposition to capitalism, racism, and patriarchy. For example, it stood against patriarchy at the International Women's Day night march and against capitalism at the May Day protest.[55] GHAP believed that the city's nighttime scene remained the last utopia for queer Montrealers, which is why it pushed for gay liberation literature to be sold in bars, nightclubs, and bathhouses. The group drew inspiration from a long history that allowed gay men to create social bonds in bars.[56]

Nighttime raids intensified as the mayor lost his grip over the Olympic Games. In late 1975, several well-established queer spots were raided, including Baby Face, named after owner and ex-wrestler Denise Cassidy, and the legendary disco-hub Lime Light, Montreal's largest discotheque where one of three dance floors catered exclusively to a gay clientele. During these raids, officers feigned routine checks for drug trafficking and underage drinking.[57] Similar raids rocked Rocambole, P.J.'s, Buds, and Taureau d'Or. In January 1976, the Montreal Club Baths franchise, which had been facing problems with municipal authorities in getting its licence approved, was raided and thirteen individuals were arrested as bawdy-house found-ins.[58] "The repression accompanying the Olympics preparation in Montreal has caused some dislocation and demoralization," lamented a columnist in the queer magazine *The Body Politic*.[59] It is important to point out that repression was not unique to Montreal as this orchestrated campaign extended to other Olympic event sites scattered between Quebec City and Toronto.[60]

But the pre-Olympic crackdown took a forceful and dramatic turn over the course of a weekend in May 1976. At Neptune Sauna, eighty-nine men were arrested in a late-night raid when officers equipped with axes and crowbars smashed down doors and busted into the venue.[61] Reinforcing traditional norms and heteronormative ideals, police told management that they "were cleaning things up." Police further underscored this paradigm by conflating homosexuality with violence when it suggested that raids at gay establishments could help identify "potential terrorists."[62] Speaking to the *Montreal Gazette*, Henri Labelle – a gay-nightclub manager and, later, a Concordia University lecturer – suggested that many well-known Montrealers frequented Neptune Sauna, including a former mayor's son, a government minister, a secretary to the Catholic archbishop, and a couple of off-duty police officers. On the night of the police raid, however, each had been able to elude police by dashing out the back door. In the context of this research, the revelation, whether true or not, matters little. What Labelle's story does suggest, however, is that there is truth behind the "nocturnal self" and the common maxim that queer folk lived two lives: "Gay from nine in the evening until five in the morning and straight the rest of the time." Meals, breakfast or dinner, eased the transition from one world to the other.[63]

As Ross Higgins notes, historically, language politics had segregated queer activism in Montreal.[64] However, the crackdowns on nightlife, adding up to hundreds of arrests, created the perfect climate for the creation of the bilingual Comité homosexuel anti-répression (CHAR) on 20 May 1976.[65] In fact, it came on the heels of additional raids at Stork Club, Studio One, and Jilly's (at the last, officers barged into the Bishop Street lesbian bar in a swat-like manoeuvre armed with rifles and cameras).[66] The moment was ripe for action. Two hundred people attended the assembly on 20 May, which was organized to denounce ongoing raids and sexual repression. Community pushback would reach its apex one month later when three hundred CHAR supporters held what was then the largest gay rights demonstration in Canadian history. Supporters marched through the city, and since the procession made its way past the Montreal office of the Quebec premier, COJO's headquarters, and City Hall, it connected the pre-Olympic crackdown to

Figure 5.2
Front page of *The Body Politic, Gay Liberation Journal*, August 1976.

political interests. For thousands, the pre-Olympic violence typified the rawness of urban modernism.

Another facet of the pre-Olympic crackdown revolved around racial profiling. Predominantly coordinated by officers from Police Station 10, these incidents occurred at nighttime in the vicinity of bars and hotels frequented by tourists. The documentary *Station 10* (1973), produced by the National Film Board, offers insight into the station's handling of various disturbances and crimes, illustrating how officers employed certain categories, like race and nationality, to chase leads and search premises.[67] This very station was assigned the responsibility of overseeing the pre-Olympic cleanup campaign a few years later. As the Summer Olympic Games approached, the station's officers enforced the city's anti-loitering bylaw to clear Black sex workers from public spaces. Additionally, they summoned immigration officers to deport those who had been apprehended. A spokesperson for the police stated that this operation against street-based sex workers thwarted the establishment of a satellite operation near downtown nightclubs by what they referred to as the "Black American mafia." In the span of several days, the police arrested fifty individuals and deported eighteen women. In fact, during the Games, the police arrested an additional eighteen Black American sex workers near the Olympic Village; they were likewise deported after being handed over to immigration officers.[68] Speaking to the tabloid *Le Petit Journal*, an officer said that they coordinated with immigration officers because the anti-loitering bylaw "was no longer enough" to contain the influx of sex workers.[69] Effectively, the officer revealed that the authorities' goal was not simply to clear streets – since this could be achieved with the anti-loitering bylaw – but also to completely eradicate public displays of sex from the city. This collaborative effort, which brought into sharp relief politics of race and immigration, led to 748 arrests in 1975 under the guise of prostitution-related offences.[70]

During the Olympics, the world witnessed the largest Canadian military operation since World War II. Security was first budgeted in 1973 as a mere $500,000 expenditure, but its price tag followed the way of the rest of the 1976 Games and ultimately cost organizers an estimated $100 million, with many additional expenditures assumed by contributing agencies.[71] The Olympic Village itself was protected by a ten-foot barbed-wire fence and patrolled, like other parts of the city, by armed officials. Fondly remembering the Summer Olympics and all its contradictions, historian Bruce Kidd notes that the strategy behind the conspicuous display of force was to safeguard the success of the Games, especially in the wake of the 1972 Munich massacre and similar acts of terrorism around the world. This fierce display of military strength may have been justified, seeing as the Official Report of the Olympic Games cited only three "breaches of security" – a Canadian athlete smuggled a friend into the Olympic Village, a journalist managed to meet Queen Elizabeth II, and a spectator jumped over a barrier to join decathlon champion Bruce Jenner for a victory lap.[72] Nevertheless, and despite a heavy police and military presence, *Le Petit Journal* claimed that the Games had been a goldmine for sex workers and pickpockets: "Since mid-July [1976], business has been good for prostitutes and pickpockets in Montreal. As with every major event of international significance, a whole fauna of pickpockets and public courtesans descended on the metropolis. If crime dropped significantly, it was because of the presence of so many police officers and armed soldiers on our streets and around the Olympic complex in the east end of the city. Nevertheless, criminals continued their clandestine activities."[73] Although surveillance and security were for the benefit of the athletes, many participants and Montrealers reported being troubled by the heavy-handed display during the two-week event.

Following the Games and throughout the following months, queer community organizers shared legal information by printing and distributing pamphlets in bars and nightclubs. Relaying this information helped community members deal with the repercussions of police raids.[74] Nightspots served as vital channels for activists to share information. As novelist Marie-Claire Blais writes in *The Nights in the Underground* (1978), a whole network of relationships is made possible in bars; it is where students, labourers, lovers, and transients find a welcoming home. However, by the end of the decade, certain activists perceived bars and nightclubs as commercialized establishments that were vulnerable to violent police raids: "Many gays are sick of disco music and we want to create and innovate, under less stereotypical conditions, an uncommercialized queer culture," wrote political activist Pierre Vallières.[75] Similar discourse emerged from *Long Time Coming* as lesbians raised the problem of queer nightspots being entangled with organized crime as men controlled the ownership and management of lesbian nightspots. By November 1974, a group of lesbians led a boycott of one such establishment, Chez Madame Arthur.[76] Eventually, CHAR's activism paved the way for the creation of the Association pour les droits des gai(e)s du Québec (ADGQ) in October 1976, which quickly became the main entity for gay rights in Quebec. In fact, the ADGQ's raison d'être was to push the Quebec government to amend section 10 of the Charter of Human Rights and Freedoms and prohibit discrimination on the basis of sexual orientation.[77]

Gay Rights in Quebec: Post-Olympic Raid on Truxx

À BAS LA DRAPOLICE[78]
– Comité de communication de l'ADGQ (1977)

Repression continued after the 1976 Summer Olympic Games. In the summer months of 1977, officers patrolled known gay hangouts, notably La Fontaine Park, where they harassed, terrorized, and assaulted individuals and, in certain cases, brought men into dimly lit parking lots for vicious beatings. In a letter sent to elected officials, media outlets, civil rights groups, and police officials, the ADGQ argued that these events only occurred in the darkness of night and were, in all likelihood, the work of a Night Patrol unit.[79] It is worth noting that the Night Patrol consisted of approximately thirty officers who were dressed in civilian attire and patrolled in unmarked vehicles.[80] Despite public outcry, police repression continued during the following months. On 19 October 1977, police raided the Dominion Square Tavern downtown and arrested twenty-two men on charges of being found-ins. This escalation set the groundwork for the raid at Truxx (1426 Stanley Street), the most infamous bar raid of the period.[81]

On a Friday night, sometime between 21 and 22 October 1977, 155 queer men and women were arrested at Truxx: 145 were charged as found-ins in a bawdy-house, 8 with gross indecency, and 2 with drug possession.[82] Numerous men described the nightmarish events that unfolded.[83] Some had been sitting, drinking, or dancing and others were cruising with undercover agents who feigned sexual interest. At a certain point, lights flooded Truxx and illuminated a pathway for uniformed officers who sported bulletproof vests and wielded machine guns and rifles. A police source told the *Montreal Gazette* that officers had followed protocols: "It's standard policy for police to come equipped with machineguns and bullet-proof vests during major raids."[84] The armed officers hurled insults at and drew weapons on the clients and staff. They arrested scores of men and in the process bruised, shoved, frisked, and intimidated.[85] Montreal police offered two reasons for the militarized raid. In one version it claimed to have been acting on a tip that Truxx's dance floor had been used as a playground for gay sex. In another, it told a *Montreal Gazette* reporter that the goal was to stamp out the "epedemic [*sic*] of armed robberies committed by homosexuals."[86] Later, officers recalled the "indecent acts" they had witnessed, which amounted to hugging, kissing, and groping at the bar and on the dance floor. In the washroom, they allegedly saw men masturbating and, occasionally, performing sexual acts.[87]

The event was the largest police assault on a Canadian queer community since the decriminalization of homosexuality in 1969 and the largest mass arrest in Quebec since the 1970 October Crisis. Those arrested during the Truxx raid were detained for fifteen hours and were forced to undergo a sexually transmitted infection test, a cavity search, and a blood test as a condition of their release.[88] *The Body Politic* reviewed the legal framework that allowed police to charge individuals under bawdy-house laws:

> According to section 179(1)(b) of the Criminal Code, a "common bawdy house" is defined as a public place resorted to "for the purposes of prostitution or the practice of acts of indecency."
>
> Since the bar's owner, Mr Salvagio [*sic*], decided to plead not guilty to the charges of keeping a "bawdy house," the burden of proof rested with the city of Montreal. The Court had already heard the corroborating testimony of the five morality squad officers involved in the raid, and their precise and circumstantial statements seemed to justify the merits of the charge.
>
> In fact, during ten days preceding the raid, plainclothes officers observed activities inside the bar. The numerous allegations of "gross indecency" and "indecent acts" – which were described at great length and in minute detail – constitute the basis of the proof of the charge.[89]

Following the dramatic raid, the ADGQ held an emergency meeting on the afternoon of 22 October.[90] It concluded that a quick and energetic response from the community was necessary, and immediately organized a spontaneous nighttime protest. At midnight, at the intersection of Sainte-Catherine and Stanley streets, protestors slowly started arriving. What started as a timid response quickly turned into the largest gay protest in Canadian history, supplanting the march that had been held on 19 June 1976.[91] Two thousand protestors came together to create an atmosphere that, according to reporters, was reminiscent of 1960s protests. Moreover, the power of place and location was made clear that evening as organizers reaffirmed the queer community's rootedness downtown. However, and despite the demonstration's peaceful procession, the Morality Squad and the anti-riot unit reasserted police power when they charged at the crowd with unexpected force.[92]

The night was at once a time of repression and a time for action. Perhaps counterintuitively, the violent raids and the anti-queer crackdowns convinced closeted individuals to come out in support of gay rights.[93] "The police did us an enormous favor," stated ADGQ president Claude Beaulieu: "We've been swamped with calls from people who never had any interest in gay organizations before … Now, they're prepared to take a stand." One Montreal businessman confirmed this: "I am a citizen of this country. I pay my taxes and I have never considered myself a militant of any sort. But because I am gay, I can no longer sit idly by and watch the police arrest innocent people. I'm mad."[94] While anti-repression work was being done at night, queer rights progressively became mainstream. Representation increased in popular culture, which helped raise awareness for rights advocacy. A week after the Truxx raid, on 27 October, the ADGQ convened with the Commission des droits de la personne and presented a twenty-page document that outlined the organization's demands concerning the 1975 Quebec Charter of Human Rights and Freedoms. The next day, Denise Cassidy, owner of Baby Face, wrote to Normand Caron, secretary of Ligue des droits et libertés (LDL), seeking the organization's backing for amendments related to "sexual orientation" in the charter.[95] The adoption of the charter had helped redefine the norms of social inclusion, but the recent protests and activism forced the Parti Québécois to modify section 10. Bill 88, which the party introduced and supported unanimously, prohibited anti-gay discrimination when it came to housing, employment, and access to public space.[96]

On 18 March 1978, the Comité de défense des accusés du Truxx (CDAT) held a dance at UQÀM to celebrate the community's recent legal victory and also raise funds for the ongoing trial. The CDAT used the dance floor to form alliances and integrate political activism into nightlife. The legal battle was but one of the multi-faceted ways that the community still faced stigmatization. Truxx found-in cases were eventually dropped half a decade later, in December 1983.[97]

Corridart (1976)

By November 1975, after Drapeau had lost total control over the Summer Olympic Games and had turned to working closely with the Police Department in eradicating sexual activity from downtown, Melvin Charney spearheaded a second "shout in the street" – a public art exhibition that would, much like *Montreal, plus or minus?*, question the character of modern urban life.[98]

Charney, as official planner and designer for *Corridart*, pushed to have the exhibition on Sherbrooke Street, to recall its history as a place of ritual and pageantry. Before being transformed into a thoroughfare for cars, it had been a street for processions, parades, and festivals. Charney understood that Sherbrooke Street's history was essentially Montreal's history. The exhibition, a critique of the evolution of North American city streets, underscored the transformation of streets from human scale to the domination of commerce and capital during the mid-twentieth century.[99] And through its name, *Corridart* evoked and mirrored Montreal's other "corridors," like those of the newly built climate-controlled underground city, that were lined with bright boutiques, cinemas, restaurants, and stores. Therefore, *Corridart* was an artful critique of mass consumerism that was designed to "change the living conditions in [Montreal]."[100]

From 7 to 31 July 1976, Sherbrooke Street was supposed to be given back to the public and become a "street-museum." To this end, Charney tried but failed to shut the street to traffic in order to restore the street's sidewalks to their early-twentieth-century width.[101] Since car traffic would continue, *Corridart*'s exhibits would take place in "transitional spaces" that emphasized everyday urban life in Montreal. These are what art critic René Viau described as *entre-lieux* – spaces that function between the world of social change and the modern city, such as balconies, courtyards, gardens, entrances, terraces, squares, alleys, paths, and any other areas accessible to the public.[102] In these spaces, organizers set up temporary stages for plays, readings, and recitals. But to realize this, they also had to uproot healthy trees and rescind parking spots. Along the exhibition's five-and-a-half-mile-long stretch, artists were scheduled to perform at various moments of the day and night. In total, *Corridart* cost $386,000, which was only 5 per cent of the $8 million allocated to "crowd-pleasing events." And despite being a tiny fraction of the cost for the entire Summer Olympics, *Corridart* was the provincial government's largest contribution to the program's visual arts division. In fact, Laurent Lamy, COJO's head of visual arts, described it as "the backbone" of the whole Arts and Culture Program.[103] *Montreal Star* journalist Cynthia Gunn even argued that for the duration of the Olympics – at the very least – Sherbrooke Street could be ranked alongside an international nucleus of beautiful and humane streets, comparable to Paris's Champs-Élysées, London's Park Lane, Rome's Via Veneto, and New York's Fifth Avenue. Sherbrooke Street was "alive with color, art, music, history and information," she argued.[104]

According to one critic, *Corridart*'s success hinged on its ethnographic qualities, found in artworks by Jean-Claude Marsan, Marc Cramer, and Françoise Sullivan. Another critic argued that the true spirit of the exhibition was captured in two works: Pierre Ayot and Denis Forcier's *La croix du Mont Royal sur la rue Sherbrooke*, a giant replica of Montreal's famous lighted Mount Royal cross lying on its side, and Melvin Charney's *Les maisons de la rue Sherbrooke*, a house facade akin to those of a movie set and erected across from the École des Beaux-Arts.[105] Quite simply, *Corridart* evoked a multitude of urban planning failures under the Civic Party by highlighting "ruined city site[s]."[106] The exhibition stood in odd visual juxtaposition to official Olympic streamers that had been created by internationally acclaimed architect and designer François Dallegret. His multicoloured streamers hung across Montreal and gave it a festive atmosphere.[107] Montreal residents, however, felt and knew that *Corridart* was a veritable reflection of everyday life in Montreal – more so than Dallegret's jovial streamers.

As the creative force behind the exhibition, Charney had pushed for the idea of historicizing Sherbrooke Street to scrutinize Montreal's planning problems. Preoccupied by the failures of the city's evolution as a functionalist city, Charney's activism was separate from movements like Save Montreal

(1973–85) or Héritage Montréal (1975–) – the latter being especially concerned with the protection and preservation of colonial relics.[108] Charney, who found heroic matter in Quebec's popular architecture, was much more sympathetic to Montreal's working-class tenements, like those that had been demolished during the push for material modernity in the late 1950s and those that burst into flames during the Red Weekend in 1974. By giving weighty importance to urban planners and architects – crucial actors in the production of spatial forms and arrangements – *Corridart* historicized mid-twentieth-century Sherbrooke Street. Simply put, it was a powerful and provocative critique of reformist policies that explored how street life had been neglected in order to make way for automobiles and commerce. In a very perceptible manner, *Corridart* followed *Montreal, plus or minus?*'s intellectual mission by forcing people to think about the social cost of modern urban development.

Unsurprisingly, many artists took part in both exhibitions, including Bill Vazan, Michael Haslam, John Honeyman (the graphic designer for both), and Jean-Claude Marsan.[109] The relationship between Marsan and Charney was extensive; both spent years lecturing at the Université de Montréal as professors of architecture. During *Montreal, plus or minus?*, Marsan was wrapping up his doctoral research on the socio-political history of architecture in Montreal, and by the time *Corridart* took shape, he had published what would become his magnum opus, *Montreal in Evolution* (1974).[110]

Although conceived by Charney to illustrate the street's history and morphology, the exhibit *Mémoire de la rue Sherbrooke* was executed by Marsan and his students.[111] Like all other artists who contributed to *Corridart*, Marsan had given a lot of thought to the history of capitalism in Montreal. In fact, his photo exhibit, which showed how Sherbrooke Street appeared before it had been transformed by unbridled development, was touted as the true reason behind Mayor Drapeau's fiat. A city lawyer confirmed that the images used by the professor had particularly upset the mayor and the city's executive committee.[112] The images, along with the accompanying texts, described how residents in areas adjacent to Sherbrooke Street – Saint-André Street, Saint-Norbert Street, and Milton-Parc – had contested, fiercely, the Civic Party's hegemonic project.[113] These communities, Marsan effectively argued, had been reduced by the political and financial elites.

The outspoken artists behind *Corridart* did not constitute a fringe artistic segment either. Claude Péloquin, one of Quebec's most revered poets and experimental artists, wrote an opinion piece in which he argued that Drapeau was in the process of replacing the heart and soul of the city for shortsighted financial gains: "Montreal by Night is dead … Thank you Mr Drapeau for killing the woman I loved."[114] This cri de cœur came on the heels of a decision by the mayor to close the Esquire Show Bar, a beloved downtown jazz club. A few weeks later, a journalist for *Le Jour* echoed similar sentiments when he reported on the Corridart Affair. In fact, his article recalled the way that other artists, like Lili St-Cyr, had described the city's transformation during the 1960s. "Montreal is dead," he wrote. "That's what the *Corridart* artists had been trying to tell us. And they were right."[115] The artists' protest, a visual and public art display during Jean Drapeau's most celebrated event, was trenchant and thought-provoking. And such a powerful message demanded a response.

***

On Sunday, 11 July, three weeks after the largest gay rights demonstration in Canadian history, Mayor Drapeau took a drive down Sherbrooke Street in his Lincoln Continental. "I went around by car," Drapeau later stated, "I did the round trip, both ways, slowing down or stopping in certain cases to see what was attached to the construction scaffolds … It shocked me. It humiliated me. It insulted me to realize that Sherbrooke Street would become a dump, for certain of those things were certainly things you find in dumps or headed there."[116] While he drove around, Drapeau saw the finger pointing and the protest art, and he saw how artists had made a mockery of his endeavour to make Montreal the greatest city in the world. The following Tuesday night, Drapeau's flippant remark about how parts of the exhibition looked like they should be headed to the dump became a reality.

When John Gordon, assistant director of COJO's art program, heard from a source that something was about to go down, he phoned Melvin Charney. They immediately drove toward Sherbrooke Street to see what that meant. In the middle of a cool and rainy night between 13 and 14 July 1976, on orders from the executive committee of the City of Montreal, five teams of municipal workers – paid overtime and escorted by police – made their way

Figure 5.3
City employees dismantle Corridart's *Mémoire de la rue Sherbrooke* in the dead of night with the help of a crane, 13–14 July 1976.

down Sherbrooke Street to dismantle *Corridart*. The employees proceeded in a flotilla of cranes and a score of trucks and followed orders that instructed them to rid Sherbrooke Street of artworks. On an otherwise dark and silent Tuesday night, under the glare of floodlights, city employees unmoored, destroyed, and expelled the artworks from public sight. Using hex keys and crowbars they began with Marsan's *Mémoire de la rue Sherbrooke* (fig. 5.3). Gordon pleaded with them to halt – or at least pause – their destructive assignment. His interference was met with police officers placing him in custody and hauling him off to jail, though no charges were filed.[117]

The fact that authorities had assigned police officers to stand by city employees during the process provided clear evidence that the undertaking held the potential for violent confrontations. But more telling still was the fact that they had acted under the cover of darkness and hidden from public scrutiny. This destruction could not have happened during the light of day when Sherbrooke Street bustled with residents and tourists. As dawn broke on 14 July, Montreal residents read the executive committee's rationale in the *Montreal Star*: "the exhibit violated by-laws on the occupancy of public domain and were a safety hazard."[118] Once the process was underway, the city stayed on course the next day, loading the facades of Charney's *Les maisons de la rue Sherbrooke* in a dump truck and hauling the artwork to the city pound on Louvain Street. And in the following days, employees returned to Sherbrooke Street to pry out the works that had been too cumbersome or difficult to remove from the street.[119] Some were dismantled by the artists themselves, both out of solidarity and out of fear that city workers would damage their works. Eventually, everything that had to do with *Corridart* – including street performances and public activities – was cancelled.

In the wake of *Corridart*'s destruction, reporters, artists, civil rights organizations, and politicians from across Canada underlined the surreptitious nature of the manoeuvre. They contended that the censorship of art had been a crime against the freedom of expression and a political manoeuvre against social change.[120] It was a clear display of Drapolice in action, argued others.[121] Given that *Corridart* was mostly funded by the province, one McGill University political science professor claimed that it was an unprecedented and a historical moment in municipal-provincial relations: "This is undoubtedly the greatest blow the Montreal administration has ever administered to the provincial government. It's unbelievable! The furtive nighttime destruction of state approved artworks (since doing so in broad daylight would have required too much courage) is nothing but first-rate imbecility."[122]

On the night of 15 July, some demonstrators marched on Place des Arts and read an anti-censorship manifesto. The protest took shape following reports that the mayor's office had cancelled the "terrasse de lecture," a youth-oriented, free, and festive street kiosk coordinated by the city's head librarian to promote literacy and an openness to different cultures during the Summer Olympic Games.[123] The following day, MCM councillor Nick Auf der Maur and Simonne Monet-Chartrand of the Ligue des droits de l'homme organized a street demonstration in solidarity with the city's arts and culture industry.[124] And during the Games' five-hundred-odd cultural events – which included Quebec folk dances, ballets, plays, concerts of symphonic and chamber music, and shows that were part of the Arts and Culture Program – artists read an official statement in solidarity with *Corridart*: "It is with regret that we must ask ourselves in the face of the world: What is freedom to Montreal? It is the freedom of powerful, small-minded men to efface what they find offensive. It is the freedom of demolition crews to emerge by night and, guarded by police, to destroy without notice a work of art. It is freedom accorded to the rulers of our city but to no other citizens. It is the freedom of a police state."[125] The statement reminded those who had come to revel in the glory of the Summer Olympic Games that Montrealers were under intense police surveillance. It was a message that poets echoed during the *Solstice de la Poésie Québécoise*. On the night of 23 July, they read a manifesto that also questioned the connection between the Games, modern capitalism, and police and military presence in the city.[126]

Acting as a gatekeeper of cultural tastes, Drapeau was the mastermind behind what everyone had seen as a covert, yet brazen, act of censorship. While the executive committee argued that *Corridart* had been dismantled because it did not comply with the bylaw concerning the occupation of public space and that it was a hazard to public safety, artists knew this to be a pretext because the Police Department had vetted the site before it opened to the public. "Mr Drapeau saw how *Corridart* was a flagrant critique of his *œuvre* and he could not resist the temptation to obliterate it," observed a journalist in *La Presse*.[127]

Afterlife and Trial

As had been the case with nightclub and bathhouse raids, the raid on *Corridart* took place at night. In the competing visions of order that clashed under the cover of darkness, the mayor opted to preserve the city's "integrity" and, in his view, keep it clear of obscene debris.[128] Indeed, the mayor seized the opportunity provided by the 1976 Summer Olympic Games to clear public spaces of nonconforming sexual and artistic forces. This began in 1975 with the crackdown on gay clubs, and continued with the destruction of street art.

Only after the end of the Games were the artworks released to the creators. The city held it all for forty days and nights, without due process, which meant the affair had begun to fade from public conversation. In late August 1976, Drapeau was invited to testify before members of the National Assembly's Commission permanente des affaires municipales et de l'environnement to explain the outrageous cost of the Summer Olympic Games. When the subject of *Corridart* surfaced, he offered the following statement: "This affair along Sherbrooke Street was one of the most incredible farce, fraud, I go as far as the word fraud, that could be imagined."[129] Saint-Jacques MNA Claude Charron retorted by asking under what right he had destroyed publicly funded art and why he did so at night: "you hate critiques, you hate opposition, you're afraid of admitting your administration's wrongdoings, not only when you've demolished homes, but even when you've demolished pictures of those homes. You're afraid of facing responsibility for actions you took under the cloak of darkness ... you've acted like a dictator, an emperor, as you've always done with the City of Montreal."[130] Stopping short of labelling Drapeau a demagogue, Charron, a queer Montrealer who was cognizant of the presence of political and police powers "under the cloak of darkness," voiced the public's frustration as he advocated for the artists.

In the fall of 1976, months after they regained procession of their artworks and saw the extent of the damage, thirteen *Corridart* artists filed a $355,000 lawsuit against the City of Montreal and COJO for wasted time, damage to reputation, loss of prestige, inconvenience, and financial loss.[131] Anticipating a long and unpredictable trial, the artists funded their legal fees by creating more art – notably postcards published by Véhicule Press.[132] As art historian Louise Descoteaux notes, although they brought the City of Montreal and COJO to court, the plaintiffs and their lawyers were clearly after Mayor Drapeau.[133] When Drapeau was called to testify in mid-January 1981, he reiterated his claim that *Corridart* had been aesthetically worthless, demeaning to the city's appearance, and contravened city bylaws. In short, it was antithetical to Montreal's triumphant message to global visitors. His testimony, however, contradicted what other appellants said, and he denied full responsibility for the artworks' removal. For instance, when he was asked why the works had been removed at night, he pleaded ignorance, stating that it was probably to avoid a traffic jam along Sherbrooke Street.[134] And he remained defiant: he stood by his claim that the undoing of *Corridart* had been neither an act of censorship nor an assault on the laws governing the freedom of expression. This stance received support from some politicians and citizens, including David Stewart of the non-profit Macdonald Stewart Foundation, who stated that *Corridart*'s message was an insult to Montreal: "I was born on Sherbrooke St I work on Sherbrooke St and I live on Sherbrooke St. If people want obscenity, that's fine with me. But not in the street. Art, according to the dictionary, means something beautiful, gay. There's nothing in the definition of art that says it should be obscene or provocative."[135] Ironically, Stewart's NIMBYism – speaking as a wealthy elite about "his" city and "his" street – personified *Corridart*'s anti-capitalist critique, its entire raison d'être. Incidentally, Charney observed how those who railed against the exhibition's artistic merit were mostly anglophone Montrealers; others, he noted, were happy to see an artistic representation of *their* city.[136]

At the trial, artists, art experts, critics, and politicians debated the resoundingly awkward notion of beauty and aesthetics. The debate exemplified the twentieth century's seismic shift in culture and the way that it had totally transformed people's ways of comprehending reality and art production. In fact, the discourse typified what historian Eric Hobsbawm claimed was the end of "traditional privileged status of 'the arts' in the old bourgeois society, that is to say their function as measures of good and bad, as carriers of value: of truth, beauty and catharsis."[137] By focusing on the concept of "beauty," the trial sidestepped the whole array of urban issues that was at the heart of *Corridart*.

In the end, Superior Court Justice Ignace J. Deslauriers ruled in favour of the city. *Corridart*'s lack of beauty created a malaise, and the judge described the whole exhibition as a failed anti-modernist critique by Marxists who disapproved of urban reforms.[138] Artists could not believe that Deslauriers, like Drapeau, dismissed the value of their art and that he held a narrow understanding of artistic expression, one rooted in the tricky notion of beauty.[139] Needless to say, Deslauriers's decision sent a shockwave across the country. Energized by overwhelming public support, the artists brought their case before the Quebec Court of Appeal. To finance this appeal, they created *Corridart 1976–*, an oversized book of prints published by the artist-run print workshop and gallery Graff. Its preface states: "*Corridart 1976–*, produced by artists for the defense of a cause which concerns all artists, rises against totalitarianism and interference … [*Corridart 1976–*] affirms the will to maintain within art its function of free expression and reaffirms the position of the artists involved and the testimony of the experts."[140] The Corridart Affair would be settled out of court twelve years later in 1988. Under a new mayor, the city awarded $85,000 to the plaintiffs. After paying legal fees, each artist received a meagre compensation of roughly $3,000.[141]

Conclusion

The repression of Montreal's gay community and the censorship of artistic works allowed Mayor Drapeau to curate an image of the city designed to appeal to international visitors and secure its global appeal. At night, police officers equipped themselves with crowbars to pry their way into bathhouses and nightclubs, and city employees used the same tools to pry apart the artworks lining Sherbrooke Street. Ultimately, night was a moment for authorities to express control over public and social spaces through structure, regulation, and control.

This chapter shows how the Civic Party was concerned with optics in an increasingly globalized world and how, in response, activists used city streets to defy its vision and authority. It shows the extent to which nighttime reproduced some forms of power, while also providing opportunities for resistance in other settings. The battleground between repressive power and cultural resistance was heightened in the months leading up to the Summer Olympic Games. Defiance, however, took different forms. For instance, in lieu of well-established platforms and institutions like those offered to Melvin Charney for his exhibitions, Montreal's queer folk resorted to community organizing and street demonstrations. Experiencing the Civic Party's rueful urban reforms and its repressive manoeuvres, Montrealers challenged and fought modernism and its ties to commerce and capital. And at every step along the way, the municipal administration received help from the police to quell challenges and defiance, whether it meant raids on queer nightspots or supervising city employees who had to dispose of artworks.

According to artists, the Corridart Affair had been an "inglorious night incarnating the triumph of reactionary forces."[142] Its censorship occurred because the exhibition's message posed a direct threat to the Civic Party's aims and goals to make Montreal a global city. Much later in the artists' continued fight for justice, an out-of-court settlement was reached. By then, Jean Doré was serving as mayor of Montreal under the MCM, while Jean Drapeau had retired from politics and taken on the role of ambassador and permanent delegate to UNESCO (1987–91). For their part, citizens of the whole province had to contend with an Olympic debt of $1.5 billion, which the province finally finished paying off thirty years after the Games in 2006.[143] Like the events that transformed liquor legislation and those that led to the Night of Terror and the Red Weekend, the crackdown on art and the attack on the queer community forced the Quebec government to intervene and resolve the problems created by the Civic Party. In many ways, this, plus the financial fiasco of the Summer Olympic Games, was the end of Jean Drapeau's obsessive edifice complex. As it became increasingly clear that Montreal would not evolve into the metropolis he desired, he tempered his ambitions and refocused the Civic Party's attention on local needs. But in addressing those, the Civic Party continued to refine the city's image at night by cracking down on street-based sex work – and on that occasion, the federal government was forced to intervene.

6

SEX WORK AND SEXIST BYLAWS

For Mayor Jean Drapeau, the 1978 election came with challenges and challengers that, in stark contrast to earlier elections, nearly prevailed over the Civic Party. Throughout the campaign the opposition contended that the party misunderstood Montrealers' thirst for policies that met their everyday needs. Thus, in the wake of that election, after the Civic Party won a slim victory with 60 per cent of the vote, it appointed young and ambitious politician Yvon Lamarre to chair the executive committee to show that it was serious about meeting the everyday needs of residents.[1]

Lamarre, who remained chair until Drapeau retired in 1986, responded to opponents and critics by making it his mission to improve Montrealers' quality of life. In particular, he focused on human-scale "beautification" projects, like upgrading old commercial streets with new street lights, pedestrian malls, and decorative paving and planters, which revitalized and enlivened the city. Lamarre also went on to establish what one reporter called the municipal administration's most laudable endeavour – the Maisons de la culture de Montréal, a project that placed the Sherbrooke Street municipal library at the centre of a network of branches promoting literature, poetry, theatre, art, music, and films. In 1981, two years after the Civic Party announced the project, the first branch opened in the low-income neighbourhood of Hochelaga-Maisonneuve, and within a decade another seven opened in adjacent neighbourhoods.[2] In 1979 the city also launched the Commission d'initiative et de développement économiques de Montréal (CIDEM) to stimulate economic growth. Under Lamarre, the CIDEM assumed responsibility for public housing by creating Opération 10,000 logements. This beautification project was created to reduce the outflow of middle-class residents to the suburbs by offering financial incentives to real estate developers and middle-class buyers.[3]

But as Lamarre beautified Montreal through urban renewal, high culture, and housing projects, he also embarked on a parallel mission that promised to refine the city's image. "The Drapeau-Lamarre administration continues its 'beautification campaign' by waging war against soliciting, prostitution, and drinking in public space," reported *La Presse* in May 1980 after City Hall passed anti-prostitution and anti-drinking bylaws.[4] While the idea of banning public drinking was straightforward – the city would clamp down on public inebriation, especially in parks and in tourist-heavy Old Montreal – the idea behind the bylaw that banned prostitution and soliciting was flawed and impractical. Unlike public drinking, prostitution and soliciting were devoid of material evidence and would be based on when and how women occupied public space. Moreover, because both bylaws were designed to make public space more visually appealing, each had little to no effect on discreet and upscale markets. People who could afford to pay for sex or drinks on private properties or in licensed establishments could continue their transactions; meanwhile, officers would patrol streets, cracking down on presumed sex workers and drinkers.[5] The city wanted to eradicate the visibility of sex workers, and as this chapter demonstrates, this process was inextricably linked to policing gender, race, and language. By enacting these bylaws, City Hall had placed nighttime at the centre of ongoing debates over profiling women and, crucially, their right to the city in 1980s Montreal.

The idea that the Civic Party's anti-prostitution bylaw could be implemented without pushback was more than impractical: it was illegal, for it was the municipal administration's attempt at circumventing a 1978 Supreme Court of Canada decision that amended the Criminal Code. The Supreme Court had ruled that for prostitution to be an offence it had to be "pressing and persistent." This decision posed a social and legal problem for Canadian municipal authorities because local police departments could not provide evidence of "pressing and persistent" soliciting. According to *Maclean's*, following the ruling, major streets across Canadian cities had turned into "sexual supermarkets."[6] In Montreal, street-based sex workers returned to the Red Light district in such volume that one police officer claimed that "no male [could] go through the area without being automatically accosted," and one journalist wrote, "decent folk off in search of the traditional 'steamie' have noticed the St Lawrence Main is as bad as it was before Jean Drapeau's 1950s clean-up."[7] The ruling had quashed the department's authority in establishing and limiting an unofficial zone of toleration for sex workers. Moreover, the Supreme Court decision emboldened both clients (pedestrians and drivers alike) and sex workers to use the Red Light district's streets as a meeting place. It was this feedback loop – adding both supply and demand – that led to the regrowth of the sex industry in the district. And because the tenement rows that housed brothels during the 1950s had been bulldozed, sex workers now worked from the district's streets.

Civic Party councillors who made their way home from City Hall at night found themselves strolling among sex workers who whispered solicitations from sidewalks. They claimed that the area was besieged with nuisances that were linked to street-based sex work like traffic, noise, and the public consumption of alcohol and drugs. The sex industry's proliferation, they further claimed, constituted a threat to the city's image. Thus, the project of policing sex work was not simply a contest over the limits of permissible sexual practice and social conduct in public space. It was also the site of an institutional struggle over the boundaries of the criminal justice system itself.

The anti-prostitution bylaw, with its vague language, was also widely perceived as a tool granting police excessive discretion over what women could do in public spaces. Just days after City Hall passed the anti-prostitution bylaw, a coalition of rights activists known as the "groupe de pression 80–81," which included city council members of the opposition as well as members from queer, feminist, and labour rights groups, protested its inherently sexist framework.[8] The bylaw tapped into long-standing traditions in policing, where an officer's decision to arrest often relied on their interpretation of "arrestable behaviour" – an appraisal based on a woman's appearance, the company she allegedly kept, and the time and place in which she was apprehended. As the following paragraphs demonstrate, the anti-prostitution bylaw allowed police to disproportionately monitor Black and Indigenous women – particularly those who spoke English – as they patrolled public space at night.[9] Moreover, the chapter also shows that this renewed attempt to govern nighttime public space was not an isolated case. Rather, it was part of a long and continuous history of police using prostitution (by)laws to target women who were not of the dominant race or ethnic group and were thought to threaten the social order.[10]

Despite mounting complaints, Civic Party councillors assured the public that the anti-prostitution bylaw was practical because it not only cleared city streets from unwanted soliciting but also made them "safer." This claim, which councillors repeated for months, incensed feminists and rights activists who responded by evoking the irony of "protecting" male residents from the "dangers" of soliciting sex workers. "I would love for [councillors] to see how women are solicited on city streets, day and night," commented one woman, "unlike yours, her safety is always at risk."[11] Critics railed against the fact that men enacted a bylaw that shielded them from sex workers but failed to address the long history of sexual violence and dangers that women faced in public space. Furthermore, the bylaw also gave a political dimension to the most innocent practice – "remain[ing] in a public place" – which allowed police to clear parks and streets of innocent bystanders. The spatial mobility of the trade made it seem particularly hard to control, and its regulation even more urgent. Although the Civic Party paid scant attention to critics, the mounting letters, rallies, and protests set the tone for a long legal battle between the party and civil rights groups. Ultimately, the anti-prostitution bylaw typified the Civic Party's political agenda because its focus rested upon upholding the city's image and new-found global reputation rather than safeguarding its population from veritable dangers. Under these circumstances, the governance of nighttime public space became a terrain where profound questions about sex, gender, and the right to the city emerged.

This chapter examines the administration's response to the shifting nature of sex work in the late 1970s and early 1980s. During this period, as architects and planners put much thought into the beautification of residential areas to recreate lively, safe, and attractive streets for residents and business in the aftermath of hallmark events like Expo 67 and the 1976 Summer Olympic Games, the sex industry's visibility on nighttime city streets increased.[12] City administrators contended that beautification and sex work were diametrically opposed. Therefore, rather than create safe conditions for sex work or focus on the social and economic factors that gave rise to it, the Civic Party held fast to its strategy of removing sex from public view. Similar to instances of morals policing examined in previous chapters, the vagueness of the administration's 1980 anti-prostitution bylaw allowed police to engage in surveillance of sex-related business and would be based on officers' dubious ability to discern individuals who contributed to the industry, which often brought to the forefront anxieties relating to race, language, and gender.

Eventually, the bylaw was struck down by the Supreme Court of Canada in a swift and decisive ruling because it overstepped the exclusive federal responsibility for dealing with prostitution. The ruling, however, was quickly answered by the Civic Party's enactment of an anti-soliciting bylaw in 1983, which was presented under the pretense of prohibiting vendors from "soliciting" in public space. Although the party had support from members of the public, police, merchants, and some feminists who were leading congruent campaigns against prostitution and pornography, the anti-soliciting bylaw was also met with challenges from civil rights, labour, and sex work activists.[13]

Because similar police crackdowns happened across Canada during the early 1980s, a growing movement for sex workers' rights started to take shape. In different cities, sex workers challenged local bylaws and mainstream stigma by organizing for working rights at a moment when the global pandemic of HIV/AIDS surfaced. Again, rather than addressing health concerns, local politicians fixated their efforts on having the federal government change the Criminal Code and ease the restrictions on prosecuting sex workers. In June 1983, following sustained pressure from Jean Drapeau and mayors of Toronto, Calgary, and Vancouver, the federal government convened the Special Committee on Pornography and Prostitution to examine the place of the sex industry within Canadian society. Ultimately, and a few months before Drapeau's retirement, the Criminal Code was amended. Revisiting these anti–sex industry campaigns sheds light on a chapter of Montreal history that is frequently shocking but also full of resistance, surprising alliances, and remarkable legal gambits.

Street-based Sex Work in the Late 1970s

The situation was such that no man could walk through Sainte-Catherine and Saint-Laurent streets without being solicited … It's a little discouraging to work in this sector because [prostitution] is eternal.[14]
– City of Montreal lawyer, 1980

As previous chapters have shown, street-based sex work increased in the aftermath of municipal crackdowns on the old bawdy-house system. In Montreal this became more visible on sidewalks and in parks that were already associated with vice and where police were less inclined to enforce prostitution laws. At times, however, police coordinated cleanup operations in these same spots to maintain the image of law enforcement and to meet previously established arrest quotas.[15] But following a 1978 Supreme Court of Canada ruling on the nature of "soliciting," the number of street-based sex workers grew, not only in Montreal but also across Canadian cities. Stretching back to Canada's first Criminal Code in 1892, and essentially unchanged until 1972, prostitution was treated as a "status" offence associated with vagrancy: "being a common prostitute or nightwalker is found in a public place and does not, when required, give a good account of herself." In 1972 it was repealed because it was unjust to arrest a person for reasons of identity alone. While this legal reform addressed some of the recommendations that had been made by the Royal Commission on the Status of Women in Canada (1970) concerning the Criminal Code's sexist and anachronistic terms, the soliciting law that replaced it focused on behaviour by prohibiting individuals from soliciting in a public place for the purpose of prostitution.[16]

Enforcement of this legislation was problematic, however, and a case reached the country's highest court after Debra Hutt, a Vancouver sex worker, was arrested and charged by an undercover police officer. She appealed on the grounds that she had entered the officer's car with his consent and had identified herself as a sex worker and discussed terms for her services. In February 1978, the Supreme Court ruled that for a person to be charged with soliciting, his or her behaviour had to be "pressing and persistent," and also indicated that a private car on a public thoroughfare did not constitute a "public place."[17] Immediately following this decision, all cases where the evidence of soliciting was based on a woman's physical overtures in public were thrown out of court. The decision limited the power of police officers because they could not provide evidence that sex workers' propositions were pressing and persistent. As a result, following the Hutt decision, police departments across Canada lobbied municipal administrations to create tougher anti-soliciting bylaws. Police departments and municipal administrations, including Jean Drapeau's Civic Party, embarked on a multilateral political campaign to amend the Criminal Code.

***

Street-based sex work flourished amidst soaring unemployment during the early 1980s, while also being profoundly reshaped by the HIV/AIDS pandemic.[18] These developments led investigative journalists and filmmakers to produce thought-provoking content about the sex industry. For instance, two journalists wrote a book-length ethnographic report about sex workers. Louise, a sex worker, expressed her thoughts on the "catch and release" system, explaining to the journalists how her legal troubles hindered her hopes for a better life: "You spend the night in a cell and the next morning the police take you to the Municipal Court. There, the judge gives you a fine … Then you go home and you can start working again!"[19] Louise could laugh at the authorities' attempt to control and eliminate the industry, but as the authors' report emphasized, her trade was more often than not characterized by substance abuse, male domination, and harsh legal penalties.[20] Several films also provided insight into the legal and social implications of sex work. For instance, *Nose and Tina* (1980) showed how Linda M., a Winnipeg-based Indigenous massage parlour worker, managed despite legal difficulties; *Not a Love Story: A Film About Pornography* (1981) followed Montreal stripper Linda Lee Tracey in her pursuit to understand the contours of the sex industry; and Genie Award winner for Best Feature Length Documentary *Plusieurs tombent en amour* (1979) offered a comprehensive and humorous exposé of Montreal's sex industry in lengthy testimonies from sex workers, queer and transgender community members, clients, a pimp, and police officers. Recorded after the Hutt decision, *Plusieurs tombent en amour* illustrates how street-based sex work greatly varied according to geographic location, economic background, gender identities, and sexual orientation.[21]

Table 6.1
The number of sex work-related offences in Montreal, 1974–87

Year	Criminal Code–Common Bawdy-House (Section 193): number of offences	Criminal Code–Soliciting or Communicating (Section 195): number of offences	Municipal bylaw	Number of offences
1974	64	439		
1975	140	581		
1976	371	512		
1977	351	375		
1978	183	64	Traffic Bylaw 333	?
1979	119	16	Traffic Bylaw 333	?
1980	254	25	Anti-prostitution Bylaw 5464	?
1981	286	11	Anti-prostitution Bylaw 5464	? ?
1982	98	7	Anti-prostitution Bylaw 5464	401
1982			Traffic Bylaw 333	16
1983	100	8	Anti-prostitution Bylaw 5464	339
1983			Traffic Bylaw 333	204
1983			Anti-soliciting Bylaw 6249	73
1984	321		Anti-soliciting Bylaw 6249	853
1985	675		Anti-soliciting Bylaw 6249	1,189
1986	692	1,621		
1987	299	2,335		

Note: As the authors of the report point out, there may be several people charged for one offence. A charge of keeping a common bawdy-house may involve several people.
Sources: Gemme et al., *Report on Prostitution in Quebec*, 64–6; Gemme, *Street Prostitution*, 43, 61, 106.

Because the Hutt decision undermined the Montreal Police Department's ability to enforce soliciting laws, officers resorted to a street-regulating bylaw to clear sex workers from streets and parks. Article 2b of traffic bylaw 333 allowed officers to arrest pedestrians for "strolling or loitering at night in the streets, lanes, fields, yards or other places in the City and who cannot satisfactorily account for his presence there."[22] The bylaw was an adequate tool insofar as it allowed police to uphold an anti–sex work agenda despite the Hutt decision or the legal hurdles placed by the Supreme Court. For instance, a *Montreal Gazette* journalist who joined two Morality Squad officers for a night beat along Sainte-Catherine Street – "prostitution alley" as the officers called it – reported that the officers had enforced the bylaw to arrest and fine several women.[23] A few weeks later, officers cleared the streets of twenty-six sex workers in the span of thirty minutes by again enforcing that bylaw.[24] Quite simply, the data shows how the department weaponized the bylaw to replace section 195 of the Criminal Code: charges under the Criminal Code decreased 89 per cent from 1975 to 1979 while those under traffic bylaw 333 skyrocketed 210 per cent from 1978 to 1979.[25] Still, an internal police report maintained that the Morality Squad faced persistent challenges because the traffic bylaw was only enforceable at night and in public space, which meant that police could do nothing about sex work in vehicles or in nightclubs.[26] Table 6.1 shows the pattern of arrests under various bylaws as well as bawdy-house and prostitution laws in Montreal from 1976 to 1987.

Officers also managed the proliferation of the sex industry by profiling the race and spoken language of women in public space. According to Marie Arrington, activist and founding member of the Vancouver-based Alliance for the Safety of Prostitutes, Montreal's street-based sex work, like that of other Canadian cities, comprised a large number of Black and Indigenous sex workers.[27] Summertime, as previous chapters have demonstrated, was a lucrative season for sex workers, and many came to the city's Red Light district hoping to earn their share of profits. During tourist season in 1979, for instance, transient Black sex workers and pimps moved to Montreal from Halifax, Vancouver, Toronto, and American cities. And as the aforementioned internal police report reveals, it was these English-speaking Black women and men that officers of the Morality Squad profiled and charged.[28] The police report, sent to executive committee chair Yvon Lamarre, also claimed that transient sex workers crossed the Canadian border illegally, which compounded the illicitness of the industry. But this assumption was debunked by a group of researchers who found that Black-American sex workers were overrepresented in arrests, although they accounted for only 1.7 per cent of street-based sex work. They conclude: "Thus, either this is really a marginal phenomenon following enforcement of the law, under which prostitutes are handed over to immigration authorities who deport them, or they work secretly or with false identity papers."[29]

The Police Department's anti-Black racism reached the public spotlight that year for two additional reasons. First, the endemic problem of racial profiling received attention during a public consultation on the future of the Police Department.[30] Second, and more infamously, on the last day of that public consultation, police officers singled out Black youths for night-time loitering in Sainte-Bernadette Park after white neighbours had cavilled about teens lingering after a soccer game. "Why can't Haitians stay in the park like others?" protested one youth. His line of inquiry, however, only led to an officer placing him under arrest. As tensions mounted between Black bystanders and police, officers started beating and verbally abusing Haitian community members with inexplicable viciousness.[31] In the days and weeks that followed, Haitian community members, backed by close to two dozen anti-racist groups, protested the department's anti-Black racism on the streets and in court. What would become known as Le Comité du 20 juin furthered the agenda for police reform by bringing into conversation five items that could minimize police brutality and profiling: multicultural training, diversity recruitment, police and community dialogue, reform of police deontology, and reduction of discretionary powers.[32]

Despite clear assertions of authority, particularly at night, Montreal police consistently voiced frustration over their limited control of public spaces, especially after the 1978 Hutt decision. By the end of 1979, Montreal chief of police Henri-Paul Vignola sent a letter to Yvon Lamarre requesting that the Civic Party help in "amending the laws so that they may … help protect society."[33] This request came on the heels of an important meeting between the Canadian Association of Chiefs of Police (CACP) and federal Justice Minister Jacques Flynn. The CACP stressed the need for tougher "anti-prostitution laws," notably through amendments around requiring proof that solicitation had been pressing and persistent, considering a motor vehicle to be a public place, and enabling prosecution of men as well as women for soliciting.[34]

Translocal Co-operation: Anti-Prostitution Bylaw 5464

The expansion and contraction of sex workers' rights during the postwar period suggested shifting ideas about the sex industry and policing in urban Canada. Whether authorities understood the industry based on gender, notions of public and private space, or temporality, each aspect influenced how sex work would be regulated.

A clear example of this understanding materialized in May 1980 when Montreal passed two bylaws that gave police additional power over public space. Anti-prostitution bylaw 5464 and anti-drinking bylaw 5465 immediately transformed the requirements for charging someone for prostitution, public drinking, and nighttime loitering. These bylaws were purportedly enacted under the municipal powers derived from the provinces, which allows cities to regulate street usage and restrict activities that encourage criminality. It is no exaggeration to claim that once enacted, they immediately transformed the culture of the city. In fact, the anti-drinking bylaw disrupted plans for the celebration of Quebec's national holiday, Saint-Jean-Baptiste Day, which was only a few weeks away. Because the bylaw prohibited public drinking and noisy activities after midnight, Saint-Jean-Baptiste Day organizers were left with the dreadful task of disentangling the French-Canadian holiday from alcohol consumption. The president of the Corporation des fêtes de la Saint-Jean, the organization that planned the celebration, sent a letter to Lamarre and Chief Vignola requesting tolerance and collaboration – in short, for the city to forget about the bylaw it had just enacted. In the end, authorities decided to tolerate public drinking and noise during the fete. But since Montrealers assumed that police would enforce City Hall's anti-drinking bylaw, the fete was "not celebrated with as much gusto as in previous years."[35]

Anti-prostitution bylaw 5464 was not administered with the same level of flexibility: it was ruthlessly enforced. This led to many charges and arrests within days of it being passed, pleasing the authorities. Because it was applied alongside the anti-drinking bylaw, they reported a significant decline in loitering, disorderly conduct, and drunkenness in the Red Light district.[36] Officers enforced both bylaws in the downtown area as well. There, they allegedly dismantled another "ring of prostitution" involving Black Americans when they arrested and charged dozens of sex workers and pimps whose networks extended from borderland cities like Buffalo and Detroit to southern states like Florida and Georgia. One can assume that some of the women would have been familiar with Québécois snowbirds.[37]

The anti-prostitution bylaw no longer required officers to prove that soliciting had been pressing and persistent when making an arrest and charging sex workers because it prohibited "any person to remain in a public place for purposes of prostitution or to approach another person for the same purposes in such a place."[38] The bylaw was clearly part of the administration's "beautification campaign." This was confirmed when Yvon Lamarre maintained that prostitution could not take place in broad daylight, in public space, and at the expense of people and tourists.[39] His comment effectively revealed that Montreal authorities, like authorities in other major cities, tolerated "invisible" forms of sex work (like escort services, massage and body rub parlours, and brothels) unless public complaints or concerns brought to light the criminal underclass.[40] What was most telling about his comment was how the Civic Party approached street-based sex work. Rather than responding to the economic and social factors that gave rise to it or attempting to regulate health hazards, the city allocated resources to the police. And, as Lamarre told reporters, this was for the benefit of out-of-towners.

From the start, many recognized the anti-prostitution bylaw as a flawed regulation because it punished female sex workers and – consistent with sexist laws that exempted customers from punishment – it left male clients completely free from penalty.[41] In feminist outlets and in the mainstream press, critics challenged authorities to end the long history of prosecuting women for physical overtures: "Why are women always being policed? Why is it serious for a woman to wink at a man when men whistle, catcall, and honk at women every single day? … But that's not a big deal, it's not 'soliciting.' Why are you policing our behaviour?"[42] A journalist confronted a police lieutenant by asking him to explain why clients were not charged under the bylaw, but he had little to say on the subject: "it's unthinkable and illogical," he surmised, "we can't charge him for paying."[43] The civil rights association Ligue des droits et libertés also weighed in on the debate and railed against the administration for enacting a bylaw that reinforced sexist hierarchies of power and privilege. The association argued that aggressive anti–sex work policing was to blame for the problems that plagued the sex industry, which is why it would soon challenge the bylaw in court. Furthermore, statements like the above were echoed by academics and labour rights activists.[44]

How, then, did sex workers react after being charged under the new bylaw? Like many other Montrealers during this period, they organized and brought the city to court. Fernande St-Martin-Poitras, who was arrested in the so-called prostitution alley on the night of 19 June 1980, challenged the bylaw's legitimacy. Her case, marked by irregular and shoddy police work, reveals how court sentences often relied on unsubstantiated police accounts during trials. After being found guilty, she appealed on the grounds that she had been tried without supporting evidence and, crucially, that the bylaw was ultra vires. Municipal Court Judge Bernard Tellier heard St-Martin-Poitras's appeal in 1981, and although he ruled in her favour based on the testimonies of the initial hearing, he dismissed the ultra vires claim. In the context of this chapter, perhaps the most important aspect of that decision concerned the connection between the bylaw and the Criminal Code: "The Court finds that the section of the Criminal Code deals directly with prostitution, whereas bylaw 5464 simply touches on one aspect of it – safeguarding against the proliferation of brothels, soliciting-areas or disorder and any other ill-famed space, thereby allowing citizens to exercise their right to move freely and peacefully in public space and on city streets, in particular."[45]

As the legal battle against the bylaw made its way through the courts, a parallel and intensifying discourse on the recognition of sex workers' rights began to emerge. For example, two trans sex workers formed Calling Out Against Discrimination (COAD), a paralegal defence group that supported Montreal sex workers and publicized police misconduct. It highlighted how sex workers were arrested for loitering without warnings; it revealed that police kept women in holding cells for weeks before standing trial; and it exposed sexual misconduct during interrogations. Above all, it empowered sex workers by informing them of their rights and encouraging pleas of not guilty, court defences, and appeals.[46]

Feminists and sex workers organized, seized editorial space, and mocked the authorities' sexist interpretation and control of public space. One of the most evocative pieces was penned by six women and published in both *Le Devoir* and *La Presse*. Their open letter to city councillors openly ridiculed the gendered experience of modern public (night)life. The humorous letter, written after councillors claimed to have been harassed by sex workers on Saint-Laurent Boulevard, took aim at the administration's unchanging attitude about the place of women in society. It parodied a line of questioning usually reserved for women who, though the victims of harassment, were asked about clothes, being in public space after dark, and regular sexual partners. It mocked police work and twisted warnings characteristically reserved for women: "In our society this kind of inconvenience is inevitable for men. You shouldn't expect to be able to wander, day and night, on any street without taking risks. It's up to you to take the necessary precautions. In order to gain more confidence, you should take self-defence classes."[47] As criticisms mounted, elected officials continued to claim that the bylaw had transformed the streets of Montreal into harassment-free zones. By the end of 1980, one Civic Party councillor asserted that the anti-prostitution bylaw created an environment that allowed residents to "walk on any street at any given hour without the fear of being harassed by these undesirables."[48]

The police, however, faced persistent problems when administering the bylaw: figuring out which women were sex workers and what to do about male clients. Police had been profiling women with mixed results in the Red Light district, and because soliciting had not dropped as much as they had hoped, it led to myriad complaints. Women – students, office workers, and "honest" homemakers – disclosed that men harassed passersby with catcalls and offers for sex. Upset Sainte-Catherine Street merchants grumbled about the undesirable customers that the sex industry attracted. Amidst this public pressure, the Police Department embarked on an entrapment campaign by placing undercover policewomen in the district. The ruse proved successful: the department arrested eighteen men within two hours. But in a frustrating twist, the entrapped johns were never prosecuted because they fell beyond the purview of the anti-prostitution bylaw. As a city lawyer reminded reporters, "the law was brought in to clear the streets of prostitutes, not clients."[49] The statement reiterated how male norms of reason and respectability guided the city's position. Rather than targeting all segments of the sex industry, the city focused on women who offered sex but not men who sought and bought it.

Rights groups invoked the bylaw's sexist legal framework to articulate legal challenges. By the end of 1980, another sex worker, Johanne Meli – who also had been arrested during a crackdown in prostitution alley – challenged the bylaw at the Quebec Superior Court on the grounds that it was vague and gave police discretionary and discriminatory powers.[50] Although the Superior Court ruled in favour of the City of Montreal, the legal challenge forced city administrators – who feared that the case might reach the Supreme Court of Canada – to amend the bylaw so that clients would face penalties too, adding fines of up to $1,000.[51] Although sex workers would still bear the brunt of police harassment, the amendment was widely recognized as a good thing because it no longer discriminated based on gender and based on penalizing only one of the participants in the transaction.[52] A few weeks later, on the night of 29 June 1981, the Morality Squad orchestrated a crackdown during which it arrested seven sex workers (male and female) and issued $100 fines to two male clients.[53]

As these developments unfolded, Canadian city mayors met to discuss the proliferation of street-based sex work. About a week after Montreal adopted its bylaw in 1980, mayors voted on a proposal to pressure the federal government to amend the Criminal Code's prostitution clause.[54] Although this proposal was rejected, it set the tone for a long legal battle that pitted municipal authorities, federal lawmakers, and sex work activists against one another. On 31 July 1981, Mayor Drapeau and Toronto's Mayor Art Eggleton met for a day-long meeting to discuss economic development, housing, energy, and federal-municipal relations. Mayor Eggleton landed at Dorval early that morning and immediately made his way to City Hall for a presentation by police officers and city lawyers on "prostitution and street nuisances." Because they were the mayors of Canada's two largest cities, Eggleton and Drapeau believed that their combined clout could pressure the federal government to adopt stricter rules against prostitution, especially against "homosexual prostitution."[55] Both sought to curb the proliferation of the sex industry, whether queer or straight. Yet, they tackled it on different geographic scales: Montreal's was scattered across the Red Light district and downtown while Toronto's was mostly located along and near Yonge Street, where people could witness a concentration of all forms of sex.[56] After discussing a host of other urban issues, the men spoke to the media to reiterate their common goals. Afterwards, they departed from City Hall, leaving behind their concerns to tour

Drapeau's most treasured attractions: the Floralies Gardens, Man and His World, and the Opera Pavilion, where they dined.[57]

But as municipal leaders campaigned for stricter laws, sex workers continued to challenge bylaws that were already in place. At the height of summer in 1981, sex worker Wesley Krehbiel challenged Montreal's anti-prostitution bylaw at the Quebec Superior Court, arguing that it was in the purview of criminal law and therefore beyond the city's authority. Krehbiel had been arrested downtown, near Dominion Square, as part of an offensive against an alleged "homosexual prostitution ring." Although there is scarce evidence that any of the community's downtown hubs (like bathhouses, nightclubs, and bars) served as fronts for sex work, police officers enforced the bylaw to intimidate patrons.[58] Indeed, the intimidation of Montreal's gay community continued years after the provincial government amended the Quebec Charter of Human Rights and Freedoms in 1977 to include sexual orientation as prohibited grounds for discrimination.

A few months later, the case against Risa Goldwax – a sex worker arrested for soliciting outside the Sheraton-Mt Royal Hotel at night – was heard at the Quebec Superior Court. The evidence and facts did not matter to the court. Rather, Goldwax and her lawyer maintained that the bylaw was ultra vires.[59] A few months later, Justice Gérald Ryan sided with Goldwax and declared, "the pith and substance of bylaw 5464 remains the regulation of the exercise of the profession of prostitution which is not prohibited by the competent authority, that is, Parliament. In my humble view, the City of Montreal, through its bylaw 5464, is legislating on criminal matters."[60] This decision was not the pivotal victory sought by Montreal sex workers, however. Two years later, Goldwax reappeared in court after the city appealed the decision and made one last attempt to make the fight against prostitution its own. Moreover, in the meantime, as litigation made its way through the courts, the bylaw continued to be enforced. "That bylaw has kept our prostitute population down quite a bit," a detective of the Montreal Morality Squad stated. "We have had a few girls in from Buffalo, and as soon as they found out about this bylaw, they got on their horses and rode on."[61] As one twenty-one-year-old sex worker put it, the bylaw allowed police to "come down really hard on us."[62] Montreal's anti-prostitution bylaw was a critical instrument for nighttime governance, which explains why the city was so determined to preserve it.

Throughout 1982, couriers carried letters back and forth between mayors who largely echoed Drapeau's wish to find a viable solution to the escalating prominence of street-based sex work. In February, Vancouver Mayor Michael Harcourt wrote to Justice Minister Jean Chrétien on behalf of the mayors, requesting the federal government to amend the Criminal Code in order to curtail street-based sex work. Jean Drapeau, as well as the mayors of Edmonton, Regina, Winnipeg, Toronto, Quebec City, and Halifax supported the letter. The battle for nighttime public space was truly nationwide. In fact, several weeks later, Vancouver, like Montreal and Calgary, adopted its own anti-prostitution bylaw, and Niagara Falls sent a petition to Chrétien demanding amendments to the Criminal Code "to effectively combat prostitution."[63] Amidst the prevailing political consensus against street-based sex work, a voice of opposition emerged. It came from Ottawa mayor Marion Dewar who, after consulting with several feminist organizations, concluded that the Criminal Code's prostitution clause should be completely removed.[64]

Anti-Soliciting Bylaw 6249

In 1982 Jean Drapeau suffered a series of physical setbacks. In February he slipped and broke his hip in the underground parking at City Hall, and in July he had a mild but disabling stroke that partially paralyzed his left side.[65] After a short convalescence, and despite these painful misadventures, the mayor believed that he was still fit to complete another four-year term. Probably unsure whether it would be his last campaign, he ran during that year's election. And for the first time since 1957, he failed to win a majority of votes in what was the biggest turnout in Montreal's electoral history (55 per cent of the city's 700,000 eligible voters headed to polling stations). But the opposition was split, and Drapeau stayed in power. However Pyrrhic the Civic Party's victory, it was still victory.[66]

Several weeks after the municipal election, the legal battle over street-based sex work escalated when a case involving Calgary's anti-prostitution bylaw reached the Supreme Court of Canada. Calgary lawyers cited Montreal's 1969 anti-demonstration bylaw to argue that bylaws – whether to curb protests or prostitution – were based on the same governing principle.[67] But Supreme Court justices noted the logical fallacy to equate the two by stating that Montreal's anti-demonstration bylaw was a temporary tool (lasting thirty days when enacted) and that it concerned parades and assemblies, obviously different from prostitution.[68] On 25 January 1983, the Supreme Court sided with appellant sex worker Lenore Jacqueline (Jackie) Westendorp and struck down the Calgary bylaw as being an attempt by the city to enact criminal sanctions, something within exclusive federal jurisdiction. The ruling set a precedent that would impact Montreal several months later.

During the early to mid-1980s, sex work activism was on the rise nationwide. This development can be explained by two important factors. First, translocal anti-prostitution politics created growing momentum for sex workers' rights. This emerged not only out of challenges to local bylaws but also out of mainstream stigma and precarious labour conditions. The shared experience of police repression during the late 1970s was a key factor in the advent of Canada's first organized sex worker advocacy group in Toronto, Better End All Vicious Erotic Repression (BEAVER). Like its American counterpart, Call Off Your Old Tired Ethics (COYOTE), BEAVER called for the decriminalization of prostitution and campaigned on positioning sex work firmly in the discourse of labour, choice, and civil rights.[69] Over the following years, other rights groups emerge, like the Vancouver-based Alliance for the Safety of Prostitutes (1982) – which established a pimp-free zone and was sympathetically profiled in *Hookers on Davie* (1984) – and another Toronto-based group, the Canadian Organization for the Rights of Prostitutes (CORP), founded in 1983.[70] Cognizant of the profession's history, CORP criticized politicians for enabling local police departments to use force. "The law forces us into the gutter and then punishes us for being there," it reasoned.[71] Over the following years, CORP would fight for the decriminalization of prostitution and the legalization of sex work. In Montreal, informal groups like La Piaule and PIAMP (or PIMP, a project to aid juvenile sex workers) offered free and around-the-clock services for street-based sex workers.[72]

The second factor driving activism emerged out of the community-based need to combat the HIV/AIDS epidemic. In Montreal, activism materialized in response to social discrimination and media prejudice against gays, Haitians, Indigenous Peoples, injection-drug users, and sex workers.[73] For the most part, as queer historian and organizer Gary Kinsman recalls, this activism developed in response to state inaction.[74] In fact, throughout the early 1980s, all of the necessary energy to deal with the epidemic came from affected communities. Gay men, for instance, employed "safer sex" to promote survival, fight stigmatization, encourage community development, and raise self-esteem. Necessary information about the virus was distributed by activist organizations like the Montreal AIDS Resource Committee, a division of Gay Montreal that was founded in January 1984.[75] Throughout the 1980s and into the 1990s, the epidemic completely transformed the disco-all-night ethos and anything-goes sexual attitudes. Critically, the outbreak prompted authorities to enforce mandatory HIV tests on sexually active individuals, which granted moral reformers a facile argument that linked hygiene and sex. Consequently, it renewed the political discourse for cleanup campaigns.[76]

As sex workers organized and distributed pamphlets, and as gay activists and racialized community members responded to the HIV/AIDS epidemic, the mayors of major Canadian cities met in early June 1983. Montreal played host to a day-long private meeting where mayors aired their grievances about public displays of hard-core pornography and sex work. "We're joining our efforts to get Criminal Code amendments to help keep our cities clean," Mayor Drapeau told members of the press, and emphasized that the goal was to create a united front so that the federal government would act.[77] Throughout this period, sexual entertainment had become big business, increasingly mass produced, commoditized, and subject to market norms of content and price, which is why Canadian mayors attacked all aspects of it.[78] Beyond city officials, opposition to the sex industry manifested itself in the emergence of a feminist anti-pornography movement, which viewed certain depictions in the industry as contributing to male violence against women and girls, including misogyny, rape, and battering. As historian Eryk Martin notes, activists incorporated emotions like hate, terror, humiliation, joy, humuor, and bravery into their broader activism while assessing the industry and expressing anger. For example, a militant group of women that called itself the Wimmin's Fire Brigade orchestrated nighttime firebombs of Greater Vancouver sex shops. They triumphantly declared that the arsons had been an "act of self-defense against hate propaganda!"[79]

The mayors reconvened a week after the Montreal meeting at a summit in Moncton and reiterated the need for federal government action on matters of hard-core pornography and sex work.[80] This time, however, the outcome was almost instantaneous. In mid-June 1983, the federal government established the Special Committee on Pornography and Prostitution (Fraser Committee) to consider competing views on the place of the sex industry in Canada. As sociologist Deborah R. Brock argues, although the committee's position started on the premise that gender inequality and sexual exploitation are part of Canadian society, it rapidly transformed into a contemporary example of hegemony in action.[81] Jean-Paul Gilbert embodied this shift, transitioning from Montreal's chief of police (1965–70), where he championed anti-sex industry campaigns, to a criminology professorship at the Université de Montréal, and ultimately becoming one of the seven commissioners.

Having old friends involved on the Fraser Committee allowed Mayor Drapeau to remain bullish about the city's anti-prostitution bylaw, and against sex work more generally. He argued that the bylaw concerned the use of Montreal streets and sidewalks, and that, as such, it did not contravene federal law like Calgary's bylaw. But behind closed doors, and like a seasoned chess player who could see several moves ahead, he knew that Canada's Supreme Court having struck down Calgary's anti-prostitution bylaw meant a similar fate was in store for Montreal's. Immediately, he instructed lawyers to draft a separate bylaw that could also address street-based sex work.

In October 1983, the city enacted anti-soliciting bylaw 6249, which applied anti-prostitution clauses into traffic and disturbance bylaw 333 and muddled the meaning of "obstruction" and "disturbances" in public space.[82] Later, Drapeau would claim that the anti-soliciting provisions did not constitute an attempt to control or punish prostitution per se. Rather, it concerned the occupancy of public space and was enacted as a mechanism to clamp down on unauthorized commercial activity in public space. He stated that it was created to protect "the right of people who don't want to be solicited on the streets" and emphasized the disturbances caused by loud restaurateurs advertising menus and thieves peddling stolen goods.[83] But this was all smoke and mirrors. Within the first few months, four hundred sex workers accounted for 90 per cent of those charged under this new bylaw. The Alliance for the Safety of Prostitutes heard about officers enforcing the bylaw ruthlessly. It heard about police driving past sex workers, and a van following:

"The policeman says, 'Hi! How are you?' to the women that are working and drives on. Then the paddywagon comes and charges the women with soliciting. In court it's the policeman's word against theirs."[84] The remaining 10 per cent somewhat reflected Drapeau's official statement. Peddlers had been charged for selling fruits, vegetables, and ice cream in public space.[85]

This latest bylaw re-energized rights groups, lawyers, and political opponents. In newspapers, the Ligue des droits et libertés reasoned that the bylaw was a structural power grab that gave police too much autonomy.[86] Lawyers expressed similar mistrust and commented on its wording: "It is so vague," stated one, "it gives police the power to arrest a man for introducing himself to a woman on the street."[87] And the opposition at City Hall saw it as the latest in a series of bylaws that transformed police work into petty "babysitting," which led councillor Sam Boskey to speculate on the overlapping nature of the city's beautification program and police work: "Residents have petitioned the city to carry out specific actions within municipal jurisdiction, such as improving lighting, creating no-parking zones, changing street directions, increasing the frequency of police patrol – and the administration has not lifted a finger. Instead, we get a repressive bylaw that applies to the whole city."[88]

Despite widespread opposition, Montreal chief of police André De Luca contended that the bylaw offered his department an effective tool with which to combat street-based sex work. In fact, he defended it at a Fraser Committee hearing by stating that it had enabled his department to issue hundreds of charges relating to soliciting for the purposes of prostitution in 1983 and 1984. And yet, De Luca could also bemoan the lack of power to arrest and detain under municipal bylaws – what is often referred to as catch-and-release – stating that nighttime crackdowns amounted to a veritable "cat-and-mouse game."[89]

***

The power struggle between municipal authorities and the sex industry could be observed in a select few neighbourhoods. Throughout this period, Carré Saint-Louis became one of these hotspots. It was a site for the sex industry and for organized crime, sometimes a deadly arena over which factions fought.[90] The transformation of the bohemian square – from a site for counterculture, students, and intellectuals to one for sex and drug trafficking – can be traced back to the mid-1950s. As discussed in previous chapters, the city's efforts to curb the informal economy led to the transformation of the Red Light district's built environment, and these efforts were subsequently followed by city-wide raids on nightspots during the mid- to late 1960s. These developments led sex workers to seek out new areas where they could solicit without having to worry about disrupting formal commercial activity or the business and wealthy classes. By the late 1970s, approximately two dozen sex workers had found the quieter residential areas near La Fontaine Park and Carré Saint-Louis more convenient. Consequently, by night, these public spaces transformed into playgrounds for heterosexual men, influenced by the interactions between female bodies and male desire.

This development drove nearby residents and office workers absolutely mad about the sex industry. In letters and petitions sent to authorities (including the mayor, the police chief, the crown attorney, directors of the Morality Squad, and the Quebec justice minister), residents expressed profound concern about the new geography of sex work and crime, and envisaged the decline and decay of residential neighbourhoods. "For about six months," wrote one family to Mayor Drapeau, "it has been impossible to drive on our street, and even in front of our home, without witnessing people selling themselves at all time of the day or night."[91] The mayor, who received several dozen letters expressing similar frustrations, remained adamant, however, and responded to such complaints by recalling the war he had waged against the sex industry in the 1950s and pledged to make Montreal "safe," as he had done in the past.[92]

Indignant residents drew connections between the authorities' crackdown on the Red Light district and downtown and the geographic shift of sex work to their residential neighbourhood. This shift, they further stated, also brought and nourished other forms of criminal activity and nuisances, like drug dealing, robberies, and alcohol consumption. Similar to other anti-prostitution campaigns of that era, citizens described themselves as concerned parents and taxpayers, which reflected their social backgrounds and the rhetorical positions they adopted in their letters.[93] They saw themselves as victims, and claimed that the sex industry added traffic, loitering, noise, and vice. Monica Berger, wife of Liberal MP David Berger, was one of these concerned citizens. Speaking from her affluent home overlooking Carré

Saint-Louis, she told *Maclean's* that along with her neighbours she had formed an action committee to reduce traffic in the area.[94] They hypothesized that if traffic could be reduced, then there would be fewer clients for sex workers – thus forcing the women to leave. The city welcomed this strategy and applied it as a short-term solution, diverting traffic and reversing one-ways so that drivers could no longer lap Carré Saint-Louis or prowl the area looking for sex. All streets between Saint-Laurent Boulevard and Saint-Denis Street were rerouted into northbound one-ways, which led to a 90 per cent drop in automobile traffic.[95]

Incidentally, it was the anxiety over Carré Saint-Louis that galvanized the political career of Jean Doré. Before venturing into municipal politics, the charismatic and bilingual labour lawyer had honed his skills first in student politics and then as a television host on Radio-Québec (present-day Télé-Québec). In 1984, two years before the municipal election, the soon-to-be mayor of Montreal won a seat on council and became leader of the opposition at City Hall after running a meticulous campaign that vowed to curb street-based sex work in the neighbourhood. Doré spent considerable time hearing from disconcerted women who described the deterioration of their neighbourhood. They could not walk near Carré Saint-Louis, they claimed, because clients and sex workers alike routinely mistook them for sex workers.[96] Once elected to city council, he helped orchestrate a crackdown in the area, which shifted the geography of street-based sex work back to the Red Light district.[97] Indeed, groups across the political spectrum – from the police to liberal-minded action committees and from Jean Drapeau's conservative Civic Party to Jean Doré's progressive MCM – supported the crackdown on the sex industry. "If this goes on we'll just keep moving them until they go right off the tip of the island and then they'll have to do business in the Saint-Lawrence River," joked the chief of the local police station.[98]

In 1984, after successfully defending the anti-soliciting bylaw at the Quebec Superior Court,[99] the city administered it and the bawdy-house legislation with uncompromising force in preparation for the long-awaited papal visit. This process started in May when officers raided two gay bars, Quai Quête and Aux Bécosses, and arrested nearly two hundred men.[100] The most infamous raid, however, occurred in June and involved fifty Morality Squad officers. That night, in the dark, smoky first-floor disco-bar Bud's, officers

Figure 6.1
One thousand protestors took to the streets after the raid at Bud's, 3 June 1984. Some of the placards read: "Build prisons quickly, there are about 500,000 gays left to lock up!" and "Repeal the bawdy house laws!"

entered and arrested 188 clients and employees under the bawdy-house legislation. Like hallmark events of the previous decades, the city would finalize preparations for the religious pilgrimage by refining its image. The crackdowns on nonconforming community members would be for the benefit of incoming globetrotting tourists and media. For Montreal's queer community, this heteronormative enforcement of city space was painfully reminiscent of 1960s and '70s raids. As one anonymous source reported, the community felt equal amounts of shock, fear, anger, and bitterness as police kept the men in custody for fourteen hours and charged them with being found-ins at a common bawdy-house and for gross indecency.

In response, and as with the 1977 Truxx raid, community pushback was instantaneous. The Association pour les droits des gais et lesbiennes du Québec (ADGQ) organized and held a demonstration the following night. About one thousand protesters rallied downtown to support a full judicial inquiry into systematic discrimination based on sexual orientation (see fig. 6.1). Daniel Gravel of the ADGQ understood the crackdown as a pre-papal cleanup campaign and told the *Montreal Gazette*: "There was a major sweep before Expo 67 and one before the Olympic Games." For community members, the pattern was easy to see: civic reforms, HIV/AIDS cleanup campaigns, and hallmark events – each had been grounds for police to crack down on gay nightspots. Under the watchful eyes of armed riot police, the crowd marched and cycled east along Sainte-Catherine Street toward what was slowly becoming the new Gay Village. Protestors chanted and brought traffic to a halt, creating a significant and impactful demonstration on that balmy summer night.[101] In a way, and despite police raids, it served to reaffirm the community's deep connection to the city, effectively conveying the message that the night belonged to everyone.

In late July, just a few weeks before the pope's visit, and possibly fuelled by a recent ruling by the Quebec Court of Appeal, which upheld Montreal's anti-soliciting bylaw, the Police Department coordinated a crackdown in the Red Light district.[102] Over the span of two nights, officers questioned 155 suspected sex workers, pimps, burglars, and drug dealers and arrested 25 on various charges: armed robbery, possession of drugs, obstructing police work, and breaking bail and parole conditions.[103] That crackdown, however, failed to shield the city from an actual terrorist attack that claimed the lives of three French tourists and left dozens more injured at Montreal's Central Station. The American terrorist later claimed that he had been influenced by cosmic forces that compelled him to "end the unholy Vatican."[104] In the aftermath of the crackdowns on the queer and sex worker communities and the cleanup following the attack, the city set the stage for Pope John Paul II's Apostolic Visit, which would become the largest religious pilgrimage in Canadian history. Despite the steady drizzle, on 11 September, the pope conducted Mass at Jarry Park before a crowd of three hundred and fifty thousand.

During the subsequent months, news outlets reported that the streets of Montreal remained a veritable battleground between law enforcement and the sex industry. The latter was supported by organized crime syndicates, including influential Quebec biker gangs. Women of different ethnic backgrounds – Black, white, and Indigenous, hailing from places like New York, Buffalo, Philadelphia, Vancouver, Toronto, and Frobisher Bay – were constantly on the move under the control of these gangs. At the same time, however, sex workers found themselves beneficiaries of the protection afforded by these hard-edged gangs because they ran a racket that, unliked the services offered by pimps, operated in collusion with the police.[105] Sex worker Miss Pat recalled the arrangement: "Back then, bikers made you pay 'protection' downtown. 'Protection' is a strong word through [*sic*] because they were never there when it was you and a trick in a tourist room. It was more of a management fee. There was a restaurant downstairs from the Miami tourist room and if you got taken away to jail, they'd come and pick you up and if you had a bad trick, they'd take care of him. We paid $100 a week and outside girls from Ottawa and Halifax paid up to $100 a day. They never harassed the women for sex though."[106] Throughout the 1970s and '80s, both local and out-of-town sex workers paid exorbitant fees to gangs in order to work downtown. In return, bikers paid the police to leave them alone. This arrangement was important for women of colour, especially Indigenous and Black sex workers, like Miss Pat, who were profiled and regularly harassed by the police.[107]

***

In February 1985, the Fraser Committee submitted its report after receiving more than five hundred briefs from concerned organizations and individuals in the course of its two-year-long $1.6 million inquiry. The report declared that sex work was a widespread phenomenon in Canada, particularly in urban centres. To supplement the presentations and briefs, the federal Department of Justice commissioned sixteen separate research projects on pornography and prostitution.[108] Ultimately, the committee's final report advocated for the decriminalization and the regulation of sex work. Those interested in the subject were well served by Montreal's newspapers: each allocated ample editorial space to legal pundits and sex workers, allowing for an assessment of reactions to the committee's recommendations. As all three levels of government scrutinized the content of the Fraser Report, activists across the country took to the streets advocating for sex workers' rights. In Montreal, the Alliance for the Safety of Prostitutes held a peaceful demonstration in the Red Light district. Also coinciding with release of the report, and perhaps as a calculated promotional move, Rita Picard released her memoir. The book, written while she was incarcerated, traced the story of how she managed to become one of the city's most reputable and famous madams. During a promotional interview with *Le Journal de Montréal*, a journalist raised the topic du jour and wondered what Picard thought of the Fraser Report. Her response was unambiguous. She scoffed at the idea that Jean Drapeau, police officers, and conservative members of the public would ever entertain decriminalizing prostitution.[109]

Finally, on 2 May 1985, Brian Mulroney's Tories tabled Bill C-49, which largely shelved the Fraser Report's recommendations and addressed solely the concerns of police, municipal politicians, and residents' organizations.[110] Among other things, the bill made it clear that soliciting in a public place for the purpose of prostitution need not be, as the Hutt decision had outlined, "pressing and persistent." The bill replaced the "soliciting" law with the "communicating" law, which maintained public order by making sex work less visible, and therefore less of a nuisance to the public. Because the bill gave municipal authorities greater control over soliciting, Canadian mayors welcomed it. Mayor Drapeau supported it with the "greatest satisfaction" and asked that members of the Canadian Parliament adopt it as soon as possible.[111] Meanwhile, sex workers and activists criticized it harshly. "Every woman should be outraged by this bill," said Valerie Scott of CORP. "It denies not only prostitutes but also all women free access to their city and freedom of association." Scott recognized the bill's vague terms as giving police too much power, and she feared that it would lead to "massive arrests on the street."[112]

In the end, Parliament passed Bill C-49 on 20 November 1985, and one month later it was enacted into law. According to one legal scholar, for all intents and purposes, the legislative amendment was a return to the 1972 vagrancy offence, which made sex workers easy "targets."[113] During the ensuing months, the responsibility for enforcing the new law in Montreal was divided between the Morality Squad and specialized morality officers who were assigned to districts where sex work was prevalent. According to researchers, and in contrast to other Canadian cities, the Montreal police implemented a system of quotas to bolster motivation among both officers and their superiors. The enforcement policy dictated that officers had to apprehend a minimum of one sex worker and one client per week, thus ensuring that both parties in the transaction were treated equally, at least theoretically.[114]

After adoption of Bill C-49, the battle over public space emerged as a paramount priority, if not a major undertaking, for city authorities.[115] In January 1986, the Police Department returned to the Red Light district in what the chief municipal court prosecutor described as "a long night for the prostitutes."[116] This action, however, was met with a spontaneous nighttime protest organized by the pan-Canadian Alliance for the Safety of Prostitutes. Between sixty and one hundred supporters gathered in the Red Light district to voice their opposition both to the civic administration and to the Criminal Code's amendments. After dark, the supporters – mainly students and advocates for women's rights – gathered to denounce police crackdowns on sex workers, which evoked a new political discourse.[117] The following year the National Action Committee on the Status of Women took a similar position when it demanded that the government repeal the Criminal Code's prostitution legislation.[118]

***

Since 1954, Jean Drapeau had stood for every civic election, his presence so entrenched that it felt as though he had become part of the city itself. And for a long time, it appeared that nothing – not opposition, not age – would make him step aside. For example, a couple of years after his stroke, Drapeau told a reporter: "I still work much the same hours I always did," and followed that statement by boasting about his industriousness: "Today, I was up at 4 a.m. and in to work by 5 a.m. I need to eat only once a day and I thrive on my work."[119] But then, five days before Bill C-49 was enacted into law, he fell in his office and cracked a vertebra. This event would prove to change the course of civic politics. Upon assessing his failing health and his chances at being reelected, he made the difficult decision that his political career would end upon the completion of his term in office.

Thirty-two years later, on the 1986 campaign trail, Montrealers were presented a new set of candidates. Claude Dupras, long-time Tory organizer and the Civic Party's new mayoral candidate, replaced Drapeau only in guise. He vowed to maintain his predecessor's policies by enforcing the Criminal Code's prostitution legislation "as strictly as possible." His opponent, MCM party leader Jean Doré, took a progressive stance on sex work. In a departure from the inflammatory rhetoric he had employed during the 1984 by-election, Doré declared his support for decriminalizing prostitution. He assured voters that the MCM would implement bylaws aimed at curbing soliciting without penalizing sex workers. The party would achieve this by creating halfway houses for those who wished to quit the business.[120] Dupras, striking an alarmist tone, rejected the idea and claimed that, under Doré, the city would transform "into the bordello-ridden, wide-open town it was in the 1940s and early 1950s."[121] Clearly, the Civic Party's goals would remain the same, with or without its founding leader. In fact, Dupras's platform hearkened back to a time that preceded the Civic Party itself – when Drapeau and Des Marais, with the help of Pax Plante, had governed under the Civic Action League and had reshaped the night and its economies.

On 9 November 1986, the Civic Party lost its bid for another term to the MCM, and Jean Doré became mayor. Despite new political winds, and contrary to Doré's campaign promises, the arrests of sex workers increased during subsequent months. In December 1986, for instance, undercover female agents were deployed in a major crackdown on clients, resulting in the arrest of 201 clients within a span of two weeks.[122] Although most policewomen expressed uneasiness posing as sex workers, a few disclosed that they had grown accustomed to this line of work. According to a group of researchers, one even took "a mischievous pleasure in arresting clients." "We observed her in action," they reported, "and can confirm that even an alert client would be taken unawares."[123] Therefore, far from ending the policing of street-based sex work, Jean Doré and the MCM upheld anti–sex work policies, especially in the Red Light district. Ultimately, this campaign displaced the boundaries of the sex industry farther away from the city's financial centre and into the Hochelaga-Maisonneuve neighbourhood.[124] The sum of this transformation, claimed one supervising officer, completely changed the image of the Red Light district and downtown. "It is no longer a prostitution supermarket," he asserted.[125] HIV/AIDS remained a critical aspect of the industry's development too. In fact, the group of researchers observed that the city was only beginning to comprehend the impact of HIV/AIDS on sex workers and police work. They hypothesized that by the end of the millennium HIV/AIDS more so than legal measures and civic governance would deter clients. Alternatively, they further hypothesized, the enforcement of prostitution laws might cease due to widespread fear of the epidemic among police officers.[126]

Conclusion

At the tail end of his political career, Jean Drapeau revisited an issue that had brought him to power decades earlier. During the mid-1950s and early 1960s, Drapeau had governed under hallmark policies aiming to make Montreal modern and vice free. As central components of his project of rule, these policies served to eradicate sex work from the city's nighttime landscape. Part of that endeavour involved the reorganization of the Police Department, thereby enabling the removal of corrupt officials from within its ranks. However, in the late 1970s and early 1980s, Montreal's problems did not stem from immoral police officers or corrupt politicians, but rather from the perceived weakness of the Canadian Criminal Code. Where the legislation faltered, Montreal authorities acted, leading to the enactment of anti-prostitution bylaw 5464. Understandably, the bylaw was declared ultra vires by the Supreme Court of Canada four years later, in 1984, after long-fought court battles by civil rights lawyers. Montreal sex workers – like Fernande St-Martin-Poitras, Johanne Meli, Wesley Krehbiel, and Risa Goldwax – fundamentally transformed the 1980s urban political discourse nationwide.

But as litigation made its way through the courts, the Civic Party remained adamant about municipal powers, and in 1983 it enacted anti-soliciting bylaw 6249. That same year, Canada's justice minister, seeing the contested nature of nighttime city streets, commissioned an inquiry. The Fraser Committee (1983–85) was formed to address two remarkably different demands, one involving feminist concerns about the prevalence of degrading images of women in pornography, and the other involving frustrations expressed by police and municipal officials about the governance of city streets. The resulting report eventually led, in December 1985, to amendments to the Criminal Code dealing with prostitution. Thus, instead of attempting to protect sex workers, especially amidst the growing HIV/AIDS pandemic, or addressing the economic reasons that fuelled the sex industry, the federal government passed a law that further marginalized sex workers.[127]

Across Canada, police departments had been dealing with myriad complaints coming from residents, merchants, and politicians who demanded that police, politicians, and legislators prosecute and displace sex workers from *their* neighbourhood. By the mid-1980s, these complaints had, each in their own way, affected the geography of sex work. At the centre of this national wrangle was Montreal's extremely proactive Civic Party. Ultimately, according to Jean Drapeau, Bill C-49 was exactly what Montreal needed from federal legislators.[128]

EPILOGUE: DAWN

We're entering a new era in Montreal.[1]
– Jean Doré, 9 November 1986

The 1986 Montreal municipal election brought one political era to an end and swept into power a party of new leaders who had a different agenda and an alternative vision for the city. In total, fifty-five MCM members were elected, including the new mayor, forty-one-year-old Jean Doré. Meanwhile, the Civic Party was virtually wiped out from city council – winning only one seat. The lopsided result gave Montreal newspapers much to consider, and each assessed the historical moment's significance. "Yesterday was a day of great mourning," reported *La Presse*, "we buried the party of Jean Drapeau."[2] Striking a different tone, the *Montreal Gazette*, which had endorsed the MCM during the campaign, claimed that it was a "humiliating and inglorious end" for the Civic Party, and the MCM's victory signalled "a turning point perhaps without parallel in Quebec since Jean Lesage's Liberals ushered in the Quiet Revolution."[3] And *Le Devoir* – the newspaper that had thrown its weight behind social reformers in the 1950s and created the momentum for Jean Drapeau's political career – offered a neutral statement: "Montrealers have bet on change, on a new team. It is the duty of the elected not to disappoint them."[4] Perhaps anticipating a colossal loss for the Civic Party, Jean Drapeau remained at home on the night of the election. Late in the evening, once the result was announced, he phoned the venue where supporters had gathered and spoke with party leader Claude Dupras. He simply told his successor: "C'est la vie." In response, Dupras thanked Drapeau and spoke in a heartfelt way, calling him Montreal's "second creator," the one who brought the city into modern life.[5]

Jean Drapeau had brought grandeur to Montreal, a grandeur that had instilled a sense of civic pride into his middle-class political base. During the second half of the twentieth century, as the threads of global urban connectivity tightened, Montreal surged forward, transforming itself with a velocity that left the mayors of the world's metropolitan centres green with envy. It was a transformation driven mainly by the vision of a single man: Jean Drapeau. Few leaders in the world could claim to have achieved what Drapeau had – a vast, interconnected public transit system, an international exposition that captured the world's imagination, and an Olympiad. With each of these monumental achievements, Drapeau's Montreal was thrust into the ranks of the world's most modern cities. Indeed, Montreal's mayor would be remembered internationally as the one who had turned Montreal from a declining, crime-beleaguered city into a global hub, and it was something that he recapped when he announced his retirement in June 1986: "My reward is the feeling that I have contributed to cleansing public affairs, to have significantly contributed to transforming the city we already loved into a city we love even more, into a city foreigners have learned to discover on site and even from afar." "Montreal today," he proudly proclaimed, "is open to the world."[6]

Urban life could be vastly improved, argued mid-twentieth-century reformers and technocratic modernists like Jean Drapeau, if specific rules and regulations were implemented to manage nighttime's disorder and moral dangers. When Drapeau was elected mayor in 1954, honesty, morality, and respectability became the guiding tenets of urban governance, which was a definitive change in tone and rhetoric from the preceding administration. These principles held the promise of transforming Montreal into a global city, and to this end his party, the Civic Action League (CAL), generated a normative discourse about the city's appearance and reputation, especially at night. The tenets of this urban reform movement would continue when Drapeau returned to power in 1960. Under the Civic Party, and for over a quarter-century, the city at night became a battleground over changing ideas of heteronormativity and respectability. Crucially, moral order concerned not only informal economies but also sexuality, artistic expression, dissent, and labour. Throughout the second half of the twentieth century, the CAL, and then the Civic Party, worked in concert with the Montreal Police Department, orchestrating a campaign that sought to rid the city of behaviours deemed nonconformist, behaviours that defied the norms of a society being carefully constructed. This campaign did not just focus on Montrealers – it swept up tourists and visitors as well, anyone who found themselves drawn into the city's informal economy or engaged in actions outside the acceptable bounds of conformity. What emerged from this effort was more than a mere reshaping of a city's nightlife: it was a comprehensive transformation of Montreal's very identity. This book shows how the regulation of the night became a means to redefine not only urban culture but also the very social fabric of Montreal – altering the way the city appeared and how it regulated sex, alcohol, labour, art, and protest. Behind this transformation stood the figure of Mayor Jean Drapeau, whose vision of a modern, disciplined city could not be achieved without first asserting control over the night. It was through force – through the rigid, unrelenting control of the city after dark – that Drapeau moulded Montreal into the image he envisioned. It put an end to an older version of Montreal and guided it on a trajectory consistent with the management of reputable urban space, carving a space within a global network of cities.

When Jean Doré became mayor of Montreal, the former labour lawyer sought to avoid the autocratic style favoured by his charismatic predecessor. Debating the merits of policy or holding discussions over local issues was something that Jean Drapeau had expressly avoided. At the height of his career, Drapeau could walk into a press conference and announce a new project, bypassing public hearings. "The public is not interested in discussion – only results," he lectured.[7] Doré's new municipal administration promised to inform and listen to Montrealers by increasing services, holding question periods at council meetings, and allowing residents to challenge controversial projects in their neighbourhoods.[8] Moreover, the MCM confronted issues that the Civic Party had refused to entertain in the late twentieth century, like police reform and long-standing practices related to racial profiling.[9] The city's first openly gay councillor, Saint-Jacques district's Raymond Blain, exemplified another aspect of this new era as he worked to create dialogue between the city and its queer community.[10] Throughout his tenure, Councillor Blain bridged the cleavage between his gay and working-class constituents by focusing on shared concerns, like public security and affordable housing.[11] Meanwhile, issues championed by other civic groups, like La rue, la nuit, femmes sans peur (Take Back the Night), were considered when the MCM looked into improving women's safety in public space.[12] In their first year, the newly elected officials made a concerted effort to understand how residents were experiencing urban space. They did not just want to observe; they wanted to actively collaborate with Montrealers to reshape the city. This was a bottom-up strategy, with the goal of confronting the complex issues that Montreal's multicultural population was navigating, a clear departure from the policies of former mayor Jean Drapeau, whose politics had been forged in the early twentieth century. It was, indeed, a new era.

However, the initial honeymoon quickly faded. Despite a noticeable change in tone and rhetoric, the MCM's actions ultimately failed to meet expectations. Sexual policing continued to shape the city and structure how residents experienced the city at night. Although less frequent, raids of queer night scenes and of erotic performances resumed, which showed that the administration and its police department remained committed to moralizing urban space.[13] The reality was that Jean Drapeau and the Civic Party had changed the political culture so much that many policies had become deeply embedded in city institutions and public attitudes. For one thing, the mid-twentieth-century reformers had shifted local policies and expectations concerning sex, labour, art, and protest to such a degree that the new administration was hesitant to usher in profound change. By the early 1990s, a new wave of political opposition would arise to challenge the MCM.

***

This book encompasses a range of different people who are not usually brought within the same analytical framework: politicians, sex workers, hospitality industry labourers, performing and visual artists, residents and tourists, queer community members, and the protective services workforce. For all their differences, they found themselves, in one way or another, caught in the whirlwind of the reformist agenda. This agenda, as we have seen, was tied to policing, part of a long tradition of moral regulation, and pursued against a backdrop of heightened suspicions of nonconformity as a threat to public safety. Bylaws were adjusted to criminalize a variety of perceived nuisances: sex, immorality, noise, dissent, and loitering. Moreover, by disturbing the night's economies, police drove certain industries deeper into the shadows, creating the conditions in which predators could flourish, and thus creating the means to reinforce segregation between acceptable and unacceptable nighttime cultures.

Clearly, the politics of policing were based on an understanding of the relationship between morality and order, and this formed the backbone of the municipal administration's project during the second half of the twentieth century. And because order was more fragile when darkness fell, the control over night – its economies and politics – became a central issue for urban reformers. Labour, sex, art, and protest, as well as sites of leisure and consumption, were reorganized in the process to suit the desires of politicians who envisioned the development of Montreal within a global network of cities. By reconceptualizing the boundary between legitimate and illegitimate culture within the context of new perceptions of urban space and public behaviour, Montreal's elected officials made it their mission to have the city rank among global cities. The night became a battleground, where social and sexual norms, once rooted, were suddenly up for renegotiation, and where the struggle over labour, culture, and artistic expression took on a new meaning. Indeed, the nighttime economy became a central cultural and economic issue during the late twentieth century – crucial not only to Montreal but also to many cities in their urban regeneration programs.[14] But, what Montrealers had known in the first half of the twentieth century was being transformed completely, as the city's officials sought not just to govern but also to mould Montreal into something bigger, something global.

In many ways, Montreal's transformation fell short of Mayor Drapeau's dream. It did not become the "first city" of the twenty-first century. In fact, when the mayor retired, Montreal's importance had dwindled among a host of North American cities. Its strategic location and its industries faltered as globalization and multinational corporations shifted production to different parts of the world. During this period, Montreal, like other major metropolitan areas of North America, had to adjust to the emergence of a global economy, a new international division of labour, and a "redefinition" of world cities as electronic crossroads of information, money, and power.[15] But Mayor Drapeau belonged to a different era, and many of his convictions, including the belief that so-called moral and honest behaviours would contribute to a better city, did not evolve with the passage of time. In this sense, one must understand how the "combined commercial, cultural, and infrastructural development,"[16] as previous researchers allude to it, was inextricably connected to nighttime regulation and order. This, in many respects, shaped the city's development throughout the years.

Throughout the second half of the twentieth century, the night was a moment when people of various backgrounds could comingle, protest, spend money, and get an intense feel for Montreal. The contest over nighttime public space evolved as property owners, merchants, pedestrians, authorities, police, sex workers, and civil rights activists articulated different concerns regarding gender, sexuality, labour, and art. This book contributes to a wider understanding of mid- to late-twentieth-century urban transformations and shows how Montreal's was enabled by a greater control and regulation of night. Over the course of this period, municipal leaders and police took steps to regulate and control the night by enacting and enforcing bylaws in nightspots and in public space where different artistic and sexual expressions were visible. Because night was a time when different rules applied, and when power expanded and contracted, it also became a moment when people could challenge the political order, a terrain where the boundaries of authority were contested ferociously. In the end, there was only one thing upon which all sides agreed: the struggle for the city's future played out at night.

NOTES

INTRODUCTION

1 Stuart Keate, "The Unhorsed Galahad of Montreal," *Maclean's*, 15 July 1948.

2 Stanké, Morgan, and Plante, *Pax, lutte à finir avec la pègre.*

3 In a bombshell publication, Plante detailed the inner workings of Montreal's organized crime. The blurb on the book's cover boldly promised a shocking exposé: "The former assistant chief of police in charge of Morality explains how police and civil authorities protect gambling, betting, and prostitution industries." All fifteen thousand copies of his book sold out within two weeks. See Plante, *Montréal sous le règne de la pègre.*

4 The *Oxford English Dictionary* defines lucifugous as "[creatures] shunning the light." Stanké, Morgan, and Plante, *Pax, lutte à finir avec la pègre*, 97.

5 This perception of the night city as the strange, irrational other of the daytime city was part of a long tradition that was informed by industrial, political, and religious morals. For more, see Nead, *Victorian Babylon*, 103, and Valverde, *The Age of Light, Soap, and Water.*

6 For example, see Fischer, *The Streets Belong to Us*; Lvovsky, *Vice Patrol*; Francis, *Red Light Neon*; Littauer, *Bad Girls.*

7 For a first-hand account, see Weintraub, *City Unique.* Also see the collection of oral histories compiled by the Centre d'histoire de Montréal: Charlebois and Linteau, *Quartiers disparus*; and Charlebois and Lapointe, *Scandale!*; and the interviews in Higgins, "A Sense of Belonging."

8 Picard would spend a total of eighteen years and six months in prison for sex work. In fact, her autobiography, written while she was imprisoned, came on the heels of Mayor Drapeau's final attempt to control the sex industry in the 1980s. Picard, *Ma vie dans les bordels.*

9 See the 1970s probe into organized crime by Dutil, *La lutte au crime organisé au Québec.* Also see de Champlain, *Histoire du crime organisé à Montréal de 1900 à 1980*, 390–2.

10 Namaste, *C'était du spectacle!*, 65; Podmore, "St Lawrence Blvd as 'Third City,'" 194–6; Gemme, *Street Prostitution.*

11 See Lapointe, *Nettoyer Montréal*; Brodeur, *La délinquance de l'ordre*; Morton, *At Odds.*

12 Patenaude, *Le vrai visage de Jean Drapeau*, 106–7.

13 Mckenna and Purcell, *Drapeau*, 140–1.

14 See Claire Harting, "Ex-prostituée, Brigitte se confie: 'Pour me venger d'être traitée de fille de vie, je me suis fait payer…,'" *Photo-Journal*, 26 October–2 November 1966.

15 A recent survey argues that the Quiet Revolution lasted from 1959 to 1983, significantly overlapping with Jean Drapeau's terms in office (1954–57, 1960–86). While this book is neither about the city's rapport with the politics of the Quiet Revolution nor about Quebec's shifting political landscape during that era, it is important to note that Montreal underwent a profound transformation in its politics of labour, language, and sex – changes that, in turn, shaped the entire province. See Mills, *The Empire Within.* For more on the social and political facets of the Quiet Revolution, see Pâquet and Savard, *Brève histoire de la révolution tranquille.*

16 On the evolution of the city's built environment – the way it managed its heritage and went ahead with modernist development (including the underground city) – see Germain and Rose, *Montréal*, 66–91.

17 Linteau, *Une histoire de Montréal*, 274–7; Poirier, "Expertise, Local Knowledge, and the Construction of the Automobile as an Environmental Risk in Montreal," 409.

18 Sections of the periodical were published in French, English, Spanish, Italian, and German. Jean Drapeau, "The Mayor Introduces 'Montréal '64,'" *Montréal '64* 1, no. 1 (May 1964), 3. XCD00-P3542, AVM. Along the same lines, see Jean Drapeau, "Montréal, ville dynamique," *Le Devoir*, 19 June 1965.

19 Antoine de Saint-Exupéry's book *Terre des Hommes* (1939) was adopted as

Expo 67's central theme because its humanistic values aligned with the exposition's insistence on global openness. The organizers may not have been aware, however, that a quarter-century earlier, the French author had described his time in Montreal (lodged at the Windsor Hotel) as torturous. Regardless, the name Terre des Hommes [Man and His World] was used for the exposition and the subsequent permanent exhibition held from 1968 to 1981. On Saint-Exupéry in Montreal, see Schiff, *Saint-Exupéry*, 375–8.

20 In 1967, metropolitan Montreal had a population of over 2.5 million; by 2001 it had a population of 3.4 million, not quite attaining half of *Horizon 2000*'s provisional forecast. *Horizon 2000*, 1967. VM097-02-01-02-01, AVM.

21 This understanding of the urban night draws from night studies literature. For more, see Gwiazdzinski, Maggioli, and Straw (eds.), *Night Studies*.

22 Tellingly, the purchases of show tickets experienced a genuine explosion throughout the 1960s and 1970s. Linteau, *Une histoire de Montréal*, 287.

23 Podmore, "St Lawrence Blvd as 'Third City,'" 199; Straw, "The Urban Night," 192.

24 Brian Stewart and James Ferrabee, "What Makes Drapeau Run? The Image Is Rooted in Faith, Fear of Failure: 'I Have to Keep Producing,' he says," *Montreal Gazette*, 21 July 1970.

25 For example, during the council meeting on 17 December 1970, the city introduced bylaws that prohibited newspaper vending machines and the occult sciences – fortune-telling and palm and tarot card reading. City of Montreal, By-law 4176, Prohibition from Practicing Occult Sciences and Predicting the Future for a Consideration (17 December 1970); City of Montreal, By-law 4177, Amendment to By-law 1254 Concerning News-Kiosks and Newsstands for the Sale of Newspapers, Periodicals, etc., as Already Amended by By-laws 1443, 1638, 1658 and 3729 (17 December 1970).

26 For more on this transition, see High, *Deindustrializing Montreal*. For more on the link between the post-industrial city and the nighttime economy, see Andy Lovatt, "The Ecstasy of Urban Regeneration."

27 XCD00-P3542 to XCD00-P3546, AVM. Also see Al Palmer "Le soir, dans Montréal/Montreal, after dark," *Montreal '64* 1, no. 1 (May 1964): 26–7; "Le ministère provincial du tourisme lance une affiche mettant en vedette, 'Montréal, la nuit,'" *La Presse*, 30 October 1965.

28 Later, Drapeau told journalists: "I like art, music, painting … [Montrealers] know that when I try to aim a little higher it's not to leave them behind. It's

to rise with them." He was a remarkably cultivated man who held a broad knowledge of Western history, spanning from classical antiquity to the Age of Enlightenment to the Progressive Era. Indicatively, he kept a well-worn copy of Niccolò Machiavelli's *The Prince* at his desk and frequently told reporters that it served as a useful template for his own politics. Bill Bantey, "Mayor Starts Crusade for Opera," *Montreal Gazette*, 9 November 1964; "25 years of Drapeau," *Montreal Gazette*, 22 September 1979.

29 Dossier Émile Nelligan, P100-06-3-D004, AVM.

30 Le mandate du maire Drapeau ([Radio] CJMS), 20 November 1955, 6m55s. P100-02-9-D001-P003, AVM. Also see "L'opéra de Montréal, maintenant ou jamais": conférence de Jean Drapeau, 8 November 1964, P100-02-02-9-D002-P015/6, AVM.

31 Fresco, *Red Mitten Nationalism*, 34–5. The Olympic Games was an element that comprised what one political scientist called Montreal's "politics of global imagineering." Paul, "World Cities as Hegemonic Projects." Also see Léveillée and Whelan, "Montreal: The Struggle to Become a 'World City.'"

32 "Cahier spécial: L'exposition Ramsès II à Montréal," *La Presse*, 27 May 1985; Alan G. Artner, "A Powerful 'Ramses II' in Montreal," *Chicago Tribune*, 27 June 1985.

33 For example (one of many), Jean Drapeau personally chauffeured internationally renowned artist Jean Marais when he came to Montreal, offering the Frenchman a guided visit of the city's recent progress and achievements. Lysiane Gagnon, "Pour Jean Marais Jean Drapeau s'est fait Cicérone," *La Presse*, 24 December 1965.

34 Like mid-century reformers and technocrats, Montreal's own believed that they were effecting change, enhancing the city's efficiency, hygiene, and rationality. For more, see Sassen, *The Global City*; Sammartino, "Mass Housing, Late Modernism, and the Forging of Community"; Gold, *The Practice of Modernism*; Mercure Jolette, "Réinventer Montréal"; Nerbas, "William Zeckendorf."

In large part, all of this was made possible by Jean Drapeau. On the North American continent, Drapeau was comparable to New York City public official Robert Moses and to Chicago Mayor Richard J. Daley, whom he met on several occasions. All three were seminal thinkers whose power, measured in decades, was exercised without challenge. Caro, *The Power Broker*; Bennett, "The Mayor among His Peers: Interpreting Richard M. Daley."

35 Lefebvre, *Rhythmanalysis*, 68; Melbin, *Night as Frontier*, 8. Also see Williams, "Night Spaces."

36 Montreal's emphasis on tourist development took flight during this period. See Broadway, "Montreal's Changing Tourist Landscape"; Levine, "Tourism-Based Redevelopment and the Fiscal Crisis of the City."

37 Fischer, *The Streets Belong to Us*, 2, 7.

38 On the topic of the city's yellow press, feminist historian Viviane Namaste writes that its substance not only dealt with female performing artists but also covered, in a much more general way, gossip about Montreal's nightlife. Namaste, *Imprimés interdits*, 27, 147.

39 Nead, *Victorian Babylon*, 192.

40 This growth continued until the 1970s when it eventually reached a plateau. On mid-century population growth and demographics, see Linteau, *Une histoire de Montréal*, 243–6, 267–70.

41 For example, during the nineteenth century, Indigenous people were prohibited from being in Victoria, British Columbia, at night and "prevented from returning until morning" unless they could show documentation legitimating their presence by a white employer. Edmonds, "Unpacking Settler Colonialism's Urban Strategies," 6, 12.

42 See Namaste, *C'était du spectacle!*

CHAPTER ONE

1 Poutanen, *Beyond Brutal Passions*, 316–18.

2 Lévesque, *Making and Breaking the Rules*, 117. For a full exploration of the role of law enforcement and elected representatives in the Canadian sex industry, notably concerning the spread of race-based hierarchies, see Ross, "'Your Town Is Rotten'"; Strange, *Toronto's Girl Problem*; Bertram, "The Other Little House"; Edmonds, "Unpacking Settler Colonialism's Urban Strategies," 13–16.

3 Four major inquiries – Rainville (1894), Cannon (1909), Coderre (1924), and Cannon (1944) – had negligible effect. On early-twentieth-century nightlife, see Marrelli, *Stepping Out*; Blais-Tremblay, "Jazz, Gender, Historiography."

4 Lapointe, *Nettoyer Montréal*, 16. Also see Lapointe, "'Beaucoup trop Chicago,'" 26.

5 Namaste, *Imprimés interdits*, 45–6.

6 Schlör, *Nights in the Big City*; Schivelbusch, *Disenchanted Night*; Baldwin, *In the Watches of the Night*; Browne, *Dark Matters*.

7 Hermann, *Capitalism and the Political Economy of Work Time*, 59–60; Kealey and Palmer, *Dreaming of What Might Be*; Bradbury, *Working Families*, 36–9.

8 Nye, *American Illuminations*, 64. For more on the Montreal context, see Cooper, *Montreal*, 108–9; Olson, "'A Profusion of Light'"; Niemeyer, "Nuit électrique."

9 Kenny, "City Glow," 103.

10 In 1950, more new theatres opened in Quebec than in any other province, and with 83 motion picture theatres, Montreal ranked second behind Toronto's 124 theatres. *Motion Picture Theatres, Exhibitors and Distributors 1950*, R-9.

11 Hawrysh, "Une ville bien arrosée," 54.

12 Winifred Bambrick, "Montreal Night Club," *Montreal Standard*, 7 April 1945.

13 Heap, *Slumming*, 7–8.

14 Namaste, *C'était du spectacle!*, 12; Lam, *Show Girls*; Mansbridge, "In Search of a Different History," 8.

15 Palmer, *Montreal Confidential*, 66. Between columns, Palmer wrote *Sugar-Puss on Dorchester Street* (1949), a pulp fiction novel of 1940s Montreal nighttime culture.

16 Gilmore, *Swinging in Paradise*, 167. For more on informal segregation, see Backhouse, *Colour-Coded*.

17 Palmer, *Montreal Confidential*, 80.

18 While estimates of Montreal's brothels range from one to three hundred, about three-quarters of all sex work occurred in the Red Light district. Lévesque, *Making and Breaking the Rules*, 117–18.

19 Ibid., 119–21. Gauvreau, Olson, and Thornton, "The Harsh Welcome of an Industrial City," 378.

20 Myers, "Deserting Daughters," 28.

21 See Herland, "Organized Righteousness against Organized Viciousness."

22 The Committee of Sixteen had established links with American reformers who were preoccupied with these urban issues. Quoted in Lévesque, "Éteindre le *Red Light*," 196.

23 Lévesque, *Making and Breaking the Rules*, 131. For more on the inquiry, see

Brodeur, *La délinquance de l'ordre*. Chapter 5 in Podmore, "St Lawrence Blvd as 'Third City.'"

24 Charlebois and Lapointe, *Scandale!*, 97–8. On the progressive movement in the United States, see Part II, "The Reformer," in Caro, *The Power Broker*.

25 For photos of the area before it was demolished, see Guillaume, "A Heuristic Archive," in *Photogenic Montreal*.

26 Myers, *Caught*, 169–74.

27 Blair Gilmour, "St Lawrence-Main," *Maclean's*, 15 September 1940. Also see oral histories in Guillaume, "A Heuristic Archive," in *Photogenic Montreal*, 194.

28 Charlebois and Linteau, *Quartiers disparus*, 78, 82, 90.

29 Proulx, *Les bas-fonds de Montréal*, 11–13.

30 In 1919, a papal charter from Pope Benedict XV granted full autonomy to the campus, and the following year it received its civil charter from the Quebec Legislative Assembly and adopted the name Université de Montréal. The institution would remain in the neighbourhood until 1943, at which point it moved to Mount Royal's slopy summit.

31 Charlebois and Lapointe, *Scandale!*, 143; Lacasse, *La Prostitution féminine à Montréal*, 131. Also see Proulx, *Le Red Light de Montréal*.

32 During the early twentieth century, condoms, vaginal sponges, and douches provided a degree of protection while Salvarsan was used against infections. Lévesque, *Making and Breaking the Rules*, 125–6.

33 Proulx, *Le Red Light de Montréal*, 33.

34 Lapointe, *Nettoyer Montréal*, 325; Morton, *At Odds*, 5; Charlebois and Lapointe, *Scandale!*, 150–3.

35 Houde served the following terms: 1928–32, 1934–36, 1938–40, and 1944–54. At the provincial level, Houde served as MPP for the Conservative Party of Quebec (1923–27) and, later, as its leader (1929–32). He also won a seat as an independent MP in Papineau (1949–53) while he was mayor of Montreal. See Dupont, "Camillien Houde, politicien de carrière."

36 Hugh MacLennan, "A Shiver When an Era Ends," *Saturday Night*, 9 October 1954; Brittain, Canell, and Duncan, *His Worship, Mr Montréal*.

37 Marsolais, "Les inclinations fascistes de Camillien Houde et son internement durant la guerre," 154–5.

38 See Burns, "Montreal: A Helluva Town," in *Life on the Home Front*, 177–99;

Weintraub, "War: The Home Front," in *City Unique*, 27–58. For more on the historical relationship between the sex industry and port cities, see Carminati, "'She Will Eat Your Shirt.'"

39 St-Cyr, *Ma vie de stripteaseuse*, 158. For more on the connection between Montreal and the Manhattan Project, see Sabourin, *Montreal and the Bomb*.

40 Weintraub, *City Unique*, 85; Gilmore, *Swinging in Paradise*, 187.

41 City of Montreal, By-law No. 1715, By-law Concerning the Curfew (2 September 1942).

42 During the early postwar period, the Juvenile Morality Squad would increase from five members in 1941 to twenty-eight in 1946 and eighty by the early 1950s. Throughout this period, the squad's mandate broadened, as did the definition of who was best suited for work with youths. In 1947, the Montreal force deemed policewomen, who had been summarily fired at the close of World War I and absent for decades, useful for police work. By the 1950s, Montreal employed the largest contingent of policewomen in Canada (twenty). Myers, *Youth Squad*, 55–73.

43 Turmel, *Le Service de police de la cité de Montréal*, 170.

44 "If a tremendous improvement is not forthcoming in this regard in the very near future, we will be forced to resort to very drastic action, such as placing Montreal out-of-bounds for all troops not actually serving here." *Minutes of a Conference held at headquarters, – Military district number four, Montreal Qué. On the 13th of January, 1944 in connection with Venereal Disease Control*, 1. Fonds Commission d'enquête présidée par le juge François Caron. 1925–1957, P043, S4, SS2, D02 – Maladies vénériennes (1942–1952), AVM.

Historian Andrée Lévesque notes that during the Depression, the federal government had halved its contribution to combatting sexually transmitted infections despite the increase in cases. In a revealing, possibly exaggerated anecdote, crime-buster Pax Plante recalled a university medical science professor saying that "at least 80 per cent of students have had a sexually transmitted infection." Lévesque *Making and Breaking the Rules*, 127; Stanké, Morgan, and Plante, *Pax, lutte à finir avec la pègre*, 132.

45 Letter from Dufresne to Renaud on 1 February 1944. P043, S4, SS2, D02 – Maladies vénériennes (1942–1952), AVM.

46 McKenna and Purcell, *Drapeau*, 84.

47 Blair Fraser, "VD… No. 1 Saboteur," *Maclean's*, 15 February 1944; "This Is What VD Costs!," *Maclean's*, 1 March 1944.

48 Letter from Dufresne to Asselin, 13 March 1944, P043, S4, SS2, D02 – Maladies vénériennes (1942–1952), AVM.

49 Straw, "La prostituée dans la nuit," 61–2, 67–8.

50 Lucien Cannon, *Rapport de la Commission Royale nommée pour s'enquérir des activités de la Sûreté provinciale et de la Police des liqueurs, dans le district de Montréal, depuis le 26 août 1936 jusqu'au 15 mars 1944* (Quebec: Gouvernement du Québec, 1944).

51 The group's first request, filed in December 1945, along with its second filed in October 1946, were both rejected because of imprecise indictments of corruption. Turmel, *Le Service de police de la cité de Montréal*, 179–82; Charlebois and Lapointe, *Scandale!*, 206.

52 According to incumbent mayor Adhémar Raynault, who had fought against illicit activities during World War II, the underworld overwhelmingly funded Houde's campaign. Although he ran for mayor several times after – as described in a bitter autobiography – he failed to create any political momentum. As a result, he ended up devoting the rest of his life to small-time livestock farming in Repentigny. Raynault, *Témoin d'une époque*, 171–83.

53 Brittain, Canell, and Duncan, *His Worship, Mr Montréal*.

54 Burrows and Palardy, *Montreal by Night*.

55 David Willock and Louis Jaques [*sic*], "Montreal Night Life: Entertaining Night-outers Is Fabulously Big Business in Canada's Gayest City," *Montreal Standard*, 28 April 1951.

56 Wallace Ward, "The Quebec of the Visitors," *Saturday Night*, 67 (12 July 1952) quoted in Neatby, "Meeting of Minds," 490.

57 Stuart Keate, "The Unhorsed Galahad of Montreal," *Maclean's*, 15 July 1948.

58 Stanké, Morgan, and Plante, *Pax, lutte à finir avec la pègre*, 97.

59 Plante served this role from 1939 to 1946. Plante, *Montréal sous le règne de la pègre*, 8.

60 Turmel, *Le Service de police de la cité de Montréal*, 182; Lapointe, *Nettoyer Montréal*, 164.

61 Stuart Keate, "The Unhorsed Galahad of Montreal," *Maclean's*, 15 July 1948.

62 Stanké, Morgan, and Plante, *Pax, lutte à finir avec la pègre*, 159–60; Leon Harris, "Former Crime-buster 'Pax' Plante Back, Has Book on Quebec's Justice Situation," *Montreal Gazette*, 10 September 1971; Morton, *At Odds*, 173.

63 Alexis Gagnon, "L'Assemblée législative adopte la nouvelle loi des liqueurs alcooliques," *Le Devoir*, 2 May 1941; *Loi modifiant la Loi des liqueurs alcooliques*, 9 May 1941. Lois annuelles du Québec, Bibliothèque de l'Assemblée nationale du Québec.

64 Palmer, *Montreal Confidential*, 135.

65 Cited in Gilmore, *Swinging in Paradise*, 176.

66 Plante, *Montréal sous le règne de la pègre*, 9; Stuart Keate, "The Unhorsed Galahad of Montreal," *Maclean's*, 15 July 1948; Letter from Pax Plante to F. Dusseault, 18 December 1947. P043, S4, SS2, D02 – Maladies vénériennes (1942–1952), AVM.

67 Ken Johnstone, "How Plante and Drapeau Licked the Montreal Underworld," *Maclean's*, 1 December 1954, 13.

68 D'Amours and Keshen, "La campagne de prévention des infections transmises sexuellement durant la Second Guerre mondiale," in *Une histoire des sexualités au Québec au XXe siècle*, 107; Stanké, Morgan, and Plante, *Pax, lutte à finir avec la pègre*, 143.

69 Kaufman, *Searching for Justice*, 71.

70 See Charlebois and Lapointe, *Scandale!*; Lapointe, *Nettoyer Montréal*; Straw, "Montreal and *The Captive City*."

71 Vaz, "The Metropolitan Tax-Driver," 29–32. City permits skyrocketed from 848 in 1945 to 4,295 in 1952. See Warren, *Histoire du taxi à Montréal*, 93–5.

72 City of Montreal, By-law No. 1800, By-law Concerning Taxi-Cabs, Automobiles for Hire and Hackney-Coaches (5 April 1946).

73 Letter from Plante to chief of police Albert Langlois, 30 December 1947. P043, S4, SS2, D02 – Maladies vénériennes (1942–1952), AVM; Warren, *Histoire du taxi à Montréal*, 114–15.

74 Letter from Plante to Aurel Lemay, Police des Liqueurs, 8 January 1948. P043, S4, SS2, D01, AVM. "Contrôle des taxis," *La Presse*, 23 October 1947; Lucien Champeau, "Photo et nom des chauffeurs de taxis," *La Presse*, 31 January 1948; "Pour les chauffeurs de taxi," *La Presse*, 2 February 1948.

75 "Permit Check System to Aid Taxi Drivers," *Montreal Star*, 25 October 1947.

76 Pax Plante, "Pour déraciner la prostitution," *Le Devoir*, 8 February 1950. For more on the role of the taxi industry in clandestine commercial networks, see Gallas, "The Price of the Ride in New York City."

77 *The Criminal Code and Other Selected Statues of Canada* (Ottawa: F.A. Acland, [1927] 1928), 80–1. As Podmore observes, the onset of Plante's rise

within the Police Department led to a peak in arrests for street-based prostitution in 1946, reaching a total of 2,832, and a markedly sexist bias in arrests pertaining to loitering. Podmore, "St Lawrence Blvd as 'Third City,'" 192.

During the 1950s, the vagrancy law was reformed. For more on those reforms, see Ranasinhe, "Reconceptualizing Vagrancy and Reconstructing the Vagrant."

78 Larsen, "Canadian Prostitution Control between 1914 and 1970," 139.

79 See Morality Squad reports from 1946 to 1948, P043-4-2-D04, AVM.

80 Francis, *Red Light Neon*, 71.

81 Backhouse, *Petticoats and Prejudice*, 230.

82 Bright, "The Other Woman."

83 Picard, *Ma vie dans les bordels*, 30–40, 115–16; Morality Squad Report (1947–1948), P043-S4-SS2-D04, 3_1947–48, AVM.

84 This was a common practice in North American cities. For example, the testimonies of innocent women who had been victims of police shake-downs and extortion in New York City came to light during the 1931 Hofstadter Committee probe into corruption in the magistrate's courts and police department. See Adler, *A House Is Not a Home*, 176.

85 Albert Langlois (1899–1964), a decorated veteran of the Canadian Army, was named Montreal's chief of police in March 1947. See Report by Chief J. Albert Langlois sent to Joseph-Omer Asselin, [morning] 15 March 1948, P043-S4-SS2-D01, AVM. Another letter was sent that same afternoon, which charged Plante with negligence and unauthorized publicity of ongoing investigations. "Ex-Police Chief Langlois Dies Month after Accident Injuries," *Montreal Gazette*, 29 January 1964.

86 Stuart Keate, "The Unhorsed Galahad of Montreal," *Maclean's*, 15 July 1948; *Mémoire présenté par Me Pacifique Plante au Comité Exécutif de la Cité de Montréal en réponse aux accusations portées contre lui par le directeur du service de la police*, 13 April 1948. P043-S4-SS2-D01 – Pacifique Plante – 1938, 1947–1948, AVM.

87 Communiqué de Pax Plante après suspension, P100-06-1-D005, AVM.

88 Plante, *Montréal sous le règne de la pègre*, 12–13.

89 Pax Plante, "La parole est au public," *Le Devoir*, 18 February 1950; "Voici les vrais coupables," *Le Devoir*, 18 February 1950; Lapointe, *Nettoyer Montréal*, 214–17.

90 See Plante, *Montréal sous le règne de la pègre.*

91 Jean Drapeau, "Discours à CJAD," 22 January 1958, 13. P100-02-2-D008, AVM.

92 Charlebois and Lapointe, *Scandale!*, 219.

93 "La ville ne veut pas payer les frais sténographiques," *La Patrie*, 6 March 1951; Brodeur, *La délinquance de l'ordre*, 141.

94 Morton, *At Odds*, 164.

95 François Caron, *Jugement: Enquête de la Police Municipale*, 8 October 1954. P043-4-1-3, AVM; Raynault, *Témoin d'une époque*, 190.

96 J.-O. Asselin was the chair of the executive committee from 1940 to 1954, Fernand Dufresne was the chief of police from 1931 to 1946, and Albert Langlois was the chief of police from 1947 to 1954. Langlois would eventually clear his name at the Quebec Court of Appeal and was able to make a comeback in 1957. He retired in 1961. Charlebois and Lapointe, *Scandale!*, 243–4.

97 Leon Harris, "Former Crime-buster 'Pax' Plante Back, Has Book on Quebec's Justice Situation," *Montreal Gazette*, 10 September 1971. According to co-founder J.-Z.-Léon Patenaude, Pierre Des Marais convinced Drapeau to run for office during an evening at his retreat in Saint-Marc-sur-Richelieu. Patenaude, *Le vrai visage de Jean Drapeau*, 51.

98 Moreover, to qualify for membership, candidates had to meet ten requirements, the first of which was an excellent moral and financial reputation: "To be a candidate for the CAL [one must] 1. Have an excellent reputation from a moral and financial standpoint." Patenaude, *Le vrai visage de Jean Drapeau*, 106–7.

99 Frank Kennedy, "Hoodlum Squads Run Wild in Roughest Election Yet," *Montreal Herald*, 26 October 1954.

100 Jean Drapeau was adamant about the trio's egalitarianism. Le Mandat du maire Drapeau ([Radio] CJMS), 20 November 1955, 3m15s. P100-02-9-D001-P003, AVM.

101 Brian Stewart and James Ferrabee, "What Makes Drapeau Run? The Image Is Rooted in Faith, Fear of Failure: 'I Have to Keep Producing,' he says," *Montreal Gazette*, 21 July 1970.

102 The paragraph draws from chapters III and V in McKenna and Purcell, *Drapeau.*

103 Groulx fanned the flames with antisemite remarks in 1933–34 in *L'Action*

nationale. Anctil, *History of the Jews in Quebec*, 161–2. Also see "Postscript" in Mordecai Richler, *Oh Canada! Oh Quebec! Requiem for a Divided Country* (Toronto: Penguin, 1992), 244–60.

104 Drapeau was undoubtedly imbued in far-right antisemitic politics during the 1930s. He kept copies of the Jeunes Laurentiens manifest, published speeches of the Jeune-Canada and Joseph Goebbels, and hundreds of articles published by the extremist press: *Deutscher Fichte-Bund*, *Le Patriote*, and *Le Miroir*. Dossiers 1930–1938 and 1931–1941 – Antisémitisme, P100-09-04, AVM.

Jean Drapeau also associated with the Ordre de Jacques-Cartier, commonly known as "La Patente." Founded in 1926, the secret society aimed to counterbalance the influence of anglophone societies (like the Knights of Columbus, the Orange Order, and the Freemasons) by furthering the religious, social, and economic interests of French Canadians. Lamonde, "Les Jeune-Canada ou les 'Jeune-Laurentie?,'" 190. For more on fascism through both local and national contexts, see Théorêt, *The Blue Shirts*.

105 Letter from Jean Drapeau to Anatole Vanier, 27 February 1934. Dossiers 1931–1941 – Antisémitisme, P100-09-04, AVM.

106 "Le trophée Villeneuve," *Le Quartier latin*, 11 March 1938; Jacques Rohan, "Le débat," *Le Quartier latin*, 5 March 1939; J.D., "Les vainqueurs à Québec," *Le Quartier latin*, 8 March 1940.

107 His university friends also remembered him as an avid table tennis player and a reliable chauffeur. "Épitaphes," *Le Quartier latin*, 14 March 1941.

108 See Comeau, *Le Bloc populaire*.

109 Lapointe, *Nettoyer Montréal*, 19.

110 Sancton, "Montreal," 77.

111 Turmel, *Le Service de police de la cité de Montréal*, 234.

112 Gilmore, *Swinging in Paradise*, 191; Weintraub, *City Unique*, 85.

113 Son honneur le maire Jean Drapeau à sa conférence de presse du 15 novembre 1955: entretien avec René Lévesque, 3m10s, 20m30s. P100-02-9-D001-P002, AVM.

114 City of Montreal, By-law No. 926, Concerning Food Establishments and Restaurants (9 May 1927).

115 Podmore, "St Lawrence Blvd as 'Third City,'" 178–9, 194; Straw, "La prostituée dans la nuit," 68, 75.

116 Both Lacasse and Podmore trace the geographic shift of the sex industry –

from "residential" brothels to streets, restaurants, and cafés – as leading to a "masculinization of the prostitution system." This reorganization, resulting in a significant increase in violence against sex workers, is largely considered the most transformative moment in the history of Montreal's sex industry. Podmore, "St Lawrence Blvd as 'Third City,'" 196, 209; Lacasse, "La fin d'un univers féminin," 97–106. Also see Lévesque, "Le Bordel," 30.

117 In an interview with Ross Higgins, an informant stated that when sex workers began frequenting the Hawaiian Lounge in 1948–49, authorities heightened their surveillance of the club and closed the place down. Higgins, "A Sense of Belonging," 272.

118 Dutil, *La lutte au crime organisé au Québec*, 140–2.

119 See Chapter 5 in Picard, *Ma vie dans les bordels* and Chapter 6 in Adams, *Martha Adams*.

120 According to Toronto tabloids, pimps began flocking to the city following crackdowns in Montreal. See Chenier, "A Place Like the Continental," in *Any Other Way: How Toronto Got Queer*. Herbert Manning, "What Virtue Has Done to Montreal," *Maclean's*, 1 October 1955.

121 According to one article, Montreal had more clubs per capita than New York City. David Willock and Louis Jaques [*sic*], "Montreal Night Life: Entertaining Night-outers Is Fabulously Big Business in Canada's Gayest City," *Montreal Standard*, 28 April 1951.

122 Gilmore, *Swinging in Paradise*, 193.

123 Mademoiselle X, "Ce que je pense de nos cabarets," *Le Magazine Maclean*, November 1961, 14.

124 Two thousand of the six thousand union members lost their jobs according to local 382 organizer Gaston Ramat. Herbert Manning, "What Virtue Has Done to Montreal," *Maclean's*, 1 October 1955.

125 Gilmore, *Swinging in Paradise*, 198.

126 Weintraub, *City Unique*, 85–6; Herbert Manning, "What Virtue Has Done to Montreal," *Maclean's*, 1 October 1955.

127 "L'incident de la brique," *La Presse*, 14 May 1955.

128 The mayor met with the owners of Café Minuit, Beaver, Montmartre, Figaro, Chanteclerc, Palm, Rigolo, Tabou, Can-Can, Rainbow, Casino français, and Café de l'Est. "Drapeau Meets Nitery Owner Delegation, Says No!," *Montreal Gazette*, 19 May 1955; Louis Robillard, "Propriétaires de clubs de nuit chez M. Drapeau," *Le Devoir*, 20 May 1955.

129 "57 cabarets perdent leur permis municipal," *Le Devoir*, 5 June 1956.

130 City of Montreal, By-law No. 2129, By-law to Amend By-Law No. 1025 concerning Posters, Photographs, Statues, etc. (1 September 1953).

131 Namaste, *Imprimés interdits*, 106.

132 Other notorious periodicals included *Tous les secrets de l'amour, Montréal confidentiel, Flirt et potins, Minuit, Jour et nuit*, and *Nouvelles et potins*. Ibid., 27–9; Straw, "Tabloid Expo," 230.

133 Morton, *At Odds*, 26, 50.

134 City of Montreal, By-law No. 2223, By-law to Prohibit Pin Ball Machines or Bagatelle Games (30 March 1955); "Pinballs Seized by Police," *Montreal Gazette*, 11 January 1956; "Machine Controls Player, So Pinball Operator Fined," *Montreal Gazette*, 19 April 1957.

135 The Police Department received $10.7 million from the city's $112.9 million budget. Jacques Delisle, "Budget municipal adopté à l'unanimité au conseil," *La Presse*, 1 April 1955.

136 "Morality Offences Total 1,982 in '55," *Montreal Gazette*, 3 January 1956.

137 Hydro Quebec, Canadian Industries Ltd, the Royal Bank of Canada, and the Canadian Imperial Bank of Commerce all erected their head office on this street. Leslie Roberts, "The Autocratic Regime of Jean Drapeau," *Maclean's*, 18 April 1964.

138 Like cities across North America, Montreal struggled with rats and other pests, many of which thrived in degraded housing and certain neighbourhood environments. Unique to Montreal's Red Light district, however, was the discourse surrounding the link between the neighbourhood's deterioration and its illicit nightlife. Drouin, "De la démolition des taudis à la sauvegarde du patrimoine bâti," 26. For more on the history of pest control in America, see Biehler, *Pests in the City*.

139 Kardos, "Political Power," 93–101, 103–7; Ruddick, "The Movement for Public Housing," 105–6; Boyko, *Les Habitations Jeanne-Mance*.

140 At the time, the Canadian public broadcaster was searching for a site to consolidate its services. In the end, however, the public broadcaster moved into the Faubourg à m'lasse, a working-class neighbourhood in the east end. *Family-City: Cité des Ondes (Radio and TV City): A Project of Slum Clearance and Renewal at the Heart of Montreal* (September 1957). VM166-S1-SS1-D5577, D244-4-3, AVM; Choko, Collin, and Germain, "Le logement et les enjeux de la transformation de l'espace urbain," 249.

141 City of Montreal, By-law No. 2325, By-law to Create the Greater Montréal Council of Arts (18 April 1956).

142 The GMCA was supported and funded by donations, contributions by municipal corporations, and 1 per cent of sales tax paid to the city by the provincial government. An Act to Amend the Charter of the City of Montréal (assented to, the 23rd of February, 1956), dossier – Création, P100-04-1-D001, AVM.

143 Léon Lortie, *The Greater Montréal Council of Arts after Three Years of Existence: The President's Report*, January 1960, dossier – 1959–1960, P100-04-1-D001, AVM.

144 Robert Duffy, "Is Drapeau a Match for Duplessis?," *Maclean's*, 22 June 1957.

145 Ibid.

146 "Danger de guerre entre le maire Drapeau et le chef A. Langlois," *Le Devoir*, 4 May 1957; "Violente sortie du chef Langlois: 'L'enquête Caron fut une fumisterie et ses instigateurs m'attaquent encore,'" *Le Devoir*, 31 July 1957.

147 Myer Negru, "Drapeau-DesMarais Keep Langlois Busy: Cold War Growing Hotter over Explanations, Clarifications, Probes," *Montreal Gazette*, 13 September 1957.

148 "Campagne syndicale contre la Ligue d'action civique," *La Presse*, 18 October 1957.

149 Weintraub, *City Unique*, 270; Robert Duffy, "Is Drapeau a Match for Duplessis?," *Maclean's*, 22 June 1957.

150 See Chapter XVII in McKenna and Purcell, *Drapeau*.

151 See electoral pamphlet, *Ralliement du Grand Montréal. Greater Montreal Rally*, 28 October 1957.

152 For a detailed account of the expropriation process in Montreal, see the collection of testimonies and photographs in Charlebois and Linteau, *Quartiers disparus*, 46–109.

153 The speech was shared widely, and it was also translated for the city's anglophone newspapers. "To Quit or Hold On?" *Montreal Star*, 23 January 1958; Conférence de Me Jean Drapeau, *Lâcher ou tenir? (sous les auspices de la Ligue d'action civique)*, P100-02-2-D008, AVM.

154 Jean Drapeau, *Qui va payer?*, 24 February 1958, 14. P100-02-2-D008, AVM; Bill Bantey, "Drapeau Says English Face Racial Politics," *Montreal Gazette*, 25 February 1958.

155 Despite a considerable physical distance, Plante kept an intellectual connec-

tion with Quebec. In the 1970s, a coda to a prior life, he participated in the Commission d'enquête sur le crime organisé and gave a book-length interview to journalists. Plante remained in exile in Jocotepec, Mexico, until he died on 9 August 1976 due to complications from a cerebral embolism. "Pax Plante sera inhumé à Jocotepec," *Le Devoir*, 11 August 1976.

156 *Présentation de H. Marcel Caron au Comité exécutif de la cité de Montréal, Mardi le 2 août 1960*. VM166-1-1-D0042, AVM; Myer Negru, "Report Spotlights Problems of City," *Montreal Gazette*, 3 August 1960.

157 Al Palmer, "Exotic Shows Subdued: 'Shadow Squad' Checks Night Club Attractions," *Montreal Gazette*, 10 January 1958.

158 "Nettoyer la jungle montréalaise des indésirable qui l'habitent," *Montréal-Matin*, 15 July 1960; "Le juge Blain suggère de priver le quartier interlope de toute protection de la police," *Le Devoir*, 15 July 1960.

159 "'Main' Cafes Told to Curb Trouble," *Montreal Star*, 20 October 1960.

160 Herbert Manning, "What Virtue Has Done to Montreal," *Maclean's*, 1 October 1955.

CHAPTER TWO

1 Quoted in Kuplowsky, "A Captivating 'Open City,'" 7, 49.

2 Higgins "A Sense of Belonging," 180–7. Also see Thérèse Masson, "Montréal by Night," *Liberté* 5, no. 4 (July–August 1963): 352; Caron, "Taming the Jungle in the City"; Podmore, "Queering Discourses of Urban Decline."

3 "'Time' Cover Listed in Obscenity Cases," *Montreal Gazette*, 23 January 1960; "Langlois Appeals to Public: Police Deserve Support," *Montreal Gazette*, 30 January 1960; "Magazine Cover Case to Court," *Montreal Gazette*, 6 February 1960.

4 "Lutte sans merci du Conseil municipal aux journaux jaunes," *Montréal-Matin*, 11 March 1958. For more, see Namaste, *Imprimés interdit*.

5 Between 1945 and 1960, the number of automobiles quadrupled throughout Quebec. By 1961, 55 per cent of households on the Island of Montreal owned a vehicle. The gradual access to automobiles was encouraged by several factors, including technological progress, cost-effective production, credit, urban sprawl, and economic prosperity. Linteau, *Une histoire de Montréal*, 250. On civic politics and Canadian car culture, see Penfold, "'People Drive Automobiles.'"

6 "The Candidates Present Their Views," *Montreal Gazette*, 27 October 1962.

7 "Le président Lucien Saulnier 'rêve' d'un Montréal à la grandeur de l'île pour 1967," *Le Devoir*, 30 October 1963.

8 Jack Zolov & Marc Beaudet, *Adultes avec réserve…*; Podmore, "St Lawrence Blvd as 'Third City.'"

9 La Chambre de commerce du district de Montréal, *Une étude sur l'accueil touristique à son honneur le maire Jean Drapeau*, [dans le cadre de la] Semaine d'éducation touristique du 17 au 25 avril 1963, 14. VM166-D142-A-(1963–1966), AVM; Masson, "Montréal by Night," 355.

10 St-Cyr, *Ma vie de stripteaseuse*, 32.

11 Ibid., 271, 274. On 19 March 1965, on Radio-Canada's *Les Couche-tard*, she stated: "I was sorry to see so many modern buildings coming up in Montreal."

12 Gérard Vallières, "The Cops on Montreal's Night Patrol Say Things Are Changing – For the Worse," *Weekend Magazine*, 17 December 1972.

13 For example, see Tousignant, *Gabor Szilasi.*

14 See municipal court sample of police reports (1961–63), P076-3-D682, AVM. "La police arrête 65.6 filles de vie par mois," *Le Petit Journal*, 30 October 1960.

15 To name but two examples, see early-1960s Los Angeles and Chicago. Davis and Wiener, *Set the Night on Fire*, 43; Balto, *Occupied Territory*, 154–89.

16 "The New Head of the Police," *Montreal Gazette*, 6 July 1961.

17 For instance, see Germaine Bernier "Montréal et sa trame sonore," *Le Devoir*, 17 August 1961; Germaine Bernier, "L'univers féminin: Le bruit 'signe de puissance' a aussi ses adorateurs," *Le Devoir*, 15 February 1965; Pierre Perrault, "J'habite une ville," *Le Devoir*, 19 June 1965.

18 Rudy, Kenny, and Fahrni, "'An Ocean of Noise,'" 262; Golan, "Soundscapes of Urban Development," 132.

19 Procès-verbal, 8 January 1965. VM074-6-D066, AVM.

20 Hasegawa, "Late-Night Noise Hazards," 156; Rudy, Kenny, and Fahrni, "Railways and the Urban Soundscape," 219; Stoever, "'Just Be Quiet Pu-leeze.'" Also see Chapter 5 in Thompson, *The Soundscape of Modernity*.

21 Jean Drapeau, *Jean Drapeau vous parle* (Montreal: Les Éditions de la Cité, 1959).

22 Bill Bantey, "Ex-Mayor Wants 'Cells' across Quebec," *Montreal Gazette*, 23 January 1958; Pierre Vigeant, "Une campagne d'épuration à l'échelle

provincial," *Le Devoir*, 20 March 1958; "M. Drapeau se rétablit," *Le Devoir*, 20 March 1958.

23 Barbeau insisted that the best choice for Quebec independence was Jean Drapeau. Raymond Barbeau, "Je m'explique," *Liberté* 4, no. 21 (March 1962), 153–4; Patenaude, *Le vrai visage de Jean Drapeau*, 64. For a thorough analysis of the politics of corporatism within the French-Canadian context, see Warren, "Le corporatisme canadien-français comme 'système total.'"

24 "Me Jean Drapeau parle de 'Cette histoire de minuit et une minute,'" *Le progrès du Saguenay*, 14 September 1959; "Au Lac-St-Jean M. Paul Levasseur l'emporte," *Le progrès du Saguenay*, 17 September 1959.

25 Founder and secretary-treasurer of the CAL, J.-Z.-Léon Patenaude, was infuriated by Drapeau's use of funds for primetime slots at CHLT-TV. He conveyed his bitterness by comparing Drapeau's devious and treacherous traits to mid-twentieth-century dictators like Francisco Franco, António de Oliveira Salazar, and Juan Perón. See Patenaude, *Le vrai visage de Jean Drapeau*, 31, 117–18.

26 For more on the transformations characteristically associated with the Quiet Revolution, see Pâquet and Savard, *Brève histoire de la révolution tranquille.*

27 See images of René Lévesque and Jean Drapeau. Raymond Masse, "Me Drapeau a prêté son serment," *La Presse*, 1 November 1960; Myer Negru, "City, Province Move Closer," *Montreal Gazette*, 1 November 1960; "Drapeau New Montreal Mayor," *Globe and Mail*, 25 October 1960.

28 The city's financial contributions during the Great Depression were a major factor in this default. It is also noteworthy that, during the Great Depression and until the early 1950s, municipalities were responsible for most of the public spending tied to the growing welfare state. Linteau, *Une histoire de Montréal*, 233–4.

29 Frederick Wright, "Montreal's New Government," *Montreal Gazette*, 30 September 1940.

30 As Collin and Bherer write, Class C councillors' involvement in debates at City Hall dampened the enthusiasm of interest groups, who withdrew from regular involvement in municipal affairs. Collin and Bherer, "One Island, Several Cities: Montreal and Its Immediate Suburbs," in *Montreal: The History of a North American City*, 142–3.

31 Sancton, *Governing the Island of Montreal*, 32.

32 Eventually, Quebec Premier Antonio Barrette commissioned an inquiry into Montreal's byzantine political structure. See Paul Champagne, *Rapport de la Commission d'étude du système administratif de Montréal (2 volumes)* (Quebec: Gouvernement du Québec, 1960–1961).

33 "Election Aftermath Includes Quotes, Familiar Faces," *Montreal Gazette*, 25 October 1960.

34 On democracy at City Hall, see Bourassa and Léveillée (eds.), *Le système politique de Montréal*, and Adam, *La démocratie à Montréal*.

35 Myers, *Youth Squad*, 42–3.

36 Paul Dubois, "Ball Rolling, Force in Good Hands – Cmdr. Way," *Montreal Gazette*, 23 March 1962.

37 Turmel, *Le Service de police de la cité de Montréal*, 260.

38 For instance, the city's youth squad educated underaged boys the era's heteronormative imperative by engaging in "a crackdown on the sexual corruption of youths." Myers, *Youth Squad*, 43.

39 Higgins, "A Sense of Belonging," 298.

40 McKenna and Purcell, *Drapeau*, 140–1.

41 In October 1961, the city extended their contracts to March 1962. Way, however, was the only one to fully complete his contract. Gaubiac terminated his contract prematurely, heading back to Paris in November to mourn his son. "Way and Gaubiac Term Extended," *Montreal Gazette*, 20 October 1961; "Paris Expert Won't Complete Mission Here," *Montreal Gazette*, 10 November 1961.

42 Gaubiac told journalists, "I don't want to know anything about Canada before I get there. I won't read a book or a paper. I want to go and see for myself." "Frenchman to Aid Montreal Police," *The Daily News*, 22 December 1960.

43 "Scotland Yard Man Going to Montreal," *The Times*, 6 December 1960.

44 "Gaubiac Coming to Teach, Hopes to Learn," *Montreal Gazette*, 22 December 1960.

45 The year-long study was estimated to cost the city about $30,000. Throughout this period, newspapers covered their work with great interest, and journalists who had special access wrote about their refined tastes for wine, whisky, literature, dance, music, and art. Bill Bantey and Jim Ferrabee,

"Drapeau Police Experts Arrive: 'Open Eyes, Open Ears,'" *Montreal Gazette*, 3 January 1961; "M. Gaubiac M. Way: La vie qu'ils mènent à Montréal," *La Presse*, 21 January 1961.

46 Unlike Pax Plante, who lived a public life, both officers preferred working away from the spotlight and in privacy. During their off-duty hours, they retreated to their hotel rooms to read or watch television. Raymond Guerin, "M. Gaubiac M. Way: La vie qu'ils mènent à Montréal," *La Presse*, 21 January 1961; Marcel Godin, "Gaubiac chez les Kinsmen," *La Presse*, 8 February 1961; Paul Dubois, "Cmdr Way Nears End of Work in City, Press Conference Today Last Function," *Montreal Gazette*, 22 March 1962.

47 "Une nuit au poste," *La Presse*, 21 January 1961; "North End Dance Hall Raided in Drive against 'Goofballs,'" *Montreal Gazette*, 21 January 1961. As Myers writes, Montreal, like other cities during the late 1950s and 1960s, saw a rise in teenaged drug and alcohol use, which led authorities to devise various programs. Myers, *Youth Squad*, 167–8.

48 "'Solve Liquor Problem,'" *Montreal Gazette*, 21 January 1961.

49 "Le budget de la police sera haussé," *Le Devoir*, 2 March, 1961.

50 Lucien Champeau, "Gaubiac et Way surpris de voir Montréal si peu protégée la nuit," *La Presse*, 7 March 1961.

51 "Commander Way Leaves," *Montreal Gazette*, 23 March 1962.

52 Turmel, *Le Service de police de la cité de Montréal*, 236.

53 "Hull Chief Accepts Police Task Here," *Montreal Gazette*, 5 May 1961.

54 Jean Drapeau kept an article on Henri Gauthier, a reformer who ended Hull's notorious corruption. With a red pen, Drapeau stressed and underlined the following section: "[Gauthier] told us nice things about the former Hull chief of police, Adrien Robert, who holds the same position in Montreal. 'I was an alderman when the city of Hull hired him. He came from Montreal, where he returned. We really regretted losing him. He was very good. He is a sincere man, *and he could not be bought*. I liked him.'" Arthur Prévost, "Henri Gauthier, le doyen des entrepreneurs de pompes zfunèbres," *Le Petit Journal*, 15 September 1963, dossier Service de la Police, P100-02-3-D002, AVM. For more on Hull and the Surveyer Inquiry see, Cellard, "Le petit Chicago."

55 "The New Head of the Police," *Montreal Gazette*, 6 July 1961.

56 The bylaw replaced bylaw 247 (1899) and bylaw 978 (1928). City of Montreal,

Bylaw No. 2655, By-law Concerning the Police Department (29 June 1961). Andrew Way and André Gaubiac, Reorganisation of the Police Department (29 June 1961), 1. v. 900, 9-1. VM095-S2-D01, AVM.

57 Raymond Masse, "Dès lundi, à Montréal: Décentralisation du service de la police," *La Presse*, 30 June 1961.

58 Andrew Way and André Gaubiac, *The Montreal Policemen's Brotherhood and the Labour Contract [strictly confidential]* (10 July 1961), 1. v. 900, 9-1, VM095, S2, D01, AVM.

59 Ibid., 7–8.

60 A directive from Lucien Saulnier's office instructed officers not to accept bribes and small gifts under any circumstances. McKenna and Purcell, *Drapeau*, 140–1.

61 Roger Champoux, "Un nettoyage et de grand style," *La Presse*, 16 November 1961.

62 Podmore, "St Lawrence Blvd as 'Third City,'" 222–3.

63 Al Palmer, "Dancing-Girls, 'Cons' – Out in Latest Cabaret Cleanup," *Montreal Gazette*, 22 November 1961.

64 Paul Dubois, "Police Continue Night Raids to Curb Protection Racket," *Montreal Gazette*, 28 September 1962; "Grande offensive de la police," *La Presse*, 28 September 1962.

65 Namaste's research on transgender performers reveals that these artists did not have to pay contributions to the underworld because they brought revenue to the establishments. Their contribution came from encouraging customers to drink and spend more money. Namaste, *C'était du spectacle!*, 26–8. Also see Higgins, "A Sense of Belonging," 298–9.

66 Paul Dubois, "Night Life – Shooting and Fight," *Montreal Gazette*, 1 October 1962.

67 Paul Dubois, "Planned Prevention of Crime Robert's Successful Formula," *Montreal Gazette*, 6 December 1962; Pierre Leger, "La 'Main' disparaîtra maintenant ou jamais," *La Patrie*, 23–9 May 1963.

68 Paul Dubois, "Night Patrol Reinstated, 12 Constables to Serve," *Montreal Gazette*, 29 December, 1962.

69 "Voici à l'œuvre … La Patrouille de nuit," *Nouvelles-Illustrées*, 14 March 1964.

70 "Tough Policing Has Made Milder Street," *Montreal Gazette*, 26 January 1963.

71 Paul Thurston, "When Midnight Tolls, the Night Patrol Moves In," *Montreal Gazette*, 10 August 1968; "The Cop," *Montreal Gazette*, 27 April 1968.
72 *Rapport Way-Gaubiac: réorganisation du Service*, 1961. VM095-2-D01, AVM.
73 In 1936, as the number of motor vehicle deaths and injuries skyrocketed, the Traffic Institute was founded to train police in crash investigations. "Commander Way Leaves," *Montreal Gazette*, 23 March 1962.
74 Paul Dubois, "New Police Code Unveiled," *Montreal Gazette*, 15 June 1962.
75 Abdel-Fattah, *Étude de la main-d'œuvre policière*, 57.
76 "Montreal on the Move!," *New York Times*, 19 November 1961. See Fond VM166-D142-A-(–1962), AVM.
77 Gabeline, Lanken, and Pape, *Montreal at the Crossroads*, 72.
78 "Perceptions from Abroad," in *The 60s*, 180–9.
79 Bradbury, *Working Families*, 38–9.
80 Rudy, Kenny, and Fahrni, "Railways and the Urban Soundscape," 225; Rudy, Kenny, and Fahrni, "'An Ocean of Noise,'" 261–88.
81 Hervé Lépine, "Quand la police fera-t-elle observer le règlement qui interdit le klaxon?," *La patrie*, 16 July 1961.
82 For example, see Smith, "The 'Hell of Modern Sound.'"
83 Ibid. Cities around the world adopted similar strategies to bring about silence and order to streets. As some researchers have demonstrated, at times these strategies were based on racist and class-based assumptions. See Bijsterveld, *Mechanical Sound*, 135; Golan, "Soundscapes of Urban Development"; Stoever, "'Just Be Quiet Pu-leeze.'"
84 "Usage du klaxon: La police sévira contre les abus," *La Presse*, 16 June 1962; Léo Nadeau, "Montréal deviendra-t-elle une ville silencieuse?," *La Patrie*, 28 January 1962.
85 "Night Garbage Collection Will be Tested by City," *Montreal Gazette*, 22 February 1961.
86 Georges Langlois, "Cauchemar des nuits d'été," *La Presse*, 3 August 1960; Germaine Bernier, "L'univers féminin: Le bruit 'signe de puissance' a aussi ses adorateurs," *Le Devoir*, 15 February 1965.
87 "Noisy Night Construction Issue: City Plans to Curb Practice," *Montreal Star*, 31 July 1963; Alfred Ayotte, "Quand finiront nos tourments?," *La Presse*, 17 April 1964; "Night Work Cutout Is Order" *The Monitor*, 27 August 1964.
88 "Sus au bruit!," *La Presse*, 13 January 1965.
89 Eleven men died over the course of the metro's construction. Their lives

would be remembered by Drapeau on the metro's opening day. Malcolm Daigneault, "The Dream Comes True – Métro Opens," *Montreal Gazette*, 15 October 1966.

90 L'équipe de Liberté, "L'équipe de Liberté devant Montréal (essai de situation)," *Liberté* 5, no. 4 (July–August 1963): 282.

91 MacLennan, *Return of the Sphinx*, 219.

92 Lortie, "Montreal 1960: The Singularities of a Metropolitan Archetype," in *The 60s*, 105–7.

93 "Noise-makers Getting the Silent Treatment," *Montreal Star*, 26 December 1964.

94 "Le conseiller Niding fait cesser le travail de nuit," *Guide du Nord*, 25 June 1964.

95 He requested that "deafening work" such as pile driving and cement pouring be restricted between 6 p.m. and 8 a.m., and completely forbidden on weekends. Letter from John Lynch-Staunton to Mayor Drapeau, 13 August 1963. Dossier Service de la Police, P100-02-3-D002, AVM.

96 "Strict Work Hours Sought by Councillor," *Montreal Star*, 19 June 1964.

97 "Noise-makers Getting the Silent Treatment," *Montreal Star*, 26 December 1964.

98 "Construction Jobs: City Bans Late Work," *Montreal Star*, 16 January 1965; Myer Negru, "During Night Hours: Anti-Noise Bylaw Strengthened," *Montreal Gazette*, 16 January 1965.

99 "La ville va sévir contre les entrepreneurs qui sans permis font du bruit, la nuit," *La Presse*, 18 January 1965; "Contre le bruit durant la nuit," *Le Devoir*, 18 January 1965.

100 Don Foley, "Could City Be Quietest? City Councillor Has a Dream," *Montreal Star*, 14 August 1965.

101 For example, Stoever notes that in New York City, noise-abatement proponents have historically used noise as a wedge issue to enforce "divisions of race, class, ethnicity, and nationality within one's self and between 'others.'" Stoever, "'Just Be Quiet Pu-leeze,'" 164.

102 City of Montreal, Amendment No. 3072 to By-law No. 1448, Concerning Noise (8 January 1965). See Procès-verbaux: Volume 66, Janvier 1965–Avril 1965, VM074-6-D066, AVM.

103 "Les Montréalais pourront enfin dormir la nuit," *Le Journal de Montréal*, 9 January 1965.

104 Roger Champoux, "Grand méfait du petit égoïsme," *La Presse*, 20 Janaury 1965; Albert Brie, "Le bruit de ma ville," *La Presse*, 22 January 1965.

105 Raymond Guérin, "Le Carnet: Ah! Cette 'engeance'!," *La Presse*, 18 June 1965; Gilbert Moore, "Qu'on embellisse la ville, mais sans nous casser les oreilles!," *Photo-Journal*, 18–25 August 1965.

106 Pol Chantraine, "Face à l'ennemi public No. 1: Pourquoi pas un permis de faire du bruit à tous les ivrognes de la Métropole?," *Photo-Journal*, 26 October–2 November 1966.

107 Lucien L'Allier, "Where There's a Will, There Can Be a Subway," *Montreal Gazette*, 14 October 1966.

108 In a 4 January 1963 letter to Mayor Drapeau, the Office of the High Commissioner for the United Kingdom wrote: "Way was awarded the Honour of a Companion of the Order of St Michael and St George in Her Majesty's New Year's Honours. I am sure that your strong recommendation made a powerful contribution to this result." Commander Andrew Way Decoration, P100-02-3-D002, AVM.

109 Address by Jean Drapeau, 26 March 1962. Dossier, Way, Andrew – Réception le 26 mars 1962. P100-02-3-D002, AVM.

110 Paul Dubois, "Gilbert Shuffles Police Force for Up-to-the-Minute Methods," *Montreal Gazette*, 22 April 1966.

111 Michel Auger, "Les effectifs de la police de Montréal seront de nouveau en partie centralisés," *La Presse*, 1 April 1970.

112 St-Cyr, *Ma vie de stripteaseuse*, 271.

113 Marcel Huguer, "Même si les racoleuses sont moins nombreuses, la prostitution n'a pas pour autant diminué ses activités," *Le Journal de Montréal*, 4 March 1965.

114 Preparation for the event required not only modern infrastructure but also a sizable police force. From 1954 to 1971, the most significant increase in police personnel occurred in 1966 with the addition of 241 constables, which was made in anticipation of Expo 67. Turmel, *Le Service de police de la cité de Montréal*, 258.

CHAPTER THREE

1 For more on the event, see Moyes and Palmer (eds.), *Expo 67 and Its World*.

2 Gaudette et al., "D'un stade mal-aimé à un stade oublié," 9.

3 *Victoriatown. Réaménagement urbain* (Montreal: Service d'urbanisme ville de Montréal, 1962), 3–5. VM097-02-05-D108, AVM.

4 Ibid., 7; "Hanley Says Fair Would Help End 'Point' Slum," *Montreal Star*, 13 December 1962; Fred Poland, "Plan to Redevelop Brings Out the Irish in 'Point' Residents," *Montreal Star*, 26 December 1962.

5 The city bought over 75 per cent of the neighbourhood's land and dwellings over a period of eight years. Williams, *Blacks in Montreal 1628–1986*, 72. Also see Kardos, "Political Power," 148–68.

6 McKenna and Purcell, *Drapeau*, 150–1.

7 Roger Newman, "Quebec Viewpoint: Clip Joints Mar Montreal's Image," *Globe and Mail*, 30 December 1966. For a local response to that article, see "Mauvaise publicité à Toronto: Certains clubs nuisent à la bonne réputation de Montréal," *Dimanche-Matin*, 15 January 1967.

8 Instead of the common "B-girl," I use the term "B-drink hustler" to emphasize the fact that these individuals were "hustling" drinks for their employer and were not exclusively "girls." In fact, (trans)women and men in drag often posed as B-drink hustlers. Additionally, I chose this term because it is the one favoured by Marlowe, a B-drink hustler, female impersonator, and, later, trans author. See Marlowe, *Mr Madam*, 22, 81–2.

9 Namaste, *C'était du spectacle!*, 29–30; Littauer, *Bad Girls*, 60–1. Occasionally, men hustled drinks in gay bars too, although I've only encountered the term "B-boy" once. See Higgins, "A Sense of Belonging," 208.

10 Straw, "Tabloid Expo," 228.

11 Tim Burke, "Police Launch Night Club War," *Montreal Star*, 26 July 1966.

12 Florian Bernard, "Montréal adopte des règlements sévères contre la prostitution dans les cabarets," *La Presse*, 10 March 1967; "Step Against Prostitution: New Bylaw Cracks Down on Bar Girl Mingling," *Montreal Star*, 10 March 1967. For more on the link between the hospitality and sex industries, see Dunae, "Sex, Charades, and Census Records," 271; Lévesque, *Making and Breaking the Rules*, 118.

13 This professional subculture included a shared jargon, personal networks, tracking and protecting earnings through creative accounting, and shielding from prosecution by co-operating with bartenders to disguise livelihoods. Littauer, *Bad Girls*, 53, 80.

14 See Pépin, "Le pouvoir des provinces canadiennes de légiférer sur la mora-

lité public," 884–5; Durand, "Analyse de la production et de l'application d'une norme pénale."

15 As Australian historian Dian Kirkby writes, historically "barmaid" and "prostitute" were terms often used interchangeably because of the former's close link with men's "immoral" habits. Kirkby, "Writing the History of Women Working," 4, 16.

16 Thinel, *Rapport de la commission d'enquête sur le commerce des boissons alcooliques*, 120, 126–7.

17 "Surveillance accrue par une Régie des débits de boisson," *La Presse*, 19 May 1971.

18 Ian Adams, "A Big Town Becomes a Great City," *Maclean's*, 3 December 1966.

19 See de Champlain, *Histoire du crime organisé*, 258–64.

20 Jean-Claude Trait, "La pègre a déjà loué des milliers de chambres et d'appartements," *Le Petit Journal*, 17 April 1966.

21 Straw, "Tabloid Expo," 224; Marcel Huguet, "'La police ne protège pas la pègre,'" *Photo-Journal*, 20–27 July 1966; "La Mafia à Montréal," *La Presse*, 30 November 1966.

22 Marquis, "Constructing an Urban Drug Ecology in 1970s Canada," 32–4.

23 For more on the historical link between fairs and crime, see Larson, *The Devil in the White City*, and Walden, *Becoming Modern in Toronto*.

24 For more on the etymology of "B-girl," see Littauer, *Bad Girls*, 54.

25 See Marlowe, *Mr Madam*, 22, 80–4.

26 This description draws from the rich history of American B-girls in Littauer, *Bad Girls*, 60–8.

27 Quoted in Namaste, *C'était du spectacle!*, 30–1.

28 See court cases R. c. Colabro (1965) and R. c. Théodore (1966) in Durand, "Analyse de la production et de l'application d'une norme pénale," 51. Also see Namaste, *C'était du spectacle!*, 33.

29 Claire Harting, "Quand les girls effeuillent leur vie … Dans les coulisses de 'Montreal by Night,'" *Photo-Journal*, 26 October–2 November 1966.

30 "Il faut de toute urgence empêcher l'exploitation des 'poissons' dans les cabarets," *Dimanche-Matin*, 2 October 1966; "Ici, on ne boit pas sur le bras!," *Le Journal de Montréal*, 12 June 1969; Paul Dubois, "Gilbert Wants Bars Better Lit, No Sitting with Customers," *Montreal Gazette*, 15 August 1966.

31 Roger Newman, "Quebec Viewpoint: Clip Joints Mar Montreal's Image," *Globe and Mail*, 30 December 1966.

32 "Tourist Time … Not Like It Used to Be but Going Up, Up and Up," *Montreal Gazette*, 22 May 1965.

33 Sismondo, *America Walks into a Bar*, 244–5.

34 Durand, "Analyse de la production et de l'application d'une norme pénale," 62.

35 "Le directeur Gilbert entre en lutte contre les clubs de nuit mal éclairés," *La Presse*, 15 August 1966.

36 "Fleecing Complaints: Shady Night Clubs in the Spotlight," *Montreal Star*, 15 August 1966.

37 Tim Burke, "Police Launch Night Club War," *Montreal Star*, 26 July 1966.

38 Ibid.

39 Bylaw project, "La conduite de certains employés dans les établissements où l'on sert des boissons alcooliques." City of Montreal, executive committee Meeting Minutes, 8 February 1967. VM074-6-D071, AVM.

40 City of Montreal, By-law No. 3416, Behaviour of Certain Employees in Establishments Dispensing Alcoholic Beverages (9 March 1967).

41 See Annex I and II for a list of American "anti-mingling" bylaws in Durand, "Analyse de la production et de l'application d'une norme pénale," 47. On San Francisco, see Littauer, *Bad Girls*. On Miami, see Lee, "American Greed."

42 "Step Against Prostitution: New Bylaw Cracks Down on Bar Girl Mingling," *Montreal Star*, 10 March 1967; Maurice Archambault, "Échec au racolage et à la prostitution," *Montréal-Matin*, 10 March 1967; Florian Bernard, "Montréal adopte des règlements sévères contre la prostitution dans les cabarets," *La Presse*, 10 March 1967.

43 Malcolm Daigneault, "Clubs 'On the Main' Face Big Crackdown," *Montreal Gazette*, 12 April 1967.

44 Al Palmer, "Visit a Cabaret? Well, Don't Chat with Employees," *Montreal Gazette*, 12 April 1967; Podmore, "St Lawrence Blvd as 'Third City,'" 229.

45 "Une bien drôle de façon de combattre la prostitution," *Le Monde du Spectacle*, 20–6 March 1967.

46 Martin Pronovost, "Le juge sort du tiroir un vieux règlement municipal!," *La Presse*, 25 July 1967; Guy Lessonini, "Grandeurs et misères du Montréal by night," *Le Nouveau Samedi*, 21 March 1970.

47 Limoges, *La Prostitution à Montréal*, 65–8.

48 Martha Adams published her autobiography during a sensational 1972 court case – highly reminiscent of the Caron Inquiry. Adams was accused of prostitution and of running, from her own apartment, a brothel involving forty women. Provincial morality squads claimed that her network extended to Boston, New York, Vancouver, Toronto, Halifax, and Quebec City – making Montreal the headquarters of a vast North American sex work ring. The trial's scandalous edge revolved around her lawyer's claim that known police officers, lawyers, magistrates, and politicians were regular clients. In 1973, she was convicted for the fourteenth time and sentenced to one year in prison. See Affaire Martha Adams, 1 January 1972, Dossier Moralité 961.31, VM166-1-1-D2999, AVM.

49 Adams, *Martha Adams*, 136–8.

50 For more, ibid., Chapter 5.

51 Picard, *Ma vie dans les bordels*, 71.

52 Namaste, *C'était du spectacle!*, 62.

53 Hargray et al. v. City of Montreal [1971], Montreal Municipal Court. Colette Hargray was not employed by Bar des Arts, therefore her case was dismissed without costs; Monique Kemp was found guilty and sentenced to $20 and costs; Jeannine Fournier's charge was dismissed without costs; Dawne Kye was found guilty as charged and sentenced to $50 and costs; Lucie Russell was found guilty as charged and sentenced to $25 and costs; Leo-Paul Champagne was found guilty as charged and sentenced to $50 and costs.

54 "Nightclub 'Mingling' Bylaw Facing Challenge in Court," *Montreal Gazette*, 11 April 1967; "Writ Halts Mingling Court Case," *Montreal Gazette*, 12 April 1967; L'Abbé v. City of Montreal (1967) [1968], QB 419.

55 Rumilly, *Histoire de Montréal: Tome V 1939–1967*, 229–49, 269–80.

56 Hubert Bauch, "After 19 Years, Expo Still Makes Montreal Glow," *Montreal Gazette*, 1 May 1986.

57 The Indians of Canada Pavilion at Expo 67 challenged Canada's Centennial celebrations and its nation-building mission. For more on Indigenous participation in the Expo project, see Moyes and Palmer (eds.), *Expo 67 and Its World*.

58 Marsan, *Montreal in Evolution*, 364–70. See Barbeau, Maroist, and Ruel, *Expo 67 Mission Impossible*.

59 Fitz, "On & Off the Record," *Montreal Gazette*, 24 July 1967; Claude Asselin,

"Les ouvriers de la relève nocturne: Des gens font leur métier pour que leurs concitoyens dorment en paix," *Photo-Journal*, 26 October–2 November 1966; Podmore, "St Lawrence Blvd as 'Third City,'" 225, 231.

60 "On & Off the Record," *Montreal Gazette*, 8 May 1967; "Trois autres danseuses 'topless' appréhendées," *La Presse*, 8 May 1967; Raymond Drouin, "Il n'y aura pas de seins nus à Montréal, Durant l'Expo…," *Dimanche-Matin*, 2 April 1967; "Pendant qu'on traque les 'topless,' les 'gros légumes' font des orgies," *Le Monde du Spectacle*, 10–16 April 1967; Lise Lapierre, "La loi existe ou n'existe pas," *Photo-Journal*, 4–11 October 1967.

61 "Arrestation de sept femmes," *La Presse*, 18 May 1967.

62 Namaste, *C'était du spectacle!*, 45–6.

63 Lacasse, *La Prostitution féminine à Montréal*, 47.

64 Rioux v. R. [1968], QB 876. The pimp (who was charged on the night of 7 July 1967) appealed the charge, and the court dropped the case on 12 June 1968.

65 "Ten Persons Arrested in Raid on Two Clubs," *Montreal Gazette*, 20 July 1967; "Descentes et arrestations dans des cabarets," *La Presse*, 20 July 1967.

66 The history of policing the African company can be traced back to March 1959 when a similar event unfolded. For more on policing, nudity, and race, see Chapter 1 in Templeton, "Polyrhythmic Dance Currents."

67 Hébert, Lever, and Landry (eds.), *Dictionnaire de la censure au Québec*, 65–6.

68 Oswald Mamo, "Les danseuses aux seins nus n'étaient pas indécentes," *La Presse*, 26 January 1968.

69 See Austin, *Fear of a Black Nation*.

70 "Le règlement 3416 vaut aussi pour les hommes," *La Presse*, 20 April 1970.

71 Leon Levinson, "Nightclubs Lose Bids for Restaurant Permits," *Montreal Gazette*, 30 June 1970; Michel Auger, "La police ferme les cabarets 'Chez Paree' et le 'Béret Bleu,'" *La Presse*, 24 December 1970; "Montréal veut obtenir la fermeture du 'Béret Bleu,'" *La Presse*, 27 August 1971. See Soccio v. Régie des alcools du Québec (1971) [1972], QCA 283.

72 That night police also raided Chez Pierre-le-Grand and Café Rialto. "Quand les moines s'en vont en tôle…," *La Presse*, 15 May 1968.

73 L'Abbé v. City of Montreal (1968) [1969], QB 1098; Jean Denechaud, "Le règlement interdisant aux danseuses de se mêler aux clients déclaré valide," *La Presse*, 9 November 1968.

74 "Pour ou contre le règlement 3416 interdisant aux employés de cabarets de fraterniser avec les clients?," *Le Journal de Montréal*, 29 February 1968.

75 Claude Jodoin, "L'opération nettoyage: razzia dans 13 clubs qui 'nous' coûte cher et qui rapporte peu!," *Le Journal de Montreal*, 20 July 1970; Claude Jodoin, "Raids 'rituels' dans les clubs: à pas de tortue, cette fois … et pourtant aussi efficaces," *Le Journal de Montréal*, 27 July 1970; Jodoin, *Montréal insolite*, 19.

76 Guy Lessonini, "Grandeurs et misères du Montréal by night," *Le Nouveau Samedi*, 21 March 1970.

77 Interview with Dennis Brown (1982) quoted in Gilmore, *Swinging in Paradise*, 226.

78 For more on those strikes, see Prévost, Gagné, and Phaneuf, *L'histoire de l'alcool au Québec*, 132–5.

79 Bernier, Brault, and Parent, "La Régie des alcools du Québec."

80 "Déclaration ministérielle," *Journal des débats de l'Assemblée nationale*, 12 November 1968, Bibliothèque de l'Assemblée nationale du Québec.

81 Palmer, *Montreal Confidential*, 134.

82 For a Canadian overview, see Heron, *Booze*.

83 Thinel, *Rapport de la commission d'enquête*, 77.

84 See the front-page headline of *Le Devoir*, 29 June 1970; Dan Karon, "City Report Charges: 'Liquor Laws Encourage Underworld,'" *Montreal Gazette*, 30 June 1970; Letter from "a Friend" to Justice Omer Côté, 21 April 1970, VM001-4-2, 721-1, AVM.

85 *Mémoire de la ville de Montréal à la Commission d'enquête sur le commerce des boissons alcooliques au Québec* (Montréal: 1970). VM001-4-2, 721-1, AVM.

86 Ibid., 12. The report came on the heels of a provincial inquiry into justice reform, which stressed the role that organized crime held in the nighttime economy. Prévost, *Crime, Justice, and Society*.

87 Ibid., 18.

88 Jean-Paul Gilbert, "Une affaire prioritaire," *Le Devoir*, 29 June 1970.

89 Jérôme Choquette, *Journal des débats de l'Assemblée nationale*, 30 March 1971, Bibliothèque de l'Assemblée nationale du Québec; "1,000 Police in Drive: City Will Enforce Liquor Laws," *Montreal Star*, 29 July 1970.

90 Thinel, *Rapport de la commission d'enquête*, 126–7.

91 Lois annuelles du Québec 1971, ch. 20 *Quebec Liquor Corporation Act* (10 July 1971).

92 Pierre-L. O'Neill, "La RAQ scindée en deux organismes," *Le Devoir*, 19 May 1971.

93 The Commission held authority over twenty-three different liquor permits, including those for restaurants, bars, pubs, taverns, and cabarets. Lois annuelles du Québec 1971, ch. 19 *Liquor Permit Control Commission Act* (7 July 1971).

94 Ibid., Division V, no. 81.

95 Lacasse, "Le travail des danseuses nues," iv–v.

96 "Deux ministres sont d'accord," *La Presse*, 19 May 1971; Derek Hill, "Mass liquor law reform urged for more access," *Montreal Gazette*, 19 May 1971.

97 Durand, "Analyse de la production et de l'application d'une norme pénale," 3.

98 Danny Vear, "Moralité publique: Montréal à nouveau déboutée en cour," *Le Devoir*, 26 February 1993.

99 Shirley Lacasse, "Le travail des danseuses nues," v.

CHAPTER FOUR

1 Lise Lapierre, "D'après Monsieur le Maire Aucun danger au Vaisseau d'Or," *Photo-Journal* 8–15 October 1969; Fançoise Kayle, "'Le Vaisseau d'Or' vient d'appareiller," *La Presse*, 9 September 1969.

2 Le Vaisseau d'Or, *Menu, Les secrets du chef, Carte des vins*. Dossier Le Vaisseau d'Or – Artistes, P100-06-3-D006, AVM.

3 "Concert du 4 septembre 1969," Orchestre du Vaisseau d'Or. Inauguration 1969, P100-06-3-D002, AVM.

4 Nelligan, "Ship of Gold," in *Ship of Gold*, 11.

5 "Montreal's 'Night of Terror,'" CBC *Television News Special*, 8 October 1969.

6 Sancton, *Governing the Island of Montreal*, 109.

7 *Rapport d'enquête sur la conduite de certains membres du corps de police de la ville de Montréal* (Quebec: Commisison de police du Québec, 1971), 121. VM095-S3-D04, AVM.

8 Sensational descriptions of a lawless Montreal made it to the front page of numerous newspapers, including *The Jerusalem Post*, *Evening Standard*, *New York Times*, *The Evening News*, *The Washington Post*, and *The Chicago Tribune*. Also see Médam, *Montréal Interdite*, 107–8.

9 Mills, *The Empire Within*, 104–5.

10 See "Days to Remember: The Sir George Williams Narratives," in Austin, *Fear of a Black Nation*, 129–56.

11 Dagenais and Saunier, "Tales from the Periphery," in *Municipal Services and Employees in the Modern City*, 16.

12 Turmel, *Le Service de police de la cité de Montréal*, 256–7.

13 City of Montreal, By-Law No. 3926, By-Law Relating to Exceptional Measures to Safeguard the Free Exercise of Civil Liberties, to Regulate the Use of the Public Domain and to Prevent Riots and Other Violations of Order, Peace and Public Safety (12 November 1969).

14 See Dupond v. City of Montreal et al. [1978] 2, SCR 770; André Beauvais, "Montréal luttera contre le jugement du juge Gaston Lacroix," *La Presse*, 16 April 1970; Marx, "The Montreal Anti-Demonstration By-Law."

15 Blais, *St Lawrence Blues*, 157, 195.

16 For a legal review of the labour dispute, see Dontigny, "L'efficacité du cadre légal particulier de la négociation collective visant les pompiers municipaux québécois."

17 *Rapport d'enquête sur la conduite de certains membres du corps de police de la ville de Montréal*, 38. VM095-S3-D04, AVM.

18 "La nuit de la grève marquée de 18 méfaits," *La Presse*, 16 December 1943; "De graves dégâts par les flammes durant la grève," *La Presse*, 15 December 1943.

19 See Dagenais, *Des pouvoirs et des hommes*, 130–1.

20 Jean-Jacques Bertrand, *Journal des débats de l'Assemblée nationale*, 8 October 1969, Bibliothèque de l'Assemblée nationale du Québec.

21 Quoted in McKenna and Purcell, *Drapeau*, 208. Gilbert expressed his apprehension to both municipal and provincial authorities between 20 July 1966 and 31 December 1968. Moreover, he organized several meetings with the management of the SQ, the RCMP, and representatives of the Canadian Armed Forces to establish a plan in the event of a strike. *Rapport d'enquête sur la conduite de certains membres du corps de police de la ville de Montréal*, 15. VM095-S3-D04, AVM.

22 An unsympathetic letter from MTC president Lucien L'Allier unleashed the fury. Jacques Lafrenière, "CTM: une lettre de M. L'Allier a finalement déclenché le conflit," *La Presse*, 21 September 1967.

23 Warren, *Histoire du taxi à Montréal*, 191–2.

24 By the following year members of the Comité d'entr'aide joined the Mouvement de libération du taxi (MLT), a more militant and radical group. Ibid., 194, 205.

25 "Saulnier: négociations dès le retour au travail," *Le Devoir*, 18 October 1967.

26 To offset losses, Drapeau announced a lottery scheme designed to attract participants from across Canada and the United States. Optimistically, he forecasted that it would generate an additional $32 million a year. See Morton, *At Odds*, 189; "Drapeau recourt à la taxe 'volontaire': Une loterie municipale en mai," *La Presse*, 3 April 1968.

27 McKenna and Purcell, *Drapeau*, 206–7.

28 Lucien Rivard, "1,500 policiers manifestent à l'hôtel de ville," *La Presse*, 24 February 1968.

29 See "Le Défilé de la Saint-Jean-Baptiste," and "Téléjournal," *Radio-Canada*, 24 June 1968.

30 Ouimet, "Le lys en fête, le lys en feu," 101–3. Jacques Lanctôt later revealed that Nightstick Monday had a direct impact on the political kidnappings of 1970. See Pierre Turgeon, "J'étais un Robin des Bois [entrevue avec Jacques Lanctôt]," *Liberté* 32, no. 5 (1990): 109.

31 The title is a clever wordplay on the homophonic Terre des Hommes. Meaning "silencing men," *Taire des hommes* at once taunts autocratic officials riding on Expo 67's coattails and evokes the city's censorship and its repression of activists in June 1968. Gélinas and Harel, *Taire des hommes.*

32 "Escouade anti-émeutes forte de 450 policiers à Montréal," *La Presse*, 3 July 1968; "Pas de gaz Mace 'pour le moment,'" *La Presse*, 8 October 1968; Joseph Hanafin, "Anti-riot Squad Planned for City," *Montreal Star*, 3 July 1968.

33 Service de la police de Montréal, *Unité Mobile: Étude sur la structure et les méthodes d'opération lors de manifestations violentes* (18 September 1968). VM095-S3-D12, AVM. For more on the history of protests in Los Angeles during this period, see Davis and Wiener, *Set the Night on Fire.*

34 "City Soon to Form 180-man Riot Squad," *Montreal Gazette*, 24 August 1968. For an international perspective of 1968 protests, see Suri, *Power and Protest.*

35 See Austin, *Fear of a Black Nation*; Warren, "L'Opération McGill français."

36 Gerald Clark, "What Happens When the Police Strike," *New York Times*, 16 November 1969; J.-C. Fortin, "La police: les émeutiers, on les attend!," *Le Petit Journal*, 9 September 1968.

37 Resolution No. 30487/1-2, minutes of the executive committee, 23 October 1968. VM074-6-D075, AVM.

38 Between June 1968 and October 1969, 2 officers had been killed on duty and more than 250 injured. Sancton, *Governing the Island of Montreal*, 108.

39 By July 1969, the MPB hired Inbucon Services Limited, a consultation firm,

to determine appropriate salaries for its members. See *Rapport sur l'évaluation relative de fonctions*. VM095-S3-D08, AVM.

40 Jacques Lafrenière, "Grève Générale des 18,000 employés municipaux," *La Presse*, 14 January 1969.

41 Daniel Marsolais, "Attentat chez Drapeau," *La Presse*, 29 September 1969; "Le maire n'a pas eu à démolir sa maison," *La Presse*, 5 December 1969; "Drapeau Buys Watchdog," *Toronto Daily Star*, 6 January 1970.

42 *Rapport d'enquête sur la conduite de certains membres du corps de police de la ville de Montréal*, 20. VM095-S3-D04, AVM.

43 Claude Masson and Jean-Paul Charbonneau, "Pourquoi les pompiers sont-ils, eux aussi, entrés dans la ronde de la contestation?," *La Presse*, 7 October 1969.

44 Jean-Paul Charbonneau, "Murmures de grèves chez pompiers et policiers," *La Presse*, 4 October 1969; "Police, Fire Pay Raises 'Not Enough,'" *Montreal Gazette*, 3 October 1969; *Rapport d'enquête sur la conduite de certains membres du corps de police de la ville de Montréal*, 35–9. VM095-S3-D04, AVM.

45 The interview aired on 13 November 1971. Quoted in Adam, *La démocratie à Montréal*, 268.

46 Letter from William A. Huebner to Jean Drapeau, 26 October 1970. P100-06-3-D004, AVM.

47 Reid, *The Shouting Signpainters*.

48 "'On veut Drapeau!' criaient les pompiers," *La Presse*, 6 October 1969. The event was labelled "la marche des pompiers sur le 'Vaisseau d'Or.'" *Rapport d'enquête sur la conduite de certains membres du corps de police de la ville de Montréal*, 34. VM095-S3-D04, AVM.

49 Lise Lapierre, "D'après Monsieur le Maire Aucun danger au Vaisseau d'Or," *Photo-Journal*, 8–15 October 1969.

50 McKenna and Purcell, *Drapeau*, 191.

51 Ibid., Chapter XXIX. The schism between Chief Gilbert and his officers can be explained by the fact that the staff at the police headquarters were not part of the bargaining unit represented by the MPB. *Rapport d'enquête sur la conduite de certains membres du çorps de police de la ville de Montréal*, 11. VM095-S3-D04, AVM.

52 Under the previous union agreement, a Montreal police officer with three years of service earned $7,300 annually. The union bargained for a $1,900 yearly increase over the next two years to reach parity with Toronto police

salaries. The appeal tribunal, however, settled on awarding $1,100. Jean-Paul Charbonneau, "Vive insatisfaction des dirigeants de la Fraternité des policiers," *La Presse*, 7 October 1969; "A Montreal Policeman Explains Strike," *New York Times*, 9 October 1969.

53 *Rapport d'enquête sur la conduite de certains membres du corps de police de la ville de Montréal*, 24–5, 37–8, 89–97, 104. VM095-S3-D04, AVM.

54 Ibid, 90–1.

55 Ibid., 6.

56 Ibid., 91.

57 Grèves: Pompiers – 1969. VM074-3-D085, AVM.

58 Lucien Saulnier, 7 October 1969. Grèves: Policiers – 1969. VM074-3-D086, AVM.

59 He arrived in St Louis at 12 a.m. on Tuesday and was back in Montreal on the same day at 9:30 p.m. Déclaration du maire en lien avec la crise (bombe), 10 October 1969. P100-02-9-D005-P006, AVM.

60 A folder at the City of Montreal archives is filled with letters – from citizens, scholars, bankers, religious leaders, politicians, and many others, including telegraphs from the leader of the opposition – praising his remarkable sangfroid. Grèves: Policiers – 1969. VM074-3-D086, AVM.

61 Gérard Cellier, "La SQ est débordée: 30 hold-up," *Montréal-Matin*, 8 October 1969.

62 *Rapport d'enquête sur la conduite de certains membres du corps de police de la ville de Montréal*, 7. VM095-S3-D04, AVM.

63 "Deux policiers battus par des voyous," *La Presse*, 8 October 1969.

64 *Rapport d'enquête sur la conduite de certains membres du corps de police de la ville de Montréal*, 82–3, 91–2. VM095-S3-D04, AVM.

65 Ibid. 70–83, 109–19.

66 Gerald Clark, "What Happens When the Police Strike," *New York Times*, 16 November 1969.

67 Pierre Vennat, "L'armée est à Montréal: Québec mate la police," *La Presse*, 8 October 1969; "L'armée est appelée," *Montréal-Matin*, 8 October 1969.

68 Jay Walz, "Montreal: It Was Unbelievable: A Big City without Police or Firemen," *New York Times*, 12 October 1969.

69 By 1900, and for sixty years, Sainte-Catherine Street was "well established as *the* retail shopping street of Montreal." See Sifton, "Montreal's Fashion Mile," in *Fashion: A Canadian Perspective*, 203–26. Also see Linteau, *Sainte-Catherine Street*, 9–10.

70 "Laughing Hoods Move In," *Montreal Gazette*, 8 October 1969; "Montréal, un nouveau Belfast!: Pillage, saccage, scenes incroyables…" *Montréal-Matin*, 8 October 1969.

71 Nye, *When the Lights Went Out*, 3, 124–5.

72 *Rapport d'enquête sur la conduite de certains membres du corps de police de la ville de Montréal*, 124. VM095-S3-D04, AVM.

73 Nick Auf der Maur, "Lessons on Fighting City Hall: A Study of Montreal's 'Mouvement de Libération du Taxi,'" *The Last Post* 1, no. 3 (April 1970): 20–3.

74 Warren, *Histoire du taxi à Montréal*, 201.

75 *Rapport d'enquête sur la conduite de certains membres du corps de police de la ville de Montréal*, 126–7. VM095-S3-D04, AVM.

76 Michel Roy, "Une fusillade fait 3 morts devant la Murray Hill," *Le Devoir*, 8 October 1969.

77 Warren, *Histoire du taxi à Montréal*, 208.

78 "Murray Hill Lot a 'War Zone,'" *Montreal Gazette*, 8 October 1969; Frank, "The 'Ingredients' in Violent Labour Conflict," 91; "Murray Hill dévastée," *La Presse*, 8 October 1969; Ray Doucet, "Two Guns Used at Murray Hill," *Montreal Gazette*, 13 November 1969.

As Warren notes, institutional change to the taxi industry came years later when Quebec Premier Robert Bourassa – whose electoral district held the highest concentration of taxi drivers in Canada – acted on the Alfred Bossé Report (1970). Warren, *Histoire du taxi à Montréal*, 208–11.

79 Auf der Maur, *Quebec*, 15; McKenna and Purcell, *Drapeau*, 214.

80 Douille de la balle tirée le 7 oct 1970 [*sic*] soirée émeute dans le salon du Vaisseau d'or. Dossier 1970 [*sic*]. P100-02-4-D005, AVM.

81 "Un 'soir d'aubaines,' une nuit de pillage," *La Presse*, 8 October 1969; "L'activité était toute dans les rues…," *La Presse*, 8 October 1969; "Pendant que Lucien Saulnier est à Québec, le maire Drapeau examine 'le Vaisseau d'Or,'" *La Presse*, 8 October 1969.

82 Christiane Desjardins, "'Tenez M. le maire, ces 10 000$ sont à vous,'" *La Presse*, 16 August 1999.

83 Gérard Lebel, *Journal des débats de l'Assemblée nationale*, 8 October 1969, Bibliothèque de l'Assemblée nationale du Québec.

84 Jean-Jacques Bertrand, *Journal des débats de l'Assemblée nationale*, 7 October 1969, Bibliothèque de l'Assemblée nationale du Québec.

85 "L'armée est appelée," *Montréal-Matin*, 8 October 1969.

86 According to a report, the military personnel used knowledge from this first mission for Operation Essay, the Canadian Forces' code name for the October Crisis mission. See Campeau, "L'intervention militaire en octobre 1970," 29; "Me Rémi Paul demande l'assistance de l'armée canadienne," *La Presse*, 8 October 1969; Parizeau, "L'armée et la Crise d'octobre," 62. Also see Lucien Saulnier's testimony to the House of Commons Standing Committee on Broadcasting, Films, and Assistance to the Arts, 27–8 November 1969, quoted in Bouthillier and Cloutier (eds.), *Trudeau's Darkest Hour*, 53–4.

87 André Plante telegraph to Lucien Saulnier at 9:44 a.m., 8 October 1969. Grèves: Pompiers – 1969. VM074-3-D085, AVM.

88 Jay Walz, "Montreal: It Was Unbelievable: A Big City without Police or Firemen," *New York Times*, 12 October 1969.

89 "Policiers et pompiers reprennent le travail," *La Presse*, 8 October 1969.

90 See photo of the union leaders and the executive committee signing the contracts. Paul-Henri Talbot, "29 octobre 1969," 29 October 1969, P833-S5-D1696-0769-004, BANQ.

91 From the 1954/55 to 1970/71 fiscal year, the Police Department's budget increased from $9.6 million to $49.7 million, while total municipal expenditures rose from $116.5 million to $444.7 million. Turmel, *Le Service de police de la cité de Montréal*, 256–7.

92 Sancton, *Governing the Island of Montreal*, 111.

93 See Chapter 4 in Levine, *The Reconquest of Montreal*. Also see Sancton, *Governing the Island of Montreal*, 76–8.

94 The crowd burned effigies of Mayor Drapeau, Lucien Saulnier, Premier Jean-Jacques Bertrand, and Justice Minister Rémi Paul. "Une mer de manifestants déferle rue Craig," *Le Devoir*, 30 October 1969; Mills, *The Empire Within*, 156–7.

95 "Press conference given by the chairman of the executive committee of the city of Montreal, Mr Lucien Saulnier, in the executive committee chamber, at 18.00 hours, Saturday, the 11th of October 1969." Grèves: Policiers – 1969. VM074-3-D086, AVM.

96 "Protesters Arrested in City Hall March," *Montreal Gazette*, 13 November 1969.

97 Brian Stewart, "Protest Ban Now Law," *Montreal Gazette*, 13 November 1969.

98 It was Diefenbaker's government that had obtained the passage of the Canadian Bill of Rights. Marcel Pépin, "Trudeau désapprouve le règlement de Montréal," *La Presse*, 15 November 1969.

99 City of Montreal, By-Law No. 3926, Relating to Exceptional Measures to Safeguard the free Exercise of Civil Liberties, to Regulate the Use of the Public Domain and to Prevent Riots and Other Violations of Order, Peace and Public Safety (12 November 1969).

100 Leon Harris, "First Victim of Bylaw: Ban Halts Vietnam Parade," *Montreal Gazette*, 14 November 1969.

101 Michel Auger, "À la demande de la police: Pas de défilé du Père Noël," *La Presse*, 15 November 1969.

102 Laurin, *Des luttes et des droits*, 82.

103 Mills, *The Empire Within*, 119–20.

104 Solange Chalvin, "Le Font commun des Québécoises descendra dans la rue, ce soir," *Le Devoir*, 28 November 1969; Gilles Gariepy, "Le Front commun des Québécoises veut défier le règlement 'qui mène droit vers le fascisme avoué,'" *La Presse*, 28 November 1969; O'Leary and Toupin, *Québécoises deboutte!*, 23; "Women Marchers Pick Jail over Fine," *Montreal Gazette*, 15 August 1970.

105 Laval Le Borgne et Lucien Rivard, "150 femmes manifestent 'assises' sur la rue St-Laurent," *La Presse*, 29 November 1969.

106 Guy Deshaies, "La requête des manifestantes pourrait entraîner l'abrogation du règlement 3926," *Le Devoir*, 1 December 1969.

107 For more on the history of left-wing feminism in 1960s and '70s Montreal, see Ricci, *Countercurrents*.

108 "Contestation du règlement anti-manifestation: Atmosphère inusitée à la Cour municipale," *La Presse*, 1 December 1969.

Two weeks after the FCQ's protest, trade union leaders organized another nighttime protest in defiance of the bylaw. Writers, artists, intellectuals, and students joined the protest. When the Police Department's anti-riot unit confronted them, the march turned into a sit-in protest, too. Michel Auger, "Troisième manifestation contre le règlement antimanifestation," *La Presse*, 11 December 1969.

109 Leon Levinson, "Protest Ban Declared Illegal," *Montreal Gazette*, 15 April 1970.

110 Marx, "The Montreal Anti-Demonstration By-Law," 348.

111 "Women Marchers Pick Jail over Fine," *Montreal Gazette*, 15 November 1970.

112 Clément, *Human Rights in Canada*, 86–7.

113 For more on the October Crisis, see Brault, *Les orders*; Chapter 7 in Mills, *The Empire Within*.

114 Thomas, *A City with a Difference*, 26; Sancton, "Montreal," in *City Politics in Canada*, 73.

115 That night, following his compelling triumph, Drapeau delivered a fiery twenty-minute speech about law, order, and democracy. Discours de Jean Drapeau, le soir des élections municipales, dans le hall d'honneur de l'hôtel de ville, 25 October 1970. P100-02-9-D004-P006, AVM.

116 Report by Chief Jean-Jacques Saulnier, "Violence appréhendée et manifestations à l'occasion du conflit qui s'envenime entre le Journal La Presse et des employés appuyés par de nombreux autres syndiqués ou organisations syndicales." City of Montreal, executive committee Meeting Minutes, 27 October 1971. VM074-6-D082, AVM; Auf der Maur, *Quebec*, 97.

117 Pierre Richard, "La marche tourne à l'affrontement," *Le Devoir*, 30 October 1971.

118 In the days leading up to the march, Louis Laberge requested that "all unionized workers of Quebec" take part in the march. Executive committee Meeting Minutes, 27 October 1971. VM074-6-D082, AVM.

119 Ménard, "Le lock-out de *La Presse*," 19.

120 Quoted in ibid., 21.

121 Ibid. Auf der Maur, *Quebec*, 92–7; Gentile, "'À bas la répression contre les homosexuels!,'" in *Une histoire des sexualités au Québec*, 201.

122 Strato Liberopoulos, "Police Mobile Unit Jails 200 Monthly," *Sunday Express*, 24 March 1974.

123 O'Leary and Toupin, *Québécoises deboutte!*, 30, 124–8; Ménard, "Le lock-out de *La Presse*," 22–5.

124 Cited in Auf der Maur, "The Trigger Was the La Presse Affair," *Last Post* (December 1971–January 1972): 10. I have italicized "our" to denote the clear opposition between "us" – the labour movement – and "them" – Power Corporation, the Civic Party, and the Montreal Policemen Brotherhood.

125 Auf der Maur, *Quebec*, 98–9; Mills, *The Empire Within*, 199–200. *La Presse*'s activities resumed on 10 February 1972 after a long, drawn-out negotiation. For more on that process, see the memoir by then–employment and workforce minister Cournoyer, *Dans le feu de l'action*, 162–75.

126 Jean-V. Dufresne, "Les nuits rouges: Drapeau blâme les pompiers d'avoir attendu jusque-là," *Le Devoir*, 5 November 1974.

127 In the months preceding the strike, the Canadian government held a symposium in Montreal on the very question of inflation. See Conference

Board in Canada, *Perspective on Inflation: A Symposium Held in Montreal, January, 1974: A Report* (Ottawa: Conference Board in Canada, 1974). Also see Cowie, *Stayin' Alive.*

128 Cournoyer, *Dans le feu de l'action*, 176.

129 Ibid., 239–40; Bernard Descôteaux, "Montréal roule de nouveau," *Le Devoir*, 20 September 1974.

130 Jean-Paul Charbonneau, "Incendie dans deux casernes de pompiers," *La Presse*, 9 October 1974.

131 Réjean Tremblay and Jean-Paul Charbonneau, "Les pompiers refusent d'obéir," *La Presse*, 1 November 1974.

132 Allison, *Rapports d'enquêtes*, 13.

133 Jean-V. Dufresne, "Montréal sans pompiers," *Le Devoir*, 1 November 1974.

134 André Béliveau, "Week-end Rouge," *Le Magazine Maclean*, February 1975, 30.

135 *La Presse* reported Jean L'Abbé saying, "I've heard enough from [Jean Cournoyer], I'm going to submit my resignation to my members immediately. We haven't been able to resolve this conflict in a professional manner; there's no point in having a union if it's to always be flouted." Réjean Tremblay and Jean-Paul Charbonneau, "Les pompiers refusent d'obéir," *La Presse*, 1 November 1974.

136 André Béliveau, "Week-end Rouge," *Le Magazine Maclean*, February 1975, 30–2.

137 Marcel Adam, "Bourassa doit mettre fin à ce gâchis de l'administration Drapeau," *La Presse*, 1 November 1974.

138 Fires broke out at a lumber yard in Verdun, the Old Doctors Hospital on Côte-des-Neiges Road, and in Saint-Jacques Ward. The following day, it hit the former Knights of Columbus Hall in Rosemont, near the future Olympic site. "Bourassa Won't Intervene: 2,400 Firefighters Off the Job," *Montreal Gazette*, 1 November 1974; Rene Laurent and Steve Kowch, "Drapeau Enters Talks as Chiefs Battle Fires," *Montreal Gazette*, 2 November 1974.

139 For a condensed timeline, see "Three-day Fires List: Arson Suspected," *Montreal Gazette*, 4 November 1974.

140 Glen Allen, "Anguish Smoulders in Burnt-out District," *Montreal Gazette*, 4 November 1974.

141 André Béliveau, "Week-end Rouge," *Le Magazine Maclean*, February 1975, 30.

142 Ibid.

143 In his autobiography, tailor businessman Alvin Cramer Segal wrote that despite being far from the heat of the action, his factory was firebombed. Segal, *My Peerless Story*, 97–8.

144 "Montréal en otage: policiers et pompiers font la grève," *Tout le monde en parlait*, 2007.

145 Cournoyer, *Dans le feu de l'action*, 243.

146 Claude Gravel, "Mésentente sur le sens de l'accord avec les pompiers," *La Presse*, 4 November 1974.

147 Robert Bourassa, *Journal des débats de l'Assemblée nationale*, 1 November 1974, Bibliothèque de l'Assemblée nationale du Québec; "Les services d'incendie de banlieue ont fait leurs 'preuves,'" *La Presse*, 4 November 1974; Glen Allen, "Anguish Smoulders in Burnt-out District," *Montreal Gazette*, 4 November 1974; "Montréal fait appel à la banlieue," *La Presse*, 1 November 1974.

148 Michel Auger, "L'incendie de l'hôtel LaSalle: Visait-on le maire Drapeau?," *La Presse*, 4 November 1974; "Canada: Montreal's Striking Firemen Back at Work," *Reuters*, 4 November 1974; "Canada: Fires Deliberately Lit in Montreal as the City's Firemen Continue Their Strike," *Reuters*, 3 November 1974.

149 Andrew Phillips, "Homeless Try to Cope: 'It's All Gone,' Victim Cries," *Montreal Gazette*, 4 November 1974; Pierre Bertrand, "Les sinistrés poursuivent conjointement la ville de Montréal et les pompiers," *Le Jour*, 5 November 1974.

150 They had been paying $38 for their unit before it went up in flames. "Montréal en otage: policiers et pompiers font la grève," *Tout le monde en parlait*, 2007.

151 Christiane Berthiaume, "Les victimes sont toujours les mêmes: les démunis…," *La Presse*, 5 November 1974.

152 Jean-Luc Duguay, "Le triste défilé des sinistrés du week-end rouge," *Le Devoir*, 5 November 1974; Evelyn Dumas, "Plus de 60 familles ont vu brûler leur maison," *Le Jour*, 4 November 1974.

153 "Montréal en otage: policiers et pompiers font la grève," *Tout le monde en parlait*, 2007; Glen Allen, "Anguish Smoulders in Burnt-out District," *Montreal Gazette*, 4 November 1974; Bob Olsen, "More than 100 Homes," *Toronto Star*, 4 November 1974.

154 "Un compromis hâté par Québec a fait rentrer les pompiers," *Le Devoir*, 4 November 1974; Evelyn Dumas, "Drapeau reprend sa campagne," *Le Jour*, 4 November 1974.

155 Evelyn Dumas, "Oui, il y a des responsables," *Le Jour*, 4 November 1974; Claude Gravel, "Le bilan d'un désastre," *La Presse*, 4 November 1974; Ingrid Saumart, "Les syndicats disent: le maire Drapeau est le grand responsable," *La Presse*, 5 November 1974.

156 Milner, "The Montreal Citizens' Movement, Then and Now," 2.

157 See Thomas, *A City with a Difference*.

158 AVM holds a box filled with litigation files and hundreds of photographs pertaining to buildings and structures that were damaged by fire and water during the Red Weekend – including an automobile repair shop, a hostel, a grocery store, Alvin Cramer Segal's textile factory, a laundromat, and scores of apartment complexes. Many shops were damaged when an accidental fire ravaged the intersection at Mont-Royal and Papineau streets on the night of 1 November, including a bazaar, clothing stores, jewellery stores, and a newsstand. Archives de Montréal dossiers de litige, VM007-Y-1-D20 to D-51, AVM. Allison, *Rapports d'enquêtes au Procureur général de la province de Québec*, 4.

159 Allison, *Rapports d'enquêtes au Procureur général de la province de Québec*, 3–5.

160 "Quatorze incendies criminels," *La Presse*, 18 June 1975; Dave Thomas, "Arson Widespread in '74 Walkout: Charges Urged for Firemen's Strike," *Montreal Gazette*, 18 June 1975.

161 Cournoyer, *Dans le feu de l'action*, 243.

162 "Le maire Drapeau est accusé de vol," *Le Devoir*, 12 November 1971; "Le 'Vaisseau d'Or' cadenassé," *Le Devoir*, 14 January 1971; McKenna and Purcell, *Drapeau*, 187–95.

163 Advertisement *Montreal Gazette*, 3 April 1970.

In the mid-1960s, after meeting with representatives of New York's Metropolitan Opera and the City Opera, Drapeau and Wilfrid Pelletier flew to Europe to meet with directors of leading opera houses, including those in Paris, London, Brussels, Berlin, Cologne, Munich, Vienna, and Milan. The Montreal Opera, however, would be founded later, in 1980, not by the city but by the Ministère des affaires culturelles du Québec. "Visit To Operas Set," *Montreal Gazette*, 4 September 1964.

164 In fact, Adam openly wondered if Montreal was under an authoritarian regime. Adam, *La démocratie à Montréal*, 7, 64.

CHAPTER FIVE

1 Michael Hoffman, "It Wasn't Art, but 'Pollution' Drapeau Says of '76 Exhibit," *Montreal Gazette*, 22 January 1981; "What Happened When the Mayor Took a Drive Down Sherbrooke St," *Montreal Gazette*, 6 October 1979; Gilles Lesage, "La XXIe Olympiade: Montréal est prêt!," *Le Devoir*, 17 July 1976.

2 *Corridart* was initially proposed by *Châtelaine*'s first editor-in-chief Fernande Saint-Martin. For more on the planning and development of the exhibition, see Gauvin, "*Corridart* Revisited."

3 McKenna, *À propos de l'Affaire Corridart*.

4 With the assistance of Jean-Serge Champagne and David Moore, Sullivan conceptualized twelve panels and six small exhibition cases. Each was placed on the sidewalk in front of the homes where important intellectuals and artists had lived – including Norman Bethune, Paul-Émile Borduas, Claude and Pierre Gauvreau, Françoise Loranger, Muriel Guilbault, and Émile Nelligan. They were also placed in front of important nocturnal meeting spots like Carré Saint-Louis, Swiss Hut, and Casa Pedro. D41-2015-002T, Folder DR2000:0004:005:0006, S3.SS02, AP041 Fonds Melvin Charney, CCA.

5 McKenna, *À propos de l'Affaire Corridart*; Annette Kuhn, "Culture Shock: The Rape of Sherbrooke," Folder 2012:0015:022:010, AP041, CCA.

6 Normand Lépine, "À la suite de 'pressions énergiques' c'est Drapeau qui a obtenu le retrait de 'Quiet Days,'" *Le Devoir*, 10 November 1970; "Le directeur de l'escouade de la Moralité: 'Je serais en faveur de la prostitution légalisé,'" *Le Journal de Montréal*, 27 June 1971.

In another instance, Montreal authorities invoked the Criminal Code's obscenity laws to confiscate copies of *Sex and the Office Girl* (1972). Michel Roy, "Les saisies de films: Choquette reçoit une délégation de la FQIC," *Le Devoir*, 20 March 1973. For more on erotic cinema during this period, see Straw, "Tabloid Porn in Quebec." On discotheques, see Rose-Anne Giroux, "Le problème de la pollution par le bruit est encore mal défini," *La Presse*, 24 September 1970.

7 The Montreal Olympics was the subject of international controversy. Taiwan boycotted the Games because Canada refused to call it the Republic of China. Twenty-nine countries from Africa plus Iraq, Sri Lanka, and Guyana boycotted it too when the International Olympic Committee refused to ban New Zealand from competition after its men's national rugby team had

toured apartheid South Africa despite the UN's calls for a sporting embargo. Macintosh, Greenhorn, and Hawes, "Trudeau, Taiwan, and the 1976 Montreal Olympics."

8 Sylvestre, *Les homosexuels s'organisent au Québec et ailleurs*, 140.

9 For more on the link between gay community building and nightspots, see Chapter 6 in Higgins, "A Sense of Belonging."

10 The 1976 Summer Olympic Games benefitted many Montrealers who relied on the tourist economy. Examples include the 30 per cent increase in cab-ride fares between 1975 and 1976 and the influx of hotel chains downtown: Hyatt Regency, Four Seasons, Holiday Inn, Ramada, Travelodge, and the Meridien Group. Warren, *Histoire du taxi à Montréal*, 262–3; Broadway, "Montreal's Changing Landscape," 41.

11 Saint-Pierre, "Illusions et désillusions autour de l'idée de vouloir changer le monde," in *Déclics, art et société*, 195; Claude Jasmin, "De l'art 'pop' pour qui aime les choses insolites," *La Presse*, 22 May 1965. Also see Lortie, *The 60s.*

12 Sloan, "*Montréal plus ou moins*, 1972," 51.

13 According to the Museum's press office, no politician toured the exhibition. Michael White, "Montreal Plus Or Minus? The Minus Sign Won the Day," *Montreal Gazette*, 2 September 1972.

14 Bernard Morrier, "Corridart: le jugement rendu vers la fin mai," *Le Devoir*, 31 January 1981.

15 See issues no. 23 and no. 25 of *The Body Politic.* For more on bathhouse raids, see Hooper, "'Enough Is Enough.'"

16 In the Territories and Maritime provinces, where the Olympic spotlight was distant, charges under the bawdy-house provisions were rare. Fraser, *Pornography and Prostitution in Canada*, 410.

17 For more on the politics of the charter and gay rights, see Tremblay, "Mouvements sociaux et opportunités politiques."

18 Previous studies have mapped out how local and national police departments enabled the largest peacetime security operation in Canadian history for the Olympics. See Kinsman and Gentile, "Sexual Policing and National Security," in *The Canadian War on Queers*; Kidd, "'The Army's Presence Will Be Obvious,'" in *Surveilling and Securing the Olympic*; Clément, "The Transformation of Security Planning for the Olympics."

19 See Dupras, *La Drapolice.*

20 Charles Lazarus, "What's Going Up and Where," *Montreal Star*, 13 September

1975. For a comprehensive assessment of mid-1970s projects, see Chapter 3 in Gabeline, Lanken, and Pape, *Montreal at the Crossroads*.

21 Frederick Louder, "Montreal's Downtown Moves East," *City Magazine* 1 (1975): 36.

22 Perrin, "'Whose City Is It?,'" 133–4; Florian Bernard, "Montréal sonne le glas du quartier chinois," *La Presse*, 19 February 1974.

23 For over a quarter-century, City Hall had been threatening to seize and demolish areas of Chinatown. The threat first arose in 1942 over owed taxes, and it reappeared a decade later when the city was looking to relocate Radio-Canada offices. Louder, "Montreal's Downtown Moves East," *City Magazine* 1 (1975): 38.

24 Gabeline, Lanken, and Pope, *Montreal at the Crossroads*, 75–7.

25 Chan, "Ethnic Urban Space," 68–70.

26 Jocelyne Lepage, "Melvin Charney: montréalais, québécois, et psychanalyste du bâtiment," *La Presse*, 31 January 1987.

27 Melvin Charney, *Montreal, plus or minus?*, 19.

28 They performed at Alexis Nihon, Place Longueuil, Place Versailles, Côte des Neiges, Place Ville-Marie, and Frères Dupuis between June 15 and July 28. Mauve, "La femme et la ville," in *Montreal, plus or minus?*, 110–15; Michael White, "Museum of Fine Arts Takes a Hard Look at Montreal," *Montreal Gazette*, 10 June 1972.

29 Tom Shively, "Mer de Champlain," in *Montreal, plus or minus?*, 115.

30 Norman Pascoe, "'Underside' of City Exposed by Tours," *Montreal Star*, 15 July 1972; Lise Blais, "Excursions pour connaître l'"autre métropole,"" *La Presse*, 1 July 1972.

31 Gary Michael Dault, "Montreal, plus or minus? Melvin Charney on Montreal's Planning Woes," *Artscanada* no. 169/170/171 (Early Autumn 1972).

32 The previous year's exhibition had attracted twenty-five thousand people. Michael White, "Montreal Plus Or Minus? The Minus Sign Won the Day," *Montreal Gazette*, 2 September 1972.

33 Ibid.; Virginia Nixon, "Montreal Plus Or Minus? You Make the Choice," *Montreal Gazette*, 17 June 1972.

34 Gilles Toupin, "Si Montréal m'était contée," *La Presse*, 17 June 1972.

35 McKenna and Purcell, *Drapeau*, 265–7.

36 Chan and Forsyth, "'Welcome to the Olympic Victims Hotel'"; Clément,

"The Transformation of Security Planning for the Olympics," 28; Auf der Maur, *The Billion-Dollar Game*, 132.

37 Wright, "The Political Economy of the Montreal Olympic Games," 17; Marsan, *Montreal in Evolution*, 390–1; Sancton, "Montreal," 83.

38 For a comprehensive rundown of how this all tied back to the mayor's office, see Auf der Maur, *The Billion-Dollar Game*. Also see Morin, *La Cathédrale inachevée*.

39 "COJO-ABC: Snyder dément toute collusion," *Le Soleil*, 12 January 1974; Gérald Godin, "Corruption à la ville de Montréal: le cas Snyder," *Québec-Presse*, 26 May 1974.

40 See Malouf, *Rapport de la Commission d'enquête sur le coût de la 21e olympiade*.

41 Howell, *The Montreal Olympics*, 5.

42 Malouf, *Rapport de la Commission d'enquête sur le coût de la 21e olympiade*, 8–9.

43 The inquiry focused exclusively on the period from 1969 to 1976. Malouf, *Rapport de la Commission d'enquête sur le coût de la 21e olympiade*, 31–7; Marsan, *Montreal in Evolution*, 394.

44 Nathalie Petrowski, "Rencontre avec Melvin Charney: La mémoire de Corridart," *La Presse*, 12 June 2000.

45 "Olympic Crackdown," *The Body Politic*, August 1976. Upon reviewing queer activism during the 1970s, Ron Dayman wrote: "Ironically, in seeking public support and boasting about its exploits through crude coverage, the police instead succeeded in disgusting enough gay people to push them to react." *Le Berdache* (May 1981): 51; Le collectif de l'ADGQ, "Editorial," *Le Berdache* (May 1981): 3.

46 Hooper, "Queering '69."

47 For a comprehensive overview, see Ross Higgins, *De la clandestinité à l'affirmation*. Also see Tremblay (ed.), *Queer Mobilizations* and Korinek, *Prairie Fairies*.

48 For more on *Mainmise* and *Sexus*, see Robillard, *Quebec Underground 1962–1972 – Tome: 2*; Higgins, *De la clandestinité à l'affirmation*, 113.

49 Out of Gay McGill emerged Montreal Gay Women (1973), which hosted Canada's second and third national lesbian conferences in 1974 and 1975. Podmore and Chamberland, "Entering the Urban Frame," 197; "No Liquor: McGill Dance Cancelled," *Gay Times*, May 1975; Guindon, "La contestation

des espaces gais au centre-ville de Montréal depuis 1950," 163–4; Ron Dayman, "Les anglophones gais s'organisent," *Le Berdache* (May 1981): 49.

50 Andrea Hildebran, "Genèse d'une communauté lesbienne: un récit des années 1970," in *Sortir de l'ombre*, 207–33.

51 "Aquarius Raid Start of Police Anti-gay Clean-up Campaign," *Gay Times*, April 1975.

52 Russell, "The Offence of Keeping a Common Bawdy-House," 298; "À propos de l'incendie du sauna Aquarius...," *Gay Montreal*, 29 June 1976.

53 For a detailed account of the group's short-lived history, see Noël, "Pratiques politiques et formation de l'identité gaie au Québec."

54 Madeleine Daoust, "Les Femmes," in *Guide de Montréal*, 278.

55 "Position du Groupe homosexuel d'action politique," S2, D1, Dossier de Danny Frankel, F0001, GHAP, AGQ; "Gays Join May Day Marchers," *Gay Times*, May 1975.

56 "Contributions to the discussions at the National Gay Conference 1975," presented by the Revolutionary Marxist Group (Canada) and the Groupe Marxiste Revolutionnaire (Québec), 25 June 1975, Dossier de Mark Wilson, Pièces 17–26, F0001, Fonds GHAP, AGQ.

Recent literature asserts that "bars have functioned as *the medium* for the historical emergence of gay public life in the United States." Of course, this statement rings true for queer communities in cities across the globe. Lucas Hilderbrand, *The Bars Are Ours*, 1. For more on Montreal's long history of gay bar culture, see Higgins, "A Sense of Belonging."

57 Lime Light was raided on 17 October and 7 November and *Baby Face* on Halloween. "On est tanné de se faire écœurer et il est plus que temps de s'organiser," Dossier de Mark Wilson, pièces 1, 01-16, F0001, GHAP, AGQ. For more on *Baby Face*, see Chamberland, "Remembering Lesbian Bars."

58 Ron Dayman, "Olympics Clean-up Strikes Again," *The Body Politic*, April 1976.

59 John Blacklock, "Olympics Circus Brings More Repression," *The Body Politic*, April 1976.

60 The Olympic Games involved twenty-six venues spread over several cities – including, but not limited to, sailing in Kingston, football in Ottawa and Toronto, and handball in Sherbrooke and Quebec City – each of which was subject to surveillance. Clément, "The Transformation of Security Planning

for the Olympics," 32. See *Games of the XXI Olympiad, Montréal, 1976, Competition Sites*, COJO, 1975–1976, BANQ. "Olympic Crackdown," *The Body Politic*, August 1976.

61 They charged eighty-five as found-ins and the bath's four directors as "keepers of a bawdy-house." Ron Dayman, "Le CHAR ou l'année gai 1976," *Le Berdache* (May 1980): 50.

62 "The Police and the Press," *The Body Politic*, August 1976; Kinsman and Gentile, *The Canadian War on Queers*, 311.

63 Fitzgerald, "What Police Raid Means to Homosexuals," *Montreal Gazette*, 17 November 1977; Korinek, *Prairie Fairies*, 23.

64 Ross Higgins, "Pour une histoire gaie de Montréal," *Sortir* (April 1983): 7.

65 Stories about the pre-Olympic crackdown reached international audiences and garnered solidarity from groups from across the Commonwealth, New York, and Denmark. "Police Repression: A National Struggle," *NGRC Forum* 1, no. 2 (Summer 1976); Bouchard, "Le milieu gai à Montreal," in *Guide de Montréal*, 244–5.

66 Jilly's was a dimly lit discotheque whose crowd was mostly francophone. Daoust, "Les Femmes," 279; "The Police and the Press," *The Body Politic*, August 1976.

67 Scott, *Station 10*.

68 Most of those arrested were from New York City, Buffalo, and Washington, DC, and worked from hotels and tourist rooms. "Les prostituées font des jeux … une affaire d'or," *Le Journal de Montréal*, 22 July 1976.

69 "Des noirs de New York tentent de s'accaparer de la prostitution à Montréal," *Le Petit Journal*, 31 August 1975.

70 "Pour préserver l'image de Montréal pendant les Jeux Olympiques la police déclare la guerre à la prostitution," *La patrie*, 1 February 1976.

71 Security included 8,940 Canadian soldiers who guarded Olympic venues, hotels, and transit hubs in Montreal, and satellite venues in Bromont, Kingston, and Toronto. They worked in liaison with 1,376 RCMP officers, 1,140 Sûreté du Québec officers, 533 Ontario Provincial Police officers, 1,606 Montreal police officers, 424 officers from four other municipal police services, and 2,910 private security guards. Kidd, "'The Army's Presence Will Be Obvious,'" 162, 167.

72 Ibid., 172.

73 "Grâce aux jeux olympiques les prostituées et les pickpockets ont fait des affaires d'or," *Le Petit Journal*, 1 August 1976. Also see Michel Auger, "Les crimes graves à la baisse pendant les jeux," *La Presse*, 21 July 1976.

74 "Olympic Crackdown," *The Body Politic*, August 1976.

75 Pierre Vallières, "Chronique," *Le Berdache* (May 1981), 31. An ad for a new discussion group echoed this suggestion: "The Féministes lesbiennes de Montréal is a recently formed group that has taken on the task of providing lesbians with opportunities to meet outside of clubs." "Communiqué," *Les Têtes de pioche*, June 1977 in *Les Têtes de pioche*.

76 As Podmore and Chamberland write, the story of the Chez Madame Arthur boycott fits into a broader set of lesbian activisms that "politicized urban public spaces in Montréal in the 1970s and 1980s." Podmore and Chamberland, "Entering the Urban Frame," 207.

77 See Ron Dayman's correspondence with Simone Chartrand (24 April 1977). 24P-630: 23/4, Fonds d'archives de la ligue des droits et libertés, Archives UQÀM.

Over the following months, the group made use of the city's extensive nocturnal network by organizing dances. Eventually, they also distributed *Le Berdache*, a journal founded in 1979 that drew inspiration from Indigenous culture and attempted to decolonize Montreal's queer settler community. See Ménard, "Du berdache au Berdache," and Sivry, "Traces militantes éphémères," in *Sortir de l'ombre*, 236.

78 *Gai(e)s du Québec* 1, no. 5 (November 1977). Fonds d'archives de la Ligue des droits et libertés (LDL), 24P-630: 23/2, Archives UQÀM.

79 24P-630: 23/4 Discrimination pour orientation sexuelle, Fonds d'archives de la ligue des droits et libertés, Archives UQÀM.

80 "Il y a patrouille de nuit et patrouille nocturne," *La Presse*, 1 April 1975.

81 Higgins, *De la clandestinité à l'affirmation*, 129.

82 Bertrand Desjardins and Claude De Cotret, "Super-descente chez les homos," *Le Journal de Montréal*, 23 October 1977; Roger Drouin, "Pourquoi s'archarner contre les homos…?," *Le Journal de Montréal*, 24 October 1977.

83 "Communiqué de presse," Folder D4, F0129, Comité de défense des accusés du Truxx, AGQ. Association pour les droits des gai(e)s du Québec, "Communiqué: ADGQ statement to October 26, 1977 Press Conference," Folder D1, F0129, Comité de défense des accusés du Truxx, AGQ.

84 Lévesque, "Du Truxx au poste de Police," in *Sortir*, 38; Joel Ruimy, "Homosexuals fighting back after raid," *Montreal Gazette*, 27 October 1977.

85 Lévesque, "Du Truxx au poste de Police," in *Sortir*, 33–40; B. Desjardins, "1,500 homosexuels se déchaînent!," *Le Journal de Montréal*, 24 October 1977; Joel Ruimy, "Homosexuals fighting back after raid," *Montreal Gazette*, 27 October 1977.

86 Christopher Bain and Steve Kowch, "City Homosexuals protest police machine-gun raid," *Montreal Gazette*, 24 October 1977.

87 Russell, "The Offence of Keeping a Common Bawdy-House," 303. A musical, depicting a fictionalized account of the raid, was created by playwrights Paul Ledoux and Terry Last. It tells the story of a group of revellers who become embroiled in activism in the raid's aftermath. Ledoux and Last, *The Night They Raided Truxx*.

88 "Press Release," 3 November 1977, Folder D4, F0129, Comité de défense des accusés du Truxx, AGQ; Roger Drouin, "Un homo indigné," *Le Journal de Montréal*, 24 October 1977.

89 Stuart Russell, "'Bawdy house' or not? Truxx trials being," *The Body Politic*, June–July 1978.

90 "ADGQ Statement to October 26, 1977 (Press conference)," 27 October 1977, Folder D1, F0129, Comité de défense des accusés du Truxx, AGQ.

91 Sivry, "Traces militantes éphémères," in *Sortir de l'ombre*, 244–5.

92 "Les homos et la police: C'EST LA GUERRE," *Le Journal de Montréal*, 24 October 1977; "Il n'y a pas eu de violence, clame la police," *Le Journal de Montréal*, 24 October 1977.

93 Joel Ruimy, "Homosexuals fighting back after raid," *Montreal Gazette*, 27 October 1977.

94 John Fitzgerald, "What police raid means to homosexuals," *Montreal Gazette*, 17 November 1977.

95 24P-630: 23/4; *Gai(e)s du Québec* 1, no. 5 (November 1977). 24P-630: 23/2, Fonds LDL, Archives UQÀM.

96 For a full summary of the events leading to the ascension of Bill 88, see *Gai(e)s du Québec*, 1 February 1978. Also see *Journal des débats de l'Assemblée nationale*, 7 and 15 December 1977, Bibliothèque de l'Assemblée nationale du Québec.

97 The dance helped raise $2,775. "Dans-bénéfice du 18 mars 1978 Pour la

défense des accuses du Truxx," Folder D6, F0129, Comité de défense des accusés du Truxx, AGQ. "Tous et toutes à la danse du 18 mars!," *Gai(e)s du Québec,* March 1978.

98 By early 1976, he completed a study of streets in Canada for the federal department of urban affairs: "Streetworks: Generating Public Open Space"; Cynthia Gunn, "He'd Turn Streets into Parks," *Montreal Star*, 26 February 1976; Anne Bower, "Rage under Wrecker's Ball," *The Financial Post,* 15 March 1975; "Growth by Destruction," *Time*, 15 April 1974.

99 McConathy, "CORRIDART," 36.

100 Charney, *Corridart dans la rue Sherbrooke.*

101 Gauvin, "*Corridart* Revisited," 15.

102 René Viau, "Quand Montréal voyait (trop) grand," *Liberté* 47, no. 3 (2005): 165–70.

103 Cynthia Gunn, "A Street Where Art Lives," *Montreal Scene*, 10 July 1976.

104 Ibid.

105 Gilles Toupin, "CORRIDART: l'histoire d'une rue," *La Presse*, 10 July 1976; McConathy, "CORRIDART," 45.

106 "The work focuses [*sic*] an urban configuration: a city square at the intersection of two main streets. The intention was to create a metaphor out of a ruined city site." Folder DR2012:0012:131:005, AP041, CCA.

107 Conceptually, Michael Haslam's *Télétron* was the closest piece to Dallegret's work. It was a phone booth where the public could pick up a receiver and "hear the street" and messages "from the underground: poetry, music, strange sounds." Haslam said: "I definitely wanted a multilingual package, and I strove to get other people to participate. I had people do tapes in French, English, and German. It was accessible and appealing, and people would listen to them." McKenna, *À propos de l'Affaire Corridart.*

108 It should be noted, however, that an image of the key moment in the 1973 demolition of the lavish nineteenth-century Van Horne mansion, once the home of railway magnate Sir William Cornelius Van Horne, was used for *Corridart*. The mansion's destruction spurred the heritage preservation movement. Ultimately though, much of Save Montreal's activism sought to safeguard residential housing. Hammond, "Architecture, Photography, and Power," in *Photogenic Montreal*, 223; Perrin, "'Whose City Is It?'"

109 Gauvin, "*Corridart* Revisited," 113.

110 Influenced by pioneering urban historian Lewis Mumford, his first book

has since undergone many reprints and re-editions, which, over time, increased its length from 423 to 730 pages. Marsan, *Montreal in Evolution*. Gilles Toupin, "Il est interdit d'afficher!," *La Presse*, 24 July 1976.

111 Gauvin, "*Corridart* Revisited," 76–8.

112 Randy Gledhill, *L'Affaire Corridart Postcards* (Montreal: Éditions Véhicule, 1977), PC N6546 .Q42 .M6 1977, Library, CCA; "Corridart Show Was 'Politics, Not Art': City Lawyer," *Montreal Gazette*, 31 January 1981.

113 Couture, "L'exposition *Corridart*," 17. For more on community activism in Milton-Parc, see Hawley and Roussopoulos (eds.), *Villages in Cities*.

114 Claude Péloquin, "Merci à M. Drapeau d'avoir tué la femme que j'aimais," *La Presse*, 25 June 1976.

115 Robert Lévesque, "Le point du jour," *Le Jour*, 16 July 1976.

116 "What Happened When the Mayor Took a Drive Down Sherbrooke St," *Montreal Gazette*, 6 October 1979.

117 The paragraph draws from Gledhill, *L'Affaire Corridart Postcards*, PC N6546 .Q42 .M6 1977, Library, CCA; Annette Kuhn, "Culture Shock: The Rape of Sherbrooke," Folder 2012:0015:022:010, AP041, CCA; Angèle Dagenais, "L'Allier 'prie' Drapeau de reconstituer Corridart," *Le Devoir*, 15 July 1976; Jean-Pierre Charbonneau and Andrée Lebel, "Montréal ordonne de démolir Corridart," *La Presse*, 14 July 1976.

118 Richard Lévesque, "City Tears Down 'Obscene' Corridart," *Montreal Star*, 14 July 1976.

119 Choquette, "Corridart," 46–7.

120 Letter from the president of the International Association of Art Critics, Virgil Hammock, to Jean Drapeau. Joan Lowndes, "Editorial: Fascist Suppression in Montréal," *Vanguard*, September 1976, 97P-615 :02/3, 97P – Fonds Laurent Lamy, Archives UQÀM; Edmund Alleyn, "Un geste fasciste," *La Presse*, 17 July 1976; Claude Turcotte, "Le boycottage par les artistes s'amorce avec difficulté," *La Presse*, 16 July 1976; René-E. Boulay, "Le démantèlement de Corridart," *La Presse*, 17 July 1976.

121 Robert Lévesque, "Le point du jour," *Le jour*, 16 July 1976.

122 Daniel Latouche, "Un saccage culturel," *Montréal-Matin*, 15 July 1976.

123 Bernard Morrier, "Un groupe d'artistes met la Ville en demeure de rétablir Corridart," *Le Devoir*, 23 July 1976; Robert Lévesque, "Une deuxième affaire Corridart," *Le Jour*, 17 July 1976.

124 Claude Turcotte, "Le COJO ne poursuivra pas Montréal pour Corridart," *La Presse*, 17 July 1976.

125 The message was reprinted in several outlets. “Destruction in the Dark,” *Montreal Gazette*, 15 July 1976; “Message lus en appui à Corridart par des artistes avant la présentation de spectacles du programme Art et culture,” quoted in Choquette, “Corridart,” 279.

126 The manifesto was republished in the poetic journal *Dérives* and signed by Nicole Brossard, François Charron, Madeleine Gagnon, Louis Geoffroy, Philippe Haeck, Gilles Hénault, André Roy, Jean Simoneau, and Patrick Straram. “Le solstice de la poésie québécoise,” *Dérives* 5/6 (1976), 29–30. Also see Patrick Straram, *Dérives* 5/6 (1976), 45.

127 Claude Turcotte, “Corridart: une colère de Jean Drapeau,” *La Presse*, 17 July 1976; Gilles Toupin, “Il est interdit d’afficher!,” *La Presse*, 24 July 1976; Angèle Dagenais, “L’Allier ‘prie’ Drapeau de reconstituer Corridart,” *Le Devoir* 15 July 1976; Claude Turcotte, “L’Allier crie à la censure et ordonne à Montréal de reconstruire Corridart,” *La Presse*, 15 July 1976.

128 Michel Roy, “La honte d’une folle nuit,” *Le Devoir*, 15 July 1976; François de Massy, “M. Drapeau se sentait dérangé,” *La Presse*, 15 July 1976.

129 Jean Drapeau, *Journal des débats de la Commission permanente des affaires municipales et de l’environnement*, 25 August 1976, Bibliothèque de l’Assemblée nationale du Québec.

130 Claude Charron, *Journal des débats de la Commission permanente des affaires municipales et de l’environnement*, 25 August 1976, Bibliothèque de l’Assemblée nationale du Québec.

131 Pierre Ayot, Jean-Claude Thibaudeau, Michael Haslam, Marc Cramer, Danyelle Morin, and Guy Montpetit v. City of Montreal and COJO [1981] QSC, 28.

132 Gledhill, *L’Affaire Corridart Postcards*, PC N6546 .Q42 .M6 1977, Library, CCA.

133 Louise Descoteaux, “Corridart: La censure,” 106–11.

134 “L’ordre de démanteler Corridart serait venu de Jean Drapeau,” *Le Devoir*, 7 October 1980; Martha Gagnon, “On n’enveloppe pas un diamant dans du papier journal,” *La Presse*, 22 January 1981; “Drapeau n’a vu aucun art dans *Corridart*, certains ont bien appliqué la décision de Drapeau,” *Le Journal de Montréal*, 27 January 1981.

135 Martha Gagnon, “Les avocats qualifient Drapeau de dictateur,” *La Presse*, 30 January 1981; Bernard Morrier, “Drapeau, un ‘dictateur,’” *Le Devoir*, 30 Janaury 1981; “Razing 1976 Art Exhibit ‘Dictatorial,’ say Lawyers,” *Mon-*

treal Gazette, 30 January 1981; Michael Hoffman, "Corridart a Failure to Urban Planner," *Montreal Gazette*, 28 January 1981.

136 Gilles Toupin, "Il est interdit d'afficher!," *La Presse*, 24 July 1976.

137 Hobsbawm, *Fractured Times*, xiv.

138 Ignace J. Deslauriers, "Contre l'art comme outil de contestation," *Le Soleil*, 1 June 1981.

139 97P-615 :02/3, 97P Fonds Laurent Lamy, Archives UQÀM. Ayot et al. v. City of Montréal and COJO [1981], QSC

140 Madeleine Forcier, "Preface," in *Corridart 1976–* (Montreal: Graff, 1982). PC N6546 .Q42 .M62 1982, Library, CCA.

141 *Corridart* returned to the limelight forty years later when Mayor Denis Coderre axed a plan to revive Ayot's *La croix du mont Royal* as part of a retrospective of the artist's work. Jeanne Corriveau, "Montréal accusée de censure," *Le Devoir*, 22 September 2016.

142 Laurent Lamy, "The Appeal of the Corridart Artists," in *Corridart 1976–*, PC N6546 .Q42 .M62 1982, Library, CCA.

143 "Quebec's Big Owe Stadium Debt Is Over," *CBC News*, 19 December 2006.

CHAPTER SIX

1 Over 38 per cent of Montrealers voted for the left-libertarian Montreal Citizens' Movement (MCM) or the Municipal Action Group (MAG) – a centrist party born in 1976 from a bitter split between radicals and moderates within the MCM. See Milner, "The Montreal Citizens' Movement," 3.

Lamarre considered himself a businessman "first and foremost" and self-described "conservative in everything I do." Anthony Wilson-Smith, "Lamarre: The Pragmatic Power at City Hall," *Montreal Gazette*, 9 October 1982.

2 Willie Chevalier, "Les Maisons de la Culture de Montréal," *Vie des arts* 30, no. 120 (Septembre–automne 1985): 42–5.

3 For more on Opération 10,000 logements, see Vickers, "From *Balconville* to *Condoville*, but Where Is Co-opville?" and Rose, "Local State Policy and 'New-Build Gentrification' in Montréal."

4 Michel Girard, "Plus question de racoler ou de boire de l'alcool dans les rues de Montréal," *La Presse*, 27 May 1980.

5 Pierre-Paul Gagné, "La prostitution à Montréal: Un commerce de luxe difficile à contrôler," *La Presse*, 23 July 1980; Gemme et al., *Report on Prostitution in Quebec*, 111–12.

6 Kevin Doyle, "The Sexual Debate," *Maclean's*, 15 April 1985.
7 "City's Prostitution Bylaw Upheld," *Montreal Gazette*, 13 January 1981; Ted Blackman, "Hustlers Regain Grip on the Main," *Montreal Gazette*, 15 November 1979.
8 Alain Duhamel, "Des règlements abusifs, disent les conseillers de l'opposition," *Le Devoir*, 27 May 1980; Florian Bernard, "Levée de boucliers contre les deux règlements sur le racolage et l'alcool," *La Presse*, 3 June 1980; "Un groupe tente d'obtenir le rappel des règlements 80 et 81," *La Presse*, 4 June 1980.
9 See Rutland, "Profiling the Future."
10 Backhouse, *Petticoats and Prejudice*, 230; Bertram, "The Other Little House."
11 Louise Perreault, "Non mais, faites-moi rire!," *La Presse*, 30 July 1980; Nathalie Pérusse, "Et les femmes alors?," *La Presse*, 22 August 1980.
12 According to research, street-based sex work remained linked to the night during the mid-1980s: "there is a very great difference between daytime and evening activity levels … the peak hours are from 10:00 P.M. to 1:00 A.M." See Gemme, *Street Prostitution*, 145–6.
13 For more on feminism and sex work, see Mensah and Laberge, "Évolution du discours féministe."
14 Pierre-Paul Gagné, "La prostitution à Montréal: D'abord, nettoyer la 'Main,'" *La Presse*, 19 July 1980.
15 Gemme, *Street Prostitution*, 65.
16 Brock, *Making Work, Making Trouble*, 32.
17 Hutt v. The Queen [1978] 2, SCR; Larsen, "Urban Politics and Prostitution Control," 29.
18 For a comprehensive labour history of Montreal during this period, see High, *Deindustrializing Montreal*.
19 Texier and Vézina, *Profession, prostituée*, 69–70.
20 Ibid., 322–3.
21 See testimonies provided by pimp "Slim," trans sex worker Nadgia, and madam Rita Picard in Simoneau, *Plusieurs tombent en amour*.
22 City of Montreal, By-law No. 333, To Prevent the Obstruction of Pedestrians or Traffic and the Disturbance of the Public Peace in the Streets, Lanes, Highways and Public Places in the City (19 June 1905) [as amended in December 1977].

23 Ray Doucet, “Morality Laws Look a Great Deal Different… in Dead of Night,” *Montreal Gazette*, 3 May 1979.

24 Pierre Daigneault (Agent Analyste, Moralité) and Claude Lalonde (Lieutenant, Moralité), “Etat de la prostitution à Montréal depuis le jugement ‘Debra Hutt,’” memorandum to the cabinet of the Director of the MUC LSC? Police Department, 3. Dossier – Prostitution – Rencontre avec le maire de Toronto, P100-07-D106, AVM.

25 Ibid., 1–2. Michel Girard, “Plus question de racoler ou de boire de l’alcool dans les rues de Montréal,” *La Presse*, 27 May 1980.

26 Daigneault and Lalonde, “Etat de la prostitution à Montréal depuis le jugement ‘Debra Hutt,’” 5.

27 Arrington, “Under the Gun,” in *Good Girls/Bad Girls*, 174.

28 Daigneault and Lalonde, “Etat de la prostitution à Montréal depuis le jugement ‘Debra Hutt,’” 4. Also see Scott, *Station 10*.

29 Gemme, *Street Prostitution*, 160–3.

30 Rutland, *Un échec éternel*.

31 Jean-Claude Leclerc, “Une charge de la police rue Bélanger,” *Le Devoir*, 23 June 1979.

32 Le Comité du 20 juin, “Communiqué de presse,” 2 July 1979, 24P-630: 08: 03/1. Fonds LDL, Archives UQÀM; André Cedilot, “350 manifestants contre le racisme et la brutalité policière,” *La Presse*, 7 July 1979; Rutland, *Un échec éternel*, 6. Also see Aurélien and Rutland, *Il fallait se defender*, and Mills, *A Place in the Sun*.

33 Letter from Chief Vignola to Chair Lamarre, 27 November 1979. Dossier – Prostitution – Rencontre avec le maire de Toronto, P100-07-D106, AVM; “Flynn Plans Move to Tighten Laws on Prostitution, Police Chiefs Say,” *Montreal Gazette*, 27 November 1979.

34 Brock, *Making Work, Making Trouble*, 50.

35 City of Montreal, By-law No. 5465, By-law Amending By-law 333 Entitled “By-law to Prevent the Obstruction of Pedestrians or Traffic and the Disturbance of the Public Peace in the Streets, Lanes, Highways and Public Places in the City” (26 May 1980); “La police a fermé les yeux: Des fêtes tièdes,” *La Presse*, 25 June 1980; “Lift Drink Ban for Fete, City Asked,” *Montreal Gazette*, 10 June 1980; André Cédilot, “L’alcool banni des rues de Montréal à la St-Jean,” *La Presse*, 6 June 1980.

36 "Cops' Lightning Raid Shakes Hooker Row," *Montreal Star*, 20 July 1980; Pierre-Paul Gagné, "La prostitution à Montréal: D'abord, nettoyer la 'Main,'" *La Presse*, 19 July 1980; "Le '5464' existe toujours," *Le Journal de Montréal*, 7 May 1981.

37 Pierre-Paul Gagné, "La prostitution à Montréal: La 'filière américaine,'" *La Presse*, 24 July 1980.

38 City of Montreal, By-law No. 5464, To Forbid Any Person to Remain in a Public Place for Purposes of Prostitution or to Approach Another Person for the Same Purposes in Such Place (26 May 1980).

39 "Sonia: 'On sera toujours là,'" *La Presse*, 19 July 1980.

40 O'Connell, "The Impact of Bill C-49 on Street Prostitution," 120.

41 See Backhouse, "Nineteenth-Century Canadian Prostitution Law Reflection of a Discriminatory Society."

42 Mireille Lachance, "Et les hommes qui racolent," *La Presse*, 1 August 1980; O'Leary and Toupin, *Québécoises deboutte!*, 44.

43 Madeleine Berthault, "Quand les hommes racolent…," *La Presse*, 21 July 1980; "Peu de clients sont arrêtés," *La Presse*, 22 July 1980.

44 Beaumier, "Les voix des femmes à la Ligue des droits de l'homme du Québec," 236; Pierre-Paul Gagné, "La prostitution à Montréal: La définition de 'sollicitation' peut présenter des risques," *La Presse*, 21 July 1980; Pierre-Paul Gagné, "La prostitution à Montréal: Des opinions divergentes," *La Presse*, 26 July 1980.

It is important to note that the LDL began as a civil liberties association. In 1974, however, it explicitly rejected its civil libertarian roots and embraced a human rights platform. Its new mandate considered the unique problems confronting the poor, women, the elderly, youth, and minorities. In 1978, it renamed itself to reflect its "social" mandate, thereby stepping away from its original "legal" origins. Clément, *Human Rights in Canada*, 95.

45 Fernande St-Martin-Poitras v. City of Montreal [1981], Montreal Municipal Court, 10.

46 Harvey Shepherd, "'Hookers' Unite to Fight Bylaw," *Montreal Gazette*, 10 September 1980; "Prostitutes to Fight New Law," *The Record*, 9 September 1980. Also see Crago interview with Miss Pat, "Sex Work," 23.

47 Lise Dunnigan (Ste-Foy), Anne Gauthier (Québec), Francine Saillant (Québec), Nicole Cloutier (Rosemont), Suzanne Messier (Québec), Maria De Koninck (Lac St-Charles), "Comment pouvoir circuler seul!," *Le Devoir*,

8 August 1980; "Du sort réservé aux filles," *La Presse*, 14 August 1980; "La grande peur de nos notables," *La Presse*, 21 August 1980.

48 L.A. MacDonald, "Bylaw Pushes Prostitutes Out," *Sunday Express*, 2 November 1980.

49 "City Won't Press Charges Against Men for Soliciting," *Montreal Gazette*, 15 December 1980; "Police Enforcing Bylaw Despite Legal Challenges," *Montreal Gazette*, 11 November 1980.

50 "'Hooker' Bylaw Challenged," *Montreal Gazette*, 7 November 1980; Anne Penketh, "Prostitution Law Opponent Clears a Legal Hurdle," *Montreal Gazette*, 24 December 1980.

51 "Prostitutes' Clients Hit as City Tightens Law," *Montreal Gazette*, 16 June 1981; Yvon Laberge, "Prostitution: le règlement amendé," *La Presse*, 17 June 1981; By-law, No. 5697, By-law Amending the By-law to Forbid Any Person to Remain in a Public Place for Purposes of Prostitution or to Approach Another Person for the Same Purposes in Such Place (5464) (18 June 1981).

52 "Tinkering with Sex Laws," *Montreal Gazette*, 17 June 1981; Leo Nasager, "It Is About Time Ladies Got a Break," *Montreal Gazette*, 30 July 1981.

53 Raymond Gervais, "Le nouveau règlement 5464: Deux clients de prostituées appréhendés par la police," *La Presse*, 1 July 1981.

54 Harvey Shepherd, "Municipalities Disagree on Issue of Prostitution," *Montreal Gazette*, 11 June 1980.

55 "Official meeting between mayor Art Eggleton of Toronto and Mayor Jean Drapeau of Montreal, to be held in Montreal on Friday, July 31, 1981." Dossier – Prostitution – Rencontre avec le maire de Toronto, P100-07-D106, AVM; "Prostitution: Mayors Ask Tougher Law," *Montreal Gazette*, 1 August 1981.

56 Mayor Eggleton's presentation reiterated what he had said a few months earlier in Regina: "This problem in the City of Toronto has had a serious affect [*sic*] upon the reputation of our main street – Yonge Street – and on neighbourhoods nearby." Art Eggleton, "Prostitution and Street Nuisances," 9 June 1981, Dossier – Prostitution – Rencontre avec le maire de Toronto, P100-07-D106, AVM. For more on Toronto, see Ross, *The Heart of Toronto*, 105.

57 "Program of the visit of the mayor of Toronto Mr Art Eggleton, July 31, 1981," Dossier – Prostitution – Rencontre avec le maire de Toronto, P100-07-D106, AVM.

In 1980, Montreal hosted the Bureau International des Exposition's eighth international horticultural exposition. Held both on Notre-Dame Island and inside Roger Taillibert's Velodrome, its theme was the "relationship between man's socio-cultural activities and his physical environment." P100-04-4-2-D001, AVM.

58 Pierre-Paul Gagné, "La prostitution à Montréal: Les homosexuels parlent de préjugés ... et crient à l'injustice," *La Presse*, 25 July 1980.

59 Risa Goldwax v. City of Montréal [1981], QSC, 7.

60 Ibid., 22.

61 Michael Tenszen, "Montreal Police Set Back in War on Prostitutes," *Globe and Mail*, 29 December 1981.

62 "City Has Thirty Days to Appeal Decision on Prostitution Bylaw," *Montreal Gazette*, 12 December 1981.

63 City of Vancouver, By-Law No. 5521, Being a By-law to Prohibit Certain Activities on the Streets (6 April 1982); His Worship Mayor Wayne Thomson of the City of Niagara Falls, Ontario, *A Petition that the Government of Canada Enact the Necessary Amendments to the Criminal Code of Canada to Effectively Combat Prostitution* (11 February 1982). Dossier – Prostitution, P100-07-D105, AVM.

64 Letter from Marion Dewar to Jean Drapeau, 23 June 1982, dossier – Prostitution, P100-07-D105, AVM.

65 Anne Beirne, "A Sudden Shock at City Hall," *Maclean's*, 2 August 1982.

66 Jean Doré (MCM) and former chief of police Henri-Paul Vignola (MAG) split 51 per cent of the votes.

67 Calgary "The Street" bylaw 9022, first enacted in 1974, was amended by city council on 25 June 1981.

68 Westendorp v. the Queen [1983] 1, SCR 43.

69 Ross, *The Heart of Toronto*, 131. Jenness, "From Sex as Sin to Sex as Work."

70 See Dale and Cole, *Hookers on Davie*.

71 The Canadian Organization for the Rights of Prostitutes (now Sex Professionals of Canada) pamphlet, 10-001-S1-F418_a, CWMA, UOASC.

72 Gemme et al., *Report on Prostitution in Quebec*, 88, 307–10.

During the early 1980s, the sexual practices of Canadians were under the microscope as never before. A second federal committee, the Badgley Committee (1981–84), was created to investigate a variety of sexual offences against children, including juvenile prostitution. For more, see Lowman et al., *Regulating Sex*.

73 Namaste, *Savoirs créoles*. Giguère, "'Assister, informer, defender,'" in *Québe-queer*, 153–4.

74 Kinsman, "AIDS Activism," in *Seeing Red*, 317–19.

75 Silversides, *AIDS Activist*, 99.

76 Mensah, "The Idea of Community and Collective Action," in *Sex Work*, 94.

77 Harvey Shepherd, "Major-City Mayors Unite against Porn," *Montreal Gazette*, 6 June 1983; "Huit grandes villes du Canada, dont Montréal, veulent étoffer leurs règlements municipaux," *La Presse*, 7 June 1983.

78 Ross, *The Heart of Toronto*, 101.

79 Quoted in Martin, "Resisting Red Hot Video," in *Feeling Feminism*, 185.

80 "Clearing the Streets," *Montreal Gazette*, 14 June 1983.

81 Brock, *Making Work, Making Trouble*, 65.

82 City of Montreal, By-law No. 6249, To Prevent the Obstruction of Pedestrians or Traffic and the Disturbance of the Public Peace in the Streets, Lanes, Highways and Public Places in the City (17 October 1983).

A year later, seven judges of the Supreme Court struck down bylaw 5464 in a swift and decisive ruling on the grounds that it was ultra vires. "Supreme Court of Canada Quashes Montreal's Old Anti-prostitution Bylaw," *Montreal Gazette*, 13 December 1984.

83 *Presentation of the City of Montréal to the Legislative Committee on Bill C-49 submitted by Jean Drapeau*, 29 October 1985, 3–4, Dossier – Prostitution, P100-07-D105, AVM; Harvey Shepherd, "Prostitution Clampdown Main Aim of New Bylaw," *Montreal Gazette*, 18 October 1983.

84 Arrington, "Under the Gun," in *Good Girls/Bad Girls*, 178.

85 Rod Macdonell, "Bylaw Works against Prostitutes: About 400 Charges Laid since Fall," *Montreal Gazette*, 9 July 1984; Yves Hamel, "Sexe et crème glacée," *Le Journal de Montréal*, 27 July 1984.

86 Serge Labrosse, "Prostitution: un règlement déguisé," *Le Journal de Montréal*, 19 October 1983.

87 "Bylaw to Fight Prostitution 'Is Too Vague,'" *Montreal Gazette*, 22 October 1983; "Montréal truffe ses règlements anti-prostitution de trucs," *Le Devoir*, 21 October 1983.

88 Sam Boskey, "New Montreal Bylaw Poses Threat to Civil Liberties," *Montreal Gazette*, 26 October 1983; Le comité sur la police, "Exposé du RCM devant le conseil de sécurité publique," 13 June 1979, 24P-630: 08: 03/1. Fonds LDL, Archives UQÀM.

89 Fraser, *Pornography and Prostitution in Canada*, 447; David Johnston, "Soliciting Law Virtually Worthless: Police Chief," *Montreal Gazette*, 28 February 1984.

90 Angèle Dagenais, "Les résidents du square Saint-Louis sonnent l'alarme: La prostitution et le commerce de la drogue ont atteint un seuil intolérable," *Le Devoir*, 9 May 1984; Carole Thibaudeau, "Les résidents du quartier Saint-Louis en ont ras le bol des fêtards et des prostituées," *La Presse*, 9 May 1984.

During the 1970s, the Dubois Brothers, a criminal organization consisting of nine brothers, seized control of Carré Saint-Louis, which the police effectively described as the "epicentre of Montreal's drug trafficking." Dutil, *La lutte au crime organisé au Québec*, 115–16, 145–7.

91 Letter from Nanci, Patrick, Luc, and André Gervais, residents of 3718 Laval, to Jean Drapeau, 24 February 1984, Dossier – Prostitution, P100-07-D105, AVM; Lysiane Gagnon, "Sur les trottoirs de Montréal," *La Presse*, 30 April 1983; Monelle Saindon, "Les homosexuels du parc Lafontaine: une race qui disparaît?," *Le Journal de Montréal*, 23 July 1983.

92 Most letters were sent between September 1983 and May 1986. Letter from Jean Drapeau to Marc-André Gratton, 29 November 1983, Dossier – Prostitution, P100-07-D105, AVM.

93 See Ross, *The Heart of Toronto*, 110.

94 Robert Miller, "Sex on Mean Street," *Maclean's*, 15 April 1985.

95 Raymond Gervais, "La nouvelle arme contre la prostitution … le sens unique!," *La Presse*, 26 October 1984; Gemme, *Street Prostitution*, 142.

96 Lewis Harris, "Prostitution Biggest Issue as Dore Bids for Seat," *Montreal Gazette*, 26 May 1984.

97 David Johnston, "Montreal Bylaw New Weapon against Prostitution: Other Cities May Copy Cleanup Idea," *Montreal Gazette*, 27 October 1984; Picard, *Ma vie dans les bordels*, 118.

98 "Only Tougher Federal Laws Will Beat Hookers: City Officials," *Montreal Gazette*, 22 September 1984.

99 Mario Clermont claimed that the bylaw was ultra vires because it was aimed at soliciting for purposes of prostitution. He also suggested that it was illogical to prohibit unlicensed sale of services for which no licence existed or could be issued. Gemme et al., *Report on Prostitution in Quebec*, 37.

100 Montreal anthropologist Ross Higgins understands the period from 1980 to 1994 as a distinct chapter in the city's attempt to regulate queer life because

of the brutal raids at Sauna David, Bud's, and KOX/Katacombes. See Higgins, "La régulation sociale de l'homosexualité," in *La régulation sociale des minorités sexuelles*, 90–3; Ross Higgins, "Les gais dans les maisons de débauche: Montréal épurée pour la visite du Saint-Père," *Sortir*, (May 1984), 18–19.

101 Claudia Cattaneo, "Homosexuals Protest 188 Bar Arrests," *Montreal Gazette*, 4 June 1984; Paul Roy, "Les gais manifestant contre l'arrestation des '188 du Bud's,'" *La Presse*, 4 June 1984; Robin J. Douglas, "The Night They Raided Bud's," *The Body Politic*, September 1984, 13–15; Paul Roy, "La police fait 188 arrestations dans un bar gai de la rue Stanley," *La Presse*, 3 June 1984.

102 Léopold Lizotte, "Le règlement municipal déclaré valide," *La Presse*, 21 July 1984; Rene Laurent, "Court Upholds City's Bylaw on Prostitution," *Montreal Gazette*, 21 July 1984.

103 Carole Thibaudeau, "Une vaste opération de police," *La Presse*, 26 July 1984; Pierre Schneider, "Razzia chez les prostituées 60 personnes interceptées," *Le Journal de Montréal*, 26 July 1984; David Johnston, "Police Dragnet Rounds Up 150 near 'The Main,'" *Montreal Gazette*, 27 July 1984; André Noël, "La police fait sentir sa présence au centre-ville," *La Presse*, 28 July 1984.

104 "Montreal Bomb Kills 3; Note on Papal Visit Found," *New York Times*, 4 September 1984; "Brigham Talked of Cosmic Forces, Witness Recounts," *Globe and Mail*, 23 April 1985.

105 Crago and Clamen, "*Né dans le Redlight*," in *Selling Sex*, 148–9.

106 Crago interview with Miss Pat, "Sex Work," 22.

107 Brock, *Making Work, Making Trouble*, 8–9.

108 For the Montreal police's official statement, see Fraser, *Pornography and Prostitution in Canada*, 354–5; Brock, *Making Work, Making Trouble*, 67–70.

109 Michel Auger, "Les politiciens n'y changeront rien: les prostituées continueront de 'travailler' comme avant," *Le Journal de Montréal*, 28 April 1985; Picard, *Ma vie dans les bordels*.

110 Brock, *Making Work, Making Trouble*, 81.

111 "Presentation of the City of Montréal to the Legislative Committee on Bill C-49 submitted by Jean Drapeau," 29 October 1985, Dossier – Prostitution, P100-07-D105, AVM.

112 Scott, "C-49: A New Wave of Oppression," in *Good Girls/Bad Girls*, 100–1. Scott's outrage was echoed by the feminist organization National Association of Women and the Law. It opposed the bill, stating that the state

should give greater attention to the economic and social causes of sex work instead. See Graham-Cox, *National Association of Women and the Law Brief on Bill C-49.*

113 O'Connell, "The Impact of Bill C-49 on Street Prostitution," 138–41.

114 Larsen, "The Limits of the Law," 36–7; Ouimet, *La criminalité au Québec*, 302, 313; Gemme, *Street Prostitution*, 50–1.

115 Gemme, *Street Prostitution*, 48.

116 Robert Winters, "Morality Squad Targets Prostitutes and Clients in Red-Light Sweep," *Montreal Gazette*, 11 January 1986.

117 "Manifestation de soutien aux belles de nuit de Montréal," *La Presse*, 18 January 1986; Marian Scott, "March to Protest Tougher Laws on Prostitution Draws 60 Women," *Montreal Gazette*, 18 January 1986.

118 Huguette Roberge, "Haro sur 1,000 'mauvaises femmes' et leurs 500 clients!," *La Presse*, 29 March 1987.

119 "The Politics of Charm and Obfuscation: Q&A: Jean Drapeau," *Maclean's*, 13 August 1984.

120 "Le RCM veut que soit décriminalisée la prostitution," *La Presse*, 19 December 1985.

121 Irwin Block, "Durpas Vow: I'll Rid City of 'Menace' of Prostitution," *Montreal Gazette*, 9 October 1986.

122 Gemme, *Street Prostitution*, 55.

123 Ibid., 63.

124 Crago and Clamen, "*Né dans le Redlight*," 149–50; Ouimet, *La criminalité au Québec*, 302; Gemme, *Street Prostitution*, 48–9.

125 Gemme, *Street Prostitution*, 185.

126 Ibid., 327.

127 O'Connell, "The Impact of Bill C-49 on Street Prostitution," 143.

128 "Summary of the Presentation of Mayor of Montreal His Worship Mr Jean Drapeau to the Legislative Committee on Bill C-49," 29 October 1985, p. 2, Dossier – Prostitution, P100-07-D105, AVM.

EPILOGUE

1 Ingrid Peritz, "Doré, MCM Sweep to Power: New Mayor Controls 55 Seats to Rivals' 3," *Montreal Gazette*, 10 November 1986.

2 Gérald Le Blanc, "Au tour du RCM," *La Presse*, 10 November 1986.

3 Lewis Harris, "Dupras Says Civic Party Will Rise Again," *Montreal Gazette*,

10 November 1986; "Change Sweeps In," *Montreal Gazette*, 10 November 1986.

4 Paul-André Comeau, "La fin de l'ère Drapeau," *Le Devoir*, 10 November 1986.

5 André Pépin, "'J'accepte le verdict avec humilité,'" *La Presse*, 10 November 1986.

6 Michael T. Kaufman, "Jean Drapeau, 83, Mayor Who Reshaped Montreal," *New York Times*, 14 August 1999; Editorial, "The Drapeau Era," *Montreal Gazette*, 28 June 1986.

7 Ian Adams, "The Busy Little Man Who's Building Big Town," *Maclean's*, 3 December 1966.

8 See Whelan, "The Politics of Urban Redevelopment in Montreal."

9 See Rutland, *Un échec éternel*, 17–18.

10 "Homosexuals Helped Me Win: Gay Candidate," *Montreal Gazette*, 10 November 1986; Ingrid Peritz, "Doré, MCM Sweep to Power: New Mayor Controls 55 Seats to Rivals' 3," *Montreal Gazette*, 10 November 1986.

11 Blain's tenure ended prematurely when he died of complications from AIDS in 1992. For more on the political and spatial evolution of Montreal's Gay Village, see Podmore, "Sharing Montréal's Village Gai."

12 Femmes et Ville (Women and the City), "For a City with a Good Life for Women as Well," Brief presented during the City of Montreal public hearings on the Policy Statement on the arrondissement Centre Redevelopment Plan (June 1988), 46. VM086-S1-SS1- P0002, AVM. For more on Take Back the Night within the Quebec context, see Coderre and Coderre, "La marche internationale *La rue, la nuit, femmes sans peur.*"

13 For example, see Nowlin, "Indecency Law," in *Judging Obscenity*; Crawford and Herland, "Sex Garage."

14 For Montreal, this transition took shape in a multitude of ways as it energetically pursued tourism as an urban regeneration program during the second half of the twentieth century. As Levine writes, despite massive government spending on tourist attractions and related infrastructure (conservatively estimated at $7 billion between 1960 and 2000), it remains "highly questionable whether the growth of a 'world class' tourist industry has produced the fiscal windfall envisioned by architects of the city's strategy." Levine, "Tourism-Based Redevelopment and the Fiscal Crisis of the City," 104.

15 For example, see Wynn and Oke, *Vancouver and Its Region*. More generally, also see Sassen, *Globalization and Its Discontents*.

16 Germain and Rose, *Montréal*, 3.

BIBLIOGRAPHY

ARCHIVAL AND LIBRARY COLLECTIONS

Archives Gaies du Québec (AGQ)

F0001, Fonds Groupe homosexuel d'action politique (GHAP)

F0129, Comité de défense des accuses du Truxx

Archives Radio-Canada/CBC Archives

CBC *Television News Special*, "Montreal's 'Night of Terror,'" 8 October 1969. Online Archive.

Radio-Canada, "Le Défilé de la Saint-Jean-Baptiste," 24 June 1968. Online Archive.

Radio-Canada, "Téléjournal," 24 June 1968. Online Archive.

Tout le monde en parlait. "Montréal en otage: policiers et pompiers font la grève," 2007. Online Archive.

Archives de la Ville de Montréal (AVM)

Bylaws, City of Montreal

P043 – Fonds Commission d'enquête présidée par le juge François Caron (1925–1957)

P076 – Fonds Cour municipale de Montréal (1867–2001)

P100 – Fonds Jean Drapeau

VM001 – Fonds Conseil de Ville de Montréal

VM007 – Fonds Service des affaires corporatives

VM074 – Fonds Comité exécutif

VM086 – Fonds Commission de l'aménagement, de l'habitation et des travaux publics
VM094 – Fonds Service des affaires institutionnelles
VM095 – Fonds Service de la police de Montréal
VM097 – Fonds Urbanisme et habitation
VM166 – Collection de dossiers thématiques
XCD00 – Centre de documentation: Publications internes et externes
Bibliothèque de l'Assemblée nationale du Québec
Journal des débats de l'Assemblée nationale du Québec
Journal des débats de la Commission permanente des affaires municipales et de l'environnement
Lois annuelles du Québec
Bibliothèque et Archives nationales du Québec (BANQ)
P833 – Fonds La Presse
British Pathé
Reuters, "Canada: Fires Deliberately Lit in Montreal as the City's Firemen Continue Their Strike," 3 November 1974. Online Archive.
Reuters, "Canada: Montreal's Striking Firemen Back at Work," 4 November 1974. Online Archive.
Canadian Centre for Architecture (CCA)
AP041 – Melvin Charney fonds
Université du Québec à Montréal (UQÀM)
24P – Fonds d'archives de la Ligue des droits et libertés
97P – Fonds Laurent Lamy
University of Ottawa, Archives and Special Collections (UOASC)
10-001 – Canadian Women's Movement Archives (CWMA)

GOVERNMENT DOCUMENTS

Allison, George A. *Rapports d'enquêtes au Procureur général de la province de Québec au sujet des incendies survenus dans la ville de Montréal entre le 31 octobre 1974 et le 3 novembre inclusivement*. Montreal: Ministère de la Justice, 30 May 1975.

Cannon, Lucien. *Rapport de la Commission Royale nommée pour s'enquérir des activités de la Sûreté provinciale et de la Police des liqueurs, dans le district de Montréal, depuis le 26 août 1936 jusqu'au 15 mars 1944*. Quebec: Gouvernement du Québec, 1944.

Champagne, Paul. *Rapport de la Commission d'étude du système administratif de Montréal (2 volumes)*. Quebec: Gouvernement du Québec, 1960–61.

Conference Board in Canada, *Perspective on Inflation: A Symposium Held in Montreal, January, 1974: A report*. Ottawa: Conference Board in Canada, 1974.

Dutil, Jean L. *La lutte au crime organisé au Québec: rapport d'enquête sur le crime organisé et recommandations*. Montreal: Commission de Police du Québec, 1976.

Fraser, Paul. *Pornography and Prostitution in Canada: Report of the Special Committee on Pornography and Prostitution*. Ottawa: Minister of Supply and Services Canada, 1985.

Gemme, Robert, Alan Murphy, Marie Bourque, Marie-Reine Nemeh, and Nicole Payment. *Report on Prostitution in Quebec*. Ottawa: Department of Justice, 1984.

Gemme, Robert. *Street Prostitution: Assessing the Impact of the Law, Montreal*. Ottawa: Department of Justice, 1989.

Malouf, Albert. *Rapport de la Commission d'enquête sur le coût de la 21e olympiade*. Montreal: Commission d'enquête sur le coût de la 21e olympiade, 1980.

Motion Picture Theatres, Exhibitors, and Distributors 1950. Dominion Bureau of Statistics – Department of Trade and Commerce, 1950.

Prévost, Yves. *Crime, Justice, and Society*. Quebec: Quebec Official Publisher, 1969.

The Criminal Code and Other Selected Statues of Canada. Ottawa: F.A. Acland, [1927] 1928.

Thinel, Lucien. *Rapport de la commission d'enquête sur le commerce des boissons alcooliques*. Quebec: Éditeur officiel du Québec, 1971.

COURT CASES

L'Abbé v. City of Montreal (1967) [1968], QB 419; *L'Abbé v. City of Montreal* (1968) [1969], QB 1098.

Ayot et al. v. City of Montreal and COJO [1981], QSC.

Dupond v. City of Montreal [1974], QCA 402; *Dupond v. City of Montreal et al.* [1978], 2 SCR 770.

Goldwax v. City of Montreal [1981], QSC 22; *Goldwax v. City of Montreal* [1983], QCA; *Goldwax v. City of Montreal* [1984], 2 SCR 525.

Hargray et al. v. City of Montreal [1971] Montreal Municipal Court.

Hutt v. The Queen [1978], 2 SCR

Rioux v. R. [1968], QB 876.

St-Martin-Poitras v. City of Montreal [1981], Montreal Municipal Court.

Soccio v. Régie des alcools du Québec (1971) [1972], QCA 283.
Westendorp v. the Queen [1983], 1 SCR 43.

JOURNALS, MAGAZINES, AND NEWSPAPERS

Le Berdache
The Body Politic
Chicago Tribune
City Magazine
Le Devoir
Dimanche-Matin
Gai(e)s du Québec
Gay Times
Globe and Mail
Guide du Nord
Le Jour
Le Journal de Montréal
The Last Post
Liberté
Maclean's/Le Magazine Maclean
Le Monde du Spectacle
Montreal Gazette
Montreal Herald
Montréal-Matin
Montreal Standard
Montreal Star/Montreal Scene [supplement]
New York Times
Le Nouveau Samedi
La Patrie
Le Petit Journal
Photo-Journal
La Presse
Le progrès du Saguenay
Quartier latin
The Record
Saturday Night
Le Soleil

Sortir
Sunday Express
Toronto Daily Star
Vie des arts

FILMS

Bailey, Norma, dir. *Nose and Tina*. Montreal: National Film Board, 1980.

Barbeau, Michel, Guylaine Maroist, and Éric Ruel, dirs. *Expo 67 Mission Impossible*. Montreal: La Ruelle Films, 2017.

Boyko, Eugene, dir. *Les Habitations Jeanne-Mance*. Montreal: National Film Board, 1964.

Brault, Michel, dir. *Les ordres*. Montreal: Productions Prisma, 1974.

Brittain, Donald, Marrin Canell, and Robert Duncan, dirs. *His Worship, Mr Montréal*. Montreal: National Film Board, 1976.

Burrows, Arthur, and Jean Palardy, dirs. *Montreal by Night*. Montreal: National Film Board, 1947.

Dale, Holly, and Janis Cole, dirs. *Hookers on Davie*. Vancouver: Spectrum Films, 1984.

Gélinas, Pascal, and Pierre Harel, dirs. *Taire des hommes*. Montreal: N.p., 1968.

Lam, Meilan, dir. *Show Girls*. Montreal: National Film Board, 1998.

McKenna, Bob, dir. *À propos de L'Affaire Corridart*. Montreal: Multi-Monde, 2002.

Scott, Michael, dir. *Station 10*. Montreal: National Film Board, 1973.

Simoneau, Guy, dir. *Plusieurs tombent en amour*. Montreal: K Films Vidéo, 1979.

Zolov, Jack, and Marc Beaudet, dirs. *Adultes avec réserve… [Boulevard Saint-Laurent]*. Montreal: National Film Board, 1962.

BOOKS, THESES, AND ARTICLES

Abdel-Fattah, Ezzat. "Étude de la main-d'œuvre policière: Montréal, Toronto, et Vancouver." Montreal: Centre International de Criminologie Comparée (Université de Montréal), 1972.

Adam, Marcel. *La démocratie à Montréal: ou, Le vaisseau dort*. Montreal: Éditions du Jour, 1972.

Adams, Martha. *Martha Adams*. Montreal: Éditions du Jour, 1972.

Adler, Polly. *A House Is Not a Home*. 1953; Amherst & Boston: University of Massachusetts Press, 2006.

Anctil, Pierre. *History of the Jews in Quebec*, translated by Judith Weisz Woodsworth. Ottawa: University of Ottawa Press, 2021.

Arbour, Rose Marie, ed. *Déclics, art et société: le Québec dans les années 1960 et 1970*. Quebec: Musée de la civilisation, 1999.

Auf der Maur, Nick. *The Billion-Dollar Game: Jean Drapeau and the 1976 Olympics*. Toronto: J. Lorimer, 1976.

– *Quebec: A Chronicle 1968–1972; A Last Post Special*. Toronto: James Lewis & Samuel, 1972.

Aurélien, Maxime, and Ted Rutland. *Il fallait se défendre. L'histoire du premier gang de rue haïtien à Montréal*. Montreal: Mémoire d'encrier, 2023.

Austin, David. *Fear of a Black Nation: Race, Sex, and Security in Sixties Montreal*. Toronto: Between the Lines, 2013.

Backhouse, Constance. "Canadian Prostitution Law 1839–1972." In *Prostitution in Canada*, 7–18. Ottawa: Canadian Advisory Council on the Status of Women, 1984.

– *Colour-Coded: A Legal History of Racism in Canada, 1900–1950*. Toronto: University of Toronto Press, 1999.

– "Nineteenth-Century Canadian Prostitution Law Reflection of a Discriminatory Society." *Histoire Sociale/Social History* 18, no. 36 (November 1985): 387–423.

– *Petticoats and Prejudice: Women and Law in Nineteenth Century Canada*. Toronto: Women's Press, 1991.

Baldwin, Peter C. *In the Watches of the Night: Life in the Nocturnal City, 1820–1930*. Chicago: The University of Chicago Press, 2012.

Balto, Simon. *Occupied Territory: Policing Black Chicago from Red Summer to Black Power*. Chapel Hill: The University of North Carolina Press, 2019.

Beaumier, Marie-Laurence B. "Les voix des femmes à la Ligue des droits de l'homme du Québec : ouvertures, tensions, débats, 1963–1980." *Travail, temps, pouvoirs et résistances* 30, no. 2 (2017) : 235–53.

Bell, Laurie, ed. *Good Girls/Bad Girls*. Toronto: The Women's Press, 1987.

Bennett, Larry. "The Mayor among His Peers: Interpreting Richard M. Daley." In *City, Revisited: Urban Theory from Chicago, Los Angeles, and New York*, eds. Dennis R. Judd and Dick Simpson, 242–72. Minneapolis: University of Minnesota Press, 2011.

Bernier, Pierre, Marc-André Brault, and Georges-N. Parent. "La Régie des alcools du Québec." *Les Cahiers de droit* 8, no. 1 (1966–67): 63–103.

Bertram, LK. "The Other Little House: The Brothel as a Colonial Institution on the Canadian Prairies, 1880–93." *Journal of Social History* 56, 1 (Fall 2022): 58–88.

Biehler, Dawn Day. *Pests in the City: Flies, Bedbugs, Cockroaches, and Rats*. Seattle: University of Washington Press, 2013.

Bijsterveld, Karin. *Mechanical Sound: Technology, Culture, and Public Problems of Noise in the Twentieth Century*. Cambridge: The MIT Press, 2008.

Blais, Marie-Claire. *Nights in the Underground: An Exploration of Love*. Translated by Ray Ellenwood. 1978; Don Mills: Musson Book Company, 1979.

– *St Lawrence Blues*. Translated by Ralph Manheim. 1973; Toronto: McClelland and Stewart, 1985.

Blais-Tremblay, Vanessa. "Jazz, Gender, Historiography: A Case Study of the 'Golden Age' of Jazz in Montreal (1925–1955)." PhD diss. (Music), McGill University, 2018.

Bourassa, Guy, and Jacques Léveillée, eds. *Le système politique de Montréal: recueil de textes*. Montreal: Cahiers de l'ACFAS, 1986.

Bouthillier, Guy, and Édouard Cloutier, eds. *Trudeau's Darkest Hour: War Measures in Time of Peace, October 1970*. Montreal: Baraka Books, 2010.

Bradbury, Bettina. *Working Families: Age, Gender, and Daily Survival in Industrializing Montreal*. Toronto: University of Toronto Press, 2007.

Bright, David. "The Other Woman: Lizzie Cyr and the Origins of the 'Persons Case.'" *Canadian Journal of Law and Society/Revue canadienne droit et société* 12, no. 2 (Fall 1998): 99–115.

Broadway, Michael J. "Montreal's Changing Tourist Landscape." *Canadian Journal of Urban Research* 2, no. 1 (June 1993): 30–48.

Brock, Deborah R. *Making Work, Making Trouble: The Social Regulation of Sexual Labour*. Toronto: University of Toronto Press, 2018.

Brodeur, Jean-Paul. *La délinquance de l'ordre. Recherches sur les commissions d'enquête I*. Ville LaSalle: Hurtubise HMH, 1984.

Browne, Simone. *Dark Matters: On the Surveillance of Blackness*. Durham: Duke University Press, 2015.

Burns, Patricia. *Life on the Home Front: Montreal 1939–1945*. Montreal: Véhicule Press, 2012.

Campeau, Sébastien. "L'intervention militaire en octobre 1970 et la loi sur les mesures de guerre: modalités et reactions." MA thesis (History), Université du Québec à Montréal, 2009.

Carminati, Lucia. "'She Will Eat Your Shirt': Foreign Migrant Women as Brothel

Keepers in Port Said and along the Suez Canal, 1880–1914." *Journal of the History of Sexuality* 30, no. 2 (May 2021): 161–94.

Caro, Robert A. *The Power Broker: Robert Moses and the Fall of New York*. New York: Vintage, 1975.

Caron, Matthieu. "Taming the Jungle in the City: Uprooting Trees, Bushes, and Disorder from Mount Royal Park." *Urban History Review/Revue d'histoire urbaine* 47, nos. 1–2 (Fall 2018–Spring 2019): 39–53.

Cellard, André. "Le petit Chicago : La 'criminalité' à Hull depuis le début du XXe siècle." *Revue d'histoire de l'Amérique française* 45, no. 4 (1992): 519–43.

Chamberland, Line. "Remembering Lesbian Bars: Montréal, 1955–1975." *Journal of Homosexuality* 25, no. 3 (1993): 231–69.

Chambers, Stephanie, Jane Farrow, Maureen Fitzgerald, Ed Jackson, John Lorinc, Tim McCaskell, Rebecca Sheffield, et al. *Any Other Way: How Toronto Got Queer*. Toronto: Coach House Books, 2017.

de Champlain, Pierre. *Histoire du crime organisé à Montréal de 1900 à 1980*. Montreal: Les Éditions de l'Homme, 2014.

Chan, Kwok Bun. "Ethnic Urban Space, Urban Displacement and Forced Relocation: The Case of Chinatown in Montreal." *Canadian Ethnic Studies/Études ethniques au Canada* 18, no. 2 (1986): 65–78.

Chan, Sophy, and Janice Forsyth. "'Welcome to the Olympic Victims Hotel': Homelessness and the 1976 Montreal Olympic Games." *Sport in Society* 21, no. 3 (2018): 468–81.

Charlebois, Catherine, and Mathieu Lapointe. *Scandale! Le Montréal illicite, 1940–1960*. Montreal: Les Éditions Cardinal, 2016.

Charlebois, Catherine, and Paul-André Linteau. *Quartiers disparus. Red Light, Faubourg à m'lasse, Goose Village*. Montreal: Les Éditions Cardinal, 2014.

Charney, Melvin. *Corridart dans la rue Sherbrooke, Montréal du 7 au 31 juillet. 1976*. Montreal: Programme arts et culture du Comité organisateur des Jeux olympiques de 1976, 1976.

Charney, Melvin, ed. *Montreal, plus or minus?* Montreal: Montreal Museum of Fine Arts, 1972.

Choko, Marc H., Jean-Pierre Collin, and Annick Germain. "Le logement et les enjeux de la transformation de l'espace urbain: Montréal, 1940–1960." *Urban History Review/Revue d'histoire urbaine* 15, no. 3 (February 1987): 243–53.

Choquette, Pascale. "Corridart: d'un événement culturel à une affaire juridique.

Analyse des textes journalistiques et du jugement de l'affaire Corridart (1975–1988)." MA thesis (Communication), Université de Sherbrooke, 1996.

Clément, Dominique. *Human Rights in Canada: A History*. Waterloo: Wilfrid Laurier University Press, 2016.

– "The Transformation of Security Planning for the Olympics: The 1976 Montreal Games." *Terrorism and Political Violence* 29 (2017): 27–51.

Coderre, Cécile, and Sara-Maude Ivelyne Coderre. "La marche internationale *La rue, la nuit, femmes sans peur* : ses origines et sa dynamique symbolique." *Reflets* 20, no. 2 (2017): 141–80.

Comeau, Paul-André. *Le Bloc populaire, 1942–1948*. Montreal: Boréal, 1998.

Cooper, John Irwin. *Montreal: A Brief History*. Montreal & London: McGill-Queen's University Press, 1969.

Cournoyer, Jean. *Dans le feu de l'action*. Montreal: Les Éditions de l'Homme, 2012.

Couture, Francine. "L'exposition *Corridart*: un cas de controverse esthétique ou politique?" *Bulletin d'histoire politique* 9, no. 3 (summer 2001): 13–23.

Cowie, Jefferson. *Stayin' Alive: The 1970s and the Last Days of the Working Class*. New York: The New Press, 2010.

Crago, Anna-Louise, interview with Miss Pat. "Sex Work: Things That Change, Things That Stay the Same." In *Le festival du 8e art: Le travail du sexe*. Montreal: Livret de la Coalition pour les droits des travailleuses et travailleurs du sexe, 1999.

Crawford, Jason B., and Karen Herland. "Sex Garage: Unspooling Narratives, Rethinking Collectivities." *Journal of Canadian Studies/Revue d'études canadiennes* 48, no. 1 (Winter 2014): 106–31.

Dagenais, Michèle. *Des pouvoirs et des hommes : L'Administration municipale de Montréal, 1900–1950*. Montreal & Kingston: McGill-Queen's University Press, 2000.

Dagenais, Michèle, Irene Maver, and Pierre-Yves Saunier, eds. *Municipal Services and Employees in the Modern City: New Historic Approaches*. Aldershot: Ashgate, 2003.

Davis, Mike, and Jon Wiener. *Set the Night on Fire: LA in the Sixties*. New York: Verso, 2021.

Demczuk, Irène, and Frank W. Remiggi, eds. *Sortir de l'ombre: Histoires des communautés lesbienne et gaie de Montréal*. Montreal: VLB éditeur, 1998.

Descoteaux, Louise. "Corridart: La censure." MA thesis (Art History), Université du Québec à Montréal, 1993.

Dontigny, François. "L'efficacité du cadre légal particulier de la négociation collective visant les pompiers municipaux québécois: le cas des pompiers de Montréal." MA thesis (Law), Université de Montréal, 2015.

Drapeau, Jean. *Jean Drapeau vous parle*. Montreal: Les Éditions de la Cité, 1959.

Drouin, Martin. "De la démolition des taudis à la sauvegarde du patrimoine bâti (Montréal, 1954–1973)." *Urban History Review/Revue d'histoire urbaine* 41, no. 1 (Fall 2012): 22–36.

Dunae, Patrick A. "Sex, Charades, and Census Records: Locating Female Sex Trade Workers in a Victorian City." *Histoire sociale/Social History* 42, no. 84 (November 2009): 267–97.

Dupont, Claude. "Camillien Houde, politicien de carrière." MA thesis (History), University of Ottawa, 1972.

Dupont, Pierre. *Guide de Montréal*. Montreal: Quinze, 1978.

Dupras, Pierre. *La Drapolice*. Montreal: Éditions Québec-Presse, 1972.

Durand, Nathalie. "Analyse de la production et de l'application d'une norme pénale: l'infraction de fraternisation." MA thesis (Criminology), Université de Montréal, 1998.

Edmonds, Penelope. "Unpacking Settler Colonialism's Urban Strategies: Indigenous Peoples in Victoria, British Columbia, and the Transition to a Settler-Colonial City." *Urban History Review/Revue d'histoire urbaine* 38, no. 2 (Spring 2010): 4–20.

Fischer, Anne Gray. *The Streets Belong to Us: Sex, Race, and Police Power from Segregation to Gentrification*. Chapel Hill: The University of North Carolina Press, 2022.

Fougères, Dany, and Roderick MacLeod, eds. *Montreal: The History of a North American City*. Montreal & Kingston: McGill-Queen's University Press, 2017.

Francis, Daniel. *Red Light Neon: A History of Vancouver's Sex Trade*. Vancouver: Subway Books, 2006.

Frank, J.A. "The 'Ingredients' in Violent Labour Conflict: Patterns in Four Case Studies." *Labour/Le Travail* 12 (Fall 1983): 87–112.

Fresco, Estée. *Red Mitten Nationalism: Sport, Commercialism, and Settler Colonialism in Canada*. Montreal & Kingston: McGill-Queen's University Press, 2022.

Gabeline, Donna, Dane Lanken, and Gordon Pope. *Montreal at the Crossroads*. Montreal: Harvest House, 1975.

Gallas, Austin. "The Price of the Ride in New York City: Sex, Taxis, and Entrepreneurial Resilience in the Dry Season of 1919." *Journal of the History of Sexuality* 31, no. 1 (January 2022): 89–114.

Gaudette, Marilyne, Romain Roult, Mohamed Reda Khomsi, and Sylvain Lefebvre. "D'un stade mal-aimé à un stade oublié: l'Autostade de Montréal." *Urban History Review/Revue d'histoire urbaine* 46, no. 1 (Fall 2017): 7–21.

Gauvin, Kim Louise. "CORRIDART Revisited – Excavating the Remains." MA thesis (Art History), Concordia University, 1996.

Gauvreau, Danielle, Sherry Olson, and Patricia Thornton. "The Harsh Welcome of an Industrial City: Immigrant Women in Montreal, 1880–1900." *Histoire sociale/Social History* 40 (November 2007): 345–80.

Germain, Annick, and Damaris Rose. *Montréal: The Quest for a Metropolis.* Toronto: John Wiley & Sons Ltd, 2000.

Giguère, Nicholas. "'Assister, Informer, Defender': Le *Virulent* (1986–1989?), bulletin du Comité Sida Aide Montréal (C-SAM) et outil de lutte contre le VIH et le sida." In *Québequeer: le queer dans les productions littéraires, artistiques et médiatiques québécoises*, edited by Isabelle Boisclair, Pierre-Luc Landry, and Guillaume Girard, 153–69. Montreal: Presses de l'Université de Montréal, 2020.

Gilmore, John. *Swinging in Paradise: The Story of Jazz in Montréal.* Victoria: Ellipse Editions, 2011.

Golan, Arnon. "Soundscapes of Urban Development: Tel-Aviv in the 1920s and 1930s." *Israel Studies* 14, no. 3 (Fall 2009): 120–36.

Gold, John R. *The Practice of Modernism: Modern Architects and Urban Transformation, 1954–1972.* New York: Routledge, 2007.

Graham-Cox, Brenda. *National Association of Women and the Law Brief on Bill C-49: An Act to Amend the Criminal Code (Prostitution).* Ottawa: Association nationale de la femme et le droit / National Association of Women and the Law, 1985.

Guindon, Jocelyn M. "La contestation des espaces gais au centre-ville de Montréal depuis 1950." PhD diss. (Geography), McGill University, 2001.

Gwiazdzinski, Luc, Marco Maggioli, and Will Straw, eds. *Night Studies: Regards croisés sur les nouveaux visages de la nuit.* Seyssinet-Pariset: Elya Éditions, 2020.

Hasegawa, Junichi. "Late-Night Noise Hazards and the Tokyo Metropolitan Government's Countermeasures in the 1960s." *Urban History* 50 (2023): 152–68.

Hawley, Joshua, and Dimitrios Roussopoulos, eds. *Villages in Cities: Community Land Ownership, Cooperative Housing, and the Milton Parc Story*. Montreal: Black Rose Books, 2019.

Hawrysh, Michael M. "Une ville bien arrosée: Montréal Durant l'ère de la prohibition (1920–1933." MA thesis (History), Université de Montréal, 2014.

Heap, Chad. *Slumming: Sexual and Racial Encounters in American Nightlife, 1885–1940*. Chicago: The University of Chicago Press, 2009.

Hébert, Pierre, Kenneth Landry, and Yves Lever, eds. *Dictionnaire de la censure au Québec: littérature et cinéma*. Saint-Laurent: Fides, 2006.

Herland, Karen. "Organized Righteousness against Organized Viciousness: Constructing Prostitution in Post World War I Montreal." MA thesis (Art History and Communication Studies), McGill University, 2005.

Hermann, Christoph. *Capitalism and the Political Economy of Work Time*. New York: Routledge, 2014.

Heron, Craig. *Booze: A Distilled History*. Toronto: Between the Lines, 2003.

Higgins, Ross. *De la clandestinité à l'affirmation : Pour une histoire de la communauté gaie montréalaise*. Montreal: Comeau & Nadeau, 1999.

– "La régulation sociale de l'homosexualité. De la répression à la normalisation." In *La régulation sociale des minorités sexuelles : l'inquiétude de la différence*, edited by Patrice Corriveau and Valérie Daoust, 67–102. Montreal: Presse de l'Université du Québec, 2011.

– "A Sense of Belonging: Pre-liberation Space, Symbolics, and Leadership in Gay Montreal." PhD diss. (Anthropology), McGill University, 1997.

High, Steven. *Deindustrializing Montreal: Entangled Histories of Race, Residence, and Class*. Montreal & Kingston: McGill-Queen's University Press, 2022.

Hilderbrand, Lucas. *The Bars Are Ours: Histories and Cultures of Gay Bars in America, 1960 and After*. Durham: Duke University Press, 2024.

Hobsbawm, Eric. *Fractured Times: Culture and Society in the Twentieth Century*. New York: The New Press, 2014.

Hooper, Tom. "'Enough Is Enough': The Right to Privacy Committee and Bathhouse Raids in Toronto, 1978–83." PhD diss. (History), York University, 2016.

– "Queering '69: The Recriminalization of Homosexuality in Canada." *Canadian Historical Review* 100, no. 2 (June 2019): 257–73.

Howell, Paul Charles. *The Montreal Olympics: An Insider's View of Organizing a Self-financing Games*. Montreal & Kingston: McGill-Queen's University Press, 2008.

Jenness, Valerie. "From Sex as Sin to Sex as Work: COYOTE and the Reorganization of Prostitution as a Social Problem." *Social Problems* 37, no. 3 (August 1990): 403–20.

Jodoin, Claude. *Montréal insolite: Un Guide pour Oiseaux de Nuit*. Montreal: Éditions Beljo, 1974.

Kardos, Robert. "Political Power and Urban Redevelopment. Case Study: Montreal." MA thesis (Economics and Political Science), McGill University, 1969.

Kaufman, Fred. *Searching for Justice: An Autobiography*. Toronto: University of Toronto Press, 2005.

Kealey, Gregory S., and Bryan D. Palmer. *Dreaming of What Might Be: The Knights of Labor in Ontario, 1880–1990*. New York: Cambridge University Press, 1982.

Kenny, Nicolas. "City Glow: Streetlights, Emotions, and Nocturnal Life, 1880s–1910s." *Journal of Urban History* 43, 1 (2017): 91–114.

Kidd, Bruce. "'The Army's Presence Will Be Obvious' (Montreal 1976)." In *Surveilling and Securing the Olympic: From Tokyo 1964 to London 2012 and Beyond*, edited by Vida Bajc, 162–79. New York: Palgrave Macmillan, 2016.

Kinsman, Gary. "AIDS Activism: Remembering Resistance versus Socially Organized Forgetting." In *Seeing Red: HIV/AIDS and Public Policy in Canada*, edited by Michael Orsini, Marilou Gagnon, and Suzanne Hindmarch, 311–33. Toronto: University of Toronto Press, 2017.

Kinsman, Gary, and Patrizia Gentile. *The Canadian War on Queers: National Security as Sexual Regulation*. Vancouver: UBC Press, 2010.

Kirkby, Diane. "Writing the History of Women Working: Photographic Evidence and the 'Disreputable Occupation of Barmaid.'" *Labour History* no. 61 (1991): 3–16.

Korinek, Valerie J. *Prairie Fairies: A History of Queer Communities and People in Western Canada, 1930–1985*. Toronto: University of Toronto Press, 2018.

Kuplowsky, Adam. "A Captivating 'Open City': The Production of Montreal as a 'Wide-open Town' and 'Ville Ouverte' in the 1940s and '50s." MA thesis (History), McGill University, 2015.

Lacasse, Danielle. "La fin d'un univers féminin: l'Enquête Caron et la prostitution, 1945–1965." In *Les Bâtisseuses de la Cité : actes du Colloque Les Bâtisseuses de la Cité dans le cadre de la Section d'études féministes du Congrès de l'Acfas 1992*, edited by Évelyne Tardy, 97–106. Montreal: Association canadienne-française pour l'avancement des sciences, 1993.

– *La Prostitution féminine à Montréal, 1945–1970*. Montreal: Boréal, 1994.

Lacasse, Shirley. "Le travail des danseuses nues : Au-delà du stigmate, une relation de service marchand." PhD diss. (Sociology), Université de Montréal, 2003.

Lamonde, Yvan. "Les Jeune-Canada ou les 'Jeune-Laurentie'? La recherche d'un nationalisme (1932–1938)." *Les Cahiers des dix* no. 63 (2009): 175–215.

Langford, Martha, and Johanne Sloan, eds. *Photogenic Montreal: Activisms and Archives in a Post-Industrial City*. Montreal & Kingston: McGill-Queen's University Press, 2021.

Lapointe, Mathieu. "'Beaucoup trop Chicago': la campagne de moralité publique Montréalaise dans ses contextes internationaux." *Bulletin d'histoire politique* 24, 1 (2015): 20–9.

– *Nettoyer Montréal: les campagnes de moralité publique, 1940–1954*. Quebec: Septentrion, 2014.

Larsen, E. Nick. "Canadian Prostitution Control Between 1914 and 1970: An Exercise in Chauvinist Reasoning," *Canadian Journal of Law and Society/Revue canadienne droit et société* 7, no. 2 (Fall 1992), 137–56.

– "The Limits of the Law: A Critical Examination of Prostitution Control in Three Canadian Cities." *Hybrid: Journal of Law and Social Change* 3, no. 1 (1996): 19–42.

– "Urban Politics and Prostitution Control: A Qualitative Analysis of a Controversial Urban Problem." *Canadian Journal of Urban Research* 8, no. 1 (June 1999): 28–46.

Larson, Erik. *The Devil in the White City: Murder, Magic, and Madness at the Fair that Changed America*. New York: Vintage Books, 2003.

Laurin, Lucie. *Des luttes et des droits: antécédents et histoire de la Ligue des Droits de l'Homme de 1936 à 1975*. Montreal: Les Éditions du Méridien, 1985.

Ledoux, Paul, and Terry Last. *The Night They Raided Truxx*. Halifax: Dramatists' Co-op of Nova Scotia, 1979.

Lee, Raymond. "American Greed: The Eleventh Circuit Analyzes Whether Booze, Babes, and Business Can Tightrope the Line between Fraud and Deceit." *Missouri Law Review* 83, issue 3 (2018): 753–72.

Lefebvre, Henri. *Rhythmanalysis: Space, Time and Everyday Life*. Translated by Stuart Elden and Gerald Moore. 1992; New York: Continuum, 2004.

Léveillée, Jacques, and Robert K. Whelan. "Montreal: The Struggle to Become a 'World City.'" In *Leadership and Urban Regeneration: Cities in North America and Europe*, edited by Dennis Judd and Michael Parkinson, 152–71. London: Sage Publications, 1990.

Lévesque, Andrée. "Le Bordel: Milieu De Travail Contrôlé." *Labour/Le Travail* 20 (Fall 1987): 13–31.

– "Éteindre le *Red Light*: les réformateurs et la prostitution à Montréal entre 1865 et 1925." *Urban History Review/Revue d'histoire urbaine* 17, no. 3 (February 1989): 191–201.

– *Making and Breaking the Rules: Women in Quebec, 1919–1939*. Translated by Yvonne M. Klein. Toronto: University of Toronto Press, 2010.

Levine, Marc V. *The Reconquest of Montreal: Language Policy and Social Change in a Bilingual City*. Philadelphia: Temple University Press, 1990.

– "Tourism-Based Redevelopment and the Fiscal Crisis of the City: The Case of Montréal." *Canadian Journal of Urban Research* 12, no. 1 (Summer 2013): 102–23.

Limoges, Thérèse. *La Prostitution à Montréal : Comment, pourquoi certaines femmes deviennent prostituées*. Montreal: Les Éditions de l'Homme, 1967.

Linteau, Paul-André. *Une histoire de Montréal*. Montreal: Boréal, 2017.

– *Sainte-Catherine Street: At the Heart of Montréal Life*. Translated by Barbara Sandilands. Montreal: Les Éditions de l'Homme, 2010.

Littauer, Amanda H. *Bad Girls: Young Women, Sex, and Rebellion before the Sixties*. Chapel Hill: The University of North Carolina Press, 2015.

Lortie, André, ed. *The 60s: Montreal Thinks Big*. Montreal: Canadian Centre for Architecture, 2004.

Lovatt, Andy. "The Ecstasy of Urban Regeneration: Regulation of the Night-time Economy in the Transition to a Post-Fordist City." In *From the Margins to the Centre: Cultural Production and Consumption in the Post-industrial City*, edited by Justin O'Connor and Derek Wynne, 141–68. Brookfield: Ashgate Publishing, 1996.

Love, Victoria, Elya M. Durisin, and Emily Van der Meulen, eds. *Selling Sex: Experience, Advocacy, and Research on Sex Work in Canada*. Vancouver: UBC Press, 2013.

Lowman, John, M.A. Jackson, T.S. Palys, and S. Gavigan, eds. *Regulating Sex: An Anthology of Commentaries on the Findings and Recommendations of the Badgley and Fraser Reports*. Burnaby: School of Criminology Simon Fraser University, 1986.

Lvovsky, Anna. *Vice Patrol: Cops, Courts, and the Struggle over Urban Gay Life before Stonewall*. Chicago: The University of Chicago Press, 2021.

Macintosh, Donald, Donna Greenhorn, and Michael Hawes. "Trudeau, Taiwan, and the 1976 Montreal Olympics." *American Review of Canadian Studies* 21, no. 4 (1991): 423–48.

MacLennan, Hugh. *Return of the Sphinx*. Toronto: MacMillan, 1967.

Mansbridge, Joanna. "In Search of a Different History: The Remains of Burlesque in Montreal." *Canadian Theatre Review* 158 (Spring 2014): 7–12.

Marlowe, Kenneth. *Mr Madam: Confessions of a Male Madam*. Los Angeles: Sherbourne Press, 1964.

Marquis, Greg. "Constructing an Urban Drug Ecology in 1970s Canada." *Urban History Review/Revue d'histoire urbaine* 42, no. 1 (Fall 2013): 27–40.

Marrelli, Nancy. *Stepping Out: The Golden Age of Montreal Night Clubs, 1925–1955*. Montreal: Véhicule Press, 2004.

Marsan, Jean-Claude. *Montreal in Evolution: Historical Analysis of the Development of Montreal's Architecture and Urban Environment*. Montreal & Kingston: McGill-Queen's University Press, 1990.

Marsolais, Claude-V. "Les inclinations fascistes de Camillien Houde et son internement durant la guerre." *Bulletin d'histoire politique* 3 nos. 3–4 (Summer 1995): 144–58.

Martin, Eryk. "Resisting Red Hot Video: Feminism, Pornography, and the Political Utility of Emotion." In *Feeling Feminism: Activism, Affect, and Canada's Second Wave*, edited by Lara Campbell, Michael Dawson, and Catherine Gidney, 184–205. Vancouver: UBC Press, 2022.

Marx, Herbert. "The Montreal Anti-Demonstration By-Law – Bad Everywhere." *Manitoba Law Journal* 4, no. 2 (1971): 347–54.

McConathy, Dale. "CORRIDART: Instant Archaeology in Montréal." *Artscanada* 33, no. 206–207 (July/August 1976): 36–53.

McKenna, Brian, and Susan Purcell. *Drapeau*. Toronto: Clarke, Irwin & Company Limited, 1980.

Médam, Alain. *Montréal Interdite*. Paris: Presses universitaires de France, 1978.

Melbin, Murray. *Night as Frontier: Colonizing the World after Dark*. New York: Free Press, 1987.

Ménard, Guy. "Du berdache au Berdache: lectures de l'homosexualité dans la culture québécoise." *Anthropologie et Sociétés* 9, no. 3 (1985): 115–38.

Ménard, Yves. "Le lock-out de *La Presse* et l'émeute du 29 octobre 1971: un conflit d'envergure nationale." *Bulletin du RCHTQ* 28, no. 2 (Fall 2002): 5–35.

Mensah, Maria Nengeh. "The Idea of Community and Collective Action: Reflections on Forum XXX." In *Sex Work: Rethinking the Job, Respecting the Workers*, edited by Louise Toupin, Patrice Corriveau, Maria Nengeh Mensah, Colette Parent, Chris Bruckert, and Käthe Roth, 81–110. Vancouver: UBC Press, 2013.

Mensah, Maria Nengeh, and Marie-Claude Laberge. "Évolution du discours féministe sur 'la prostitution' au Québec." *Bulletin d'histoire politique* 15, no. 1 (Fall 2006): 71–80.

Mercure Jolette, Frédéric. "Réinventer Montréal: une archéologie du discours urbanistique des Trente Glorieuses." PhD diss. (Political Science), Université de Montréal, 2020.

Mills, Sean. *The Empire Within: Postcolonial Thought and Political Activism in Sixties Montreal.* Montreal & Kingston: McGill-Queen's University Press, 2010.

– *A Place in the Sun: Haiti, Haitians, and the Remaking of Quebec.* Montreal & Kingston: McGill-Queen's University Press, 2016.

Milner, Henry. "The Montreal Citizens' Movement, Then and Now," *Quebec Studies*, no. 6 (1988): 1–11.

Morin, Guy R. *La Cathédrale inachevée.* Montreal: XYZ Éditeur, 1997.

Morton, Suzanne. *At Odds: Gambling and Canadians, 1919–1969*. Toronto: University of Toronto Press, 2003.

Moyes, Craig, and Steven Palmer, eds. *Expo 67 and Its World: Staging the Nation in the Crucible of Globalization*. Montreal & Kingston: McGill-Queen's University Press, 2022.

Myers, Tamara. *Caught: Montreal's Modern Girls and the Law, 1869–1945*. Toronto: University of Toronto Press, 2006.

– "Deserting Daughters: Runaways and the Red Light District of Montreal before 1945." In *Child Welfare and Social Action: Nineteenth and Twentieth Centuries*, edited by Pat Starkey and Jon Lawrence, 15–35. Liverpool: Liverpool University Press, 2001.

– *Youth Squad: Policing Children in the Twentieth Century*. Montreal & Kingston: McGill-Queen's University Press, 2019.

Namaste, Viviane K. "Beyond Leisure Studies: A Labour History of Male to Female Transsexual and Transvestite Artists in Montreal, 1955–1985." *Atlantis* 29, no. 1 (Fall/Winter 2004): 4–11.

– *C'était du spectacle! L'Histoire des artistes transsexuelles à Montréal, 1955–1985*. Montreal & Kingston: McGill-Queen's University Press, 2005.

– *Imprimés interdits. La censure des journaux jaunes au Québec, 1955–1975* Quebec: Septentrion, 2017.

– *Savoirs créoles : leçons du sida pour l'histoire de Montréal.* Montreal: Mémoire d'encrier, 2019.

Nead, Lynda. *Victorian Babylon: People, Streets and Images in Nineteenth-Century London*. New Haven: Yale University Press, 2000.

Neatby, Nicole. "Meeting of Minds: North American Travel Writers and Government Tourist Publicity in Quebec, 1920–1955." *Histoire sociale/Social History* 36, no. 72 (November 2003): 465–95.

Nelligan, Emile. *Ship of Gold: The Essential Poems of Emile Nelligan*. Translated by Marc Di Saverio. Montreal: Signal Editions, 2017.

Nerbas, Don. "William Zeckendorf, Place Ville-Marie, and the Making of Modern Montreal." *Urban History Review/Revue d'histoire urbaine* 43, no. 2 (Spring 2015): 5–25.

Noël, Roger. "Pratiques politiques et formation de l'identité gaie au Québec: L'expérience du Groupe Homosexuel d'action politique (1975–1976)." MA thesis (Political Science), Université du Québec à Montréal, 1993.

Nowlin, Christopher. *Judging Obscenity: A Critical History of Expert Evidence*. Montreal & Kingston: McGill-Queen's University Press, 2003.

Nye, David E. *American Illuminations: Urban Lighting, 1800–1920*. Cambridge: The MIT Press, 2018.

– *When the Lights Went Out: A History of Blackouts in America*. Cambridge: The MIT Press, 2010.

O'Connell, Sheilagh. "The Impact of Bill C-49 on Street Prostitution: 'What's Law Got to Do with It,'" *Journal of Law and Social Policy* 4 (1988): 109–45.

O'Leary, Véronique, and Louise Toupin. *Québécoise Deboutte! Tome 1*. Montreal: Les éditions du remue-ménage, 1982.

Olson, Sherry. "'A Profusion of Light' in Nineteenth-Century Montreal." In *Espace et culture / Space and Culture*, edited by Serge Courville and Normand Séguin, 253–64. Sainte-Foy: Les Presses de l'Université Laval, 1995.

Ouimet, Marc. *La criminalité au Québec durant le vingtième siècle*. Quebec: Les Presses de l'Université Laval, 2005.

Ouimet, Marc. "Le lys en fête, le lys en feu: La Saint-Jean-Baptiste au Québec de 1960 à 1990." MA thesis (History), Université du Québec à Montréal, 2011.

Palmer, Al. *Montreal Confidential*. 1950; Montreal: Véhicule Press, 2009.

– *Sugar-Puss on Dorchester Street*. 1949; Montreal: Véhicle Press, 2013.

Pâquet, Martin, and Stéphane Savard. *Brève histoire de la révolution tranquille*. Montreal: Boréal, 2021.

Parizeau, Alice. "L'armée et la Crise d'octobre." *Criminologie* 13 no. 2 (1980): 47–78.

Patenaude, J.-Z.-Léon. *Le vrai visage de Jean Drapeau*. Montreal: Éditions du Jour, 1962.

Paul, Darel E. "World Cities as Hegemonic Projects: The Politics of Global Imagineering in Montreal." *Political Geography* 23 (2004): 571–96.

Penfold, Steve. "'People Drive Automobiles': Esther Shiner, the Silent Majority, and the Popular Case for the Spadina Expressway, 1971–1987." *Urban History Review/Revue d'histoire urbaine* 49, issue 1 (Fall 2021): 30–53.

Pépin, René. "Le pouvoir des provinces canadiennes de légiférer sur la moralité publique." *Revue générale de droit* 19, no. 4 (1988): 865–94.

Perrin, Eliot. "'Whose City Is It?': Save Montreal and the Fight for Democratic City Planning." *Urban History Review/Revue d'histoire urbaine* 51, no. 1 (March 2023): 117–44.

Picard, Rita. *Ma vie dans les bordels*. Montreal: Québecor, 1985.

Plante, Pacifique. *Montréal sous le règne de la pègre*. Montreal: Éditions de l'Action nationale, 1950.

Podmore, Julie. "Queering Discourses of Urban Decline: Representing Montréal's Post-World War II 'Lower Main.'" *Historical Geography* 43 (2015): 57–83.

– "Sharing Montréal's Village Gai." In *Sharing Spaces: Essays in Honour of Sherry Olson*, edited by Robert Sweeny, 129–43. Ottawa: University of Ottawa Press, 2020.

– "St Lawrence Blvd as 'Third City': Place, Gender and Difference along Montréal's 'Main.'" PhD diss. (Geography), McGill University, 1999.

Podmore, Julie, and Line Chamberland. "Entering the Urban Frame: Early Lesbian Activism and Public Space in Montréal." *Journal of Lesbian Studies* 19, no. 2 (2015): 192–211.

Poirier, Valérie. "Expertise, Local Knowledge, and the Construction of the Automobile as an Environmental Risk in Montreal, 1960s–70s." *Canadian Historical Review* 101, no. 3 (2020): 397–423.

Poutanen, Mary Anne. *Beyond Brutal Passions: Prostitution in Early Nineteenth-Century Montreal*. Montreal & Kingston: McGill-Queen's University Press, 2015.

Prévost, Robert, Suzanne Gagné, and Michel Phaneuf. *L'histoire de l'alcool au Québec*. Montreal: Société des alcools du Québec, 1986.

Proulx, Daniel. *Les bas-fonds de Montréal*. Montreal: VLB éditeur, 1998.

– *Le Red Light de Montréal*. Montreal: VLB éditeur, 1997.

Ranasinhe, Prashan. "Reconceptualizing Vagrancy and Reconstructing the Vagrant: A Socio-Legal Analysis of Criminal Law Reform in Canada, 1953–1972." *Osgoode Hall Law Journal* 48, no. 1 (2010): 55–94.

Raynault, Adhémar. *Témoin d'une époque*. Montreal: Éditions du Jour, 1970.

Reid, Malcolm. *The Shouting Signpainters: A Literary and Political Account of Quebec Revolutionary Nationalism*. Toronto: McClelland & Stewart, 1972.

Ricci, Amanda. *Countercurrents: Women's Movements in Postwar Montreal*. Montreal & Kingston: McGill-Queen's University Press, 2023.

Richler, Mordecai. *Oh Canada! Oh Quebec! Requiem for a Divided Country*. Toronto: Penguin, 1992.

Robillard, Yves. *Quebec underground: 1962–1972 – Tome: 2*. Montreal: Éditions Mediart, 1973.

Rose, Damaris. "Local State Policy and 'New-Build Gentrification' in Montréal: The Role of the 'Population Factor' in a Fragmented Governance Context." *Population, Space, and Place* 16 (2010): 413–28.

Ross, Daniel. *The Heart of Toronto: Corporate Power, Civic Activism, and the Remaking of Downtown Yonge Street*. Vancouver: UBC Press, 2022.

Ross, Margaret O'Riordan. "'Your Town Is Rotten': Prostitution, Profit, and the Governing of Vice in Kingston, Ontario, 1860s–1920s." *Journal of the History of Sexuality* 32, no. 2 (May 2023): 174–201.

Ruddick, Susan M. "The Movement for Public Housing in Montreal, 1930–1958." MA thesis (Geography), McGill University, 1979.

Rudy, Jarrett, Magda Fahrni, and Nicolas Kenny. "'An Ocean of Noise': H.E. Reilley and the Making of a Legitimate Social Problem, 1911–1945." *Journal of Canadian Studies/Revue d'études canadiennes* 51, no. 2 (Spring 2017): 261–88.

– "Railways and the Urban Soundscape: Montreal, 1850s–1950s." *Urban History Review/Revue d'histoire urbaine* 49, no. 2 (Spring 2022): 217–40.

Rumilly, Robert. *Histoire de Montréal : Tome V 1939–1967*. Montreal: Fides, 1974.

Russell, J. Stuart. "The Offence of Keeping a Common Bawdy-House in Canadian Criminal Law." *Ottawa Law Review* 14 (1982): 270–313.

Rutland, Ted. *Un échec éternel : La lutte contre le profilage racial à Montréal, 1979–présent*, mémoire présenter à la Commission de la Sécurité Publique de la Ville de Montréal (22 November 2019).

– "Profiling the Future: The Long Struggle against Police Racial Profiling in Montreal." *American Review of Canadian Studies* 50, no. 3 (2020): 270–92.

Sabourin, Gilles. *Montreal and the Bomb*. Translated by Katherine Hastings. Montreal: Baraka Books, 2021.

Sammartino, Annemarie. "Mass Housing, Late Modernism, and the Forging of Community in New York and East Berlin, 1965–1989." *American Historical Review* 121, no. 2 (April 2016): 492–521.

Sancton, Andrew. *Governing the Island of Montreal: Language Differences and Metropolitan Politics*. Berkeley: University of California Press, 1985.

– "Montreal." In *City Politics in Canada*, edited by Warren Magnusson and Andrew Sancton, 58–93. Toronto: University of Toronto Press, 1983.

Sassen, Saskia. *The Global City: New York, London, Tokyo*. Princeton: Princeton University Press, 1991.

– *Globalization and Its Discontents*. New York: The New Press, 1998.

Schiff, Stacy. *Saint-Exupéry: A Biography*. New York: Alfred A. Knopf, 1994.

Schivelbusch, Wolfgang. *Disenchanted Night: The Industrialization of Light in the Nineteenth Century*. Berkeley: University of California Press, 1988.

Schlör, Joachim. *Nights in the Big City: Paris, Berlin, London, 1840–1930*. London: Reaktion Books, 1998.

Segal, Alvin Cramer. *My Peerless Story: It Starts with the Collar*. Montreal & Kingston: McGill-Queen's University Press, 2017.

Sifton, Elizabeth. "Montreal's Fashion Mile: St Catherine Street, 1890–1930." In *Fashion: A Canadian Perspective*, edited by Alexandra Palmer, 203–26. Toronto: University of Toronto Press, 2004.

Silversides, Ann. *AIDS Activist: Michael Lynch and the Politics of Community*. Toronto: Between the Lines, 2003.

Sismondo, Christine. *America Walks into a Bar: A Spirited History of Taverns and Saloons, Speakeasies, and Grog Shops*. Toronto: Oxford University Press, 2011.

Sloan, Johanne. "*Montréal plus ou moins*, 1972: Urban Knowledge Meets Conceptual Attitude." *Journal of Curatorial Studies* 7, no. 1 (2018): 32–57.

Smith, Martyn David. "The 'Hell of Modern Sound': A History of Urban Noise in Modern Japan." In *Asian Sound Cultures: Voice, Noise, Sound, Technology*, edited by Iris Haukamp, Christin Hoene, and Martyn David Smith, 101–23. New York: Routledge, 2023.

St-Cyr, Lili, with Louis-Jean d'Amour. *Ma vie de stripteaseuse*. 1982; Outremont: Les Éditions Quebecor, 2005.

Stanké, Alain, Jean-Louis Morgan, and Pax Plante. *Pax, lutte à finir avec la pègre : un portrait-robot du célèbre incorruptible Pacifique Plante*. Montreal: La Presse, 1972.

Stoever, Jennifer. "'Just Be Quiet Pu-leeze': The *New York Amsterdam News* Fights the Postwar 'Campaign against Noise.'" *Radical History Review* 121 (January 2015): 145–68.

Strange, Carolyn. *Toronto's Girl Problem: The Perils and Pleasures of the City, 1880–1930*. Toronto: University of Toronto Press, 1995.

Straw, Will. "Montreal and *The Captive City*." *Québec Studies* vol. 48 (Fall 2009/Winter 2010): 13–23.

– "La prostituée dans la nuit: étude de la presse à sensation au Québec, 1942–1960." *Tangence* no. 130 (2022): 61–83.

– "Tabloid Expo." In *Expo 67: Not Just a Souvenir*, edited by Rhona Richman Kenneally and Johanne Sloan, 221–38. Toronto: University of Toronto Press, 2010.

– "Tabloid Porn in Quebec." *Porn Studies* (2022): 1–8.

– "The Urban Night." In *Cartographies of Place: Navigating the Urban*, edited by Janine Marchessault and Michael Darroch, 185–200. Montreal & Kingston: McGill-Queen's University Press, 2014.

Suri, Jeremi. *Power and Protest: Global Revolution and the Rise of Détente*. Cambridge: Harvard University Press, 2003.

Sylvestre, Paul-François. *Les homosexuels s'organisent au Québec et ailleurs*. Montreal: Éditions Homeureux, 1979.

Téllez Niemeyer, Valeria. "Nuit électrique: atmosphères lumineuses à Montréal au XIXe siècle." RACAR 45 (2020): 36–48.

Templeton, Melissa. "Polyrhythmic Dance Currents: Race Multiculturalism and the Montreal Dance Community." PhD diss. (Critical Dance Studies), University of California Riverside, 2012.

Les Têtes de pioche [Journal des femmes]. Montreal: Éditions du Remue-ménage, 1980.

Texier, Catherine, and Marie-Odile Vézina. *Profession, prostituée: rapport sur la prostitution au Québec*. Ottawa: Éditions Libre Expression, 1978.

Théorêt, Hugues. *The Blue Shirts: Adrien Arcand and Fascist Anti-Semitism in Canada*. Ottawa: University of Ottawa Press, 2017.

Thomas, Timothy Lloyd. *A City with a Difference: The Rise and Fall of the Montreal Citizen's Movement*. Montreal: Véhicule Press, 1997.

Thompson, Emily. *The Soundscape of Modernity*. Cambridge: The MIT Press, 2004.

Tousignant, Zoë. *Gabor Szilasi: The Art World in Montreal, 1960–1980*. Montreal: McCord Museum, 2019.

Tremblay, Manon. "Mouvements sociaux et opportunités politiques: les lesbiennes et les gais et l'ajout de l'orientation sexuelle à la Charte québécoise des droits et libertés." *Canadian Journal of Political Science/Revue canadienne de science politique* 42, no. 2 (2013): 295–322.

Tremblay, Manon, ed. *Queer Mobilizations: Social Movement Activism and Canadian Public Policy*. Vancouver: UBC Press, 2016.

Turmel, Jean. *Le Service de police de la cité de Montréal (1909–1971). Étude rétrospective sur son organisation*. Montreal: La Section Recherche et Planification du Service de Police de la C.U.M., 1974.

Valverde, Mariana. *The Age of Light, Soap, and Water: Moral Reform in English Canada, 1885–1925*. Toronto: McClelland & Stewart Inc., 1991.

Vaz, Edmund W. "The Metropolitan Tax-Driver: His Work and Self-Conception." MA thesis (Sociology), McGill University, 1955.

Vickers, Simon. "From *Balconville* to *Condoville*, but Where Is Co-opville? Neighbourhood Activism in 1980s Pointe-Saint-Charles." *Labour/Le Travail* 81 (Spring 2018): 159–86.

Walden, Keith. *Becoming Modern in Toronto: The Industrial Exhibition and the Shaping of a Late Victorian Culture*. Toronto: University of Toronto Press, 1997.

Warren, Jean-Philippe. "Le corporatisme canadien-français comme 'système total'. Quatre concepts pour comprendre la popularité d'une doctrine." *Recherches sociographiques* 45, no. 2 (May–August 2004): 219–38.

– *Histoire du taxi à Montréal. Des taxis jaunes à UberX*. Montreal: Boréal, 2020.

– "L'Opération McGill français. Une page méconnue de l'histoire de la gauche nationaliste." *Bulletin d'histoire politique* 16, no. 2 (Winter 2008): 97–115.

Warren, Jean-Philippe, ed. *Une histoire des sexualités au Québec au XXe siècle*. Montreal: VLB éditeur, 2012.

Weintraub, William. *City Unique: Montreal Days and Nights in the 1940s and '50s*. Toronto: McClelland & Stewart Inc., 1998.

Whelan, Robert K. "The Politics of Urban Redevelopment in Montreal: Regime Change from Drapeau to Doré." *Quebec Studies* no. 12 (1991): 155–69.

Williams, Dorothy W. *Blacks in Montreal 1628–1986: An Urban Demography*. Cowansville: Les Éditions Yvon Blais, 1989.

Williams, Robert. "Night Spaces: Darkness, Deterritorialization, and Social Control." *Space and Culture* 11, no. 4 (November 2008): 514–32.

Wright, George. "The Political Economy of the Montreal Olympic Games." *Journal of Sport and Social Issues* 2, no. 1 (1978): 13–18.

Wynn, Graeme, and Timothy Oke, eds. *Vancouver and Its Region*. Vancouver: UBC Press, 1992.

INDEX